HENRY RICHARD

HENRY RICHARD

Apostle of Peace and Welsh Patriot 1812–1888

Gwyn Griffiths

I'm ffrindiau bach dros y môr –
Kaliesha Lloyd,
Tyrece James,
Daniel Morgan

First published by
Francis Boutle Publishers
272 Alexandra Park Road
London N22 7BG
Tel/Fax: (020) 8889 7744
Email: info@francisboutle.co.uk
www.francisboutle.co.uk

Henry Richard: Apostle of Peace and Welsh Patriot© Gwyn Griffiths, 2012

ISBN 978 1 903427 33 0

Contents

Acknowledgements

This book resulted from a conversation I had some years ago with Mrs Ethni Jones, former Assistant Secretary of the Fellowship of Reconciliation in Wales. It is thanks to her that I set about writing it. My thanks, also, to the present Secretary, Mr Arfon Rhys, and Fellowship Co-ordinator, Ms Marika Fusser for their support and enthusiasm.

I am indebted to Mr David Hanson MP for his interest and for drawing my attention to the existence of commemorative chinaware with fine images of Henry Richard and George Osborne Morgan. My thanks to Mr Michael Freeman, Miss Carrie Canham and Miss Mary Turner Lewis of Amgueddfa Ceredigion Museum, for copies of these images and permission to reproduce them along with his photographs of the monument at Tregaron. Also of the photograph of Henry Richard's grave at Abney Park Cemetery, which I suspect may have been taken by Mr Robert Thomas, formerly Deputy Headmaster of Ysgol Uwchradd Tregaron. From time to time Mr Thomas would take children from the school to London to tidy the grave.

My thanks to Dr Fred Holley, editor of Merthyr Historian, for his assistance and advice; to Dr Bill Jones, Reader in Welsh History at Cardiff University, for drawing my attention to some little known correspondence by Henry Richard which is at Cardiff Central Library; to Mr Cyril Evans of the National Library of Wales, Aberystwyth, for a number of useful and fruitful pointers; to Mr and Mrs Hefin and Catrin Williams, Mrs and Mrs Evan and Mary Lewis, Tregaron, and Mr Raymond Daniel, Llanddewi Brefi for other photographs, practical assistance and advice.

I am grateful to Mr Brian Davies, Pontypridd Museum, for valuable background information on industrial matters particularly to do with Aberdare; to Mr Scott Reid, of Cyfarthfa Castle Museum; and to the Rev Dr D. Ben Rees, who has been unstinting in his efforts to keep alive the name of Henry Richard. Also to Councillor Ray Davies, Bedwas, and Côr Cochion Caerdydd, steadfast fighters in the cause of peace.

Thanks to Gwen, my wife, a true historian who shares my love of second-hand bookshops and whose discoveries have contributed much to my researches.

Finally, my grateful thanks to Clive Boutle, of Francis Boutle Publishers, for his skill, good taste and determination in bringing this project to fruition. As always, it has been a pleasure to work with him.

Gwyn Griffiths

List of illustrations

Bust of Henry Richard by William Davies (Mynorydd).
National Library of Wales copyright

Introduction

Henry Richard (1812–1888), was one of the great, and the best known, of nineteenth century Welshmen. His name was known to politicians, particularly those concerned with the cause of peace, in Europe and the United States of America. In Wales he was adored. He was a respected Member of Parliament for 20 years, but although a brilliant future had been predicted for him he remained a back-bencher. It is unlikely that he sought government office and in any case, politicians who stick to their principles can rarely expect to attain high office. Henry Richard did not compromise.

He was born in the small town of Tregaron in the heart of Ceredigion, Mid-Wales. His father, the Rev Ebenezer Richard, was the town's influential Calvinistic Methodist minister. While the Rev John Elias of Anglesey was the supreme Presbyterian power in North Wales, Ebenezer Richard ruled in South Wales. Henry inherited the eloquence and organising skills of his father. His mother, Mary, was a woman of influence, capable of keeping order among any unruly females in her husband's chapel. She was the daughter of a small local landowner, socially superior in status to her husband, and with money to provide her two sons with the best education available to Nonconformists at that time. The older brother, Edward Williams Richard, studied medicine at Guy's Hospital and Henry, although the son of a Presbyterian Minister, went to the Congregational College – or Academy – in Highbury. The Congregationalists, or Independents as they are usually called in Welsh-speaking Wales, were the most radical of the main Nonconformist denominations and it was there that Henry Richard found his spiritual home. That, allied to the Radical tradition fermenting in London in that time, was a good grounding for a clever and rebellious young man.

After a sometimes stormy period as a student, Henry Richard

was called to be minister of Marlborough Congregational Chapel in the Old Kent Road. He was a successful and popular minister and what was once a divided chapel with a sizeable debt became a thriving, expanding centre of worship, education and culture. He became active in promoting voluntary education in London, and to some extent in Wales. He became involved in the Peace Society, and for a few years he was both minister of Marlborough Chapel and Secretary of the Peace Society. While holding both posts he was joint organiser of three international peace conferences – in Brussels, Paris and Frankfurt. After 15 years in Marlborough he left the ministry to become the full-time Secretary of the Peace Movement. Under his guidance the society grew from a marginal, religious group of individuals who opposed war and armed conflict on moral and religious grounds to a more secular organisation. He became close to the Free Trade activists Richard Cobden and John Bright, men who saw the pacifying possibilities of trade between nations. It was internationalism in a new guise. With Richard as Secretary of the Peace Society, a new generation of pacifists emerged, men ready to challenge governments and bring pressures on them to settle disputes through arbitration instead of going to war. Henry Richard encouraged anyone who loved peace to join, whether or not they believed in the abstract notion of a Christian duty to oppose war. The Society drew closer to the radical wing of the Liberal Party, not that they – or Henry Richard – shied away from criticising whatever party was in power.

At the same time Richard remained a stout defender of Wales and Welsh interests. He became Wales's spokesman in an English press which was at best dismissive, usually contemptuous, of Wales and the Welsh. He had articles published in the London papers justifying the Rebecca Riots at a time when even the Welsh language papers showed little sympathy for them or their methods. His most celebrated defence of Wales, however, was his response to the 1847 *Reports of the Commissioners of Enquiry into the State of Education in Wales* often referred to as The Treason of the Blue Books. They were written by three English Anglicans with no understanding or sympathy for Wales, its language nor the Dissenting denominations which were displacing the Established Church in the country. The entire nation was enraged, none more so than Henry Richard. Unable to read the Welsh language papers, the English ignored, were unaware even, of the commotion in Wales – until Richard entered the fray in the London papers. He had been invited to speak on Voluntary Education in Wales in a series of lectures at Crosby Hall. He quickly departed from his subject to deliver a thundering attack on the Commissioners Report. His lecture was published in the *British Banner* and as one of the pamphlets in the Crosby Hall lectures series. Richard's lecture attracted such attention that one of the commissioners felt obliged to respond to it by publishing a pamphlet of his own in defence of the Reports![1]

The series of Peace Conferences which he and the American Elihu Burritt organised between 1848 and 1851 – in Brussels, Paris, Frankfurt and London – were hugely successful. Organising such events would be an ambitious project even today. At that time it must have been a momentous task – arranging speakers, finding suitable venues and ensuring board and lodging for the many thousands who attended. He came to know, and gained the support of many prominent European statesmen. He opposed the Crimean War, almost single-handedly as most of his friends deserted in face of the jingoism of that "popular" war. His arguments against war and in favour of arbitration between nations are as relevant today as they were in his time. He opposed war on Christian and moral grounds but his arguments were usually founded on the waste of war – in lives, money, and the poverty and suffering of working people.

Was he a Welsh nationalist? He was certainly a fervent patriot. Nationalism takes many forms. There is the nationalism perverted into aggressive imperialism bristling with animosity, greed and self-aggrandisement at the expense of others. He detested this trait of English/British nationalism which he encountered in his work with the Peace Society. There was also, among the Free Trade politicians Richard had got to know, a nationalism happy to see nations growing and thriving side by side. A nationalism leading to internationalism – an informal internationalism of peaceful, profitable intercommunication of goods and ideas among nations recognising a just harmony of interests between peoples. This, Henry Richard, as a Welshman, would have understood. When his fellow Liberals protested about Russia's oppressive treatment of the people of Poland and their language, he was never shy of telling them that that was exactly what they – the English – were doing to the people of Wales and the Welsh language. His brand of nationalism led to his internationalist vision of a Europe united in peace.

In 1868, for the first time, he stood for Parliament as a Liberal candidate for Merthyr Tydfil and Aberdare. It was the first election after the extension of the franchise and the working-class, industrial constituency was probably the most democratic in Britain. Richard was presented as one of that working class and of the same social origin as the voters. He owned no property, he was unattached to any economic interests and sympathetic to the social objectives of the people. He was returned with one of the biggest majorities of the Parliament. So it was until the end of his life, and in his latter years no one dared oppose him. He was not a wealthy man and unlike parliamentarians in that era his modest election costs were borne by his supporters and electors. Every political movement in which he was ever involved was democratic.[2]

One of his first speeches in the House of Commons was an attack on the Conservatives who had dismissed tenants for voting Liberal. Richard has been described as a gentle and unassuming person, yet on an election platform and in Parliament his attacks were scathing, laced with a sarcastic, caustic wit. We cannot imagine any present-day Member of Parliament attacking the very concept of war with his raw ferocity, facts and figures always at his finger-tips. His arguments were often based on the information he had gleaned from the Government's own official documents – he was irrefutable. He was a meticulous researcher and an enemy of colonialism. He often said that being a Welshman had taught him to loathe the warlike tendencies of the English.

Although he lived his entire adult life in London, it was said that he was more comfortable speaking or preaching in Welsh and that he would take every opportunity to do so. Tregaron, Wales and the Welsh language were his anchors. His book, *Letters and Essays on Wales* (1866), published originally in the *Morning Star* and *Evening Star*, has been described as the most important and influential work on Wales published in the nineteenth century.[3] The articles were intended to help the English understand their eccentric neighbours. They certainly had that effect – Gladstone admitted that he learnt almost all he knew about Wales from those essays and that they had completely changed his attitudes. Of greater importance, the book gave the Welsh new confidence and a pride in their own culture and nationality. It remains a stimulating read to this day. Other, earlier, speeches and writings had been translated into Welsh. A. G. Williams, the first Archbishop of Wales after the Disestablishment, grudgingly conceded that "[t]hey were the marching orders of every dissenting preacher and deacon, and were heard in every chapel in the principality".[4]

In his final years, as a member of the Lord Cross Royal Commission on Education, he fought a determined and successful battle to introduce the teaching of Welsh into schools. Had the teachers and Welsh Inspectorate acted upon the recommendations of that Commission – and it was on the issue of the language in schools alone that the Commission managed to agree – the language today would be in a much healthier condition. He was active in the establishment of Aberystwyth University and Vice-Chair of Cardiff University College. A fortnight before his death he chaired a long and arduous meeting to prepare the University of Wales Charter. He died in the home of his old friend Richard Davies, in Treborth, in sight of Snowdon and overlooking the Menai Straits.

He admired Gladstone, but when "the grand old man" acted in a manner contrary to the pacifist principles of Henry Richard, he could expect no mercy. Even in the late 1840s Richard had been dubbed the Apostle of Peace. In the House of Commons he was the Member for Wales. He was the first MP to fight Wales's corner and he inspired his own generation of parliamentarians and the next – people like T. E. Ellis – to follow his example. In an era when the reins of power were firmly in the grip of the Anglican Church, he managed to prize some of that power away from them. He was the unofficial leader of the English and Welsh Nonconformists in the House of the Commons. To quote A. G. Williams again, Richard was "a commanding figure among Nonconformists in England, [and] their supreme leader in Wales."[5] Williams also provided a lively description of Richard whom he claimed to have met a few times during the Merthyr and Aberdare election of 1868:

> A short, thick-set Welshman with a resolute mouth and keen eyes he delighted the Welsh people with the purity and beauty of his Welsh and with bursts of real eloquence. I do not believe that any political leader in Wales has ever commanded among the Nonconformists an influence so unchallenged and so profound as the influence at that time of Mr Henry Richard.[6]

He never attained a Government post – and it is unlikely that he ever desired one – but he held considerable influence. For all his efforts – and he opposed every war on principle – his failures were clear enough, while it is almost impossible to calculate his successes in terms of the lives saved by his interventions.

Chapter 1

Childhood in Cardiganshire

Henry Richard was born into a comparatively privileged family on 3 April 1812. His maternal great-grandfather was Efan Dafydd Siencyn of Cyswch, Llanfair Clydogau, poet, preacher and follower of the evangelist Daniel Rowland of Llangeitho. His paternal grandfather, also named Henry Richard, from Trefîn, Pembrokeshire, had been a teacher in Griffith Jones's Circulating Schools[1] and was born in 1730, the year Griffith Jones established his first school in Llanddowror. From a young age he showed a love of knowledge and a desire to share that knowledge. In due course he spent time as a teacher in Llanddowror where he taught Thomas Charles, founder of the Welsh Sunday School Movement, and one of the founders of the British and Foreign Bible Society. Richard later established a school near Barmouth, giving Calvinistic Methodism a foot-hold in Meirionethshire.[2]

The Rev Ebenezer Richard, father of the subject of this book, was one of two sons of that Henry Richard. The other son was the Rev Thomas Richard of Fishguard, a fiery preacher and a colourful character – but more of him later. The brothers were educated at Haverfordwest Grammar School and on leaving that school Ebenezer Richard established a school in Dinas, a village a few miles up the coast from Fishguard. He was also a private tutor to the children of Major William Bowen of Llwyngwair. Later he kept a school in Cardigan and tutored the children of Captain James Bowen, brother of William Bowen. Between them the two brothers owned most of the land of that part of North Pembrokeshire. Both were sympathetic to Methodism, which explains their friendship with Ebenezer Richard. Such was their admiration of Richard that James Bowen did his best to dissuade

Henry Richard's father, Ebenezer

him from becoming an itinerant preacher. Ebenezer Richard's military connections are ironic considering his son's lifelong campaign for peace. During his travels as a Calvinistic Methodist preacher Ebenezer Richard met Mary, daughter of William Williams of Wernfawr, Tregaron. It was a lengthy and discreet courtship, conducted mostly by letter, possibly because the – albeit modest – landowning Williams family doubted the suitability of a Methodist preacher as husband for their only daughter. However, after nine years, by which time Mary became increasingly uneasy the two were married in Tregaron parish church on 1 November 1809.[3] Ebenezer, one of the first men to be ordained by the Methodists, was appointed minister of Bwlchgwynt, Tregaron, a chapel first built in 1774. We can assume from his activities in Dinas and Cardigan that Ebenezer Richard was as enthusiastic for education as he was for religion. He did remarkable work for the Sunday school movement and was described as a man of exceptional energy and organising ability – his second son, Henry, inherited the talents of his father and paternal grandfather.

Mary was considered socially superior to Ebenezer. Her brother, Edward Williams, had enjoyed an exciting – if brief – life. Edward Williams may not have been a moral or religious influence on Henry Richard and his siblings, but financially his contribution was important. Edward was a privateersman in the service of John & Henry Clarke, Liverpool, who had been – and may still have been – licensed slave-traders. He probably attended a nautical school at Llanarth, on Cardigan Bay, which taught navigation. By 1800 he was a junior officer on the *Duke of Clarence*, originally *La Flora*, an armed vessel captured from the French. He showed promise and at the age of 26 was captain of the *Active*, another vessel captured from the French. His first voyage was to Africa and from there to Havana and back to Liverpool – one of the old slave-trade routes.[4] He contributed substantially to the family coffers and when he died in Africa on 7 April 1805, he left his father £3,500 in his will.[5] Only £900 came immediately into the hands of William Williams and the remainder was the cause of worry and legal disputes in future years. Doubtless this sum contributed to the dowry of £1,000 provided to Ebenezer Richard when he and Mary were married. It also explains how, in time, Ebenezer and Mary Richard were able to afford the education they provided for their children. According to Henry Richard's testimony at no time in his life did Ebenezer Richard earn more than £40 a year.[6]

In addition to financial security, Mary brought other talents to the marriage. For a woman of that era she was well educated. She was a determined woman able to keep the competitive and arrogant women of Bwlchgwynt chapel in order and was often referred to as "the old JP". She could organise the Sunday school when necessary and conduct a prayer meeting as well as any man.

Ebenezer's brother, Thomas, was equally fortunate in his choice of a wife, despite the scandalous circumstance of the marriage. While still in his teens Tom was impressive even when sharing the pulpit with older, distinguished preachers. His very presence would cause a flutter of anticipation among the congregation. Tom had fallen in love with Bridget Gwynne of Cwrt, Fishguard, but her father did not fancy a fiery Dissenting preacher as a son-in-law. The ardent couple would not be dissuaded. Bridget went to stay with an aunt in Manorowen who shared her father's disapproval of the courtship. There was an easy way out through the window of the bedroom and on the morning of 30 April 1819, a Mr Vaughan and a pair of horses waited beneath her window. They galloped to Llanrhian Church where Tom, Ebenezer and a few friends were waiting and the vicar of the parish performed the marriage ceremony. What Ebenezer Richard knew in advance of the plans and what was his attitude to his younger brother's romantic escapade is unclear. The terse note in the family register suggests a note of disapproval. "We enter it in our Family Register because of the near relation we bear to one

Prospect House, Tregaron, home of the Richard family

another," wrote Ebenezer. Despite its scandalous beginnings it was a happy marriage, Bridget became a faithful and devout Calvinistic Methodist and had the means to allow Tom to devote his life to the ministry.[7]

The first of Ebenezer and Mary Richard's four children was born on 24 August 1810. Edward Williams Richard was named after his late uncle, the sea captain who had died five years earlier. At the time the family lived in Tŷ Gwyn, Mary's home in Tregaron. Early in 1811 the foundation stone was laid on the other side of the river Brennig for the house that would soon become the family home. The land was given to them on very generous terms – a "lease of lives" – by Mary's cousin, John Jones of Deri Ormond. Jones, a wealthy landowner and successful London physician, had amassed a fortune of £200,000 and taken a liking to Ebenezer. He went further. After consulting with the Vicar of Llanbadarn and other church dignitaries, Jones tried to persuade Ebenezer Richard to accept ordination to the Church of England, and had even lined up a church for him. The Calvinistic Methodists were for 75 years a group of voluntary associations or societies within the Anglican Church and it was not until 1811 that they finally broke away and established themselves as a separate denomination and ordained their own ministers, so it would not have been a big step had Ebenezer accepted the offer. It suggests that a Methodist preacher was not entirely satisfactory to the Wernfawr family. Ebenezer declined the offer and there is no suggestion that this caused any offence to John Jones and their friendship was not impaired.[8]

On 4 May 1815 the family of four moved into their new house,

Prospect House, where their next child, Mary, was born. Later that year Edward took Henry to play in Dolfelin field with strict instructions to take good care of his little brother. Edward got involved in a game with other boys and Henry got too close to the edge and fell into the river. Fortunately a woman we only know as Peggy, who lived in Cyrte, Blaenau Caron, was passing and pulled the unconscious toddler out of the water. Wrapped warmly in her shawl he recovered – and so was saved the life of one who grew up to become one of Wales's most influential nineteenth-century personalities.[9]

The young brothers were a lively pair, with a love for riding and swimming. Henry, later in life, admitted that he suffered in his youth from a guilty conscience following an evening of pleasure. "I remember well when a youth having a vague uneasy conscience of guilt after a merry evening. Such was the effect of early educa-tion in forming an artificial conscience by forbidding as sinful what is perfectly innocent."[10] Swimming and riding, clearly, were not considered sinful. Cleanliness came second only to godliness in the Richard household and the boys were allowed to bathe whenever they wished. Horse-riding, despite its dangers, was the most effective way to travel. Their paternal grandfather – Henry Richard – died at the age of 80 after his horse slipped on the ice on the way home from preaching at services in Ambleston, Woodstock and Blaen-y-wern, Pembrokeshire. He broke the bones in his lower leg and died of shock a fortnight later. It is known that the young Henry Richard had at least one lucky escape when riding. When he was 10 years of age he accompanied his father to a meeting of the Methodist Association in New Chapel, North Pembrokeshire. A crow rose from a nearby field and the pony bolted. Henry was dragged along through the dirt and stones. Luckily both stirrups broke and he escaped serous injury.[11]

Henry Richard probably received his earliest education at home, taught by his mother – and by his father when he was not away preaching. Tregaron was blessed with educated people and Richard probably received private tuition from the Rev Theophilus Jones, a friend of his maternal grandfather, who lived in Lôn Penyrodyn. Jones (1762–1829) was one of the early giants of Welsh Nonconformity and had been educated at the influential grammar school, St John's College, Ystrad Meurig, where he was said to be one of the cleverest pupils of his time. We can assume that his Latin and Greek were excellent. The name of St John's Ystrad Meurig, which finally closed its doors in 1973, is held in romantic affection by Welsh scholars and poets – a school that uniquely combined the ancient Welsh poetic tradition with a classical Greek and Latin education. It raised generations of Anglican clergy – and men who defected to Nonconformity – as well as teachers who enriched the villages of Cardiganshire. Another local scholar was Daniel Jones of Camer Fach, and no doubt Henry would have been taught by him in Sunday School. There was also a school in the town taught by John Jones, a retired civil servant and his English wife. This John Jones was the grandson of John Dafydd Daniel, another leading light of early Methodism in Wales.[12]

There was no shortage of books in Prospect House. Ebenezer Richard never missed an opportunity to buy books – usually second hand – while on his travels. He bought many books when Thomas Blaencyswch's library was sold in 1811. Among them were *Aesop's Fables* and *The Vicar of Wakefield* – both showing signs of wear and tear.

Edward and Henry Richard were first sent to the Mathematical and Commercial Academy in Chalybeate Street, Aberystwyth, where there was an excellent headmaster named John Evans, who set great importance on science, mathematics and nautical studies.[13] It appears that Edward had shown some interest in a maritime career. Unfortunately he showed no aptitude for astronomy or mathematics, necessary skills for navigation if he was to follow his uncle's footsteps.

Both left Chalybeate Street without the benefits enjoyed by their contemporary, the brilliant Lewis Edwards of Penllwyn in the Rheidol valley. Edwards eventually became the first Principal of Bala Theological College, established the influential literary magazine *Y Traethodydd*, and had attended London University at the time Edward and Richard were also students in the capital. The brothers were then sent to Llangeitho Grammar School, which was much closer to Tregaron. Here there was another well-respected headmaster, John Jones of Glanleri, Borth, a village north of Aberystwyth. Jones had been educated at Ystrad Meurig, but had left the Church and joined the Calvinistic Methodists.[14] He placed great importance on theology although Lewis Edwards – who had also moved to this school – complained that he limited himself to studying the Puritan theologians. Ebenezer Richard may have sent his sons to Llangeitho as a reaction to the Anglican influences of Ystrad Meurig.

A lifelong, if uneasy, relationship continued between Lewis

Edwards and the Richard brothers in the face of some trying circumstances. One was a public and vicious reprimand Edwards received some years later from the boys' uncle, Thomas Richard, at a meeting of the Methodists Association in Woodstock. Edwards was intent on furthering his education and sought the approval of the Association. Thomas Richard responded by accusing him of pride and arrogance in language that reduced Edwards to tears. Ebenezer Richard was more measured in his use of words, but he also declined to give Edwards his support. The members, however, were taken aback by Thomas Richard's response and Edward Jones of the Tabernacle, Aberystwyth, and John Hughes of Pontrobert, spoke up in support of Lewis Edwards,[15] who was given permission to apply as a student at a newly established Presbyterian college in Belfast. In the event he chose London University, the new secular university – "that godless institution on Gower Street" – established as a reaction to the educational privileges enjoyed by members of the Anglican Church.[16] Edwards was even more enthusiastic than Henry Richard for education and he later attended Edinburgh University. In the same year that Lewis Edwards was reprimanded by Thomas Richard for wanting to pursue his desire for education, Henry Richard was given every encouragement by his uncle to attend the Highbury Congregational College. Years later, Thomas Richard sent his own son to the Anglican St David's College, Lampeter! It is no surprise that Lewis Edwards retained a degree of animosity towards the Richard family. Many years later, Edwards, having written a generous appreciation of the life of Ebenezer Richard in Y Traethodydd, complained that he never received a word of gratitude from either of the brothers.[17] Evan Phillips of Newcastle Emlyn had an interesting opinion of Ebenezer and Thomas Richard: "Ebenezer was like a plum, soft on the outside, but there was a stone in the centre. After breaking the hard exterior, like through the shell of a coconut, you discovered in Thomas Richard a heart of gentle sweetness. I never met a gentler person than Mr Richards (sic)."[18]

The lives and careers of Edward and Henry Richard ran in parallel for many years – their parents probably presumed that away from home they would be safer in each other's company. With Mary Richard's cousin, John Jones, a successful physician in London, medicine was a possible career for one of the sons. In 1825, the family heard that a Mr D. F. Nichol, a Carmarthen chemist, was seeking an apprentice and they considered this would be suitable for Edward, their eldest. It proved an unusual arrangement. Mr Nichol, it transpired, was a 21-year-old student, who had been a chemist's apprentice in Carmarthen and had gone on to St George's Hospital in London where he eventually passed to be a licentiate of the Society of Apothecaries and later proceeded to the Royal College of Surgeons. Edward was apprenticed to Messers Nichol, Fryer and Mortimer, druggists and chemists, Upper Market Street, Carmarthen. D. F. Nichol appeared to be the senior partner but he was certainly not active and it was Mr Mortimer who ran the business. Evidently the £99 which was the cost of Edward's apprenticeship was an important contribution to maintaining Nichol's London life-style and studies. The complicated arrangements were to Ebenezer Richard's advantage. It gave him time to find the £99 and find an apprenticeship for Henry, also in Carmarthen. The two sons of the Rev Ebenezer Morris, Twr Gwyn, Lledrod, a close friend of Ebenezer Richard, were doing well in the cloth trade in Liverpool and it was decided that this would do for Henry. At the age of 14, Henry Richard was apprenticed for three years to a haberdasher, John Lewis, by the town hall in Carmarthen, at a cost of £15 a year. He proved an excellent worker and was described by John Lewis as kindly and talented and he was given ample time and opportunity for study.

The boys duly became members of the Calvinistic Methodist chapel in Water Street. Edward was finding the work dreary and there are suggestions that he was having doubts about religion. He must have expressed these doubts because a letter from his father written in 1827 admits that he, too, had suffered similar uncertainties of faith in his youth. But the following year Ebenezer worried that Edward was still showing little or no concern for religion. He wrote seeking assurance that both were communing regularly at the "Lord's Table" and hoping that "their thoughts were often turned to their immortal souls". Henry returned to Tregaron on 4 August 1829, having spent his time, according to his father's entry in the family register, "with credit to himself and acceptability to his master and satisfaction to his parents. He had been admitted to full communion with the church at Water Street and received a pleasing testimonial to his character from the minister and elders." Three months later Edward returned having completed his apprenticeship "though with much difficulty to the end". There is more than a hint of relief in Ebenezer Richard's words: "He as well as his brother was received to full Communion during the time of his Servitude and was enabled to complete his time without forfeiting his membership in the Church of God. Alleluiah!"[19]

By then, Henry, hardly 18, was employed by John Matthews, a draper at the Bristol Emporium, Aberystwyth, on the princely salary of £25 a year. His employer, with whom he lodged, was completely satisfied with his work and described him as a young man of deep religious convictions. Matthews had heard him speaking publicly and praying at the Tabernacle, and hinted that he had qualities for which the word "genius" may not be inappropriate. John Evans, his old headmaster at the Mathematical and Commercial Academy in Chalybeate Street, was a deacon at the church and very soon Henry was a popular Sunday school teacher with a class of young men. He took on the duties of occasional lay preacher and although conscientious in his work at the Bristol Emporium, it was becoming noticeable that he had no intention of spending his life measuring and selling cloth.

While Henry, for the time being, was in stable employment, his brother was restless. Edward was now intent on becoming a doctor and to study at Guy's Hospital in London. With his mother's cousin, John Jones, a successful physician in the capital, and Jones's sister – Catherine – married to the celebrated surgeon, Sir Astley Cooper, his connections were excellent. Another John Jones from Tregaron, a friend of Edward's, was already a medical student in London. On 15 February 1830, Ebenezer Richard and Edward began the stage-coach journey to London. The intention was that he should find suitable employment to pay for his keep while studying in his hours of leisure. The money owed to Mary Richard from her brother, the late Edward Williams's, will was still unresolved and a matter of increasing concern. Edward Richard would lodge for the immediate future with Mr and Mrs Josiah Davies of the Welsh Calvinistic Methodist chapel in Jewin Crescent, and his father would conduct services for nine Sundays, presumably for free. It was hoped that the inheritance from Edward Williams's will would arrive before too long allowing the family to pay for their elder son's education and keep in London. The weeks passed and on 21 April Ebenezer began his return journey to Wales and still there was no sign of work for his son. Finally, on 8 May there was relief with the news that Edward had been offered work with Messers Marshall and Angus, surgeons, of 35 Greek Street, Soho, on a salary of £18 a year and his board and lodging. He quickly gained their confidence and enjoyed the work there immensely – much more than in Carmarthen.[20]

But before receiving the good news from Edward, Ebenezer Richard faced another shock, in spite of indications that Henry was restless at Aberystwyth. A letter he had sent to his father and brother in London suggested that he was just a little jealous of Edward enjoying the wonders of London. He hoped that Edward would be able to resist the "vice and infamy".

It was a few days after he had returned to Tregaron that Mary Richard told her husband that Henry was determined to go into the ministry. Henry had already discussed the mater with his mother so that she would break the news gently to him before the "official" letter arrived. When the letter came it revealed that he had never felt really happy in the work he had chosen imprudently and was finding himself "bound to a business to which I was neither qualified by nature nor inclination"[21] The "old JP" needed all her diplomatic skills to calm a husband who anticipated supporting two student sons, neither of whom was contributing towards their keep. Also, arrangements had been made to send Hannah, the youngest of the four children, away to school in Aberaeron. Ebenezer evidently felt his sons to be inconsiderate of his feelings and had been aware while he in London that Edward had been itching to see him return to Tregaron. He was obviously concerned about Edward and he wrote to him with endless advice on how to safeguard his "immortal soul" – to keep clear of sin and laziness, to be careful of the company he kept, the places he visited and the people to whom he spoke. And "never neglect prayer; (and) be diligent in worship either public or private".

Plans for Henry's future remained uncertain. He sent Edward a critical review of the performances of the preachers at the Aberystwyth Association at the beginning of May. "You expect me now, I doubt not, to give my opinion of the proceedings," he wrote. "The preaching was on the whole good. Mr M. Roberts preached better in my opinion than I have ever heard him. Mr Howells was in the middling mood, but my uncle's (Tom Richard) sermon in the chapel was the most excellent. I have seldom listened to such a discourse – it electrified the congregation."[22]

Chapter 2

Early Years in London

Ebenezer Richard revealed his youngest son's ambition to a few close friends in the Methodist Association but nothing would be decided until he went to Bristol a few weeks later and discussed the matter with "Mr Davies and other friends" – probably the Rev Dr David Davies of Charlotte Street. Dr Davies had influential friends, among them Dr Ebenezer Henderson, Principal of the Highbury Congregational College in London. On 11 June Ebenezer sent a letter to Edward with the news that he had just returned home from Bristol and was about to depart to attend the Association's meeting in Bala and was taking Henry with him. Evidently, it was decided that Henry would leave John Matthews's drapery in Aberystwyth and accompany his father on his preaching journeys until a place could be found for him at a Nonconformist academy.[1]

Henry was determined to have an education before embarking on a career in the ministry and it was decided that Highbury was the ideal place. Interestingly, the Presbyterian College at Carmarthen, which also trained ministers for the Congregationalists, Baptists and Unitarians, was not considered. It is likely that Ebenezer Richard believed the place to be "tainted" by Unitarianism, of which he disapproved. On 12 August Ebenezer Richard presented his son's cause to the Cardiganshire Monthly Meeting of the Calvinistic Methodists held, as it happened, in Bwlchgwynt, Tregaron. Without a single objection it was agreed to support Henry Richard's desire to study at Highbury, the college of another denomination. It is an indication of his father's influence within the Methodists, especially when we recall Lewis Edwards's traumatic experience when he expressed a similar desire at Woodstock earlier the same year. Henry Richard, in an article published in *The Congregationalist* in 1876, said that he had decided not to become a minister of religion without a college education, and that he went to London without any specific plan.[2] It is worth noting that Nonconformist academies had existed in Wales as well as England for a century and in general their standards were high. Many offered Hebrew, Latin, Greek and German. We find, later, that Henry Richard had at least an adequate knowledge of French, no doubt learnt at Highbury.[3]

Edward Richard does not appear to have been overworked in the surgery in Greek Street and like many an exiled Welshman we find him submitting an article to the Welsh journal *Seren Gomer*, observing the comings and goings from the window of his lodgings in Romilly Street. His writing shows an acquaintance with the satirist Ellis Wynne (1670–1734) and his *Gweledigaeth Cwrs y Byd* (A Vision of the Way of the World) and its streets of Pride, Pleasure and Lucre. He also appears to have been influenced by the eccentric literary style of the London Welsh antiquarian William Owen Pughe (1759–1835). As well as his dreams of walking the corridors of Guy's Hospital, Edward was an enthusiastic character with many passing interests. He sent his father a copy of Edward Irving's discourses, who replied that he thought them "superexcellent as a Lecture from a philosopher's chair but nothing of a pulpit sermon to the never-dying souls of perishing sinners."[4]

As soon as Edward knew that Henry would be coming to study in London he arranged temporary accommodation for him at Jewin Crescent Chapel House and set about making other plans. He promised to take time off from work to meet his brother either by the Bolt and Tun Inn or the Quadrant, Regent Street, depending on which coach he would travel. He offered to speak to Thomas Wilson, the treasurer of Highbury College, on behalf of his younger brother. Edward was only 20 years old, but he never lacked confidence, and Wilson was an important man – self-important even – who by his wealth had accumulated much power and influence. It was agreed that it would be wiser to wait for Henry to arrive before making any representations to Wilson.[5]

On 18 August 1830, Henry Richard left Tregaron for London, his permanent home for the rest of his life. On route he visited the Rev Dr David Davies in Bristol who gave him a letter of introduction to Dr Ebenezer Henderson of Highbury College. Two days later, on 21 August, he arrived in London and settled in at Jewin

Crescent. There he met David Thomas, also a Welsh speaker and the son of a Calvinistic Methodist minister in Merthyr Tydfil. In an obituary to David Thomas in *The Congregationalist* in 1876, Henry Richard recalls their first meeting. Thomas's nephew, incidentally, was D. Alfred Thomas (Lord Rhondda), the Liberal industrialist with whom Richard very briefly before his death represented the Merthyr Tydfil and Aberdare parliamentary constituency.

> Fortunately I went to lodge to the Chapel House and when I told some of the friends of my intentions, I was informed that a young man from Merthyr named David Thomas also stayed at the house, and was about to go to Highbury. We met. David Thomas a tall, slim young man, with broad shoulders and a mop of fair hair over which he had little control. He knew my father well, who had been received at his mother's house in Merthyr in the course of some of his visits to Glamorgan, because my father's work extended to all parts of the principality. He had heard him preach many times, and he cherished that deep respect for him – bordering almost on worship – which the Welsh people, especially Welsh Methodists, have for their great preachers.
>
> He welcomed me kindly and took me to meet Thomas Wilson. I will not relate the story of how I was accepted at Highbury, although it was interesting enough. All I had expected was to be sent on trial for a term to Rowell. But somehow I managed to pass with what little knowledge I had, and after going through the terrifying experience of delivering a sermon to the committee, and the examination which followed, I was allowed immediately to enter the Academy.[6]

David Thomas was a year younger than Richard and had been working in Barclay's Bank, Lombard Street, since 1827. After deciding to enter the ministry the young man from Merthyr spent nine months at a school in Rowell, Northamptonshire. After that he had been accepted at Highbury and as already noted he took Henry to meet the influential Thomas Wilson. Henry had the opportunity to present his letter of introduction from Dr David Davies to Dr Henderson. Letters of commendation had also been provided by his former employers, John Lewis of Carmarthen, and John Matthews of Aberystwyth. And there was a Statement of Approval from the Monthly Meeting at Bwlchgwynt, Tregaron, with a further note of support from Anglesey's "Methodist Pope", the Rev John Elias. He must have created a favourable impression because the college decided not to ask him to go to Rowell but to

sit an examination and preach a sermon to the college committee
– his first ever in the English language. The sermon he delivered
to the Highbury Committee must have been an ordeal. He had
probably never heard more than half-a-dozen English sermons,
let alone deliver one. Years later he referred disdainfully to the custom in his native Cardiganshire of sometimes including an
English sermon in the quarterly meetings of the Association or at
a preaching festival. It was, he said, a kind of "religious sandwich",
but with a difference. With a normal sandwich the tasty part is in
the centre but with these sandwiches the tasteless bits were in the
middle. Throughout his life he was quite dismissive of the English
style of preaching[7] although there is evidence that he soon adopted
that style himself.

Richard began his probationary period at Highbury College
together with David Thomas and four other new students. The
two Welsh students moved into their college accommodation on 6
September 1830, and there began a life-long friendship. Their
friendship – and love of Welsh preaching – often got them into
trouble. Henry admitted that both were disadvantaged at having to
preach publicly in a language and style in which neither was comfortable.

They frequently attended Sunday services in London's Welsh
chapels, especially Jewin Crescent. "There were in the (English)
Nonconformist at that time famous preachers … and I had heard
them all," he said. "But usually Mr Thomas and myself, in our
first two years at the college before we had to undertake our own
Sunday engagements, more often than not, would attend the
Welsh chapels, because to us the English ministry was cold and
formal compared to the warm eloquence of our fellow countrymen. In those days the Jewin pulpit would be filled by some of the
great preachers of the Principality – John Elias, Ebenezer Richard
(my father), Henry Rees (Liverpool), those whom I believed then
and still believe to be the incomparable masters of religious eloquence."[8] It was not long before John Elias fell out of favour with
Henry because of his "sentimental attitude" towards the Anglican
Church.[9]

Evening services at Jewin Crescent often included two sermons
and a meeting of church members – "which went on for a long
time". As they did not have money for a carriage and there were no
buses they had no choice but to walk back to Highbury. "David
Thomas with his long legs and great strides, and myself with my
short legs and rapid steps, hurrying home with all our might, and

peering into the window of any shop with a clock, full of concern that we would not reach the gates by ten." The door of the college would be locked promptly at ten after which any late-comer had to ring the bell and face the wrath of one of the teachers.[10]

Edward, the older brother, had by now been accepted as a "surgical student" at Guy's and moved to Webb Street, close to the hospital, where he joined his friend and fellow medical student John Jones, also of Tregaron. Jones was a kindly, exuberant character although his family, in the opinion of Mary Richard, were "a set of very hard people". According to Ebenezer Richard, Mary worried more about Jones than about her own sons.[11] That autumn, the first spent by Henry and Edward in London, a large number of the population, including many students, went down with some illness, possibly cholera.[12] Edward suffered from it, but his friend John Jones died of its effects. In a letter to his parents, which included a report of the funeral, Henry wrote that Edward was deeply affected by his friend's death. Jones's widowed mother claimed that, apart from herself, no one felt her son's death more deeply than Edward.

After his friend's death Edward moved to other lodgings, in Crosby Row, again very convenient to Guy's, where he was joined for Christmas 1830 by Henry. A hamper from Tregaron relieved the monotony of their usual diet, which together with Henry's company, revived Edward's spirits greatly. In the same period a note mentions that the brothers had renewed their acquaintance with Lewis Edwards who was at London University and finding it very agreeable living like a prince on "bread, cheese and porter". Early in 1831 the three travelled together back to Cardiganshire.

The Richard family had influential and interesting London connections. Among them were the Jones family of Banc yr Eidion Du (The Black Ox Bank), Llandovery, a bank eventually taken over by Lloyd's. Mary Richard, to whom they were related, for unknown reasons, disapproved of these Joneses and advised her sons to keep well away from them. This advise was ignored and when Mary discovered that Henry had been to afternoon tea with them he got a stern reprimand. He responded with one of his mother's favourite Welsh sayings – that there is no harm in taking a pearl from a frog's mouth. Edward, on the other hand, considered visiting the doctor John Jones something of an ordeal. Mary Richard was insistent that they should keep on good terms with her cousin and his family, but Edward in particular felt that the welcome in the doctor's house was not very cordial. Yet, he appeared to delight in receiving news from Cardiganshire, especially reports on the building of the Anglican St David's College, Lampeter, which would open in 1827. John Jones was the treasurer and contributed generously to the building fund. He was also happy to arrange for parcels and letters from Tregaron to be conveyed to the two brothers in London.[13]

Edward's fellow-lodger, also a student at Guy's was Llewelyn Mortimer of Trehowell, Pencaer, near Fishguard. Ebenezer Richard, from nearby Trefîn, was anxious that nothing should impair his forty years of friendship with the Mortimer family. "We are glad you notice Mr. Ll. Mortimer in your letter which I hope you will continue to do, and please to tell him that I saw his father, sisters, and brother at Fishguard last Sunday, and in tolerable good health," he wrote in a letter to Edward.

The friendship was strained during Christmas 1831, which Henry, Edward and Mortimer celebrated together, again at Crosby Row. A hamper of Christmas fare from Trehowell had been left in a cart outside a public house at Welshpool and taken by thieves. Luckily a goose, turkey and a hare arrived from Tregaron with strict instructions that all should be shared with Llewelyn. Also, a tongue and goose arrived from Rowlands of Ystrad, together with a note that there would have been a hare in the hamper – if only he had caught one! Evidently this hamper was in payment for advice or treatment regarding some ailment suffered by Rowlands. Edward often complained that as a student he was expected to provide the people of Tregaron with free medical advice.[14]

Edward was diligent in his studies, so much so that Henry complained that he seldom left his lodgings.[15] Yet Edward seems to have been the one who wrote home regularly with news, particularly of Jewin Crescent, which would interest Ebenezer Richard. Edward, in one of his letters, reported on the centenary celebrations of the 1732 revival. There were a few revivals in that period, including one in Llangeitho in 1735. Edward praised the appearance of the chapel and the singing but said that the speeches were dry and dull.[16]

After a period of study and examinations which had been successful, brilliant even, Edward failed his examinations in 1832. Henry blamed the caprices of the brutes of examiners rather than any failing in his older brother. Edward left immediately for Tregaron, leaving Henry in London. The parents were disappointed but they did not dwell on the matter. Tribulation worketh patience, was their attitude. His two sisters, Mary and Hannah, managed to borrow a gentle, sweet-tempered pony for him and when Henry eventually arrived the two spent the summer riding in the hills and down to Cardigan Bay. Henry returned to London in September but Edward, fortuitously, stayed a little longer in Tregaron. In October, Ebenezer was overcome by a strange lethargy and it was decided not to reveal news of the illness to Henry – on the assumption that the information would not reach the capital. Then, one Sunday evening in Jewin Crescent a man who had just arrived from Llangeitho told him how pleased every-one was that his father was recovering from his serious illness. "Is it possible that this can be the fact?" wrote an indignant Henry, "and I am left to know it in such a way as this!"[17]

Back in Cardiganshire Edward and his mother had taken Ebenezer for a change of air to Aberaeron which seemed to have done him the world of good. Ebenezer's main concern was that he was missing a revival that had erupted in Tregaron, with reports of 40 people joining his chapel. The revival had moved on to Llangeithio sweeping 120 "sinners" into the fold. By December Ebenezer was sufficiently recovered for Edward to return to London. Henry had some difficulty contacting Llewelyn Mortimer and Edward's lodgings. His landlady had moved to another house and although she had left a note at Jewin Crescent she failed to include her new address! Christmas came and Henry, Edward and Llewelyn feasted on a goose and a hare provided by their families in Tregaron and Trehowell. That evening Henry and Edward went to Jewin Crescent Sunday school where Edward gave a talk on the revival in Tregaron. The effect, he said, even on the hardest of men had been astonishing, with much wailing and repentance at past transgressions. "Even Evan the Tinman had joined." Edward re-sat the examinations of the Society of Apothecaries at the end of January. 1833, and this time he was suc-cessful. He lost no time in setting up a practice in Chiswell Street, Finsbury.[18]

This was the start of Henry Richard's gradual drift from the quiet conservatism of Cardiganshire Calvinism to the radicalism of the Congregationalists – a denomination led by preacher/journalists committed to change and social reform.[19] He was finding his spiritual home in a denomination with a progres-sive attitude to the issues of the day, issues towards which the bel-ligerent young man was becoming increasingly sympathetic. He was soon involved in student politics and incurring the displeasure of no less a person than the influential Thomas Wilson, treasurer of Highbury College. Wilson had assured Richard, now in his third year at the college, that he would be paid for conducting Sunday services – payment that would have enabled him to support himself. But as was the case with other students he was disappointed. Richard had enjoyed a period conducting services at Framling-ham, Suffolk, but by the time he had paid his expenses he had nothing left so he refused to go there again. Wilson was a dictator – albeit a benign one – who expected the respect and obedience due to a benefactor of his standing. Unlike others who had suffered at the hands of the great man, Henry Richard – despite his respect for Wilson's piety and generosity – was not one to sneak back into his office and beg forgiveness. Wilson decided where students would be sent to conduct services and his influence in the appointment of ministers was considerable. When Wilson decided to send Richard for two months to Croydon in the summer of 1833, Richard replied that he was happy to go there for a month, but he would be spending the second month home in Tregaron.[20]

Henry's parents were unhappy at the way their son was challenging the great Wilson and worried that their son's impetuous behaviour would be detrimental to his career. After his holiday Henry returned to London having spent a weekend on the way at the home of his friend David Thomas in Merthyr. And immediately into another row with Thomas Wilson. Wilson ordered him to go to Croydon. Henry refused, stating that he had preached all his sermons in Croydon, and he did not have time to prepare any more. His mother sent him a copy of a discourse she often used when she needed to calm stormy waters. The content of the discourse is not known but it does seem that Henry appreciated her advice. Edward, too, tried his best to persuade his brother to calm down. Edward had established himself in a busy practice although he complained towards the end of the year that His Majesty's subjects seemed to enjoy particularly good health. That Christmas the family in Tregaron sent a turkey, which according to Henry was almost as big as a sheep which had Edward and Llewelyn Mortimer hacking away at it for almost a week. Henry was inspired to write a poem in praise of the bird:

> It was glorious to sit and see Edward split
>   The limbs of that beautiful creature
> While the rich fumes arose refreshing the nose
>   And spreading delight on each feature.

Not often the mind such enjoyment can find
    In a world so sad and so murky,
So complete a delight as we felt that night
    In eating that beautiful turkey.[21]

There is an amusing description of Henry taking a Bible study class of lively and mature girls in Ware, Hertfordshire, which he himself admitted was no easy task for a 21-year-old. He said that he did his best to appear "grave and ministerial", but that he found it difficult and could not help smiling a lot at them.[22]

Henry continued to tread on Wilson's toes. His parents and older brother were convinced that he was going to ruin his career by championing causes that were fine in principle, but which gave an impression that he was not an easy young man to get on with. He was elected secretary of a committee to organise a social evening for students to meet some of the prominent Nonconformist ministers in London. He was the secretary of a student committee to prepare a petition to Parliament about disparities between Anglican clergy and Nonconformist ministers. He should have led the deputation to present the petition to Lord Holland and John Wilkes had he not been sent – deliberately? – to preach in Ipswich and could not return in time. He was the secretary of a committee formed to defend a student dismissed for disobedience. The student had protested that he was rarely sent out to preach and claimed that this was because Thomas Wilson was prejudiced against him. The students threatened to bring the matter to the attention of the "religious public unless the sentence was revoked". Henry himself wrote the letter to the college secretary. The response sulkily disapproved of the students' action but agreed to meet them. Henry Richard also established a union of the students attending the five Nonconformist academies in London as well as founding and editing a magazine for the Highbury College students.[23]

Henry was hurt at his father's lack of support for his actions and he wrote home that the campaigns did not harm his future in the least; the only ones who could be damaged were Mr Wilson and the Tutors. Edward did his best to make peace between them and went to great trouble to persuade Thomas Wilson to chair a meeting of the Bible Society at Jewin Crescent. Edward himself gave a lecture in English, which was well received. Henry stayed away!

A number of prominent Nonconformists in and around London had taken a liking to Henry Richard, among them a Mr

Challis, an influential and able man from Croydon who once told Thomas Wilson that he was a great admirer of the young Welshman's sermons. Wilson's response was that he admired Richard's ability but did not care for his temper. Adding the ambiguous proviso that "Henry has got it in him and we must get it out of him." It is not clear whether he was referring to Henry's talent or his temper. Another of Henry's admirers, a Mr Wastie, tried to secure an invitation for him to become minister of Esher Street Congregational Chapel, Kennington. A meeting was called to discuss the matter but Edward, who was as ambitious for his brother's career as for his own, unwisely attended. Not everyone shared Mr Wastie's admiration for Henry and he was accused of bringing Edward to the meeting to vote for his brother.[24]

Henry Richard was disappointed at this rebuff and that, together with overwork, made him depressed and irritable. He complained about his brother's interference. He criticised his father's old friend, the ultra-conservative John Elias of Anglesey, for a statement of support for the Anglican Church declaring that he had lost patience with the man. Edward, decisive as ever, urged him to go home and get some Tregaron fresh air in his lungs. Once there, his father decided that a few preaching engagements in Welsh would do him the world of good. Together they rode off to the Calvinistic Methodists' monthly meeting at Llanarth, on to Fishguard where they stayed with Henry's uncle, Thomas Richard and his wife Bridget, and then to Trefin, Ebenezer Richard's birthplace, where they stayed a few nights with a maiden aunt. From there they went to the Calvinistic Association being held in St David's. Henry criticised the preaching and praised the board and lodging at the home of a jolly vicar named Mr Richardson. They proceeded to Haverfordwest and then Carmarthen where Ebenezer had to "meet a Mr Charles[25] and Mr T. Evans who had been appointed by the Association to prepare a new Hymn Book for the use of the body in South Wales." In Carmarthen Henry faced a barrage of questions about his brother – was he in good health, was he likely to get married, etc?[26]

It may be that Henry Richard at this time was on the verge of a breakdown. In spite of his readiness to challenge authority he was shy and lacked confidence. He was pulled between the radical, sophisticated ideas of London and the simple, rural ways of Tregaron. He was also worried by a crisis of confidence in his Christian beliefs. Professor Ieuan Gwynedd Jones[27] suggests that from now on Tregaron, Cardiganshire and Wales were the anchors of his life. We could add the Welsh language to the list. Although London remained his home for the rest of his life, he lectured and preached in Welsh at every opportunity.

While Edward was increasingly obsessed by the poetry and ideas of Coleridge, Henry was pursuing political ideas and information. He worried about the treachery of men towards one another and "that our fellow creatures are a community of hypocrites, always deceived and deceiving one another … it was a blessing to make that discovery early."[28]

Gradually Henry recovered his health and good spirits. It is not clear whether this was due to the Tregaron air, the flannel waistcoat he received from his mother, the medicine provided by his brother together with the exhortation to take a regular plunge in the sea. Maybe a combination of them all, and perhaps the sudden appearance of £280 in the family bank account – probably money from the will of the sea captain Edward Williams. Whatever, Henry had recovered his health and spirits by the spring of 1834 and returned to London. When he arrived in Cheltenham his desire to get to the capital was such that he decided to travel overnight despite the added cost of fifteen shillings.[29]

In London he found Edward dining merrily with a group of friends, in exuberant spirits with a flourishing practice. Not only had he had advised Henry on matters of health but he had been busy furthering his brother's career in London. He kept in touch with Thomas Wilson at Highbury and influential Nonconformist leaders in London, notably Mr Challis in Croydon and Mr Wastie in Esher Street. He insisted that Henry should go to Highbury as soon as possible – but all the tutors were away on the day of his first visit. Edward arranged a meeting of the Welsh Auxiliary Bible Society in Jewin Crescent chaired by Mr Challis with Henry giving the address. It was another opportunity for the man from Croydon to hear Henry speak. "The meeting went off as well as an English Meeting in a Welsh Chapel and to a Welsh congregation could be expected to go off," observed Henry drily. Almost another month went by before Henry finally visited Thomas Wilson and it was with much relief that the family in Tregaron received the news that Henry had made peace with the great man. Wilson promised to seek a chapel for Henry to be a "supply" preacher in the short term.[30]

Wilson kept his word and Henry was sent on a month's trial to Marlborough Congregational Chapel in the Old Kent Road. David Thomas, his friend from Merthyr, had been there immediately before him and no doubt the two were competing for the same post. There are suggestions of manoeuvrings in the dark – no doubt by Edward – and that Henry may have spoken out unwisely – to the extent that Ebenezer Richard wrote to his younger son advising discretion even when speaking to "bosom friends". Henry's response was to blame his brother who "is constitutionally suspicious and never has had and never will have a perfect confidence in the sincerity of any living being except perhaps ourselves." He added: "I never discovered the slightest attempt by Thomas to injure me in the estimation of others. On the other hand he has spoken very highly of me to Wilson and others. I hate ingratitude in myself more than insincerity in another."[31]

Whatever the extent of the whispering or the plotting, Henry was invited to spend August 1835 on trial at Marlborough and at the end of the period he was invited to become the permanent minister of the chapel.

Chapter 3

The years at Marlborough

As soon as it was confirmed that Henry Richard would be ordained minister of Marlborough Congregational Chapel, Edward began making arrangements. He was anxious for his mother to come, since Ebenezer Richard's health was causing concern. Also, he wanted his mother to see his new house. The family went to considerable trouble to ensure everyone was suitably dressed so as not to embarrass Henry in front of his congregation. They began their journey on 3 November 1834, had to wait in Llandovery in order to get inside seats on the mail coach and finally arrived at St Martins le Grand at 7am on 7 November. Ebenezer wrote in the family register that "they were affectionately received and kindly accommodated at Edward's residence, 45 Chiswell Street". The old man became unwell while in London but he managed to sit through the ordination service on 11 December and dinner for the guests at the Kentish Drovers tavern in the afternoon. There were 40 ministers at the service and the Rev John Burnet and Dr Ebenezer Henderson were among those who officiated. Ebenezer Richard's health deteriorated after the ordination and the family became very concerned. Mary Richard was worried that he would die and would have to be buried in London. But with Edward in constant attendance he recovered and within a fortnight was on his feet preaching at his son's Communion Sunday on 11 December.[1] He described the service enthusiastically in a letter sent to a Mr and Mrs Jones in Lampeter:

> Last Sunday was our dear Henry's first Communion since his ordination. His mother, brother and I went to his chapel to be present on this solemn occasion. But what will be your astonishment when you learn that your old friend, Ebenezer Richard of

Tregaron, stood up to preach a sermon in English to a very important congregation in the metropolis! After the sermon, we had the great happiness of sitting at the Lord's Table while our beloved Henry officiated. It was almost more than our feelings could bear; in truth it was to us like a little heaven on earth.[2]

When Henry Richard began his work at Marlborough he soon found there was much to do. The chapel had a debt of £1,800 which would restrict his pastoral work. Although the chapel, which seated a 1,000, attracted a large congregation, not many of them were actual members. Nor was it a united church, another challenge to a young man of 23 who, as a student, had not been renowned for tact and reflection. However, he applied himself to the work with enthusiasm and energy and within seven years the debt was cleared. For many years, it had been necessary to hold the Sunday school in the gallery above the entrance. The chapel was also the only place where weekly meetings could be held and more room was needed. One of the members provided an interest-free loan and a vestry with room for 200 was built behind the chapel and opened on 10 January 1839. A total of 269 new members joined the chapel, and two Sunday schools and a literary society for young people were established during the first four years of his ministry. Richard also became involved in matters outside the church and it is mainly due to him that a British School was built in Oakley Place, Old Kent Road, a school free from the interference of Church and state.[3]

According to John Eastty in *Freeman*[4] Henry Richard was a well-known preacher before he was ordained minister of Marlborough chapel:

> As a substitute his services were eagerly sought to supply the pulpit of the most gifted metropolitan ministers, and the people were most edified and delighted … As a preacher Mr Richard was not given to extempore utterance. He read his sermons, but with an unusual grace and emphasis, accompanied by appropriate action; and the hearer was so intent upon the expression of his countenance and his earnestness of manner that he scarcely observed the turning of the leaves of the manuscript, so deftly was it done.

W. A. Essery[5] also noted that he read his sermons, but he said that Richard as a preacher never fulfilled the promise of his early years. According to Marlborough tradition "they were long, argumentative, prosy and dry." His speeches in Parliament, years later, could also be difficult, with long sentences and many clauses. In that he was not untypical of other MPs of his time. But on an election platform his speeches were direct, clear and at times electrifying.

Henry's sister, Mary, married Sam Morris, son of Rev Ebenezer Morris of Tŵr Gwyn, Lledrod, one of Ebenezer Richard's closest friends. The marriage ceremony took place in St Caron's Church, Tregaron, on 13 July 1836. They went to live in Garreg-wen, and Sam later became a deacon at Tŵr Gwyn where he ruled with a rod of iron and terrorised young preachers.[6] The following year, in the second week of March 1837, Ebenezer Richard died having just returned to Tregaron following a preaching tour of north Cardiganshire. Evidently, his loss was greatly felt. "Wales has had a great loss, Cardiganshire a greater one, Tregaron's loss was the greatest of all."[7]

Henry Richard's fifteen years at Marlborough were key to his spiritual, political and intellectual development. The Old Kent Road provided every opportunity for him to establish himself in London's Nonconformist community. He became part of the network of ministers and laymen who were prominent in education, radical politics and humanitarian circles. As a student lodging at Jewin Crescent, he got to know the influential (Sir) Hugh Owen (1804–1881) of the Poor Law Commission. Owen worked to draw Wales into the circle of the British State. Like many Anglicised members of the Welsh middle class of the time the Welsh language did not rate highly in his list of priorities. He urged his fellow countrymen to adopt the English language, the language of Empire and trade. Owen and his acolytes were responsible for Anglicising the Eisteddfod and persuading the poets to yield their privileged position to musicians and singers who would perform before the Queen and bring honour to Wales as the "Land of Song". If what Henry Richard wrote later in *Letters and Essays on Wales* is any indication of his opinions it would appear unlikely that the two would have been in accord on this matter.[8]

The headquarters of the main religious denominations and inter-denominational movements, the British and Foreign Bible Society, the SPCK, and the Society for the Abolition of the Slave Trade were all based in London. The Anti-State Church Association, later renamed the Society for the Liberation of Religion from State Patronage and Control (or simply the Liberation Society) was also based in London. We recall that Henry Richard in Highbury in 1834 was secretary of a student committee to bring pressure on Parliament to redress discrimina-

tion against Nonconformists. The Liberation Society made effective use of newspapers to promote its aims and Henry Richard
acquired those skills and before long was making good use of
them. Also published in London were influential journals with
large circulations such as *Evangelical Review*, the *Congregational
Quarterly* and the *Eclectic Review* – all spreading new ideas out to the
rest of the country. In 1841, the *Nonconformist*, edited by Edward
Miall – a close friend of Henry Richard – was established. Richard
was moving ever closer to the role of preacher/editor that was a
characteristic of the Congregational and Baptist denominations, in
Wales as much as in England. They – along with the Unitarians –
were the most politically radical of the religious denominations.
Later, in 1855, after he had left Marlborough chapel and the ministry, a daily paper named the *Morning Star* was established with
Henry Richard as joint-editor.

The 15 years at Marlborough were formative years in their
influence on Henry Richard, they were also exciting and influential years in the growth of Nonconformist politics.[9] The
Nonconformist/Whig alliance which succeeded in repealing the
Test and Corporation Acts in 1828 was dissolving, but the pressure
from Dissenting denominations for civil and a social equality was
on the increase. Issues such as the Church Rates, allowing Nonconformists to attend universities, reforming marriage and registration laws on which the Whigs were inflexible and the Liberals at
best luke-warm, inclined their advocates to alliance with the radicals inside and outside Parliament. Chartism was becoming a
powerful force in London, especially among the craftsmen of
South London among whom Henry Richard worked. Some of
Richard's friends, such as Edward Miall and Joseph Sturge, the
Quaker philanthropist from Birmingham, tried to establish a
more moderate movement – the Complete Suffrage Union –
which they considered would be less damaging to society than
Chartism. A movement they hoped would unite the working class
and the middle class in pursuit of common aims. These were also
the years when the Anti-Corn Law League was established.

Politically the most significant event of Henry Richard's time in
Marlborough was the founding of the Liberation Society in 1844.
The founder was Edward Miall, a Congregational minister in
Leicester and one of the most original and progressive thinkers of
nineteenth-century Nonconformity.[10] Also present at the inaugu-
ral meeting was the Rev John R. Kilsby Jones, himself a Welsh
Congregational minister in Leicester and translator into English of

the biography by William Rees (Gwilym Hiraethog) of William
Williams (Williams o'r Wern). Miall soon moved to London to be
closer to Parliament – lobbying is not a modern phenomenon.
Richard became a member of the Society and soon he was in close
contact with the organisation and eventually played a vital role in
its activities in Wales. With its radical ideology, mastery of propaganda techniques and the ability to adapt the organisation of
Nonconformity to its own ends, the Society was a perfect vehicle
to initiate political change, particularly in Wales. Thus, in his
formative years Henry Richard found himself at the centre of a
turmoil of activity. He became one of Edward Miall's closest
friends, he also became a friend of Richard Cobden, and Joseph
Sturge took him under his wing.[11] Cobden, a man of poor background, became a successful industrialist and merchant and a
Member of Parliament in 1841. Sturge was an advocate of Free
Trade, low taxation, cutting expenditure on arms and improving
the education system; he was later a leading figure in the Peace
Society, showing great bravery in his opposition to the Crimean
War. Sturge was also an active member of the Anti-Corn Law
League which was founded by Cobden and John Bright in 1838 to
repeal the taxes imposed on imported grain at the beginning of the
Napoleonic Wars. These protectionist policies benefited rich
farmers in England – and to a degree in Wales – but were deeply
unpopular among the poorer classes who experienced an increase
in the price of bread. The Corn Laws were eventually repealed in
1846.

These were also the years when Henry Richard discovered the
social and political issues which he, as a Welshman, would exploit
in later years. He took an interest in Welsh education which, after
Griffith Jones's drive towards literacy in the previous century, was
in decline. Among his Welsh contemporaries in London, men
who shared his concerns, were Hugh Owen, Griffith Davies the
actuary – who later became involved in a law suit with Edward,
Henry's brother – and John Davies of the Bank of England. Hugh
Owen was intent on popularising the British (i.e. non-sectarian)
Schools in Wales. Henry Richard advocated a system of voluntary
education, independent of state and church. He regarded accepting Government support to be incompatible with liberty and
opening them up to the corrupt influences of Government.[12] He
was prominent in the establishment of the Congregational Board
of Education and he was the first secretary of the Voluntary School
Association. In 1844 Richard and the Rev John Blackburn, minis-

ter of Claremont Chapel which Hugh Owen had joined after he married, visited Wales as representatives of these two organisations. They wrote two reports which were partly instrumental in setting up the first Normal Schools in Wales for the training of teachers, the first in Brecon and then in Swansea.[13]

We find him commenting increasingly on matters to do with Wales. In a letter to Edward in 1843, written during a visit to Cardiganshire, he makes a reference to "Rebecca". "I have been eye-witness of the effects of her exertions. She has been to Tregaron twice since my arrival. The first time she demolished the gate, and the second time, since 'Jack y Glover' would insist despite her warning in taking toll, she came and pulled down the house."[14] These were the years when Henry Richard became the voice of Wales in London, the years when he began a mission to explain and justify Wales to the world, above all to the abysmally ignorant English. He was the first to take to this task, writing in English although still contributing to Welsh language periodicals in his mother tongue. Although urging caution and trying to persuade them to refrain from resorting to violence[15] Richard provided an objective background to the Rebecca Riots explaining that the farmers of south-west Wales had a grievance which justified their actions. He wrote a long article for the *Daily News* explaining the troubles and arguing that there was no political significance to them. In a lecture to the Congregational Union he emphasised that the protesters were peaceful and religious, not the barbarians portrayed in the English press. He succeeded in raising awareness of the poverty and suffering in rural Wales, the increasing conflict between landowners and tenants and the inequalities of the legal and social systems. He emphasised the peaceful nature of the Welsh – some may describe it as servile – but "peaceful" was the word best suited to his argument at the time.

"For the last hundred or hundred and fifty years there is probably no part of the United Kingdom that has given the authorities so little trouble or anxiety," he wrote later in his *Letters and Essays on Wales* (1866). He went on:

> Anything like sedition, tumult, or riot is rare in the Principality. There have been only two considerable exceptions to this rule, and these are more apparent than real. The first was the Chartist outbreak in Newport in 1839. But this was almost entirely of English inspiration, and spread over only one corner of Wales, that occupied by the mixed and half-Anglicised population of Monmouthshire and the other adjacent coal and iron districts.

The great bulk of the Welsh people had no share whatever in the movement, but looked upon it with undisguised repugnance and horror. The Rebecca disturbances of 1843 undoubtedly differed widely in this respect, that they broke out in the very heart of the purely Welsh population. But the character of these also has, I believe, been greatly misunderstood in England. They had no political significance whatever, and implied no disaffection to the Government. They were merely uprisings, to which men were driven, or imagined themselves driven, by the pressure of a grievance that had become intolerable, and against which they had long in vain protested and appealed. The thing came to pass on this wise. The small farmers of Cardiganshire and Carmarthenshire were accustomed to use a great deal of lime as manure. As there were no railroads in those days, they had to send their carts for the article to the lime-kilns, a distance of twenty, thirty, and even forty miles. But so ingeniously had the local magistrates who had the administration of the turnpike trusts in their hands, contrived by the multiplication of turn-pike gates at every few miles interval along the whole line they had to traverse, to erect obstacles in the way of these efforts of their own tenants to improve the land that, as the farmers have told me themselves, the prices which they paid for the load of lime at the mouth of the kiln, was sometimes more than doubled by the time they got it home by these ever recurring highway imposts.[16]

The tenants were being heavily penalised by their landlords for improving land which they themselves owned! Henry Richard wrote the above words 23 years after the troubles. His writing at the time in the *Daily News* sparked curiosity among other papers and the *Times* – London's largest daily – sent a reporter, Thomas Campbell Foster, to investigate. (Foster befriended the tenant farmers and his reports were thorough and sympathetic.) Richard may not always have been the most objective of commentators. He was a politician long before he was ever elected to Parliament. But a politician ever ready to embrace a just cause, popular or otherwise. He took it upon himself to defend the name of Wales and champion the cause of the followers of Rebecca. Richard, although calling for calm, was taking his own course of action. The Peace Society, where he was an increasingly active member, opposed, not only war between nations, but disturbances in general – Chartism, the Rebecca riots and strikes. It is well to remember today, as we recall with admiration the actions of Rebecca rioters, that there was at the time no great support for them in Wales. The radical Welsh Congregational Minister and editor of *Y Cronicl*, Samuel Roberts of Llanbrynmair, urged "Rebecca's family … to consider and remember that every riotous and destructive action went against the spirit of Christians."[17] *Yr Eurgrawn* worried over "… behaviour that will take you (i.e. Wales) down to the depths of the mutinous Irish. It is to be hoped that it is not the children of your Sunday Schools who behave in this way." Both these North Wales papers blamed the "mobs" of the South for the disturbances.[18] The debate was fiercer in the Carmarthen papers. The English language *Carmarthen Journal*, as expected, deplored such actions. The conservative Anglican satirist David Owen (Brutus) in *Yr Haul* accused David Rees, Congregational Minister of Capel Als, Llanelli, and editor of *Y Diwygiwr*, of fanning the flames of dissent:

> 'Becca is not just one person or even two persons, but the spirit of rebellion working within the children of disobedience, that which the Rev. David Rees, Capel Als, Llanelli, and editor of Y Diwygiwr has been striving to create in the country for many days by his exhortations, month after month, 'Agitate, agitate, agitate' …[19]

In fact David Rees, in spite of his frequent calls to the people to agitate, had condemned the Rebecca uprising. "A rational Christian can only blush and be ashamed that great Carmarthen-shire has disgraced itself so deeply," he wrote.[20] Nor was *Seren Gomer* supportive of the aims of Rebecca, with its condemnation of violence. Richard showed courage in defending a cause which was not popular at the time.

There is an interesting connection here. Richard Cobden – a friend of Henry Richard's and by now an MP – was married to Catherine Anne Williams, the daughter of wealthy merchants in Machynlleth, Mid-Wales. Her brother was Hugh Williams, a young solicitor who settled in Carmarthen in 1822, had become sympathetic towards Rebecca rioters. Some suggested that he himself was "Rebecca" – the leader – although there is no evidence of this.[21] But it can be assumed that through Henry Richard's friendship with Cobden, Catherine and Hugh Williams ensured that he totally understood the history and background of the troubles.

His comparison of the Chartist movement with Rebecca as outlined in *Letters and Essays* is interesting. He criticised the Chartists, a movement he considered in essence to be English, and active in Anglicised areas of Wales. He is happier to defend the Welsh-speaking Wales.[22] Here again we have an indication of his readiness to adapt and change his views when it was expedient to do so. When Richard was the Liberal Parliamentary candidate for Merthyr and Aberdare in 1868, two years after the publication of *Letters and Essays on Wales*, he was pledging to work for the full Charter programme! It should be said, however, that his criticisms of the Chartists were moderate compared to those of David Rees in *Y Diwygiwr*. After warning the Welsh to avoid "unbecoming methods" after the Newport debacle (4 November 1839), the "Agitator" deplored the conduct of his fellow countrymen: "The lamentable, wretched and disgraceful circumstances which occurred recently, calls upon us to end our Chartist essay, very differently from how it was intended. Wales! Gird yourself in sackcloth … your character has been soiled."[23]

The Rebecca troubles had hardly subsided when another storm blew up in Wales and Henry Richard was again at the fore in defence of his nation's reputation. Thanks to Griffith Jones's Circulating Schools and Thomas Charles's Sunday Schools a high percentage of Welsh people could read and write. They could read and write Welsh – but had little knowledge of English. Standards in day schools, however, where children were taught in English – which they did not understand – were poor. English people saw the Welsh as filthy pagans and immoral barbarians. The *Morning Chronicle* declared that "Wales was fast settling down into the most savage barbarianism". The *Examiner* stated that the Welsh people "were sunk in the depths of ignorance, and in the slough of sensuality, and that their habits were those of animals, and would not bear description".[24] Welsh was denounced as a barbaric tongue and it would be better for Wales if it were dead and buried. William Williams, a successful industrialist and MP for Coventry but originally from Llanpumsaint, Carmarthenshire, asked for an investigation into the state of education in Wales. He believed that the language placed the Welsh people at a disadvantage and was an obstruction to the effective administration of the law in Welsh courts. Also, the matter of the numbers of Nonconformists compared to Anglicans in Wales was attracting interest in England. Then, in 1846, the Lord John Russell administration set up a Commission to investigate "the state of education in the Principality of Wales, particularly the means available to the labouring class to attain a knowledge of English". Three commissioners were appointed to do the work and their three volumes, *Reports of the commissioners of enquiry into the state of education in Wales*, were published in 1847. The Reports, which came to be known as *Brad y Llyfrau Gleision* (The Treachery of the Blue Books), showed the

extent of the religious change happening in Wales. The polarisa-
tion of two cultures, socially unequal – the English-speaking
Anglicans and the Welsh-speaking Nonconformists – was revealed
and brought to the attention of the politicians. But its anti-Welsh
bias delighted the London press. As for the three Commissioners
– H. R. Vaughan Johnson, R. R. W. Lingen and Jelinger C.
Symons – in Henry Richard's words, "… they were singularly dis-
qualified for their work: they had no knowledge of the language,
they had no sympathy with the people, and they fell into bad
hands".[25] By that he meant that they had relied excessively on the
evidence of minor clergymen itching to pour their vitriol on the
Nonconformists. The Welsh reacted ferociously with Evan Jones
(Ieuan Gwynedd) publishing searing articles in the Welsh language press; R. J. Derfel, with his play *Brad y Llyfrau Gleision*,
coined the name by which the *Reports* have been known ever since;
Lewis Edwards wrote scathing articles in the January and April
issues of *Y Traethodydd*, as did David Rees in *Y Dysgedydd*. Others
like Samuel Roberts and Gwilym Hiraethog gave full vent to their
fury in various journals. The English, whether they were at all
aware of the sentiments voiced so bitterly in the Welsh journals,
were happy to ignore whatever may have been written in "the barbaric tongue". But Richard, angered by the Reports, responded to
them – in the London press. Soon after the publication of the
Reports he was due to deliver a lecture in Crosby Hall in a series
organised by the Congregational Board of Education. His lecture
was *On the progress and efficacy of voluntary education, as exemplified in
Wales*. A more appropriate title would have been *A Vindication of the
Welsh People from the Aspersions of the Education Commissioners*. Soon,
he had deviated from his original subject and eloquently, and with
a firm grasp of facts and figures his lecture became an attack on the
Commissioners and a defence of the Welsh people. For two and a
half hours he held the audience spellbound.[26] His lecture first
appeared in the *British Banner*, which enjoyed a large circulation
among Nonconformists, and then in a book, *The Crosby Hall
Lectures*, along with the other lectures in the series.

Even in cold print well over a century and a half later the inten-
sity of his feelings can still be felt. He condemned the Commissioners for gathering every kind of filth about the character of the
Welsh people asking whether there was in their Reports any mention of virtues. His lecture ends with these words:

As I have been wading my way through these enormous volumes, where, I have asked myself again and again are the worthy, consistent, exemplary members of our Dissenting churches, who, in their humble stations, exemplify the power and loveliness of Christian principle, and adorn the God of our Saviour in all things – from whose stone hearths there ascends, day and night, the incense of a simple spiritual devotion, perhaps more acceptable in the sight of Him who reads the heart than the glittering pomp of priestly pageantries, or the pealing swell of cathedral music; whose homely huts, though devoid of all pretensions to the elegancies, and even many of the comforts of life, are nevertheless adorned with the beauty of holiness? Where is the record of these men's characters and virtues? That there are hundreds and thousands of such, I know. Have I not stood beneath their humble roofs, whose naked rafters were polished and japanned by the smoke of the mountain turf? Have I not sat at their uncovered deal tables, to partake of their buttermilk and oatmeal-bread, which, coarse fare though it be, they feel a hospitable pride in dispensing? Have I not knelt on the mud floor, beside the wretched pallets on which they are stretched, and learned from lips pallid with the hue of death, lessons of Christian resignation, of holy and triumphant confidence in God, such as I never learned elsewhere? Where, I say, are these men who shed the lustre of their piety over the hills and glens of my native land? I find no trace of them in these Blue Books; and, until I do find them, I utterly refuse to accept their contents as a fair representation of the character of my countrymen.[27]

In his introduction to *Letters and Essays from Wales* (1884) Richard notes that his lecture had the effect of drawing a response from one of the Commissioners with a pamphlet of his own in the form of a letter to Lord John Russell.[28] Henry Richard took the debate to London and came to the fore as a defender of Wales and the Welsh in the capital. In the words of Ieuan Gwynedd Jones he also showed that he understood the political obligations of what he was doing and turned the Report to the advantage of the Welsh people.[29] He added: "His greatness lies in the extraordinarily sophisticated way he was able to put these and other similar episodes in the recent history of the country, including Chartism, within a comprehensive historical and social framework." Also, Wales was stung by the Commissioners' Report and in the surge of indignation Henry Richard took his opportunity in what was the beginning of a sea-change in Welsh political history.

He idealised the rural, Welsh-speaking Wales, the Tregaron of his childhood, even though he spent by far the greater part of his life in London and represented urban, industrialised Merthyr

Tydfil in Parliament. This becomes increasingly obvious when reading *Letters and Essays*, a book that remains informative and stimulating to this day and described by Ieuan Gwynedd Jones as "one of the most important books about Wales to have been published in the nineteenth century".[30]

Mention must be made to Henry Richard's energetic and interfering brother, Dr Edward Richard. Since his arrival in London and lodging in the Chapel House, Edward had been an active member at Jewin Crescent. Although Henry studied at the Congregational College and became minister of the Marlborough (English) Congregational Chapel, his brother kept faith with the Calvinistic Methodists of his father. The two kept in close touch throughout their lives and collaborated to write a biography of their father.[31] Edward had literary ambitions – as did Henry, but the younger brother was content with the humbler pages of newspapers and periodicals. Edward was active with Jewin Crescent Sunday school and in the wider circle of the London Welsh. He was friendly with the minister, the Rev James Hughes, whose bardic nom-de-plume Iago Trichrug suggests that he too was from Cardiganshire. Another of his friends was Edward Cleaton, one of the chapel deacons, a woollen merchant and preacher whose family were from Llanidloes. Edward and Henry were invited to Cleaton's home for Christmas dinner 1832 where they spent an enjoyable afternoon – "a fine goose and plum pudding". But in March 1834 Edward was writing to his father that "Cleaton had left Jewin for good and become a regular attender at Dr Bennet's and is soon likely to become a member".[32] In 1835 Edward established a society he called "Y Gymdeithas Gristionogol Gymreig" (The Welsh Christian Society) which held its first meeting in Jewin Crescent on 16 February 1837, with a number of "eminent men" present.[33] His home in 45 Chiswell Hill was convenient and offered a warm welcome to preachers, students, poets and musicians from Wales. His name became known to a widening circle of friends and acquaintances bringing him into contact with every strata of London Welsh society. He was concerned about their spiritual as well as physical welfare – mindful, perhaps, of something said by his father that the work of Henry, who studied and attended the disorders of the eternal soul, was of greater importance than that of a doctor who cared for the mortal body. Edward, at this time, was grappling with ideas that the body should not be divorced from the soul and he was convinced the poor and careless Welsh in London needed more than treatment for physical ailments. With such thoughts in mind Edward established his Welsh Christian Society. His father received the news of the society's success with great pleasure.[34]

But all was not at peace in Jewin Crescent. There were continuous complaints that members were selling milk on Sundays and some of the chapel zealots wanted them to be expelled. There is a long tradition of Welsh people – particularly from the Tregaron area – in the retail milk trade in London. And Welsh people were getting into the business in increasing numbers.[35] Milk in the days before refrigeration and pasteurisation had to be delivered daily and cows had to be milked twice a day, on Sunday as on any other day. Almost a century later, herds of cows were kept almost at the heart of London. Maybe this was the disagreement which led to Edward Cleaton's departure. John Elias's insistence in 1835 that anyone who traded on a Sunday should not be allowed to be a member of a Calvinistic Methodist chapel divided Jewin Crescent bitterly. Four deacons resigned on 17 July 1842 because the chapel elders could not agree whether or not to expel a member for selling milk on Sunday.

In 1839 Edward moved to 18 Great Newport Street and in 1840 he undertook the duties of secretary of the Welsh Auxiliary Bible Society, an organisation in which he had been involved for some time. Unexpectedly, news came that on 25 October 1843 Edward had married Eleanor Anne Da Costa, a widow three years older than himself, whose address was also given as 18 Great Newport Street. Although it appears that Edward had temporarily moved out of that address and at the time of the wedding was residing at Peckham Park, Camberwell. Little is known about Eleanor, there are suggestions that she may have been Edward's house-keeper and there appears to have been rumours in Tregaron that "Uncle Edward married some French woman".[36] They were married by Henry in Marlborough Chapel. French or not, she does not appear to have interfered with Edward's activities in Jewin Crescent nor the hospitality he provided for his friends and visiting artists and dignitaries from Wales.

There followed a turbulent period in his life. Edward Richard and some members of Jewin Crescent who lived in the West End wanted to extend the Welsh Calvinistic influence. In a meeting of elders at Jewin Crescent on 14 August 1849, permission was granted to establish a branch of Jewin Crescent in Grafton Street. Edward Richard and 67 others left for the new chapel. It seems that the remaining members of Jewin Crescent watched their departure with some relief. The circumstances are not clear but a little time earlier the elders felt the need to discipline one of the members – namely Edward Richard. There is a story of officers of the law arriving in Jewin Vestry on the night of 31 January 1848 with the intention of taking Richard into custody. At the time it appears that he owed money to a number of people. There was a scuffle and some of the younger members sought to defend Richard, the lights were extinguished and he escaped in the confusion.[37] Because of this, or for some other reason that may have been simmering for a while, on 20 February 1848 Griffith Davies (the Actuary) proposed to censure Edward Richard, but failed to gain the support of the members. The matter stuttered on through the spring until Jewin Crescent decided to expel Edward from being a deacon, but the decision was not confirmed at a meeting of the Association in Machynlleth but adjourned to the Bridgend Association in August, much to Griffith Davies's dismay. At Bridgend it was decided to send representatives from all the counties of North and South Wales to London to investigate. Edward Richard felt the tide was running against him, but he would not accept the humiliation of being publicly disciplined and he issued a writ against Davies for slander – "for words spoken, or rather read" at the meeting on 20 February.[38] However, the writ was withdrawn almost at the very last minute when Richard was taken into custody on 14 June 1849. He was accused of presenting two forged receipts for rent he should have paid on behalf of Jewin Crescent for a chapel in Denmark Street, another branch of Jewin. Money, which it appears he had not transferred to the owner of the building used as a chapel. The last word on the matter was published in the *Times*: "The prisoner was then conveyed to Newgate".[39]

It is not known for how long he was imprisoned, certainly not for very long. There are a few suggestions that Edward was disorganised in matters to do with money. Back in 1843 Henry complained to his father that Edward was lazy and would sooner borrow from him than send bills out or visit those who owed him money. In the family papers there are no references to the problems at Jewin Crescent nor the imprisonment but there is a suggestion that the period between 1847 and 1850 were not years of prosperity for Edward.[40] Nor is his name mentioned as having attended the wedding of his sister Hannah to David Evans, a tanner, in 1848, who took great care of Mary Richard in the last years of her life when she went to live with them in Aberaeron. The witnesses of the wedding were Henry and Sam Morris of Garreg-lwyd, husband of Mary, his other sister.[41] Although Edward was overloading himself with work it was not the kind of work which would have endeared him to his bank manager nor bring him fame – at least not of the kind he desired. He was a man of many ambitions – including literary ones – but they were too diverse and he enjoyed little success in any of them at this time. Also, it seems that after his marriage he distanced himself from the family and he was also suffering from asthma which the unhealthy London air did little to alleviate. Edward and his wife left the city in 1849 and moved out to Finchingfield, renting a house in Great Bardfield, and 1853 they took a house in the centre of the village, which they re-named Prospect House. Soon he was again busy promoting education, establishing a thriving literary society, with such success that a new hall had to built to accommodate all the members. He was active with the Freshwell Labourers' Friendly Society – and, according to the *Chelmsford Chronicle* he was always anxious to "elevate the minds of the poor classes".[42]

Chapter 4

Early years of the Peace Society

While Edward Richard's life was in a state of confusion, Henry's fame and good name shone ever brighter. His star was in the ascendant. He was the emerging force in the peace movement. His chosen path is ironic when we recall his father's friendship with the military Bowen brothers of Llwyngwair and Cardigan, and the dubious connections of his seafaring uncle, Edward Williams. But he was caught up in the radicalism of the Congregational denomination and of the London society in which he was becoming ever more deeply immersed. He was also a man of rebellious nature. He responded publicly and fearlessly to the Blue Books at the heart of the enemy camp. Pacifism has always been a minority issue and rarely popular in the land of John Bull as Richard Cobden and others stated on many occasions. This was the time of the British Empire in its imperialistic glory.

It was in London that Richard became a pacifist. The peace movement hardly existed in Wales in the first 50 years of the nineteenth century although there were active individuals. Samuel Roberts (SR as he was usually known) of Llanbrynmair was an ardent pacifist as was William Rees (Gwilym Hiraethog) – both were Congregational ministers and editors. SR established *Y Cronicl* as a platform for his own ideas, advocating franchise reform, criticising oppressive landlordism and heavy taxation, and supporting the Peace Society. Gwilym Hiraethog took a similar stance as editor of *Yr Amserau* (The Times), also established in 1843. Yet, Welshmen had been influential in the London Peace Society – as it was first known – even if the Society was not active in Wales. Among its founders in 1816 was Joseph Tregelles Price (1784-1854), a Quaker and the ironmaster of Neath Abbey.[1] The

Society's first Secretary, Evan Rees (1790–18 21) was from Neath although he lived most of his life outside Wales. Nun Morgan Harry (1800-1842) from Lampeter Velfrey, Pembrokeshire, Congregational Minister of New Broad Street, London, was the Society's Secretary from 1837 until his death. Although the Society quickly established branches in Birmingham, Manchester and on the continent it was not so in Wales. The concept of pacifism was rarely popular – but people from time to time would get weary of war. Up to 1815 the battles against France and Napoleon attracted as much attention in Wales as in England, and as Wales was a mainly agricultural country, it was a time of comparative prosperity for farmers. And when battles were won papers like the *Cambrian* and the *Carmarthen Journal* were full of details of these triumphs. On the subject of Pacifism Richard wrote in *Y Traethodydd* (1849): "For many years all kinds of dishonour and contempt were cast upon them, not only from the nobility and those who govern us and the military corps of all ranks, those who 'from this profit attain their wealth', but from the majority of the Christians of this country, and even by many Ministers of the Gospel." Certainly what was achieved by the peace movement in Wales would bear no comparison to what was happening in the English Midlands, Yorkshire and eastern England where the Quakers were a force. The only branch in Wales was the Swansea and Neath Peace Society founded in 1817 by Tregelles Price; its aim was to work with the London society founded the year before, not to give voice to Welsh views and opinions. The few members were all Quakers and by 1835 – when Henry Richard entered the ministry – the society had all but disappeared in Wales. There were no references to it in *Seren Gomer, Carmarthen Journal* or the *Cambrian* after 1824.[2] And though there might have been fiery speeches, contributions in the collection boxes were tiny – a reliable indicator of whether a cause thrived or not in those days.[3]

Henry Richard's early years in the Peace Society were successful. The name had been changed from the London Peace Society to "The Society for the Promotion of Permanent and Universal Peace". For 30 years after the Battle of Waterloo there was a period of peace – or at least there were no wars close enough to home to concern the ordinary Briton. The first Opium War with China (1839-1842), a disgraceful example of immoral imperial interference attracted little condemnation. In Wales it was hardly mentioned. Tea, porcelain and silk from China were highly prized in Europe and North America. Since Britain produced nothing that

China wanted – except opium – the imbalance of payments was huge. Britain's answer was to offload great quantities of opium, produced on an industrial scale in Ghazipur, in the middle Ganges valley – "one of the most valuable gems in Queen Victoria's crown".[4] With an increasing number of the population addicted to opium China's Government decided to prohibit the importation of the damaging drug. Britain's answer was to go to war with China, demanding that they buy the opium, causing untold ruin and taking possession of Hong Kong island. We have no record of whether Henry Richard was involved in opposing the first Opium War but he certainly showed a clear grasp of the facts in opposing later wars with China. One piece of warped logic used at the time was that by forcing China to open its ports to the opium trade it allowed missionaries and Bibles to enter the country![5] Henry Richard was consistent in his argument that war never "opened doors" for Christianity.[6]

Richard travelled extensively in this period lecturing and addressing audiences. *Defensive War* was the title of a lecture he gave in the Hall of Commerce, Threadneedle Street, on 5 February 1845, a lecture that was published as a pamphlet later and re-printed in 1890, after his death. In this lecture he argued that the use of force was incompatible with Christianity in all circumstances and that the teaching of Christ required professing Christians to accept the path of martyrdom, if necessary, to uphold the doctrine of non-violence.

He based his arguments on Christ's teachings: "Do not oppose evil": "To no man rendering evil for evil. Providing good things, not only in the sight of God, but also in the sight of all men." The individual has ways of defending himself without resorting to revenge and spilling blood and if our faith were stronger we could venture amongst our enemies with greater safety than if we were clad in armour. Every war, he said, is an act of crime, and that included going to war for defensive reasons:

> If we admit that a defensive war is legal then everything becomes justified, because is it not terrible that 19 of the 20 most hideous recent wars to dowse the land with blood have been fought for that purpose, or at least as an excuse for it?

Where, he asks, in the New Testament does it state that deeds which are forbidden to individual Christians are legal to Christian governments?[7] Henry Richard's personal position was clear. But he never refused the aid of those who did not fully support his stance. While his own position was unequivocal, throughout his life he was pragmatic in his relationship with others. This would be the basis for the modern peace movement.

In May 1848, three years after delivering the lecture Henry Richard was appointed Secretary of the Peace Society following the resignation of the Rev John Jefferson. The year Marx published *The Communist Manifesto* was a tumultuous one. Trouble was fermenting in Ireland, the Chartists were still active, Austria and Italy were at war, the war between Germany and Denmark over the Schleswig and Holstein regions had begun. There was civil war in Switzerland, the USA and Mexico were at war and Louis-Philippe had to leave France and escape to England. Henry Richard rolled up his sleeves and began his life's great work, work that brought him into contact with some of Europe and America's most prominent politicians – and the title of Apostle of Peace.

As already suggested, Henry Richard was becoming part of an influential circle, men like Richard Cobden, the Free Trade advocate and MP, and the Quaker philanthropist from Birmingham, Joseph Sturge. Another was John Bright, also with Quaker connections and an MP since 1843. All had been active in the Anti-Corn Laws League and were members of the Peace Society. The USA also had its peace movement and their "Apostle of Peace" was the learned blacksmith, Elihu Burritt. Burritt came to London soon after Henry Richard had been appointed Secretary of the Peace Society and outlined an idea to organise a Universal Peace Congress. Together they set about developing the idea and although Paris had been their preferred choice of venue the troubles at the French capital forced them to reconsider. Their second choice was Brussels. Their aim was to hold the Congress in September, giving them just a few months to make arrangements. They travelled together to Brussels, secured the support of the Prime Minister, Charles Latour Rogier, who instructed the members of his Government to offer every assistance. One member of the Government who was particularly enthusiastic was Auguste Visschers, who agreed to be President of the Congress. On 20 September 1848 about 300 delegates from eight countries, over 200 of them from Britain and the USA, gathered for what was to be the first of a series of peace Congresses organised by Richard and Burritt. It was at this Congress that Henry Richard delivered his first speech on the international stage in which he argued that war was totally at odds with the Christian spirit. He ended a vigorous speech with a call to unmask the horrors of war:

We must exhibit war in its true colour, we must have the courage with a bold hand to tear the mask which it has thrown over its face, and regardless of the pomp and circumstance with which it is enshrouded, the sounding phrases of honour, patriotism and glory with which it is wont to conceal its true character, we must present it to the eye of the world, as it truly is – a gigantic murderer, drunk with ambition and lust, and hideously stained with the blood of its myriad victims.[8]

Visschers, at the end of the three-day Congress, said that "… the presence of the Apostles of Peace (Richard and Burritt) in our city is an event in which our population is deeply interested, and I am proud to say that the first stone of the Temple of Peace has been laid at Brussels."[9] Henry Richard found great pleasure in "… seeing citizens of eight or nine European countries, some of whom had been for centuries hating, tearing and devouring each other sitting side by side considering the best means of joining the nations of the earth in a bond of peace."[10] A new theme was introduced in an appeal by Roussel, one of the Belgian delegates, for immediate and simultaneous disarmament – not at some future date chosen by generals and politicians. The main subject of discussion at the Congress, as in the subsequent Congresses was how to arrive at the following objectives:

1. To get the nations to settle all differences of opinion and misunderstandings between them by Arbitration. That is, in the event of disagreement between one country and another, the two would be expected to ask another country that was friendly with both to reconcile them and prevent them from going to war;
2. To emphasise that no country should take sides with a country that was at war with another, nor to support the arguments of either for going to war;
3. An appeal to the nations to establish better communications with each other.[11]

The Congress was an undoubted success although the majority of delegates were from England and the USA – Henry Richard was probably the only person from Wales. The profile of the Society was raised thanks to much positive publicity. Money flowed into its coffers and the Society's monthly journal, the *Herald of Peace*, now edited by Henry Richard, was enlarged. A fund to raise £5,000 to develop the Society's activities was launched and £6,000

Elihu Burritt

was raised in a very short time.[12]

Other congresses followed – Paris (1849), Frankfurt (1850), London (1851), Manchester and Edinburgh (both in 1853). The Paris Congress was possibly the most influential and memorable. Henry Richard and Burritt travelled to Paris to instigate proceedings in April 1849. They visited members of the French National Assembly, newspaper editors and writers – among them the poet Alphonse de Lamartine, whom they met on 23 April. Richard kept a detailed diary of his impressions of the places and people he visited and wrote affectionately of their reception at Lamartine's home in the Rue de l'Université. The poet-statesman had been a Minister in the 1848 Administration, but his career and influence declined the following year. Richard was charmed by the poet's easy-going geniality, his wife, and the "pretty little white greyhound (that) leaned its face fondly against his" as he half-reclined on the sofa. Lamartine promised to do all he could to help them organise the Congress, and even considered chairing the organising committee. The only thing he would not agree to, was to be President of the Congress.[13] In the event he declined to take the chair of the organising committee, too. Henry Richard was quite fluent in French, a fact which emerges years later when in Italy and speeches in Italian were translated into French for his benefit. Auguste Visschers, who had presided at the Brussels Congress, came to meet Richard and Burritt and accompanied them on most of these exploratory meetings. They had two meetings – including a breakfast – with Alexis de Tocqueville, the French Foreign Minister, who promised every assistance. At the breakfast Richard was charmed by de Tocqueville's wife – an Englishwoman of grace and dignity – and surprised to find a dish of mashed potatoes steaming in the centre of the table. Having discussed the nutritional value of the potato, it was apparently natural that the discussion would move on to the Irish problem![14] They had difficulty getting someone to accept the Presidency of the Congress. The Archbishop of Paris declined for health reasons. Eventually the celebrated poet and writer Victor Hugo proved a successful and popular choice.[15]

In Paris, as in Brussels the previous year, there was a large representation – 670 – from Britain, including some from Wales. Doubtless some came for a pleasant few days in Paris and women in magnificent dresses mingled with Quakers in their simple garb. Alexis de Tocqueville welcomed the representatives on 22 August followed by an inspiring – prophetic, even – address by Victor Hugo. Hugo had emerged as a statesman and a member of the Second Republic's French National Assembly in February the previous year. Louis-Philippe had fled to England under the name of Mr Smith, and following a period of turmoil Louis-Napoleon Bonaparte (1808-1873), nephew of the emperor, was democratically elected President in the autumn. Eventually, the government slid to the right and Louis-Napoleon, with the aid of the military, grabbed dictatorial powers and appointed himself Napoleon III, ending Hugo's brief period in the political limelight. However, in July 1849 Hugo threw his charismatic authority behind a parliamentary commission to study the moral and material condition of France when he delivered a speech on poverty at the Assembly. A month later he opened the Peace Congress's official proceedings. The name of Louis-Napoleon was rarely, if ever, uttered at the Congress.[16] At the Congress Hugo's speech had the audience in raptures at the Salle Sainte Cécile. It was he, from the Chair, who first predicted that one day we would see a United States of Europe, corresponding to the United States of America, and that there would be a supreme court of arbitration to "legislate on disagreement and conflict and abolish injustice, and by electoral legitimacy strengthen the existing relations among the nations of Europe." He predicted the day when "bullets and shells would be replaced by votes, by the universal suffrage of nations, by the venerable arbitration of a Great Sovereign State; when a cannon would be exhibited in public museums, just as an instrument of torture is now, and people would be astonished that such a thing could have been."[17]

This was heady stuff. "The day will come when the arms of war will fall from your hands, too. The day will dawn when a war between London and Paris, St Petersburg and Berlin, Vienna and Turin will be as absurd and impossible as between Rouen and Amiens, between Boston and Philadelphia. The day will come when you France, you England, you Germany, you, all the nations of the Continent, without losing your unique and splendid identities, will melt in a larger unit, into an European brotherhood, as Normandy, Lorraine, Alsace and all the French regions did to become France."[18]

An attractive but still an abstract vision, offering no explanation of quite what he had in mind. However the response was whole-hearted and fervent. As well as the 670 from Britain there were large representations from the USA, Holland, Belgium and France. The delegates from Italy were not numerous and it is doubtful whether there many from Germany. As for the Austria-Hungarian Empire, it probably had its own ideas on how to unite Europe! Hugo's dream was short-lived. Following Louis-Napoleon's *coup d'etat* on 2 Dec-ember 1851 not much more than two years after the Peace Congress, Hugo chose exile although he retained his vision of a united Europe in the form of a European Federation. He sent a message to that effect to the Lausanne Peace Congress of 1874.

If the success of the Brussels Congress was unexpected, Paris was beyond the expectations of everyone. The Paris newspapers rejoiced in this manifestation of Peace and even the English press momentarily forgot its cynical opposition and disregard for the peace movement. A strong motion condemned the custom of lending money and raising taxes to wage war. A letter by the finan-cier Samuel Gurney, who was the treasurer of the Committee of the Peace Society, attracted great interest. He confidently expressed the opinion that unless "England" totally changed her course in respect to her military policy, the result would be bank-ruptcy and the loan-mongers would lose their money.[19] Richard Cobden, who was present at Paris although he had not attended the Brussels Congress, thought this would concentrate the minds of statesmen more effectively than any moral appeals from the Society!

After the Paris Congress, in appreciation of Henry Richard's work, a group of his admirers presented him with a cheque for

Henry Richard, Apostle of Peace

£1,000 and a handsomely bound family Bible "as a token of their high appreciation of his devoted and persevering public labours to advance the great cause of Permanent and Universal Peace". The names of the subscribers consisted of 40 men – including Cobden, Sturge and John Bright – and two women, Eliza and Anna Bell.[20]

Richard's duties as Secretary of the Peace Society now took up all his time, and following the success of the Paris Congress large meetings were held in London, Manchester and Birmingham. Richard was making a big impression on a number of influential people. In a letter to Joseph Sturge, dated 16 April 1849, Cobden wrote: "By the way, I heard from Manchester that your Mr Richard is quite a hit and that he is, according to the old Leaguers as fine a speaker as was ever heard in the Free Trade Hall." The Leaguers were the members of the Anti-Corn Law League. Sturge gave the letter to Richard who valued and kept it amongst his most treasured possessions. It was evident that Henry Richard, now at the peak of his powers, would have to take decisions on his future. He decided that arguing the case for "peace on earth" was as important as preaching about "The Prince of Peace" on Sundays. He had told the members of Marlborough Chapel of his intentions in October 1849 and early in 1850 he decided, finally, to devote his life entirely to the Peace Society. The members tried to persuade him to take a holiday at the chapel's expense before becoming the Society's full-time Secretary. Finally, after 15 busy and successful years, he left Marlborough Chapel in the Old Kent Road. He was presented with "a purse full of gold" and the 30 volumes of the *Encyclopaedia Metropolitana* magnificently bound in Russia and a pressing invitation to return to give a lecture on the Frankfurt Peace Congress – his next major project.[21] They had been 15 good years, the debts were paid, two Sunday schools and a Vestry had been erected and British Schools established in the neighbourhood providing daily education for 400 children.

Chapter 5

The Frankfurt Congress

Frankfurt, capital of trade and finance and centre of the confeder-ation of Germanic states, was to be the venue for the third in the series of Peace Congresses organised jointly by Henry Richard and Elihu Burritt. They aimed to hold the Congress in August 1850 and a huge logistical task faced them. They were expected to visit Paris on their way where a reception hosted by Ferdinand de Lesseps, the diplomat and engineer of the Suez Canal, awaited them. There they met friends from the Paris Congress, among them Victor Hugo, Garnier, Lacau and Coquerel.[1] They promised to do all in their powers to secure a good representation from France, while a few expressed concern at the political direction France was heading and how that might impair hopes of perma-nent peace.

Richard again kept a detailed diary of his journey and his impressions of the countries through which he passed. He and Burritt travelled through Flanders and Belgium and met Visschers, President of the Brussels Congress and who had helped organise the Paris Congress. They visited Antwerp, Cologne, Maastricht and we find Richard in romantic mood as he contem-plated the Rhine. "Before retiring to rest I leaned over the parapet, wrapped in a sort of dreamy excitement at finding myself at the brink of this noble stream, so consecrated by song that it seemed to the imagination almost like a river of fairy-land."[2] They arrived at Frankfurt, the birthplace of Goethe, where the Emperors of Germany were crowned, home of the Rothschild family, where Bismarck thundered against the republic. But to Richard this was the city where Luther had preached having been condemned for his "heresies" by the Catholic Church in the Diet of Worms, 1521.

Neither Richard nor Burritt knew anyone in Frankfurt, apart from Georg Varrentrapp,[3] the chief medical officer of a large asylum. He was an influential man with progressive ideas on mental health and had visited London in 1847. He welcomed them warmly and proved a valuable coadjutor. They were also warmly received and had valuable assistance from Pastor Bonnet of the French Protestant Church. Connections were made and a formal request made to Parliament for permission to hold the Congress. It was promptly given, although the Democratic Party hampered some of the work by intimidating people with threatening behaviour and language. However, everything was set and, despite the concern of some of the city dignitaries, it was agreed that the Congress should be held in St Paul's Church which seated 3,000 people. Nevertheless, Richard appears to have been getting into a state of some exasperation with the responses from some quarters:

> Nothing can be worse in its effects on the character of the people of the Continent than the perpetual meddling of their Governments in all the affairs of life, and their consequent dependence upon political action as the means of social and national regeneration. We find the most painful and pitiful illustrations of this everywhere.[4]

Getting permission to hold the Congress in St Paul's was, however, a feather in the cap of the organisers. Its semi-circular form was ideal for the event. But of even greater importance, the Paulskirche had – and has – great political significance in the history of Germany. It had been built as a Protestant Church in 1739 and for a brief period between 1848 and 1849 it had housed the Frankfurt Parliament, the short-lived assembly that tried to develop a constitution for a united Germany. The idea was opposed by Prussia and Austria and the Parliament was dissolved on 30 May 1849. The Church was not in use as a place of worship at the time of the Peace Congress – it reverted to its original purpose in 1852. Destroyed during the second world war it is worth noting that this was the first building to be restored at the end of hostilities.

Following the approval of Parliament enthusiasm for the Congress increased and the major part of the organisation was completed. Richard, Burritt and others who had now joined them, set off on a mission to find places of interest for the delegates to visit. They went to Heidelberg on the banks of the Neckar, "a city surrounded by a semi-circle of mountains of the loftiest and grandest form, clothed with luxuriant vegetation, while the castle, at once a fortress and a palace, stands, in its vast proportions and picturesque grandeur, midway between the town and mountain top, which swells its huge bulk behind."[5] A place the delegates should visit, thought Richard. They were warmly received by some of the Professors at the University apart from one who said that supporting the Congress could harm his career.

The group which had by now increased considerably in numbers, proceeded to Worms, a place of special interest to Richard. He wrote in his diary that they stood "as near as possible" to where Luther stood when he appeared before Charles V in 1521 – "one of the greatest and sublimest scenes in the history of the world". Inspired by his own thoughts and imagination he added: "A grander figure than that of the Reformer standing up in the midst of that vast array of worldly dignity and power, maintaining with meekness and moderation, the great truths upon which the weal of the world so much depended, is not to be found in the record of ages." Richard and his companions sat for a while under the large elm tree in Pfiffligheim where Luther had rested before entering Worms. Richard recalled how he broke off two small twigs to take with him "as a memento of a spot so fraught with thrilling interest".[6]

On their return to Frankfurt they needed to tie up the final preparations. Small, diplomatic decisions – such as who they should invite and their order of importance – and preparing a programme, the kind of minutiae at which Henry Richard excelled. On 12 July they were joined by Auguste Visschers and set off again to promote the Congress in northern Germany. They visited Giessen, where they were intrigued by the peasant costumes, particularly the hats of the women. At the university they were received warmly and enthusiastically and met the theologian and historian Dr Ferdinand Christian Baur, a progressive thinker who had attempted to explain the evolution of Christianity from Judaism. They were also received by Baron Justus von Liebig, the University's Professor of Chemistry, another progressive thinker. Von Liebig had been appointed to his post when he was just 21 and carried out pioneering work in agricultural chemistry. He told Richard and his companions he had made references to the subject of peace and its benefit to material and international trade in a book about to be published.[7]

On their way to Halle they passed Eisenach and Wartburg castle where Luther hid for 10 months after his return from Worms.

Here he finished translating the New Testament into German and Richard greatly regretted that they were unable to visit Luther's cell. "There are few spots on the face of the earth that I should have more liked to have stood upon than Luther's cell still shown at Erfurt, and which is preserved in precisely the same condition as it was when occupied by him 350 years ago. But I was denied this gratification, as our arrangements would not permit us to stay at Erfurt," he wrote rather sorrowfully. By 16 July they had arrived at Leipzig, "a handsome city", and met a number of professors, among them a Professor Linder; they chatted for an hour, each with his cigar – which Henry Richard fulsomely praised. He seems to have developed a taste for good cigars and enjoyed a glass of something stronger than tea from time to time.[8] Although it was unlikely that he would write, as Lewis Edwards did when he was a student in London, informing his parents that he "took some bread and cheese and porter" every night on which he lived "as comfortably as any prince in Europe".[9] Henry Richard was advised later in life when suffering from angina to take the occasional drop of strong liquor.

From Leipzig they went to Berlin where they had a guided tour of the prison, the *Musterstrafanstalt*, and were unexpectedly invited to a wedding. Such an insight to this aspect of the life of a German family, was according to Richard, a pleasant diversion for two dusty and travel-worn bachelors. On 19 July Burritt, Richard and Visschers arrived at the beautiful city of Potsdam with the intention of visiting Baron Alexander von Humboldt, the naturalist and explorer – the most famous German of his day. Their intention was to invite him to preside over the Congress. He welcomed them cordially and after a brief introduction from Visschers, Humboldt proceeded to outline his own past efforts in the cause of international peace. It was, he said, a noble and praiseworthy intention, "but I am an old man and have seen a good many Congresses and my experience does not lead me to anticipate any great results from them." He could see many problems facing the Peace Society and had some doubts about it and its activities. "However," he added, "I should be very sorry that you left me with the impression that I am opposed or indifferent to your noble enterprise. Far from it. My heart is entirely with you." He declined the invitation to be President of the Congress saying that he was too old to go to Frankfurt, but promised to send a letter of support to the Congress in which he would express his sympathy, and without mention of any doubts he had regarding its likely effect.[10]

When he realised that Elihu Burritt was an American he talked about the conversations he had with Thomas Jefferson when he had lived in the USA and warmed to the subject of slavery and his concern at seeing determined attempts inside and outside the legislature to extend the abominable system. It is obvious from Richard's diary that he had enjoyed meeting Humboldt, with the suggestion that he was not a good listener. He would interrupt regularly and continue the thread of the other speaker's conversation. The German thanked his visitors warmly and told them how much he had enjoyed speaking to them.

Richard and his companions then returned to Berlin to meet Professor August Wilhelm Heffter, a judge and the author of an influential volume on International Law published in 1844. In fact, it was the first ever book on European International Law and dealt at some length with the question of the conduct of a country which had conquered another towards the vanquished. Attempts were made to try and persuade him to preside over the Congress, but other commitments made it impossible for him to attend. They then visited Professor Ernst Wilhelm Hengstenberg, an evangelist of extreme views who was known to Richard as the author of *Commentary on the Psalms*, which had been translated into English. Richard's opinion of him was that he was "a strong reactionary and a devout believer in armies".[11]

They proceeded to Bavaria, and in their hotel in Nuremberg the landlord was alarmed when they distributed leaflets advertising a meeting that would be addressed by "The Apostle of Peace" which might attract the interest of the police. He was eventually persuaded to allow them to receive friends secretly in their bedrooms! They went on through Augsburg to Munich – in Richard's opinion the most beautiful city in the whole country. Among the professors who received them was Professor Ignatius Döllinger, Professor of Church History at Munich University, an able man, according to Richard, with a clear mind, but another who insisted that a standing army was a necessity to ensure peace among the people.[12] He was an interesting man for other reasons. He was a Catholic who years later was excommunicated for refusing to accept the infallibility of the Pope. The two returned through Ulm, Stuttgart – where everyone they talked to turned out to be atheists – and by boat along the Neckar to Heidelberg, then by train to Frankfurt.

At Frankfurt there was still work waiting them. There was going to be a large delegation from Britain and permission was required for them to travel through Belgium and Prussia without passports and without having to open their bags. They needed to arrange two steamers from Cologne, special trains as well as hotel accommodation in Frankfurt for everyone. They rushed to Darmstadt to try to persuade Heinrich Karl Jaup, former Prime Minister of the Hessen-Darmstadt region, to be President of the Congress. He was the third choice but he accepted the invitation readily. By now Richard Cobden had arrived, likewise Varrentrap, the French economist Joseph Garnier, the French politician Louis Marie de la Haye Cormenin and Jaup. With two days to go before the Congress was due to open the resolutions to be presented had yet to be drafted and it would not be an easy task. The Germans were insistent that standing armies were necessary to keep order, but Richard and Burritt could see problems from the Quakers who opposed the idea of having any kind of army. Thanks to Cobden's diplomatic skills there was agreement, although Richard worried that there could be trouble later from the Quakers who opposed the use of armed force for any purpose. It was with much relief that Henry Richard and Burritt on 21 August went down the Rhine as far as St Goar to meet the first steamer from Cologne. Over the previous two months the two men had probably done more for the cause of peace than would be achieved by the Congress during the next few days. It had been a feat of organisation and persuasion of heroic proportions.[13]

The Frankfurt Congress was the last, and in many ways the most attractive of the three Continental Peace Congresses. At least 500 representatives left Dover on 21 August, sailed to Calais, then on a night train, breakfast in Verviers, Belgium, arriving in Cologne late next evening where accommodation had been arranged for everyone. Early next morning, in two large steamers they sailed up the Rhine. In St Goar, where the mountains rise magnificently from the river banks, Henry Richard and Elihu Burritt waited for them with the Congress papers and were given a hearty round of applause for their work. A special train awaited them at Biebrich, near Wiesbaden, to take them on to Frankfurt. The arrangements were so thorough that all the delegates found their lodgings in a very short time.[14]

St Paul's Church was beautifully decorated for the morning of 22 August with the banners of the various countries hanging inside. When Jaup took the chair for the opening session the floor of the Church was filled with representatives from Britain, France, Belgium, Germany and the USA while the galleries overflowed with men and women. The presence in the galleries of one strange visitor was noted, namely General Julius Jacob von Haynau, the "Austrian Butcher", notorious for the cruel way he dealt with two uprisings, in Italy and Hungary in 1848 and 1849. His presence was, no doubt, an accident – he happened to be travelling through and spent the night in the city. Richard Cobden, in one of his speeches, made a reference to his presence pointedly noting that great military might was not necessary to quell uprisings. "In 1847," he said, "I went through all the courts of Europe, with the exception of that of the Pope, and I found Kings everywhere dressed in regimentals, their ante-rooms filled with soldiers, and their fortifications well replenished with troops. 1848 came, and all over the Continent thrones tumbled like a pack of cards. I therefore can appeal to Governments and kings, as well as taxpayers and the people, to help a cause that will bless and benefit them all."

A resolution was passed unanimously "That the standing armaments with which the Governments of Europe menace one another impose intolerable burdens, and inflict grievous moral and social evils, upon their respective communities: This Congress therefore cannot too earnestly call the attention of Governments to the necessity of entering upon a system of international disarmament without prejudice to such measures as may be considered necessary for the maintenance of the security of the citizens, and of the internal tranquillity of each state."[15]

One other interesting resolution was accepted. It was presented by Cormenin of France, condemning the practice of duelling and was said to be the first great assembly to condemn and exclude duellists on the grounds of morality, religion and reason. He was supported by the French journalist and republican politician Émile de Girardin who killed the historian and writer Armand Carrel in a duel in 1836. "I fought a fatal duel twenty years ago, and I still feel remorse for it at this moment," said Girardin. "If we were to leave no trace in Frankfurt than this resolution, we might say we have done enough."[16]

Henry Richard spoke at the end of the Congress and described how he and Elihu Burritt had arrived at Frankfurt for the first time. They knew no one in the city and on the first appearance things did not appear promising, but after they had submitted a request to the Parliament they had an immediate and positive response. He thanked the Senate of Frankfurt, the local committee and the Lutheran Consistory and called on the British contin-

gent to show how unfounded were any suspicion that their enemies were their German brothers. This was done with a hearty
cheer. He then called upon them to show that their desire was to
see a strong, free and united Germany. Once again his words were
greeted with prolonged applause.

He went on to say that he had been warned many times that the
Congress would be the subject of contempt and scorn. Then came
a typical burst of eloquence. "We would be unworthy of being the
defenders of a cause so elevating and sacred if we had not considered that we could meet the contempt of the conceited and self-
seeker, those who are now, and always have been, opposed to all
great and liberal thoughts when they are first presented," he said.
"This is my answer to them – if anyone believes that it is reasonable for intelligent beings to establish justice by force, let them
laugh. If some consider that it is a fine thing for fathers to be
dragged from the bosom of their families, and sons torn from the
arms of their parents, and sent away to be shot like dogs, and left to
wallow in their blood, and perish destitute on the field of battle, let
them laugh … If some consider that it is an honour to the philosophy and understanding of the nineteenth century that its entire
civilization rest, not on knowledge, but on brutish power, let them
laugh."[17]

Among the 500 British representatives was Samuel Roberts
(SR) of Llanbrynmair, representing Mid-Wales. If Henry Richard
had made a favourable impression on the delegates, the impression he made on SR was even greater. In his report in *Y Cronicl* he
wrote that "it would be desirable if an open door could be found
through some part of Wales for him to stand and give a voice for
Peace in Parliament."[18] Eighteen more years of agitation elapsed
before SR's dream of seeing Henry Richard representing a Welsh
constituency in Parliament became a fact.

At the end of the Congress, the Ambassador for the Duchies of
Schleswig and Holstein in the north of Germany who were at war
with Denmark asked the Congress to set up a Committee of
Inquiry to look at the matter and try to bring the hostilities to an
end. Although the rules of the Congress forbade the discussion of
on-going issues it was agreed that Sturge, Burritt – who spoke
Danish – and Frederick Wheeler would go and see whether they
could reconcile the two sides. Wheeler, an American minister, was
chosen instead of Henry Richard who had to return to London. At
first it appeared as if they were having some success, but then the
armies of Prussia and Austria joined the war on the side of the

Duchies and Sweden on the side of Denmark and the fighting continued for another year. Their efforts received fulsome praise from Baron Bunsen, the Prussian Ambassador to London at the time, who admitted to Cobden that he had more confidence in Sturge, Burritt and Wheeler than in any of the professional diplomats.[19]

Chapter 6

Hopes raised – and dashed

The activities of the Peace Society following the Frankfurt Congress continued with renewed enthusiasm and a series of meetings aimed at increasing support for the cause of peace. One meeting was held in the Yorkshire hall, Wrexham, on 12 November with Sturge, Cobden and Henry Richard speaking and Townshend Mainwairing, MP for Denbigh Borough, in the Chair.[1]

As Henry Richard became increasingly prominent in the Peace society Welsh interest grew correspondingly. "It is a matter of surprise and dismay these days, when there is so much professing of religion, that so little support and assistance for the Society and its principles … interwoven with everything that is amiable and commendable and in accord with the truth as it is in Jesus," pronounced *Y Drysorfa Gynulleidfaol*.[2] According to *Y Bedyddiwr*,[3] the Society was gaining ground and influence. In *Y Diwygiwr*[4] David Rees – the agitator – thundered his disapproval of war and asked: "What but custom could have kept such chaos from being excommunicated by Christians?" *Seren Gomer*[5] insisted that "our nation needed little persuasion to be united in its support of this splendid Society."

In fact, the Welsh language press was not totally united in its support for the peace movement. David Owen (Brutus), the caustic Anglican and conservative in *Yr Haul*, took a different line. "We received," he wrote,[6] "a pack from the Secretary of the Society, the Rev Henry Richard, and in his letter the respectable gentleman said that there is much excitement throughout the kingdom, and we can expect the Society's missionaries in Wales, to agitate in its support and signing petitions in support of Mr Cobden's motion to be presented in the next Parliament that all disputes between countries should be settled, not by the sword, but by arbitration.[7] We support all the principles of this Society … But we do not applaud the methods of the Society in presenting their case, nor do we approve the spirit of its supporters … Is it right and wise for this kingdom to disarm at the present time when insurrection and war is fermenting and working its way across the entire continent … Something whispers to us … that we will be in Samson's plight … if this kingdom is disarmed …"

Brutus was attacking, not without reason, the methods and character of some of those Welshmen who were the most ardent in their support for pacifism. One of them was William Williams (Caledfryn), a strong supporter of the Liberation Society, the Anti-Corn Law League and the Peace Society. In spite of his excellent articles in support of the Peace Society, Caledfryn – literally "Hard Hill" – was a cantankerous character; it was said of his often savage criticism of other people's poetry in *Y Gwladgarwr* that he had chosen an appropriate bardic name for himself. Samuel Roberts, too, could be excessively scathing in print – some of his contemporaries accused him of a bitterness not congenial to the pacifist spirit.[8]

The Great Industrial Exhibition in London was one of the main attractions of 1851. The Crystal Palace was built to accommodate it in Hyde Park – one of the superintendents of the work was the architect John Jones (Talhaiarn) one of the two most popular Welsh language poets of the century. (I mention his name as it will come up again.) Railways were now connecting other towns and cities with London and steam ships were drawing the nations closer together. There was a new spirit of confidence in the United Kingdom, a feeling that trade was a reviving force and that mankind was expanding rapidly in knowledge and mastering machines as well as the powers of nature. The idea of progress was slowly gaining currency – that the world was moving forward. Whether it was that idea that inspired the Great Exhibition, or whether it was the Great Exhibition that gave rise to the idea of progress, is not easy to decide. But in 1848 the first volumes of Macaulay's *History of England* were published and it is interesting to recall one of his first sentences: "The history of our country during the last one hundred and sixty years is eminently the history of physical, of moral, and of intellectual improvement." An idea was gaining currency that material progress led to moral improvement which was creating a spirit of optimism. Public opinion was more peaceful and according to Henry Richard, "a deeper sense of the enormity of war was growing up everywhere in the heart of Christian nations, and a kindlier feeling gaining ground between different countries, especially between France and England".[9] The peace movement had the ear of a large section of the public.

The Peace Society took advantage of the Great Exhibition and the fourth International Peace Congress was held in Exeter Hall from 22-24 July. Joseph Sturge rented a house close to Hyde Park where he would receive and welcome foreign visitors – the kind of arrangement we would associate with today. A large delegation arrived from France, Germany, Sweden, Belgium and Italy as well as representatives from Europe's capitals. More than 60 delegates had crossed the Atlantic with representatives from 16 states. Henry Richard's problem was to decide who, from such an array of talent, would be called to speak.[10] Cormenin and Girardin were present together with fifteen working men and women from France. The Scottish writer and historian, Thomas Carlyle, sent a particularly cordial and supportive letter, in which he said that the less war and cutting of throats that happened the better it would be for us. "One rejoices much to see that innumerable tendencies of this time are already pointing towards the result you aim at; that, to all appearances, as men no longer wear swords in the street, so neither, by-and-by, will nations," he said.[11]

Another Scotsman, the scientist – and theologian – Sir David Brewster, chaired the Congress. It was claimed that 4,000 visited the Peace Congress – how many would have attended the Congress were it not for the Great exhibition, and how many were pacifists, is questionable. But those were not issues to unduly worry Henry Richard. What he sought was attention and publicity for the Peace Society – and he got them. Debates in favour of peace and against militarism and the expansion of imperialism and in favour of arbitration and disarmament were appearing daily in the press and being discussed by commentators. Even if the *Times* and *Morning Chronicle* ridiculed the "utopian peacemongers" there were many weekly publications who took a more favourable view of the Society's efforts. Speeches by Richard Cobden, Edward Miall and others were favourably reported. Prior to the Exhibition, Richard and other members of the Peace Society had tried to persuade the organisers not to include any stands displaying weapons of war. They failed in their attempt but they managed to secure agreement that such stands would not be considered for any prizes. The Great Exhibition organisers evidently accepted the argument that this was an event to celebrate rather than destroy life.[12]

In Wales, "peace" became a respectable and popular subject for poetry competitions at *eisteddfodau*. Gwilym Hiraethog wrote a famous ode that was as peaceful in spirit as his earlier poems on *The Victory at Trafalgar* and *The Death of Nelson* had been belligerent.[13] There were some Friendly Societies who were advocating peace at the time – notably the Oddfellows, the Independent Order of Rechabites and the Ivorites, a society which conducted its activities in Welsh and supported Welsh culture.[14] The Ivorites in particular encouraged the fostering of "union and fraternity" a sentiment expressed in poems by Evan James,[15] author of the words of the Welsh National Anthem, *Hen Wlad Fy Nhadau* (Land Of My Fathers). James was an active Ivorite and wrote a number of poems to be sung to popular tunes at their dinners.[16]

Henry Richard and the Peace Society were also embarking on a campaign to warn the countries of Europe, Britain especially, that war was inevitable unless the dispute involving Turkey, Russia, France and Britain was resolved. The Society was attracting attention, its finances were in good shape and it was fashionable to be a member. Membership had expanded from a hard core of religious pacifists – in which the Quakers were active – to include political, "conditional pacifists". The founders of the Society were men, mainly Quakers, who opposed war on principle. Now others were being invited to join, politicians who opposed war as a matter of policy. They based their argument on the wasted lives, the suffering of the working classes, the damage done to the economy and to trade; the wives who were widowed and the children who were orphaned. The "conditional pacifists" wanted to settle international disputes by peaceful means, through conciliation and arbitration – but their opposition to war was not absolute. The Society had gained valuable experience in disseminating its message through newspapers and pamphlets and Henry Richard – as well as being an astute politician – was becoming skilled in these methods. In principle, Richard was a religious pacifist firmly in the Quaker camp but he was pragmatic when it came to gathering support and extending the Society's influence.

The spirit of peace lit at the Congresses of Brussels, Paris, Frankfurt and London did not last. Minor disputes in which Britain were involved had rumbled on throughout this period. There was hostility towards Greece between 1848 and 1850. The house of a Portuguese Jew, named David Pacifico, living in Greece had been burnt in an act of anti-Semitism and the Greek Government refused to compensate him. Pacifico was born in Gibraltar and could claim to be a British citizen and on this basis Lord Palmerston, the Foreign Secretary, was prepared to declare war on Greece. It did not happen but British warships blockaded the Greek coast for months – to the annoyance of France.

Then on 2 December 1851, French democracy was overturned by Louis-Napoleon bloody *coup d'etat* and the climate of western European politics changed. Politicians became nervous and others proceeded to stir the newspapers with claims that France could invade and overrun Britain whenever it felt like it. Without consulting anyone, the combative Palmerston congratulated Louis-Napoleon, suggesting that the British Government approved the *coup*. He was reprimanded, then sacked, by the Prime Minister, Lord John Russell.[17] Not that he remained long in the political wilderness. The high officials of the military and the fleet – allied to the warmongering press – grabbed the opportunity. France, the old enemy, was again a threat, and the very name Napoleon was enough to incite hostility. Lord Derby's administration collapsed and a coalition under Lord Aberdeen was established in December 1852. In the words of Richard Cobden when John Bull gets the taste of blood in his jaws he is beyond reasoning. Henry Richard kept arguing the case for arbitration and peace with as much determination as ever.

If there was any danger of the clamour drowning the voice of the Peace Society, Henry Richard would not be silenced. He was sending letters to the newspapers and writing and editing the *Herald of Peace*. Richard Cobden published a pamphlet, *1793 and 1853 in Three Letters*.[18] which attracted great attention and was roundly condemned by the warmongering English press. The influence of Henry Richard can be detected in the pamphlet – the meticulous research, style, content and the ferocity of its anti-imperialism. The pamphlet is in the form of three letters to an unnamed clergyman who had preached a sermon in memory of the Duke of Wellington. The letters compare English attitudes to France in 1853 with those when England attacked Napoleon in 1793. The justification then – and in 1853 – was that it was a defensive war to safeguard human rights and freedom. Although France declared war in 1793, the pamphlet argued that the true initiators of war were the countries circling France under the pretence of re-installing the French monarchy. France had no choice.

France in 1792, wrote Cobden in the Third Letter, was at war with
Austria and Prussia, threatened by Russia, Sweden, Spain, and
Sardinia, and assailed openly or covertly by all the despotic powers
of the Continent. Nothing was "dreaded more by her than a maritime war with England". A careful study of history showed, he
wrote in his preface to the second edition, that the British
Government had shown the same enthusiasm for going to war
with France in 1803 and 1815 as it had done in 1793. He accused
the "English" Government of creating Napoleon. "… who is
ignorant that Napoleon, the genius of that epoch, was brought
forth and educated by us – that he, until then an obscure youth,
placed his foot upon the first step of the ladder of fame when he
drove our forces from Toulon in 1793, and that it was in overcom-
ing the coalitions created by British energy, and subsidised with
English gold, that he found occasions for the display of his almost
superhuman powers?"[19] Although published under the name of
Cobden we see the hand of Richard in the research, suggesting a
different view of Anglo-French hostilities to those usually argued
by English historians. Throughout his life Richard would rely on
official Government documents and Hansard for his sources,
ensuring an accurate chronology of events. It also made it difficult
for the Government to refute his arguments. Cobden's pamphlet,
typically of Richard, is full of statistics and telling sentences, such
as this from the Third Letter: "The present generation of adults
have been educated under circumstances which forbade an impartial judgement upon the origin of the war. They were either born
during the strife of arms, when men's hopes and fears were too
much involved in the issue of the struggle to find leisure for a historical inquiry into the merits of the quarrel, or after the conclusion of peace, when people were glad to forget every thing
connected with the war, excepting our victories, and the victors."[20]
We, at the beginning of the twenty-first century can sympathise
with those sentiments. Richard would often quote the words of
Milton – "But what does war, but endless war still breed".

   The hawks of war were circling, clamouring that Louis-
Napoleon and the French were out to "avenge Waterloo" and soon
they would be landing on the undefended shores of England. It
was the time to prepare for war, and towards the end of 1852 the
Peace Society found itself in trouble. A Militia Bill was presented
to the House of Commons by Lord John Russell with the intention of creating a local militia of 70,000 young volunteers to be
trained in the use of firearms. The number expected from Wales –

not including Monmouthshire – was 4,512. If voluntary enlisting failed the Government would call up men by a system of lottery. The Peace Society, naturally, opposed the Bill and printed and distributed thousands of leaflets explaining the obligations and to ensure that young men were not misled.[21] A number of those distributing the leaflets were arrested on the grounds of sedition. *Y Cronicl* – SR's paper – reported that police in Hampshire had been ordered to destroy all Peace Society leaflets, or leaflets produced by any other organisation to dissuade young men from enlisting in the Militia.[22] The subject was raised in Parliament and 64 supporters of the Peace Society signed a letter to the Home Secretary, Spencer Horatio Walpole, accepting responsibility for the leaflet. The letter was drafted by Henry Richard, and penned in forthright – aggressive, even – language. He argued the need to explain the law in a way that would be understood by all and that the free distribution of leaflets was a well-established custom. The leaflets contained nothing but the truth and punishing distributors was nothing less than a campaign to stifle opinion and information. Others were "persuaded" to join the Militia through the use of alcohol and it was disgraceful that Christians could not resort to the truth to warn ill-informed young men.[23]

Palmerston was determined to pursue the prosecution but the Attorney General, Sir Alexander Cockburn, refused to take action and the Government had to drop the charges. Palmerston was furious, but there was nothing he could do but bluster that an adequate number of young men had enlisted voluntarily in spite of all opposition. Henry Richard responded in the *Herald of Peace* that Palmerston was well aware that he was lying, adding that Palmerston had been kind enough to offer the Peace Society some small advice, and the Society was happy to return the favour. The Society's advice was that his Lordship should hold his tongue and that he was old enough to know better than to stir up ill-feeling and prejudice towards himself and his government by his lack of courtesy.[24]

Again, there are suggestions that some would have liked to see Henry Richard in the House of Commons. In his diary he noted that he had visited Edward Miall who had recently been elected MP for Rochdale and was taking his time to acquaint himself with "the tone and spirit" of the house before delivering his maiden speech. Miall had admitted that he would have been happier if Richard had been there with him as representative of, for example, the "Carnarvonshire Boroughs" as he felt that he had not much support "among the Dissenters of the House".[25]

The Peace Society worried that the politicians would let Britain slide into another war. Or be swept on a tide of public opinion and newspaper rage. A decision was taken to organise another Peace Congress in 1853, this time in Manchester. It would be another load on the shoulders of Henry Richard but he forged ahead with typical energy and enthusiasm. A meeting was held and it was decided to raise a fund of £10,000 – £4,000 were raised within 30 minutes and another £500 before the end of the meeting. These were large sums, but there were some very wealthy men among supporters of the Peace Society – Joseph Sturge, Cobden, Miall and John Bright were all successful industrialists – men who had the power to raise substantial sums for causes they believed in. A letter calling for a Peace Congress was signed by 200 influential persons, including 19 MPs. The aim was to pacify a public agitated by the press and politicians who argued that France, under Louis-Napoleon, was about to attack Britain. Henry Richard went to Manchester some months in advance to make preparations. These were difficult – even dangerous – times, with the public in an excitable mood and it was necessary to tread warily. But the spirit of the old Anti-Corn Law Leaguers was alive and well, and George Wilson, chairman of that campaign, agreed to be President of the Congress. The Manchester Peace Congress was held over two days, 27-28 January 1853, and was attended by 600 delegates with 400 letters of support or apologies received from people unable to attend. Cobden and Bright delivered powerful speeches and a delegation from the Congress took a written address prepared by Henry Richard to the Prime Minister, Lord Aberdeen.[26]

At one of the meetings of the Congress Henry Richard delivered a speech outlining Britain's Burmese wars – a subject rarely raised today in discussions of nineteenth-century imperial history. It began with the – unfounded – claims that Britain was concerned about the safety of India's eastern boundary in Bengal before turning covetous eyes on the lucrative cotton trade between Burma and China and then at Burma's forests and mineral wealth.

Rangoon was attacked by employing Indian soldiers, a war that lasted from 1824 to 1826. The states of Arakan and Tenasserin were annexed, to be governed from the headquarters of the East India Company in Calcutta. In effect the East India Company governed the country up to the uprising of 1857. Punitive measures were forced on Burma, which included having a representative of the British Government in the court of Rangoon and payment of compensation of £1,000,000 to Britain. Also, Burma was forced to produce rice in Arakan – for the benefit of Britain, naturally. Britain also instigated the second war with Burma in 1852. The excuse this time was a fine of £100 imposed on two British traders by the Governor of Rangoon. Britain sent a fleet of warships insisting that the fine be withdrawn and the governor removed from office. Burma could do little but yield to both demands, but that was not enough either. Local officials were accused of being discourteous towards British subjects. "... England's soldiers are now spending £250,000 every month sub-duing the little people of Rangoon and the surrounding areas by the fair, gentle, kindly, enlightened, respectful, holy, self-restrained and godly use of English militarism and the East India Company," sneered SR in *Y Cronicl*.[27] Clearly Henry Richard was not alone in his criticism of the British imperialistic spirit, the interference and attacks on other countries. Great diligence was required from Richard and the Peace Society to keep abreast of all the minor wars and skirmishes happening in Britain's name in far corners of the globe. By that address, subsequently published as a pamphlet with the title *The Origin of the Burmese War* (1853), he attracted the atten-tion of others – in particular Richard Cobden. Prior to that there was indifference and ignorance in England towards British misad-ministration and aggressive policies in the Far East. Over the years Richard's attempts to draw attention to minor wars, often started without consultation, sometimes without the knowledge of the Government, would become increasingly significant. It was often due to his hard work that people got to know the truth of much that went on and how the British Empire was extending its tentacles.

Despite the ridicule of *Punch* and the sneering *Chronicle*, Henry Richard was satisfied with the Manchester Congress. Peace was back on the agenda and being discussed seriously and effectively. It was agreed that Manchester, as well as London, should be a centre of the Peace Society's activities, and that Henry Richard should spend some months there every year. Cobden and Bright took an active interest in the Society's work and were both MPs in the North of England. It was not an idea which attracted Richard greatly but he agreed to it without complaint. Throughout his life he took the view that duty should take precedence over personal preference.[28]

A second, better attended, Congress was held in Edinburgh in October of the same year. Duncan McLaren, Lord Provost of the

City, gave the Congress his wholehearted support and there was strong representation from Scotland including a number of Presbyterian ministers. *Y Bedyddiwr* regretted that among them there was not one name from Wales. "Have our fellow country-men become totally indifferent with regard to war and the gener-ous principles of this splendid Society?" it asked.[29] In two years *Y Bedyddiwr* was proclaiming its support for the Crimean war – but more of that later. Of course there was one prominent Welshman at Edinburgh – its organiser, Henry Richard. This time he was venting his condemnation of bellicose and nationalistic English bragging inflamed by the newspapers. A little earlier in an article under the title *Is National Boasting Good?* he argued how a combat-ive spirit might – indeed, was likely – to drive a country to war.[30] He attacked this English disposition for war, a point he would often make over the years. Miall, Bright and Cobden were all among the speakers. Cobden examined the question of whether it was right to go to war to support the independence of Turkey. The clouds of war were gathering.

Towards the autumn of 1853 Henry Richard received an unex-pected invitation to become Principal of Brecon Congregational College. Unexpected, because he had, on the suggestion of Cobden and others, stopped prefixing his name with the title of Reverend. As he often spoke on public platforms it was considered wise not to use the title in case people might stay away thinking it might be a preaching festival! Richard was evidently honoured and flattered to receive the invitation and gave it careful consider-ation.

He was now 41, at one of life's crossroads, and whatever deci-sion he took, there would be no turning back. He sought the opin-ion of his friend, the Rev Dr John Campbell. Campbell was a minister and editor of the outspoken *British Banner*, of which it was once said that it would be appropriate to replace the second "n" in *Banner* by a "g"! Campbell wrote him a long, fraternal, and pompous letter. The invitation from Wales, wrote Campbell, was one of high trust, fraught with great usefulness, and would enable Richard to become the benefactor of his native land, and exercise an untold spiritual influence over his countrymen. It would be a sphere of literary ease, removed from the wear and tear and agita-tions of life, and would be a permanent provision for the rest of Richard's life. Then Campbell appealed to Richard's idealism and sense of service:

> I look upon the Peace Society, as, of its class, by far the most
> important movement of the age. Next to Associations for
> Propagating the Gospel, nothing, to my view, can be compared
> with it. And, indeed, as it relates to the kingdoms and empires of
> Europe – kingdoms and empires embodying the knowledge, the
> wealth, the power of the globe itself, for the whole is centred
> there – I assign to the Peace Society a place above that even of
> missionary societies. While these Powers would laugh at them,
> they listen to the Peace Society. I look upon it as the chief moni-
> tress of Cabinets, and the chief check to the madness of states-
> men. The Peace Society talks to them in a language they
> understand. I am as confident as I am of my own existence that it
> has done more than all other things united to keep down the war
> spirit of England, and through it to maintain the peace of the
> world – that peace which is the condition of all good, and with-
> out which it is impossible for even the Gospel itself to make
> progress, or even maintain its ground. Mr Cobden alone, by his
> speeches and pamphlets, has, of late years, done more to pro-
> mote peace than all the bishops of all the Churches of Europe.[31]

At the Peace Society, he added, as in any similar organisation, the
Secretary was the lynch-pin – the life and the soul – and in that
position Henry Richard was "pre-eminently qualified". He knew
of no one so suitable for this arduous office, and the consequences
would be dire if Richard were to leave. He warned that the appeal
of the Society would be weakened if he left and influential friends
would withdraw their support. He was also completely honest
with Richard. The attraction of the Society could weaken and
membership dwindle, and he could face old age on a tiny pension.
Continuing in the post would involve no small sacrifice and much
insecurity. After receiving Campbell's letter Henry Richard came
to a decision quickly and – gratefully and gracefully – declined the
opportunity to return to Wales.

Campbell's prophecy that there could be lean years and retreat-
ing friends ahead was confirmed sooner than expected. After the
encouraging and exciting years of the late 1840s and early 1850s,
the large meetings and the enthusiastic letters and the heady
International Congresses Henry Richard could see, perhaps more
clearly than most, the cloud on the horizon. That cloud was the
Crimean War, a war described by Queen Victoria in a private letter
as "popular beyond belief".

Chapter 7

The Crimean War

The cause of the Crimean War is complex, and a good example of "John Bull" wanting to get involved in other people's quarrels and making things worse. It began as a trivial dispute between Catholic France and Orthodox Russia over who should have the rights to the Holy Places in Palestine. Louis-Napoleon insisted that the Turkish Ottoman Empire should acknowledge France as the principle authority over the Christians of the ancient Biblical lands of Canaan and the Holy Places of Jerusalem, in particular the keys to the Church of the Nativity. Tsar Nicholas I of Russia challenged the claim and the change of authority citing treaties made in 1757 and 1771 which had given these rights to the Greek Orthodox Church. The Ottoman Empire was in decline and in an attempt to keep out of trouble, the Sultan, Abdülmecid I, first of all acquiesced to France's demand. But when Russia took a stance, he changed his mind, hoping the problem would go away. France responded with a diplomatic and military offensive which included sending a warship into the Black Sea, through the Bosphorus and Dardanelles straits. This was contrary to an international treaty made in 1841 prohibiting warships from any country except those of the Ottoman Empire from using the straits. Nicholas I replied with his own offensive and placed an army on the banks of the Danube. On 2 July 1853, a few months before the Aberdeen Peace Conference, Tsar Nicholas attacked Moldova, at the time a part of the Ottoman Empire. Nicholas was accused of wanting to carve up the European part of the Ottoman Empire and of expecting support from Prussia, Austria and Britain for his plan. But France, Russia and Britain – of course! – were all awake to any opportunities to expand their spheres of influence in the region and Britain certainly did nor wish to see Russia controlling the Bosphorus and Dardanelles straits. France rapidly lost interest in the dispute regarding the Holy Places and took the diplomatic initiative of joining Britain and supporting Turkey against Russia. In October 1853 Turkey declared war on Russia and Tsar Nicholas responded by sending his warships on the last day of November to Sinop where they destroyed the Turkish fleet. This act was sufficient excuse for Britain and France to go to war against Russia, which they did by formally declaring war the following March.

Almost a year elapsed between Russia and Turkey breaking off diplomatic relations in May 1853 and Britain and France going to war against Russia in March 1854. Which would seem to have given plenty of time for reflection, but it was not so. The press whipped public opinion into a frenzy of hatred against Russia. The conditional supporters of the Peace Society, those who opposed war on political "principles" and the waste and destruction, melted away in the months leading up to war. Some became militant pro-war apologists. Many MPs who had been prominent in their support for the Peace Society were silenced, men like Frank Crossley (Halifax), Joseph Crook (Bolton), Apsley Pellatt (Southwark) and James Kershaw (Stockport), in fact, nearly all the Members of Parliament with the exception of Cobden and John Bright. Even Cobden's voice was rarely heard in this period. Bright continued to oppose the war in his speeches in the House of Commons until the beginning of 1855, but when an effigy of him was burnt in his own constituency, in Manchester, even he was silenced for a while. The number who attended the annual general meetings of the Peace Society in 1854 and 1855 dropped to 23.[1]

But in spite of the attacks on him in the press and by the public, Henry Richard stood firm. He continued to speak and publish articles opposing war in general, and the Crimean War in particular, in the *Herald of Peace* and other journals. He and the steadfast Joseph Sturge were the mainstays of the peace movement over the next few years, upholding and developing the arguments against Britain's involvement in the war.

However, there was one incident that makes us wonder whether even he had wavered at one point. The Quakers were absolute in their opposition. At the same time they believed – correctly – that there was no hope of influencing public opinion or to change the government's position. They concluded that the only way of preventing the war was to appeal directly to Tsar Nicholas himself. A deputation of three Quakers set off for St Petersburg – Joseph Sturge, Robert Charleton, who owned a large pin-making factory in East Bristol, and Henry Pease, an industrialist from Saltburn, near Darlington. They began their journey on 20 January 1854, and arrived in Russia on 2 February. They were received and given a warm welcome by the Tsar on 10 February. As a Christian, he said that he sympathised with the Quakers' position regarding war – but his response was only what might have been expected: "I have a duty to perform as a Sovereign. As a Christian I am ready to comply with the precepts of religion. On the present occasion my great duty is to attend to the interests and honour of my country." The three waited in Russia until they received his official response in writing, and on 14 February, the very day that Britain severed diplomatic connections with Russia, they began the journey home.[2]

The deputation was a failure – and revealing. It showed the extent of the difference of opinion between the religious pacifists and the political conditional pacifists. Public opinion ensured that the condemnation from the newspapers was absolute. On 21 January the *Times* called the deputation "a piece of enthusiastic folly" followed by a more vicious attack a few days later. The Birmingham *Mercury* was the only paper to show any sympathy for their effort. On 28 January the paper in a reference to Joseph Sturge, a much-loved benefactor of the city, commented that "his mission, though a mistake is a most amiable one. His benevolence, though pure waste, is still benevolence". The militaristic spirit had permeated to the marrow of public opinion. Even a regular contributor, who called himself "X", writing in the May 1854 issue of the *British Friend*, the official journal of the Quakers, chastised the three for their appeal to the Tsar.[3] He condemned the Tsar and his "despotic policies" compared to the benevolent and tolerant Turks in their governing of other countries.[4] Did "X" represent the opinions of a substantial minority among Quakers, although at variance with their official position?

Of greater interest to us, perhaps, was the position taken by Henry Richard.[5] There was no mention in the *Herald of Peace* – edited by Richard – of the journey of the three Quakers before they left, and the only reference which can be found regarding their adventure from Richard was a letter in the *Times*, a less than supportive correction. The *Times* in its article of 21 January had written that the three men were going to Russia as representatives of the Peace Society. In a letter to the paper two days later Henry

Richard denied that the three had anything to do with the Peace
Society and said that he had no knowledge of the content of their
message. This would appear to be unlikely in view of Sturge's
close involvement with the Society. In his biography of Joseph
Sturge,[6] Richard again denied that the deputation had anything to
do with the Peace Society and that his only action was to "… cordially wish God speed to the good and brave men that had under-
taken it". The *Herald of Peace* offered no defence of the three from
the ridicule and condemnation of the press. Did the pro-war jingoism and the withdrawal of the "conditional" support of the
politicians cause uncertainty even among the Peace Society? It
could be that Richard was peeved that the three Quakers had taken
their action without consulting him. Yet Richard Cobden was certainly aware of their intentions, because in a letter to Sturge he
wrote "I rather think you overrate the effect of deputing crowned
heads … If a party of Friends were now to set off on a visit to
Nicholas, it might, I think, expose them to a charge of seeking
their own glorification."[7] Cobden, who once referred to the
Quakers as "the soul of the peace movement", like Richard,
offered no words of public support to the three men. The same
was also true of John Bright. As happens in a time of war pacifists
were branded cowards and traitors. These were uncomfortable
times for the Quakers as they watched the approach of the
inevitable and the peace movement appeared more and more a
movement that prospered in a time of peace – or at least when
wars were fought well away from British shores by foreign troops
in British employ.

A few years later, Henry Richard, in his booklet *History of the
Origin of the War with Russia*,[8] based mainly on the Government's
own documents, showed that the Tsar had no intention of capturing Constantinople and that above all he "was anxious for the
friendship and alliance of England". That information had not
been made public at the time. It was clear that Nicholas anticipated the inevitable fall of Turkey – no statesman in Europe would
have disagreed with his analysis – and that he wished to make a
treaty with Britain, a country like Russia that took the greatest
interest in the fate of Turkey. Perhaps the three Quakers understood what was happening better than most.

There were indications that Henry Richard was suffering some
depression at this time – the effects of overwork, the threat of war,
personal loneliness and the loneliness of working for a movement
that was becoming less popular by the day. There is evidence,

however, that he could enjoy himself in the company of like-minded men. He describes in his diary a jolly evening spent in H. R. Ellington's house in the company of Louis Alexis Chamerovzow, the writer and campaigner on behalf of minorities – particularly the Maori – and against slavery. Chamerovzow later provided valuable assistance to Sturge and Richard when they visited Paris at the time of the 1856 Peace Treaty. "Such laughter is medicinal for mind and body, but such is the effect of early education in forming an artificial conscience by forbidding as sinful what is perfectly innocent, that I remember well when a youth having a vague conscience of guilt after a merry evening."[9] In general, however, he seemed engrossed in his work, making new, influential, friends and discussing new and stimulating ideas. Shortly after the war had begun 26 April 1854 was proclaimed by the Government "A day of Solemn Fast, Humiliation, and Prayer". It was a practice established by Henry VIII before going to war against France in 1544. Richard, Edward Miall, H. R. Ellington, J. Carvell Williams and other friends responded to the appeal for a day of fasting by spending a day in Epsom where they enjoyed an extravagant lunch. It was such an agreeable day that they decided to continue these meetings and they formed a club, which they called the Privy Council, meeting in each other's houses on the first Saturday of every month to discuss the religious and political issues of the day. The club continued to meet for many years and Henry Richard, almost to his last days, was one of the more enthusiastic attendees – and the liveliest of conversationalists.[10]

John Bright may have been silent in public on the issue of the Crimean War, but in private he revealed his opinions in a letter to a friend:

> I cannot conceive anything more unwise than to endeavour to excite public opinion to drive the Government into war with Russia in defence of Turkey. If such a war should be undertaken, I believe our children and posterity will judge us precisely as we now judge those who involved this country in war with the American colonies and with France, with this difference only, that we shall be held to be so much more guilty, inasmuch as having had the blunders and crimes of our forefathers to warn us and to guide us, we have wilfully shut our eyes to the lesson which their unfortunate policy has left us. War will not save Turkey if peace cannot save her; but war will brutalise our people, increase our taxes, destroy our industry, postpone the promised Parliamentary reform, it may be for many years.[11]

Bright argued that war could not be justified because of the cost in blood and money, the cruelty, wives left in poverty and solitude, the increase in taxes and the deterioration in Government institutions. The working class would be the one to suffer the hardship and poverty. Cobden once said that the "a" at the end of Crimea should be placed at the beginning to form "a crime". Such arguments, whether voiced publicly or privately by Richard, Cobden or Bright, were ignored and Britain rushed headlong into the madness.

The Tory Government took a political position, as did most Liberal MPs, arguing that Russia would expand and become too powerful, leading to the destabilisation of Europe. Only a minority of Liberals, including Gladstone, took the view that Russia did not have expansionist designs. They argued that Russia was a Christian country, albeit Orthodox, but preferable to Islamic Turkey.

Henry Richard set out to inform the public so that they would be more critical of what they read in the newspapers. He thundered against the war every month in the *Herald of Peace* and the line of his reasoning can be seen in his pamphlet, *Evidence of Turkish Misrule*.[12] The Turks were a barbaric race and the Ottoman Empire one of the most brutish in history. What was the British Government doing rushing to the defence of such despicable nation? They should be swept away from Europe, and even further afield if that were possible.

> The Ottoman Empire have been encamped for more than four centuries in Europe. During that time they have been brought into contact with every form of European civilisation; but they have remained so obstinately impervious to all the influences brought to bear upon them, that we are at last constrained to the conclusion that they have no capacity for civilisation, or if they have, it has certainly not been yet developed. They can fight desperately enough, but that is the note of barbarism, not of civilisation. When they cease to fight, they seem to fall into a normal state of sloth, sensuality and decay.[13]

While Henry Richard lashed the Turkish empire without mercy, he was not alone in his criticism. At the time Turkey was being reviled for its treatment of the people of Bulgaria and he quotes the reports of eye-witnesses, including the French Deist François Volney as well as a number of English writers who travelled through Turkey and many parts of its Empire. Hubert von Boehm, an officer in the service of Prussia wrote:

Of the great resources of the Turkish empire, little more has remained than a neglected and thinly-populated land, and a lazy, strengthless population. Richly as nature has endowed the land, man has recklessly turned its gifts into curses. The forests lie waste, the fields uncultivated, and the most fruitful and most beautiful districts, changed into dreary deserts are no longer able to nourish a tribe of beggars. The rule of the Turks has not built a village nor tilled an acre, nay, hardly planted a tree ...[14]

And the most damning of all, a description of Bulgaria by Bayle St John:

Wherever there is a centre of Turkish authority established, a wilderness is at once created around. The greater proportion of the Bulgarian population is dispersed in villages far from the high roads, and a wholesome terror ... is from time to time struck by invasions of armed tax-gatherers.[15]

Britain declared war on Russia in March 1854, the day after France. The war became deeply ingrained in the popular imagination – Balaclava, the charge of the Light Brigade, Florence Nightingale, and in Wales, Betsi Cadwaladr, the heroic nurse, resonating even today. It was the war from which the Irish journalist, William Howard Russell, sent his historic dispatches to the *Times*, reports of such honesty that it is arguable whether any journalist has since enjoyed the same freedom reporting from a war zone. Russell's reports of the horrors and the shambles resulted in the fall of Lord Aberdeen's government in January 1855. The war lasted until March 1856 with 25,000 British, 100,000 French and 3,000,000 Russian casualties – many dying as a result of cholera and other diseases because of the poor organisation and hygiene.

In Wales, *Yr Haul*, the Welsh-language Anglican journal reflected the general attitude. "Every gentle heart bleeds because of the sword, and although we oppose war, and our prayers are for the sword to be replaced in its scabbard, yet England is just in girding for battle, because had she and France not taken the matter in hand the freedom of the free countries of Europe would be destroyed. It is strange that there are in Wales men who are staunch supporters of the crowned head of Russia, but such people are to be found in every sect ..."[16]

One moment the Government was preparing a "Militia Bill" to oppose Louis-Napoleon, then he became "our brave and loyal ally" in a war against Russia. Samuel Roberts took little time to note the irony and remind the readers of *Y Cronicl* that the war against "old Bony" had been popular enough, as was the campaign to raise a militia to face Louis-Napoleon.[17] Britain, France and Russia had interfered in the Greek war of independence from Turkey in 1827 after other European nations had failed to get the two countries together to negotiate. At that time public opinion was in favour of Greece and against Turkey. According to *Goleuad Cymru* (1820) Turkey was a strange country. "The religion and laws of the state permit polygamy and concubinage and the governor has the right to cut off the heads of seven men every day without giving a reason for his actions to anyone." Now, two years after raising a militia to face Louis-Napoleon, Britain was fighting alongside Turkey and France in the Crimea!

In Wales, despite the calamities in the fields of battle, the war was still popular. "It troubles me," wrote Samuel Roberts, "to oppose a war that is so popular throughout our country ... But we must make a stance on this matter of conscience."[18] The English language papers in Wales, such as the *Cambrian, Carmarthen Journal, Cardiff and Merthyr Guardian* and *Carnarvon Herald*, were full of enthusiasm for the war. They carried reports of the campaigns of the Welsh regiments, the Royal Welch Fusiliers at Alma, the Welsh Regiment at Inkerman and Lord Tredegar at the Battle of Balaclava.[19] The Welsh language papers, in the main, followed that line. The Baptist *Seren Gomer* referred to "this monster" and "this madman" when referring to Tsar Nicholas I.[20] When something has gone beyond reform it must be destroyed, argued *Y Bedyddiwr*.[21] This "present campaign is merely a means used by Providence by which to destroy him and clear the way to proclaim the eternal Gospel in these vast lands and kingdoms." Using the sword to spread the Gospel – the same argument had been used to justify the Opium Wars! The Calvinistic Methodists defended the war in a meeting of the North Wales Association in 1854, stating that "Her Majesty's Government" had done everything in its power to prevent the war and that the Association "disowned all connection with unwise ideas". *Y Traethodydd*[22] published an essay on *War and Christianity* and stated that in "special circumstances war was in accord with the principles of the Christian Religion". With the exception of *Y Cronicl, Y Dysgedydd* and *Y Diwygiwr* – journals edited by Congregationalists, the denomination to which Henry Richard belonged – the Welsh language press was united in support of the war.

The argument presented in the pulpits – with the exception of the Congregationalists – was that this was a "just war" and a punishment for a Russia's sins. There were two other principles of the religious debate which needed to be addressed. The first was that it was wrong to go to war until all else had failed. As there had been some attempt at conciliation, it could be argued that this requirement had been met. The second, that a war could be fought to defend a moral order was more difficult since Britain was fighting to defend an Islamic empire alongside a Catholic state. To get around that problem a secular case was argued that this was a war to uphold international law and the balance of power. The Church of England, with its symbiotic relationship with the Government and the Monarchy, was flexible in its attitude to war. According to the Book of Common Prayer it was legal for a Christian, if required to do so by the King, to wear armour and participate in war. This placed the onus of deciding whether a war was justified on secular authority.[23]

Y Cronicl reported that St David's Day dinners had a distinctly military aspect in 1855 and the courage of Welshmen in battle became a subject for poetry competitions in *eisteddfodau*. In 1854 John Jones (Talhaiarn) voiced the sentiments of many Welsh people in the words:

Gogoniant Prydain enwog	The glory of great Britain
Yn noddi'r llesg a'r gwan	Protecting the weak and faint
Hi wna i'r Arth gusanu gwarth	She'll force the Bear to kiss the shame
Am reibio mwy na'i rhan.[24]	For plundering more than it's share.

Turkey, of course, was the "weak and faint" and Russia the "Bear".

Samuel Roberts complained that he was persecuted for his stance.[25] He added that "the secretary (Henry Richard) was heavily blamed in the course of the past two years, because he refused to justify the present war with Russia. He was denounced many times as unpatriotic to his country and a defender of Russian tyranny. He believes that the ministers of the Russian court made many fair and polite offers to end hostilities by calm judgement, concord and peace." As in all wars, those who take a balanced view of events are traitors. A hundred years after the Crimean War A. J. P. Taylor[26] noted how often the position of those who deviated from public opinion had been vindicated, especially on matters of foreign policy. So it is to this day.

In a meeting organised by the Peace Society in Neath, with the respected industrialist and founder member of the Society, Joseph Tregelles Price, in the chair, a former mayor of the borough got up and protested about the lecture. According to the *Cardiff and Merthyr Guardian*[27] he was loudly cheered by the majority of the audience. The clerk of the borough judged that some of the speeches were bordering on treason. A brass band marched in playing *God Save the Queen* and *Rule Britannia*. One young speaker had to run for his life through a back door despite the presence of Tregelles Price. Henry Richard spoke wherever he was given a hearing. He braved the popular pro-war frenzy in meetings around the end of 1855 and the beginning of 1856 – Manchester, Norwich, Bristol, Cardiff, Coventry, Luton and other places. It was decided that it would be unwise for him to speak at Newport (Monmouthshire) where posters had been put on the walls inciting people to attack him. When he went to Cardiff, he recalled years later in the *Herald of Peace*[28] that he battled for 90 minutes to make his voice heard and was accused of being the "Emissary of the Tsar". Richard responded that he was the "Emissary of the Prince of Peace". There was no welcome for the Peace Society in Cardiff. There is no doubt that Henry Richard faced real danger to his person in that period – as did Cobden, Bright and even Joseph Sturge in Birmingham.

Then came signs that public opinion was changing. Henry Richard had an attentive and respectful hearing in Swansea in November 1855. He spoke in Welsh at Ebenezer Chapel on Thursday, 21 November, on the *History of the Beginning and the Likely Consequences of the Present War*. *Y Gwron*[29] reported that the meeting had supported a motion "condemning war in general and this war in particular", even though Richard blamed France rather than Russia for starting the war. The following night he spoke in English in a meeting at the Town Hall. According to *Y Gwron* the "warmongers" were prepared to disrupt the meeting, but there was no trouble. "We never saw a more respectful, nor a more attentive meeting, in the Town Hall," wrote a correspondent. "Mr Richard spoke for over two hours, and for the second hour he had the audience in the palm of his hand, they applauded regularly along with shouts of 'Down with War'. At the end the Chairman invited questions or comments on the lecture. The Rev D. D. Evans and Mr Willet asked a few unimportant questions, to which the audience expressed a degree of displeasure. Mr Richard gave a polite reply …"

There were other signs of a change in public opinion in some

quarters. Henry Richard made his most powerful condemnation
of the war from a totally political position in the *Herald of Peace* of
January 1855. His aim was to let the people read the facts unham-
pered by the frenzy of exaggeration that was driving public opinion. In his assessment he blamed every country for the war –
except Russia! He criticised Turkey and praised the Tsar for his
patience, for his readiness to work towards peace and blamed the
public for driving the Government to war. The article was repub-
lished as a pamphlet soon after.[30] In the same month the Quakers
published *A Christian Appeal From the Society of Friends to Their
Fellow-Countrymen on the Present War*, a leaflet opposing war on religious grounds. It was an appeal to the Government to use every
Christian means to restore peace and urging the leaders to be
aware that "that which is morally or religiously wrong cannot be
politically right". More than 125,000 copies of the leaflet were distributed in London alone, Quakers paid for the leaflet to be
inserted as an advertisement in local newspapers and copies were
re-printed to be distributed in other parts of Britain. Was it coinci-
dence that both publications appeared at the same time? When we
recall Richard's cunning and his friendship with Sturge, probably
not.

Soon after the appearance of these two publication the curate of
St Andrews Church, Enfield, the Rev Dr Alfred Bowen Evans –
another Welshman? – delivered a sermon on the occasion of the
second day of National Fast and Humiliation in March 1855. The
sermon, delivered without notes, was praised and published in the
Nonconformist journal, *The Train*, and subsequently published as
a pamphlet.[31] It was noted that the church was full of very attentive
young men. Evans took a very clear position from the start – "We
are Christians – therefore we cannot fight." He systematically
destroyed the political and religious justification of war by emphasising that most of the arguments were taken from the Old
Testament, and therefore not valid. He criticised Britain for its
mismanagement of the war effort, the waste of life and displace-
ment of funds which could have been used for good causes, and
for its alliance with Turkey, a country with a history of ill-treating
its Christian population. It was the British people who should be
humiliated for sanctioning the war. Also, reports were received on
that same day of the disastrous state of the British army during the
siege of Sebastopol. Evans ended his sermon not with outright
condemnation of war but by appealing to the congregation to give
his arguments careful consideration.

One of the failures of the *Herald of Peace* at this time was the assumption that an appeal to the religious denominations would be well received and that the ministers and clergy would denounce the war from the pulpits. Richard, its editor, gave much greater space to the religious arguments against war than to the political arguments. The responses in the Welsh denominational press is an indication of the failure of the tactic. This resulted in a desire to establish a daily paper that would adopt a pacifist editorial policy. Richard Cobden had suggested the idea in a letter to Joseph Sturge in 1853. "… what an advantage it would be if … we could have a daily paper advocating peace and constantly having before the public the evils of war … It is only by a daily paper that we can really influence public opinion."[32] There was a more general desire for a more liberal paper, one that was not so pro-war and less Anglican in its sympathies than the other papers published at the time. Sturge did not pursue the matter until the middle of 1855. Henry Richard was keen on the idea, likewise Cobden and Bright, but the two politicians wanted to keep in the background. They wanted to influence the content without being seen publicly to have links with a pacifist newspaper. It would not be a paper advocating the unconditional position of the Quakers. It would oppose the Crimean War, support arbitration and a policy of non-intervention. In other words, they did not want a daily *Herald of Peace*. Henry Richard and Sturge – both unconditional pacifists – accepted that policy and Sturge went away to raise the capital. By the beginning of 1856 the finance was in place and William Haly had been appointed editor. Although there were indications that the war was about to come to an end, Sturge and Henry Richard were adamant that such a paper was necessary. In fact, it was considered that a period when public opinion was more conducive to peaceful principles could boost the circulation and help the paper to get established. The paper, named *Morning Star*, was launched on 17 March 1856, and initially Richard and Sturge left the running of the paper in the hands of Haly.[33] After a shaky start, with the paper losing money, Haly was sacked and replaced by Henry Richard and John Hamilton as joint-editors. Matters improved greatly and by the end of May, the circulation of the *Morning Star* had reached a healthy 40,000.

In the meantime, despite the warmongering Palmerston being elected Prime Minister in February 1855 following the collapse of the Lord Aberdeen coalition, public opinion was changing. Peace talks were initiated in Vienna and then Tsar Nicholas died suddenly on 2 March 1855. As public opinion in general blamed the Tsar for the war this was seen as providing an opportunity for peace. But with Palmerston announcing that he would not agree to peace before capturing Sebastopol, the peace talks collapsed and the people became uneasy again. Yet, it was becoming easier to speak out against the war.

★   ★   ★   ★

In the middle of the hurly-burly of Henry Richard's public life there was an interlude of considerable sadness with the death of his mother, Mary. Her health had for some time given concern to him and his brother Edward. Both had been urging her to lose weight and spend a little time in the Mid-Wales spa towns of Llandrindod or Llanwrtyd as she would have done with her parents in her youth. For some years she had left Tregaron to live with her daughter, Hannah, and son-in-law, David Evans the tanner, in Aberaeron. Since moving to Aberaeron, it appears that she had made as much of an impression there as she had in Tregaron. In the obituaries which followed her death in 1855 her life was celebrated as much for what she herself had achieved in life as for being the wife of a prominent man and the mother of one whose name was becoming known throughout Britain and beyond.[34]

Chapter 8

The Paris Treaty

After two years of war at a cost, to Britain of £100,000,000 and the sacrifice of 20,000 lives – four out of every five dying, not on the battle field but in the pitifully inadequate hospitals – ceasefire was agreed in February 1856. Representatives of the countries that had been at war gathered in Paris to hammer out a Peace Treaty. Henry Richard was of the opinion that the British people were tired of war and the time ripe for some public statement in support of arbitration which could be included in the Treaty. He persuaded the committee of the Peace Society to act and a powerful and influential deputation was nominated. On 14 March the deputation met Palmerston and an address, drafted by Henry Richard, presented to him proposing "some system of international arbitration which may bring the great interests of nations within the cognisance of certain fixed rules of justice and right". The Society also urged "a provision … binding the respective Governments to refer misunderstandings hereafter to the decision of an impartial arbitrator." They could see such an arrangement ripening in the fullness of time into a kind of court or congress of nations. Henry Richard, who had prepared the document and who had never deviated from his opposition to the war, was chosen to read the address – although there were Members of Parliament present, including Bright and Cobden, as well as some who had resigned from the Peace Society at the beginning of hostilities but were now returning, rather sheepishly, to the fold. The reception from Palmerston was civil if cold but he made some comments which could be construed as supportive. It was difficult for him to disagree with words like referring misunderstandings "to the decision of an impartial arbitrator".[1] Yet he made no promises to take

Joseph Sturge

any practical steps in support of the request.

In spite of Palmerston's equivocal response Richard was determined to continue with his campaign and take his memorandum
to Paris and canvass the leaders and representatives of the various
states. Again, as at the beginning of the war, his support melted
away. Without the promise of backing from Palmerston they
feared that they, and the Peace Society, would become the target of
the scorn and sneers of the press and the public. Cobden did not
see fit to venture to Paris. In a letter to Joseph Sturge[2] he said that
he had "no faith in these missions to crowned heads and despotic
governments. If you go, it must be as a matter of conscientious
duty – just as a good Catholic makes a pilgrimage to the shrine of
'our lady of Loretta' – and I must be allowed in both cases to consider it a loss of labour and money." At least his opposition was
consistent with his response when he heard of Sturge's intention
to lead a deputation to St Petersburg before the war started!

Whether from cowardice or a genuine belief that it would be a
waste of time, no one was prepared to accompany Henry Richard
on his mission. Finally he approached the courageous Joseph
Sturge and the old Quaker replied without hesitation in his
archaic language: "Thou art right; and if no one else will go with
thee, I will; and I am prepared to go not only to Paris, but if necessary to Berlin, Vienna, Turin, and even to St Petersburg should
there be time, and see if we can't get access to the various sover-
eigns whose plenipotentiaries are sitting at Paris".[3] A document
was drawn up for the various nations and the two set off for Paris,

where they were joined by the President of the Peace Society, Charles Hindley, MP for Ashton. Richard Cobden had a low opinion of Hindley whom he considered to be a weak character – "I shouldn't like to go tiger hunting with Hindley"[4] was how he expressed his opinion of him in a letter to Sturge on one occasion! At least he was, unlike Cobden, prepared to enter a lions' den in Paris.

There is a long history of nations settling disputes through arbitration. There were 81 examples of successful arbitration between Greek city-states in the years 798-640 BC. In the modern period Leibnitz, Rousseau, Grotius, Vattel, Kant and John Stuart Mill had advocated ways of maintaining peace through arbitration. The principle had been applied successfully in the nineteenth century. In 1831 the King of the Netherlands had settled a boundary dispute between Britain and the USA. In 1842, the King of Prussia, Frederick Wilhelm IV, was the successful arbitrator in a dispute over British ships seized by France in 1834 and 1835. In 1850 Louis-Napoleon settled a dispute between Portugal and the USA regarding the sinking of the USS *General Armstrong* in a Portuguese Port in 1814.[5] And as Henry Richard himself wrote in his *Memoirs of Joseph Sturge*:

> All history attests that wars often break out, not because the differences which must sometimes arise in the intercourse of nations as of individuals are incapable of a pacific solution, but because no provision has been made for referring the matters in dispute to any other than the blind and brutal arbitration of the sword.[6]

Richard and Sturge sailed for France on Thursday 20 March 1856. Richard kept a detailed journal of their time in Paris, from 20 March to 10 April.[7] They met Charles Hindley the day after they arrived and there began a period of frantic and undignified rushing in search of the representatives of the countries who would be preparing the Treaty. Above all, they were anxious to get the support of Louis-Napoleon. On their first morning they called on Athanase Laurent Charles Coquerel, a Protestant priest who had once been joint-secretary of the French peace movement. But that gentleman did not receive visitors on Fridays. Evidently such arrogance did not please Richard, but he and his companions experienced a number of similar rebuffs over the next days and weeks. Some, who could have been useful to them, they failed to meet. Others – like Louis-Marie de Cormenin who had taken a prominent part in the Peace Congresses – welcomed them warmly but were unprepared or unable to help them secure a meeting with Louis-Napoleon,[8] suggesting they should speak to someone else. So it went on, although Richard, at least, kept in good spirits and enjoyed the splendours of Paris and wrote in great detail of them. On Monday they visited the Rev Henry Rowland Bramwell, the British chaplain at St Germain, and the same evening they again met the writer and civil rights campaigner Louis Alexis Chamerovzow.

On Tuesday (25 March) they had a breakthrough, although were not be aware of it at the time. Richard, Sturge and Hindley had a meeting with Lord Clarendon who had established a base for himself at the Hôtel du Louvre. Clarendon had been Britain's Foreign Secretary since 1853 and had effectively sustained good diplomatic relationship between France and Britain during the Crimean War and had some influence with the French Emperor. They were courteously and sincerely received and Richard proceeded to explain the purpose of their journey to Paris and opined that Clarendon was the appropriate person to suggest that a clause on arbitration might be inserted in the treaty. He expanded on his ideas and read part of the address he had presented to Palmerston. Clarendon agreed that it was undoubtedly desirable for nations to find better ways of settling their differences than by going to war, and that "very often the question in dispute was not worth one day's expenditure in war, to say nothing of higher considerations".[9] Yet, there was the issue of the honour and dignity of nations and "if we did not … show a readiness to hold our own, we might expect that others would bully us". Richard responded that a *stipulated* arbitration would enable governments to refer the matter in dispute to an impartial third person, before the countries in dispute became excessively irritated. And, as in the case of Britain, before the newspapers had the opportunity to inflame public opinion. Although he did not say much, it was apparent that Clarendon understood the argument and that he himself had suffered at the hands of the press in the past. Stating that it would be difficult to get governments to agree to submit to arbitration, Lord Clarendon promised to do all he could to get a clause on arbitration inserted in the treaty. As they were leaving Sturge asked Clarendon whether he could advise them as to how they could get to meet Louis-Napoleon. Clarendon said the Emperor was overwhelmed with matters of state, but he promised to ask his co-plenipotentiary, Lord Cowley (Henry Wellesley), to help.[10]

Richard and his two colleagues were not confident that their meeting with Clarendon would bring much success so they prepared a letter for Louis-Napoleon's private secretary, Pierre-Albert de Dalmas, a solicitor and former journalist who had assisted the Emperor in the *coup* of 2 December 1852. They received an invitation to the Tuileries. Dalmas invited them to write to the Emperor and assured them he would draw it to his attention the following morning. The letter was written, but they received no response and Henry Richard, judging from the evidence of his journal, was losing patience: "If I had not a very strong conviction that it was and is our imperative duty to bring the important question with which we are entrusted before these great people, I should retire from this work in disgust, for certainly this waiting upon the great is not an occupation particularly gratifying to one's self-respect."[11]

However, the doggedness of the three brought unexpected success. Clarendon kept his promise. On 30 March he wrote to Palmerston that he wished to propose that the Congress should acknowledge the principle of settling disputes without going to war. It seems that Palmerston had no objection because on 13 April Clarendon was able to write that the Russians were ready to accept the principle of conciliation. He believed that this was sufficient for the present to satisfy the "peacemongers" in "England". Richard, Sturge and Hindley were jubilant when they heard that the Congress had accepted the clause, which appeared as Protocol 23:

> The plenipotentiaries do not hesitate to express, in the name of their Governments, the wish that States between which any serious misunderstandings may arise should, before appealing to arms, have recourse, so far as circumstances might allow, to the good offices of a friendly Power. The plenipotentiaries hope that the Governments not represented at the Congress will unite in the sentiment which has inspired the wish recorded in the present protocol.

It was not a binding declaration. In the French wording proposed by Clarendon and agreed by the other plenipotentiaries "une stipulation qui recommende de recourir à l'action *médiatrice* d'un Etat ami ..." – it was the word 'mediation' that was used, not 'arbitration'. Nor was it as binding as Richard would have desired; but it was a statement of support to an important principle. They had achieved as much, if not more, than they had hoped for. Richard could take pride in a considerable achievement – one of the very

few enjoyed by those who worked in the cause of peace during the
Crimean War. Gladstone said in the House of Commons afterwards that for the first time "the representatives of the principal
nations of Europe have given an emphatic utterance to sentiments
which contain, at least, a qualified disapproval of a resort to war,
and asserted the supremacy of reason, of justice, humanity, and
religion".[12] It provided a valuable precedent and was resorted to
three times before the end of the century. Crete's campaign for
independence in 1868 led to conflict between Greece and Turkey
– but the dispute between the two countries was settled in a congress the following year. The Protocol was again used at the
Franco-Prussian War of 1870. At the First Hague Conference of
1899, the Protocol was the precedent for proposals to create a
binding international court for compulsory arbitration to settle
international disputes and the formation of a Permanent Court of
Arbitration – often referred to as The Hague Tribunal. Two
important consequences of the Crimean War, as far as the Peace
Society was concerned, was the inclusion of Protocol 23 in the
Paris Peace Treaty and establishing the daily paper, the *Morning and
Evening Star*, which remained a powerful influence until its demise
in 1869. These were heroic feats, especially when we recall they
were accomplished at a time of public hostility towards the Peace
Society. The membership of the Society had dwindled and much
of what was achieved was due to the work of two men – Henry
Richard and Joseph Sturge.

As expected, Britain was the first to ignore the sentiments of
Protocol 23 and any regard for conciliation or arbitration. No
sooner had the guns in the Crimea been silenced than Britain was
stirring up trouble in China. On 8 October 1856, the Chinese
authorities boarded the *Arrow* in the belief that it was either a
smuggler or a pirate ship. Enraged, the British claimed that it was
an English ship – that the captain was English and it was sailing
under the Union Jack. In fact neither was true. The ship had at
one time been registered in England but that registration had
expired.[13] When the British discovered that the actions of the
Chinese were justified they blustered that the Chinese had shown
disrespect to the Union flag. The British consul in Canton
demanded that the ship be released immediately, that there should
be an apology, otherwise Canton would be bombarded in 48
hours. The bombardment duly began on 23 October and continued with no respite until 13 November. Henry Richard led an
effective campaign of protest in the press. Lord Derby raised the

matter in the House of Lords and Richard Cobden did the same in the House of Commons. During a debate that lasted four nights, Gladstone attacked Britain's villainous behaviour, a calamity heaped on calamity. Finally a motion was passed, with a majority of 16, that there had not been a satisfactory explanation for the bombardment of Canton and that a Select Committee should be appointed to examine Britain's trading relationship with China. The response of Palmerston was to dissolve Parliament and call a general election.

As often happens in such circumstances, in 1857 the Tories were returned with a majority increased to 30 seats. The so-called honour of the Union flag was more important than justice or legality. Cobden and John Bright lost their seats – not that it was a new experience for them, they had lost their seats during the Crimean War. It was futile to reason with a country in a state of insanity.

There was no longer a voice in Parliament to oppose what was happening in China and the attacks began in earnest towards the end of 1857. France joined in claiming that a missionary had been murdered somewhere in China's interior. The bombardment from Britain's warships continued without mercy. Canton was razed to the ground, a large number of women and children were killed, 7,000 houses were destroyed and 30,000 people made homeless. The Chinese were forced to sign the Tientsin Treaty (1858), compelling the country to provide accommodation for foreign representatives, and opening a number of Chinese ports to western trade, as well as providing unlimited freedom of travel to the Chinese interior for missionaries. Later that year, after further discussion in Shanghai, the importation of opium was made legal. When the Chinese refused to ratify that treaty the attacks began again, Peking was taken, the summer palace of the Emperor was destroyed and the Chinese compelled to honour the agreement allowing the opium trade to continue.

It was a matter of grave concern to Henry Richard that religious newspapers were among the most fervently in favour of the attacks on Canton. They argued that these attacks "opened doors to the Gospel". Richard responded in the *Morning Star* by asking whether those who made those arguments seriously believed that "the people of China would receive the Bible from their hands with greater joy and thanks because it had been soiled by the blood of their dear ones."[14]

In October 1857 the revolt in India, the long battle for Indian independence, began. India was being governed by the East India Company. Bengal soldiers, Sepoys, under English officers employed by the Company, had been fighting Britain's wars in Burma for decades. The Indian soldiers had long respected the East India Company officers who lived and socialised with them and together faced the same dangers. But with the passage of time an increasing number of English officers isolated themselves and began to view the natives as people with troublesome desires and needs. They no longer took the trouble to learn the language of their soldiers and they became more and more alienated from local customs. Some of the soldiers, particularly the Hindus who were of the higher Brahmin caste, were very conscious of the arrogant attitudes of the officers towards their religion and traditions. But what sparked the revolt was something relatively minor. Most Sepoys were either Hindus or Muslims and when it was rumoured that new cartridges were sealed with pig and cattle fat, which they were obliged to bite off before loading, they mutinied. A regiment of foot soldiers from Bengal refused to use the cartridges and were imprisoned. On 18 May their comrades broke into the prison and released 85 men and went on to capture Delhi. Both sides were guilty of atrocities during the revolt and such was the condemnation of the East India Company that it was effectively nationalised as a result.

Sturge was very concerned and like many well-informed British people he saw the atrocities as a consequence of decades of bad government.[15] He was certain that the revolt was the result of the oppressive treatment of the indigenous people by the British. He decided that it would be of great service if a voluntary commission, in which the Indian people had complete confidence, went to India to discover the reasons for the disaffection of the population. He got the support of John Dickinson of the India Reform Association but no one was prepared to take the responsibility of accompanying him on this hazardous undertaking. Henry Richard was about to go and take a short holiday with his brother after a period of intense activity when a letter arrived from Sturge asking him to delay his departure and requesting a meeting.

> I am very sorry to delay thy visit to thy brother, but I want to see thee on a matter of so much importance, that I must beg thee not to leave until Saturday morning. I hope to get to Broad Street by one o'clock on Friday, but I shall probably wish thee to go with me and call upon one or two other persons.[16]

When they met Sturge had already prepared an itinerary for the journey and he promised to do his best if Richard would agree to accompany him. It was obvious that Sturge had no faith that a Royal Commission set up by the Government would provide the right answers:

> I would just say, that with the strong probability that a Royal Commission would not be formed of the right men, and the great evils of unavoidable delay even if it were, I doubt very much if this would be a wise course, even if it could be obtained. The evils of the present system are admitted by all but those who are blinded by self-interest, and the dreadful injustice to the natives is palpable to the mind of every honest man who has looked at a tithe of the evidence now in our possession; and if it be possible properly to govern India in future, I doubt if there were ever a better opportunity than there is now that the old system is broken up, to introduce better methods of government, or at least to make the arrangements for doing so in a way that should convince the natives we wish to do them justice.

In his *Memoirs of Sturge*, less than ten years later, Richard added his own comments to Sturge's desires:

> Thus, in the sixty-fifth year of his age, with his health greatly enfeebled, and conscious, as we shall presently see, of his own approaching dissolution, was he prepared to leave the home that was so dear to him, to brave the dangers of climate, and all the horrors and hazards of that time of anarchy and war, with no expectation of gain or glory, but moved solely by sympathy for the wrongs of the poor natives of India, and a patriotic concern for the true honour of England. His designs, indeed, were not accomplished. After frequent and earnest consultation with gentlemen intimately conversant with India, it was felt that the disturbed state of the country, and the extreme terror and jealousy which had taken possession of the native mind, would have rendered it impossible, at that time, to conduct such an enquiry as Mr. Sturge contemplated with any satisfactory result.[17]

Chapter 9

The Morning Star *and the Liberation Society*

Reference has already been made to the establishing of the *Morning Star*, a liberal paper that would be a vehicle for presenting pacifist views and ideas. A paper to take a stance on moral issues, disarmament, conciliation by arbitration and non-intervention in foreign disputes. The first issue, 17 March 1856, costing one penny, promised "a first class London daily newspaper at the lowest possible price". It promised to be "For the people, not for Party." After a shaky start it became a success and an evening edition, the *Evening Star*, appeared. William Haly, the first editor, was sacked after three months following the paper's poor initial performance, losing money at the rate of £100 a week. Richard Cobden, who had insisted that he would take a back seat position with regard to the running of the paper, took an increasing interest in its day to day affairs. After Haly had been dismissed, Henry Richard and John Hamilton were appointed joint-editors. Cobden in letters to Henry Richard shows that he wanted direct, vigorous journalism, and that he was taking as his model the cheap American papers. "Your politics may be right or wrong, but that you must be something is beyond all doubt."[1] Matters improved quickly and by the end of May the circulation of the *Morning Star* alone had reached a healthy 40,000. Hamilton's understanding of foreign affairs was described as poor and Henry Richard took an increasingly active role in the day to day running of the paper.

An agreement was drawn up, which according to a letter from Richard to an un-named friend, was very specific as regarded their division of duties. They would meet every evening to review the last edition, discuss the next day's paper, revise the leading articles and generally consult on the policy, conduct and literary management of the paper'.[2] Clearly Cobden considered that Henry Richard had a keen understanding of foreign issues and that he was anxious that Richard should provide firm guidance on these matters. In a letter to Richard in the early days of the paper, Henry Rawson, the paper's manager, had been specific with regard to Richard's position. "I may say we wish you to take a general supervision of the affairs of the *Star*, acting as our (the proprietors) representative, and having power to act in our behalf". This was confirmed in a letter from Cobden to Richard, who wrote "I hope you will undertake the office of editor-in-chief with an absolute veto over the leading articles. And I hope you will be put in a position to exert our unquestioned authority in all departments of the *Star* office." For the first year the arrangement worked perfectly. The circulation of both papers was satisfactory and Henry Richard worked industriously and conscientiously. He withdrew from all duties except his post as Secretary of the Peace Society.

Then, one day in 1857 Henry Rawson brought a man named Samuel Lucas into the office, introduced him to Henry Richard, said he hoped they would work well together, and left. Richard assumed that Lucas's role would be to take care of the business department, which he welcomed. But Lucas quickly assumed full editorial control over the paper as well as its administration and soon Henry Richard was complaining that he no longer had any influence over its content and was even finding it impossible to get his own articles published,[3] articles on matters he considered of paramount importance – slavery, peace and the way Britain was governing India. It may be that Richard had allowed his grip on the paper to slip. But there was another factor of which he may, or may not, have been aware. It is certainly not mentioned in the letter but Lucas, a Quaker merchant, was married to Mary, sister of John Bright and had invested heavily in the paper. He was in a position to push Richard aside, which he did without ceremony. He also had investments in the Southern States of the USA, but in the paper a few years later, he sided with the North in the Civil War – to the disapproval of Cobden who advocated neutrality and an anti-war position. It was also a stance at variance with that of Henry Richard and the Peace Society. But more on that later.

Richard complained about the general direction of the paper., which had begun to publish details of horse racing and theatre reviews. Others were critical of the paper but Henry Richard withdrew quietly, presumably so as not to harm its reputation and the investments of his friends. Lucas remained editor of the paper until he died in 1865, aged 54. Charles S. Miall in his biography of Henry Richard suggested that there was a need to move with the times and give space to popular subjects. He also suggested that Henry Richard, despite his idealism, his organising and public speaking skills, lacked the "quickness of perception, versatility and grasp of multifarious details necessary in a successful newspaper editor". Whatever, his position and status at the *Star* seems to have been ill-defined from the start.

After the death of Lucas, both papers were edited until 1868 by the Irish writer and politician, Justin McCarthy. Richard quickly returned to favour and it was in the *Morning and Evening Star* that his influential *Letters and Essays on Wales* first appeared. They were published as a book soon after. McCarthy, an Irish nationalist, became an MP between 1879 and 1896 and it is probable that he had much in common with the Welshman. The papers were edited for the brief period before they came to an end in 1870 by John Morley, a journalist from Blackburn who eventually became MP for Newcastle.

★ ★ ★ ★

Eleanor, Edward's wife, died on 21 February 1861, after some months of illness. Strangely, no letter of condolences, not even one with a reference to her death, has survived.[4] Also, Edward and Henry had tried to carve out some kind of career for Eser, the son of their sister Mary and Sam Morris. He was an unusual boy, ingenious and likeable. Henry had secured employment for him at the Census Office after he had failed his exams twice at Swansea Normal College.[5] But he was never to hold down any job for long and eventually sailed to America, where he disappeared.

Henry Richard returned regularly to Tregaron to re-charge his batteries and preach or lecture in Welsh whenever he had the opportunity. He and his cat, Tiny, spent August 1861 holidaying at his sisters' homes in Cardiganshire. A letter he sent to his brother Edward from Garreg-wen, the home of Mary and Sam Morris is full of the old intimacy which seems to have disappeared during Edward's marriage. It is a letter full of the gossip Edward enjoyed. It appears that he did little else but attend preaching festivals.[6] He heard their old acquaintance, Lewis Edwards, preaching at the monthly meeting at Tŵr Gwyn, Lledrod. It seems that the two brothers did not have a high opinion of Edwards, but this time Henry was impressed.

> He took me by surprise ... He not only preached good sermons but produced very powerful effects on the people. The first evening especially he completely mastered and subdued the whole congregation. He certainly presents the most remarkable instance I have ever known of a man overcoming by sheer dint of pluck and perseverance what seemed utterly insurmountable physical defects, and becoming an effective popular speaker in despite of nature. Never was there a man so wholly unfitted for an orator. You remember what he was. His organs of speech seemed positively to refuse utterance to his thoughts. His voice was hoarse and unmusical to a degree. His lungs seemed to labour like those of a broken-winded horse and his countenance (and in that respect he is unaltered) though the features are rather fine, is singularly devoid of that nobility and power of expression by which the soul of an orator sometimes reveals itself through the flesh. Notwithstanding all this, however, he has acquired a remarkable degree of what is real eloquence ... I had some little intercourse with him both here and at Newcastle (Emlyn) and found him pleasant and genial and, I think, glad to see me. He enquired very kindly after you.[7]

Again he describes entertainingly and sometimes maliciously the preachers at the Association in Newcastle Emlyn. D. Charles Davies began well but ended rather flatly. The celebrated Edward Matthews (Ewenni) was "not at all equal to himself". Henry even found time to ponder the hats of the women in the open-air meeting on the banks of the river Teifi.

In August 1862 Henry had been packed off back to Cardiganshire again on the orders of his brother Edward, with a bottle of tonic and pills for his carbuncles. Tom Morris of Blaenwern, Sam Morris's brother, had heard that Edward had advised Henry to take the occasional glass of wine and had sent some bottles to him from his cellar. Soon, thanks to the tonic, the pills, Tom Morris's wine, the care lavished on him by his sister Mary and the sea air at Aberaeron, Henry was restored to his robust health.

★ ★ ★ ★

The following month, brimming with energy and enthusiasm, Henry Richard was back in Wales, this time in a prominent and official role. In 1862 events were held in England and Wales to mark the bicentenary of the beginning of Protestant Nonconformity – 1662 was the year when non-Anglicans were prohibited from the Universities of Oxford and Cambridge and clergy of a Nonconformist tendency were expelled from their churches. The Society for the Liberation of Religion from State Patronage and Control – formerly known as the Anti-State-Church Association – organised a series of lectures and public meetings emphasising the principle of religious equality, and redoubled efforts to build new places of worship and clear the debts of nonconformist chapels. This followed a sterile period of indifference to any reform under the Palmerston administration. One aim was to establish the Liberation Society on a firmer footing in Wales. Also, because of the depressed state of the cotton industry in Lancashire, one of the Society's strongholds, a considerable drop in subscriptions was expected.[8] Partly to make up for the anticipated deficit in the North of England the Society turned its attention to South Wales, with its huge imbalance in Parliamentary representation. In Wales, where nearly 75 per cent of its people were Nonconformists, every Member of Parliament was an Anglican – although not all were Conservatives.

Henry Richard's role in the Liberation Society had been marginal. He had toured South Wales with another representative of the Congregational denomination, John Blackburn, in 1844 and compiled reports on the state of education and religion. There are suggestions that he had, during that tour, advocated the setting up of local Liberation Society associations and for them to affiliate to the Society centrally. If so, it seems that he had made some impression. When the conference was held in Swansea in September 1862, South Wales was well represented and included the likes of the colourful Rev Dr Thomas Price of Aberdare,[9] who, possibly influenced by Henry Richard's visit of 1844, had been active in the Society. Price had been at various times a successful and effective editor of *Y Gwron* and *Seren Cymru*. He would play a controversial role in the election of 1868 when Richard became MP for Merthyr and Aberdare. Yet, Wales had not been fertile ground for the Liberation Society although it should be said that it had concentrated its energies on London and the populous towns of the North of England and the Midlands. There were language difficulties, too, and the English language papers in Wales were either hostile or indifferent to the Society's efforts. But in Britain, in general, it had been effective, and in *Y Diwygiwr*, December 1853, David Rees could claim that "It seems clear that this Society, which was mocked and scorned as a foolish affair aiming at some utopian schemes, has now become a fact of some importance."[10] Henry Richard – as one who knew Wales well – was invited to be a member of the London deputation to Swansea. He had been elected to the Society's executive three months earlier.[11]

A meeting was called to organise the conference and 40 prominent representatives of the various denominations met the delegation from London, which consisted of the Rev (as some still referred to him) Henry Richard, Edward Miall and John Carvell Williams, the Society's Secretary. About 200 people attended the conference itself, which was many more than the representatives from London had expected. As the first event organised to try to secure a fairer representation for Wales in Parliament it was promising and significant. It was the first real attempt in Wales to cast off the political yoke of the Church of England and the wealthy class of landowners who had preserved and prolonged that order. During the Conference the following resolution was passed:

> That this Conference is of the opinion that Welsh Nonconformity has never been adequately represented in the House of Commons – that while the population of Wales contains a much larger proportion of Dissenters than is found in England, Scotland or Ireland, the relative number of their Parliamentary representatives is much less than in either of those countries, and that even those who attach themselves to the Liberal Party, the majority are in the habit of treating questions deeply interesting to the friends of religious liberty with culpable remissness; that this conference is constrained to admit that, for these reasons, the Parliamentary influence exerted by Wales for the advancement of the voluntary principle has been comparatively small, and having such a conviction, the Conference is earnestly solicitous that practical steps should be taken for so improving the Welsh representation as to bring it into harmony with the views and the feelings of the population.[12]

This resolution was based on a speech and a careful analysis by Carvell Williams, a London Welshman, Nonconformist, Liberal, an excellent organiser and powerful speaker who spent a lifetime opposing the privileged position of the Church of England. Years later, in 1885, with Richard approaching the end of his life and Williams newly elected to Parliament they collaborated on a booklet with the title *Disestablishment*. In the Swansea conference Carvell Williams analysed the voting record of Welsh MPs on religious issues. The Church Rate Abolition Bill – an issue of great importance to Welsh Nonconformists – received 16 votes out of 32, and this only after great external pressures. A proposal by

Lewis Dillwyn, MP for Swansea, from a cartoon for Punch *by Spy*

Lewis Dillwyn – who was one of the speakers at the conference – to abolish sectarian distinctions in the public grammar schools, another matter of great concern to Wales, had attracted only 12 votes. Dillwyn, the MP for Swansea, although an Anglican, was a true radical. The previous year, a majority of Welsh MPs (8 to 12) had voted against Sir Morton Peto's Bill allowing Nonconformists to be buried in Anglican churchyards. This was another significant issue in Wales where 79 per cent of the worshipping population were not members of the Church of England. In 1856 Edward Miall had presented a Bill in Parliament in favour of the Disestablishment of the Irish Church. Only two Welsh MPs had supported a Bill that was of considerable interest to Wales.[13] The Welsh Members were not reflecting the opinions of the great majority of the Welsh population.

Henry Richard urged the people of Wales to claim their rights and to elect to the House of Commons representatives worthy of Wales. At another of the Swansea Conference sessions he gave an address which proved in very few years to be prophetic:

> I assert without hesitation that the living practical Christianity which to so large an extent prevails in this country is owing entirely to the influence of the voluntary principle, for whenever spiritual fire burns in the Church of England itself in Wales, it is to be traced to stolen embers from the altars of Dissent. Churchmen imagine that the country is theirs, and that we exist

only on sufferance. Hence the mingled resentment and disdain with which they look down on the persons of Dissenting ministers. But this is a gross misconception; the country is not theirs, but ours; we claim it as a rightful possession. It is ours by spiritual conquest. Our forefathers found it overrun by the enemies of all truth and righteousness, and that because of the neglect of its official guardians; and when the Nonconformists and early Methodists went forth to re-conquer the land, the clergy of the Established Church were foremost in opposing them. It is ours also by spiritual cultivation. There is no population on the face of the earth more thoroughly instructed in religion than are the people of the Principality, and this is to be attributed, not to the State Church, but to Dissenting Ministers and Sunday Schools.[14]

He proceeded to call on the Welsh people to be conscious of their political duties and be prepared to suffer for their principles. He spoke, perhaps for the first time, with the authority of a leader among his own people:

> I want you to prove your sincerity as Nonconformists by appearing at the vestry meetings and by getting your names enrolled on the register, in order that you may send men to Parliament who shall worthily represent the Principality of Wales. The question for us is not as to encountering the sword and scaffold, or fines and imprisonment, in vindication of our principles. The time for these things is gone past for ever. But we also may be required to resist temptation and endure sacrifices peculiar to our age. The questions for us are: can we withstand those social allurements by which it is sometimes attempted to anoint us with flatteries, in order to induce us to relinquish or relax our convictions? Are we prepared to encounter the frown of Squire this or Lady Bountiful that? Are we prepared to be turned out of our farms rather than betray our principles? Are we prepared at all hazards to resolve that Wales shall no longer be grossly misrepresented in the House of Commons?[15]

He praised the work and courage of Lewis Dillwyn in the House of Commons and called on Wales to elect 15-20 true Liberals to Parliament, men who would lend their support to Dillwyn. "Why do you not elect men of your own who can speak for you in that assembly?" he challenged. Before the end of the decade Wales had responded to that challenge and many farmers suffered the consequences of acting in accord with their conscience. Soon, Henry Richard himself was to be elected to Parliament and see the number of Welsh Liberal MPs grow until they represented 80 per cent of the Welsh constituencies.

A note of warning came from the Rev Dr Thomas Price of

Aberdare. Price was a well known Baptist minister, a popular lecturer, newspaper editor, active in friendly societies, and one who had long taken an interest in the Liberation Society. He took a prominent part in the two-day Swansea conference where he spoke of the problems which would have to be addressed when trying to secure MPs who would be representative of Nonconformist Wales. The majority of those who attended the chapels belonged to the poor classes, and from Cardiff to Holyhead three out of every four of the electors were under the thumbscrew of the ground landlords, the iron masters or the coal owners – all Anglicans – and would vote according to their direction. "Let us work for a few years, and the result will be different from what it is now," he cautioned. With regard to finding suitable candidates, he said: "We have but few men that can spare the time, the money, and with the status to contest our boroughs and counties, and therefore we must take the best we can. But I very much question whether we could find two better men than Mr Dillwyn and Mr Bruce. I would not exchange these two men for any other two men I know in Wales."[16]

Despite Dr Price's warnings the delegates departed in good spirits and branches of the Liberation Society were established throughout Wales with two committees, one in North Wales and the other in South Wales, to organise meetings and ensure that there would be cooperation during elections.

Joseph Sturge, the Quaker who had been one of Henry Richard's keenest supporters, died in 1859. Over the following years, at the request of the philanthropist's family, Richard worked on a biography to Sturge. *Memoirs of Joseph Sturge* was published by E. W. Partridge in 1864, a substantial volume of over 600 pages. It is a volume full of information about the peace movement and the work of the son of a Gloucestershire farm who became a successful merchant in Birmingham and a generous benefactor to many charities. The book shows the unassuming nature of Henry Richard's character, modest as to his own contribution to the Peace Society but generous in the credit he gives his old friend and mentor.[19] Sturge died three days before he should have presided at the annual general meeting of the Peace Society. He had accepted the position the previous year following the death of Charles Hindley in 1857. Of the three who went to Paris in 1856 to persuade the belligerents in the war in the Crimea to agree to alternatives to settling disputes by force, only Henry Richard remained. Following Sturge's death, another Quaker, Joseph Pease, was elected president of the Peace Society. Pease had been the MP for South Durham between 1832 and 1841 when he retired from politics. He was the first Quaker to be elected to the House of Commons and had to wait before taking his seat because he would not swear the usual oath of allegiance to the monarch. He was allowed, after a committee had discussed the matter, to make a statement of affirmation. He remained president of the Society until his death in 1872.

In July 1860 Palmerston presented a Bill to Parliament to strengthen the fortifications around Dover and Portland and the shipyards and arms depots on England's east coast. Palmerston was suspicious of Louis-Napoleon – the man he had congratulated on his *coup d'etat* twelve years earlier and who had fought alongside Britain in the Crimean War. Again, a volunteer militia was formed to train men to use firearms, a *rifle corps*, as they were called. These militias were to continue until the end of the century. The Welsh poets were back to their belligerent best. John Jones (Talhaiarn) urged Welshmen to join the militias as did Wales's other popular nineteenth-century poet John "Ceiriog" Hughes, who exhorted:

Deffrowch! Brydeiniaid dewr,   Awake! Stout-hearted Britons,
  Peidiwch ymddiried i'r môr;   Trust not in the sea no more,
Peidiwch rhoi ffydd i Ffrainc, Have no faith in the Frenchman,
  Na gwawd i'r rheiffl-gôr.[18]   Don't mock the rifle corps.

Regardless of Ceiriog's appeal, Henry Richard would not refrain from mocking the rifle corps, accusing the military men of scaring people when it would have been wiser to urge the countries to decrease, not increase, the accumulation of weapons of war. As Disraeli once admitted to John Bright: "You can't conceive how much I am bothered by these damned services; there's no satisfying them."[19] While Palmerston was thinking of war, Richard Cobden had been trying to draw Britain and France closer together through trade links. In 1860, before leaving for France on a trade mission, Cobden went to see Gladstone, Palmerston and Lord John Russell. He explained that his intentions were to persuade France to ease its trade restrictions and pave the way for greater freedom for trade between the countries. Gladstone showed great interest, Russell was indifferent and Palmerston had little interest but agreed to discuss the matter.[20] During their conversation Cobden asked Palmerston what he thought of Louis-

Napoleon. "Well," replied Palmerston, "I can hardly say. Certainly, for the eight or nine years he has been at the head of affairs in France, nothing could have been more straightforward and apparently friendly than his conduct towards us. But still there are circumstances which are suspicious. For instance, we have just received information from our consul at Nantes that he is building at that port some 80 to 100 flat-bottomed boats evidently adapted to effect a landing on a shallow beach."[21] Cobden went to Nantes and discovered that the purpose of the boats was merely to carry coal along canals and rivers. When Cobden told the French about Palmerston's suspicions they laughed heartily.

Y Diwygiwr[22] could see the sense in Cobden's thinking: "The hero of free trade spent the best part of his time this year in France teaching that country to expand its trade, and he managed to form a trade alliance between us and the French. It will do more to stop a French rush on our country than ten million *Rifle Corps*."

In April 1861, Henry Richard led a small deputation representing the Peace Society to France, presenting a written address to the French people on the same subject. The response was enthusiastic and the address was published in France's most influential newspapers and in other Continental papers.[23] In 1862 a large number of French people came to London for the International Exhibition. Richard took advantage of the opportunity to present friendly addresses published in a number of languages and signed by Joseph Pease, the President, and Richard, the Secretary.[24] Those present were urged to create a strong voice in favour of decreasing the number of soldiers and arms throughout Europe. Louis-Napoleon delivered a very peaceable speech which included a suggestion that a Peace Congress be held in Paris aimed at better European coexistence.[25] The French Emperor kept his word and in 1863 issued a formal invitation to European statesmen to come to Paris to attend a Congress aimed at safeguarding peace. Every country accepted the invitation – except Britain! Henry Richard argued passionately against Britain's decision and prepared a statement on behalf of the Peace Society which was sent to Louis-Napoleon wishing the Congress every success. If he could lead Europe towards disarmament and arbitration he would earn far greater honour than by military force. Louis-Napoleon replied with a message of approval for the sentiments expressed by the Society, assuring them of his desire to secure peace in Europe.[26]

Chapter 10

The American Civil War

In 1861, following Abraham Lincoln's election to the presidency, the American Civil War broke out. The Republican Party had campaigned for the abolition of slavery in those States where it was still legal. Seven of the Southern States announced their intention of leaving the Union, even before Lincoln began his presidency on 4 March 1861. This they did even though Lincoln in his inaugural address had said that he would not interfere with slavery in the South. War began on 12 April when the Confederate States attacked Fort Sumter in South Carolina. Lincoln responded by calling on all States to provide an army of volunteers. Four other States joined the rebels. In September Lincoln changed tack and announced that the purpose of the war was to abolish slavery – which may have been enough to persuade Britain not to intervene in the war. It lasted until 1865, and was an early example of "total war" in the modern era, employing methods that gave a foretaste of the horrors of the first world war.

As happened in the Crimean War, Henry Richard went his own way and persuaded the majority of the Peace Society to follow. In spite of his hatred of slavery he opposed the decision of the North to save the Union by resorting to arms.[1] In any case Richard believed that Lincoln's intention was not to abolish slavery but to save the Union. Gladstone agreed, while Cobden and John Bright took the opposing line. Richard believed that the majority of the Northerners who argued for going to war hated the black population just as much as the Southerners did. He worried that so many American peace supporters had joined the flow of warmongers and wrote them a strong – if kindly – letter.[2]

One of the people he wrote to was Harriet Beecher Stowe,

author of the popular novel *Uncle Tom's Cabin*, first published in 1852 – and translated and published in Welsh the following year. It is probable that Richard met Harriet and her brother the Rev Henry Ward Beecher during their visits to Britain. The American brother and sister were the great-grandchildren of Mary Roberts of Foelallt, Llanddewi Brefi, who had emigrated to America around 1775. The village of Llanddewi Brefi is just a few miles from Tregaron where Henry Richard was born. Harriet Beecher Stowe visited Britain in 1853, 1856 and 1859, and Henry Richard might have met her. Certainly felt comfortable enough to write directly to her. Henry Ward Stowe went on a lecture tour of England and Scotland in 1863 to present the Northern States' case for war and succeeded in attracting considerable support – if not that of Henry Richard. In one of his diaries Henry Richard records a long conversation he had with Richard Cobden when they discussed at length Henry Ward Beecher's style as an orator and preacher.[3] Whatever the Welsh connections, when Beecher Ward came to Britain to argue the case for the North, and announced that he himself was prepared to fight to the death for that cause, he was roundly condemned by Richard. "It is offensive," he wrote, "that the disciples of Christianity should advocate that they were promoting the cause of humanity and Christianity through the destruction of 5,000,000 men – or be destroyed in so doing." It was, he continued "one of the strangest acts of self-deception … in the history of the human race."[4]

Henry Richard's fellow-countrymen tended to support the North, their opinions formulated by the influential Welsh language paper, *Y Drych*, at that time published in Utica. *Y Drych* portrayed the war as a campaign to free the black slaves of the South from "traitors, murderers and thieves".[5] Other Welsh American papers took a similar stance. They were second to none in their patriotic fervour for the Union and the North, and attacked viciously any Welsh – or British – people who took a neutral stance or expressed sympathy to the Confederacy. Some of these articles were lifted and published word for word – and condemned – in the Caernarfon weekly, *Yr Herald Cymraeg*. *Y Drych* responded by publishing a series of letters in *Y Wasg Gymraeg a'r Argyfwng Americanaidd* (The Welsh Press and the American Crisis). Letters with such comments as "I can hardly believe that my fellow-Welshmen, in spite of their ignorance of the true nature of the revolt and massive consequences which may result from it, are ready to betray their 'blood-bought' principles, by defending the

deserting slavers in their efforts to destroy our country and establishing an empire based on slavery on its ruins."[6] One of those
who suffered a sustained onslaught of criticism from *Y Drych* was
Samuel Roberts (SR). SR had emigrated to Tennessee in 1856
with the intention of establishing a Welsh colony in Brynffynnon.
That alone was enough to arouse the fury of *Y Drych*, since the
owners of the paper wanted to establish Welsh colonies in other
parts of the country. And as SR was fiercely opposed to the war, the
attacks on him intensified and – as he was a landowner – he was
accused of being "… more of a traitor and slavery-approver than
the Southerners themselves."[7] SR fought back claiming that the
support of the American Welsh for the war was proof that an entire
community had turned its back on Christian values. SR's quarrel
with *Y Drych* continued for many years.

Henry Richard found himself in the same predicament as SR.
Both loathed slavery but did not believe it right to abolish it by
force. As for the Union, Richard supported it but he was adamant
again that it should not be sustained by force. In his opinion the
Confederate States had every right to become an independent
country if that was their wish and he offered a neutral policy and
discussions as a way of achieving peace. But on this issue, he could
not call on the support of his friends Cobden and Bright. The
American Civil War was a difficult subject for pacifists. A correspondent writing in *Y Cronicl*[8] under the name of Ioan Pedr
echoed Henry Richard's opinion: "It would appear that the
Americans have been deeply disappointed in the effect their
behaviour has had on other countries. The Northerners expected
France and Britain to give their approval, to arm and charge to
their defence. They expected Christians of all countries to fall to
their knees and seek the protection of God for their arms … But
the Parliaments of France and Britain took a neutral position and
Christians and ministers showed that the cause of the King of
Peace was dearer to them than a warring cause, even that of the
United States of America." He emphasised that the Southern
States had every right to govern themselves and that the "war had
nothing to do with slavery".[9] Was Henry Richard writing under a
pseudonym or was the editor voicing the opinions of Richard as
expressed in the *Herald of Peace*? The *Herald of Peace*, of which
Richard was the editor, was distributed to every newspaper office
throughout Britain.

According to *Yr Annibynwr*[10] the aim of the United States was to
"keep the Union together" and that abolishing slavery was "a rea-

son" offered later. Once more, it was the papers associated with the Congregationalists who were the most anxious for peace. The majority view was that the real purpose of the war was the abolition of slavery – a very noble aim. When SR wrote that the South was not entirely to blame and that the war was uncalled for, he was accused in Wales – as in *Y Drych* – of supporting slavery. It is likely that *Y Cronicl* was expressing a desire – or simply echoing Henry Richard's propaganda in the *Herald of Peace* – when he claimed that "the most powerful and clear proof of the influence of the Peace Society … (was) that Palmerston and Russell … had agreed to seek the assistance of Mr Cobden to advance the Government's policy."[11] But the enthusiasm of neither Cobden nor Bright for opposing the war lasted for very long. Richard continued to argue that the North's sole intention was to safeguard the Union. He quoted Abraham Lincoln's words: "My principle aim is to maintain the Union, and not to destroy slavery. If I could keep the Union, without releasing a single slave, I would do so, and if I could do so by releasing all the slaves, I would do that, too. What I am doing with regard to slavery, I do to keep the Union. And that which I refrain from doing, I refrain to keep the Union."[12] Richard argued forcefully, but few were listening. *Y Dysgedydd*[13] complained that the war monster was as alive as ever in spite of the odes and articles written and the lectures delivered in support of peace. *Baner ac Amserau Cymru* could not think of one example in the scriptures where a man is denounced for defending himself. After noting that every one of the founders of the Peace Society were now dead, *Y Dysgedydd* said: "If the question is asked what is the result of all this towards establishing peace, we cannot answer. Nothing is more difficult to quantify as moral influence … The Peace Society, however, has reached the point where it is now scorned." It was indeed a very low point in the history of the Peace Society and that of Henry Richard. The attention it received in the Welsh language journals was becoming less and less and there is no evidence of the formation of any new branches.

There was one incident during the American Civil War which, from a British perspective, could have led to damaging consequences. Two representative of the Confederacy, James Murray Mason and John Slidell, two ex-US Senators were passengers on a British ship, the *Trent*, on their way to Britain and France to seek diplomatic recognition for the South. On 8 November 1861, the *Trent* was boarded by the USS *San Jacinto* and Mason and Slidell taken to Fort Warren. John Bullish passions were aroused and insisted that the two be released immediately – or Britain would go to war. Before a reply had been received Britain had dispatched soldiers to Canada. Henry Richard sent an address to the religious denominations begging them to use their influence and "to stand up amid the storm, and in the name of their Divine Master, rebuke the raging tempest of human passion". Richard and Joseph Pease, President of the Peace Society, then appealed to Palmerston to refer the matter to some friendly and impartial arbitrator. Their appeal was successful and Louis-Napoleon acting as arbitrator supported the position of Britain. His decision was that the two emissaries, being on board a neutral ship and not being military persons in the service of the South, should not have been seized. The two men were released and allowed to continue their journey. Their attempt to seek recognition for the Confederate States, however, proved futile.[16] Nevertheless, it was a triumph for Henry Richard and the Peace Society. Britain could easily have become involved in the war on the Confederate side with who knows what disastrous consequences.

With the end of hostilities in sight, Henry Richard wrote in the 1865 Annual Report of the Peace Society of the:

> Inexpressible satisfaction [of seeing] the dreadful and disastrous civil war which has so long desolated America coming to a close. No imagination can conceive, no language can adequately express, the amount of evil which it has inflicted on that country and the world. Probably no fewer than 1,000,000 of young men have perished prematurely, and in every conceivable form of horror and agony, by sword, and famine, and pestilence, and misery. As to its cost in money, we shall certainly be within the mark if we say that on both sides not less than £1,000,000,000 have been withdrawn from the service of civilisation to be squandered in mutual butcherings and blood.[17]

The one bright spot, he added, was that it had abolished "the great abomination of slavery ... out of the land for ever".

It is not easy to comprehend the amount of work Henry Richard was doing at this time. He did all within his power in 1863 to dissuade Britain from attacking Japan in what is known as the Anglo-Satsuma War. It all stemmed from a brawl on the road linking Yeddo (Tokyo) and Yokohama where three Englishmen and a woman were riding when they came face to face with a procession of nobles. The normal custom in Japan was to retire from sight or kneel while the procession passed, a practice which the English group had been warned that they should observe. They ignored the advice and during the ensuing skirmish one of the Englishmen was killed and the other two injured. Britain's response was to demand £100,000 compensation and the execution of the *samurai* involved in the skirmish. Japan agreed to apologise for the incident and to pay the compensation, but this was not enough. Henry Richard, as soon as he became aware of the facts, sent a scathing article to the newspapers. This was followed up by an address to the Foreign Secretary, Lord Russell, prepared by Richard and signed by himself and Joseph Pease, reminding the Government of Britain's Treaty of Commerce with Japan. That Treaty – which had been obtained by coercion – had been broken by the irresponsible actions of the English travellers. Richard's efforts were futile and seven British warships sailed to Kagoshima on 11 August with the demand that Britain's ultimatum be honoured. There followed a pretence of negotiations and on the 14th the British Admiral ordered the bombardment to commence. This lasted for two days and Kagoshima, a city of 180,000 was burnt to the ground, a great commercial centre, in the words of Cobden, "reduced in 48 hours to a heap of ashes.". It was another example of British officials in distant lands using their military and naval forces without the authority of the Government in London. The one tiny concession to emerge from this deplorable event was a dispatch from Lord Clarendon to consular and military representatives abroad, declaring that:

> Her Majesty's Government cannot leave with Her Majesty's Consuls or naval officers to determine for themselves what redress or reparation for wrong done to British subjects is due, or by what means it should be enforced. They cannot allow them to determine whether coercion is to be applied by blockade, by reprisals, by landing armed parties, or by acts of even a mere hostile character. All such proceedings bear more or less the character of acts of war, and Her Majesty's Government cannot delegate to Her Majesty's servants in foreign countries the power of involving their own country in war.[18]

The instruction, as will be shown later, was regularly ignored, and when Henry Richard was elected to Parliament he tried to get the support of the House of Commons to prevent such actions.

Britain, however, was dissuaded from supporting Denmark in its war against Prussia and Austria in 1864, in spite of the enthusiasm of Palmerston and John Russell. Britain had, on this occasion, offered to act as mediator but when talks broke down Palmerston and Russell were anxious to intervene on Denmark's side. They

would probably have done so were it not for the withdrawal of
France leaving Britain on its own.[19] In 1864 the Poles revolted
against Russian rule. Richard argued against intervention, not on
pacifist grounds this time but because he felt that the uprising had
nothing to do with freedom but had been stirred up by Poland's
Catholic nobility.[20] Again the Peace Society managed to keep
Britain's itchy fingers out of the pie.

Chapter 11

Parliamentary ambitions

By 1863 there were signs that Henry Richard had set his mind on becoming a Member of Parliament and his brother Edward was enjoying a role as advisor and generally furthering the "project" as he called it. Cardiganshire was the seat they had in mind and the two had spent some time discussing and plotting. It appears that Edward had sent Henry a comprehensive letter full of "wise, kind and generous" advice some years earlier which had touched him greatly. According to Edward it would be a folly to embark on a contest unless success was assured. In view of the threat of civil war in America Edward was also concerned that Henry would lose some investments he had in Illinois, but promised he would make good any losses that might be incurred. With all the small free-holders in Cardiganshire, Henry was confident that he would win the seat, and he reassured his brother that his Illinois investments would not fail.[1]

The following year, 1864, Henry wrote to his brother describing his feeling of wellbeing after a "delightful plunge" in the sea. He also mentioned an enjoyable evening spent at Blaenwern, the home of Thomas Morris JP. Tom Morris was the eldest son of Ebenezer Morris, and brother of Sam, Henry's brother-in-law. Tom Morris had made a fortune as a wool merchant in Lord Street, Liverpool, and before getting expelled, had been active in Pall Mall Presbyterian Church, the oldest of the Presbyterian chapels in the city. Tom was also on friendly terms with Sir Thomas Lloyd of Bronwydd. Others present at that enjoyable evening were the Vicar of Llangynllo, near Newcastle Emlyn. "He is a jolly fellow," wrote Henry, "so fond of his glass that his living was sequestered and has only just been restored to him – a pleasant, merry, good-tempered man who far from disguising them, seemed quite ready to make merry over his own besetting infirmities. The other, his curate, was an ex-dissenting minister – a man of sense and talented as a preacher."[2] The letter also states that Louis-Napoleon had accepted a copy of Henry Richard's *Memoirs of Joseph Sturge*.

The French Emperor, despite being brought to power by a coup, was proving a peaceful leader, especially in his relationship with Britain. Although they made numerous requests, neither Henry Richard nor Sturge ever met him but he must have been well aware of their existence. Henry Richard spent some days at the end of 1863 at the home of Richard Cobden in Durnford House, Midhurst, and kept a detailed journal of their discussions. Among those recollections were Cobden's thoughts about the elegance of Louis-Napoleon's writing. Cobden was looking at the current edition of the *Herald of Peace* and the content, reproduced in full, of the Emperor's invitation to the other European powers to attend a Congress in Paris to discuss disarmament. "How admirably it is written," noted Cobden, adding: "He is a great master of style"[3] – a much better writer than orator.

There had been many suggestions that Henry Richard was considered to be a man of sufficient calibre to be an MP. Years earlier, after the Frankfurt Peace Congress, Samuel Roberts had suggested in *Y Cronicl* that Wales should find a way of sending him to Parliament. Edward Miall when first elected to Parliament had said how much happier he would have been if Henry Richard had been there by his side as a representative of Nonconformity. The door appeared to have opened for him in 1865 and in the county of his birth. It was an interesting proposition. Cardiganshire had two Parliamentary seats, one for the county and the other for the borough. The borough was safely in the hands of Edward Lewis Pryse – a moderate Liberal whose support for the Nonconformists was assured. The county constituency was the interesting one. The sitting Member was a Tory, Colonel W. T. R. Powell. In 1865 Powell was in poor health and was rarely seen in the House of Commons and there were rumours that he would not be seeking re-election. There was a gentlemen's agreement, if Powell did not stand then Sir Thomas Lloyd would stand as a Liberal with the support of the Tories.[4] A curious choice as Lloyd was an Anglican, although his family had endowed Capel-y-Drindod, Henllan, for the use of the Presbyterians, Baptists and Congregationalists. A chapel built, incidentally, as a kind of symbolic buffer to stop the

advancement of Unitarianism down the Teifi valley. He was a
Palmerstonian Whig – certainly not a Radical Liberal, and he had
little sympathy for Gladstone. Then the unexpected happened.
With Parliament within a week of being dissolved Lloyd wrote to
Powell asking him to confirm that he was retiring. Powell replied
that he was standing again and Lloyd wrote to the newspapers
announcing his withdrawal and that he would not oppose Powell.[5]
The Nonconformists, who had pledged their votes to Lloyd were
released from their promises. Henry Richard stepped forward –
not unexpectedly as the Liberation Society had been preparing the
ground. There had been speculation, and Edward Richard had
been scheming for some time. But on 20 May Edward died suddenly from a stroke at the home of his friend the Rev George
Mansfield, in Brixton.

   More surprising than the intervention of Henry Richard was
that David Davies, Rhondda coal owner and railway builder
declared an interest in contesting the seat.[6] Here was a self-made
industrialist who had invested heavily in the county, and a
Nonconformist to boot – a Calvinistic Methodist. He also appears
to have had some ancestral connections with Cardiganshire. Two
Nonconformists now wanted to stand for the seat. A meeting was
arranged to be held in Aberaeron in which Richard and Davies
would both deliver an address to decide who would be the candidate. Powell, shocked at the thought of having to fight an election,
withdrew, but not before warning Thomas Lloyd of his intentions.
Lloyd's hat was back in the ring, and Richard decided to withdraw
as those who had promised to give him their support were now
likely to return to the Thomas Lloyd fold.[7] According to H. R.
Evans,[8] however, a man by the name of Hare had been sent from
London by Richard's supporters and this man had betrayed
Richard and withdrawn his name without consulting anyone. In
the end Sir Thomas Lloyd was elected with a narrow majority, but
David Davies – with his aggressive style of electioneering – had
introduced a new style of contesting rural constituencies. Davies
felt that Richard had done him no favours by withdrawing.
Richard, after all, had withdrawn in favour of Thomas Lloyd, a
hint to the Congregationalists to support the Anglican Lloyd. It
took a while for Davies to forgive that little disservice. It showed
that there was still no united Nonconformist front in
Cardiganshire and to the fury of David Davies the old system of
the squirearchy cutting deals held sway.

   There was, however, some unease. The 1862 Liberation Society

David Davies

conference in Swansea had been influential and Welsh
Nonconformists joined in the campaign for their civil rights. A
series of conferences were held in Wales in the autumn of 1865
addressed by Henry Richard, John Carvell Williams and Edward
Miall. One was held in Aberaeron and was attended by a large
gathering of Nonconformists. Henry Richard spoke, and was followed by Edward Miall who was critical of Sir Thomas Lloyd,
who had not, he said, been to the satisfaction of the people of
Cardiganshire. He accused Lloyd of being unreliable and urged
them "to take nobody as your representative but one in whose
soundness of character you have implicit reliance – one who has
sympathy with you in your objectives, one who has earnestness of
desire to promote those objectives, and who is worthy of your suffrage. Here (turning to Henry Richard) is your man." The audience applauded wildly and Henry Richard hinted that he was
ready to contest his native Cardiganshire at the next election.[9]
Thus, almost unconsciously religious zeal was diverted into political action. Although David Davies had vowed to return it was
appearing increasingly likely that Henry Richard would be the
Nonconformists' representative at the next election. The
Liberation Society concentrated its energies on Cardiganshire. A
salaried agent, Thomas Harries, was appointed to work in the constituency and the Society's senior executives visited the county on
a regular basis.[10]

Then there came another offer. In 1867 it was announced that
an extra seat would be created to represent Merthyr Tydfil,

Aberdare, Hirwaun and Mountain Ash. The Nonconformists and Liberals quickly came to a decision that this was the seat for Henry Richard.

The spring of 1865 had been a sad time for Henry Richard. His brother died, and so too did his great friend Richard Cobden, on 2 April 1865, during the period leading up to the General Election. They had been close friends and had worked together in the cause of peace for over 20 years. In a letter to his brother Edward six weeks before he died Henry Richard recalled the time he spent in Durnford House, Midhurst, Cobden's home at the end of 1863.

> Yesterday we laid the body of Richard Cobden in the grave in the little churchyard of Lavington, about a mile from his house. He rests by the side of his boy whom he loved so fondly and whose loss he felt so keenly. The rustic church is most beautifully situated on an eminence which commands a large expanse of fertile and well-wooded country bounded by the soft outline of the Sussex Downs. The day was bright and balmy as a day in June and all things outwardly concurred to rob the grave, if anything could rob it, of its gloom. But alas! what can do so? For had we not him, the great Statesman, the eloquent orator, the gentle and generous friend, there shut up in that vault, never to see his face or touch his hand or hear his voice more. The blow had nearly paralysed me. My thoughts, purposes, hopes were so entwined around him that I seem to have lost a part of my own identity. As I joined the procession yesterday, I walked over the very road step by step and remembered the very words he said to me at different spots as we passed along. I had promised myself many another walk with him, listening to his sagacious wide-reaching thoughts and inspired by the rare moral courage that he possessed.[11]

In a Peace Conference in Newcastle-on-Tyne Richard was again expressing his sadness and depression:

> Last Friday, I stood over the grave of Mr Cobden, and to confess to you my weakness, when I looked into the vault, and saw his coffin lie there, and called to remembrance how long that man had been like a tower of strength to me, upon which I would always lean – his wisdom in council, and his undaunted courage in action – the first impulse was, as if I must retire from all share in public matters, and give them up in despair and despondency.[12]

Needless to say Richard's gloom did not last long. He rolled up his sleeves and got on with his war on war with even greater determination. Richard was not the only one to feel the deep loss when Cobden died prematurely, at the age of 60. Others felt that his death was nothing less than a tragedy and they set about establishing the Cobden Club with the motto: "Free Trade, Peace, Goodwill among Nations".[13] The club's objective was to keep alive and extend Cobden's doctrine, briefly – to avoid intervention in the affairs of other nations, to educate our own people and encourage their skill and industry, to preserve free exchange, to be as enterprising, energetic and adaptable as possible in commerce, to keep an eye on national expenditure and redeem the National Debt. Among the "brilliant gathering" at the first dinner of the club, with its Lords and Government Ministers, was Henry Richard. Gradually Richard found himself drawn in to something which, over time, became an increasing worry for him – Cobden's letters. Cobden was a prolific and energetic letter writer and his many admirers were concerned that his letters would be published piecemeal. There was an urgent need to collect and publish them to keep alive and spread his philosophy and to be a means of letting the new generation learn and share his views and plans for social, political and economic reform. There could be no better way of achieving this than through reading his letters. Cobden's friends in the Cobden Club, in particular John Bright, Thomas Thomasson and Sir Louis Mallet, were anxious to get the project under way. Unfortunately they proceeded without discussing the matter with Cobden's widow.[14] The subject of the letters will be dealt with more fully later but it appears that Catherine Cobden had asked Richard to write a biography of her husband. He certainly took a pile of Cobden's letters with him when he went on holiday to Switzerland in 1869 and started putting them in some kind of order. Pressure of work was certainly one reason why he did not continue with that project – the same difficulty he had with his *Memoirs of Joseph Sturge*, which took years to complete. He handed over the work of writing Cobden's biography to John Morley. Morley's biography, *The Life of Richard Cobden*, which acknowledges Richard's considerable contribution was eventually published in 1881.[15]

★ ★ ★ ★

Despite Henry Richard's work in counteracting the negative influences of "The Blue Books" English prejudice towards Wales and the Welsh remained strong, so much so that the 1847 *Reports of the Commissioners of Enquiry into the State of Education in Wales* were still seen by many as a true representation of Wales. As one who lived and worked in London Henry Richard was well aware of the English ignorance of, and prejudice towards, the Welsh. At best they were seen as a nation of warm-hearted, simple people speaking a guttural incomprehensible jargon, and in comparison to their Saxon neighbours without much learning and only half-civilized. To use Richard's own words, "there is a lurking conviction at the bottom of most Englishmen's hearts, that no people can be really civilised who don't talk English".[16] The libellous pronouncements, published with the full force of officialdom in the "Blue Books" 17 years earlier had yet to be erased from the common Englishman's view of the Welsh character and country. After the death of Samuel Lucas in 1865 Henry Richard found himself back in favour with the *Morning Star*, and in February 1866 the paper began publishing a weekly series of articles on Wales which continued until May. His *Letters and Essays on Wales* were first published in a book in October of the same year. Professor Ieuan Gwynedd Jones, in a lecture to mark the centenary of Richard's death, described the book as "one of the most important books about Wales to have been published in the 19th century." Its declared purpose was to interpret Wales to England, to open the eyes of Englishmen to the existence of a unique kind of nationalism on their border and to lay to rest any fears they might have about it. "But its real purpose," argued Professor Jones, "was to convince the Welsh themselves as to their nationality and the vast possibilities that existed for exploiting it for their own ends."[17] The articles attracted great interest, they were often quoted and translated and published in their entirety in the Welsh language papers. Numerous Nonconformist Associations and Assemblies passed resolutions publicly thanking Henry Richard for his work – extracts from 15 of them were included as an appendix in the 1884 edition of the book.

The picture presented of the Welsh people is positive and patriotic. He explains how the Anglican Church failed the people of Wales in its moral and spiritual duties and how the Nonconformists came and magnificently made up for its failings despite the opposition of the Clergy of the Established Church. It was this policy that made Wales a nation of Nonconformists as shown in the 1851 census. Never again would the Nonconformists seek "their religious nourishment from the somewhat withered breasts of their old step-mother [the Anglican Church]". He explained how 3,000 chapels[18] were built through the efforts of the Dissenting worshippers themselves; and the work of the Sunday schools which provided for a significant proportion of adults thirsting for learning as much as for the children.[19] A stimulus that inspired and enriched the minds of the Welsh. He gives a glimpse of folk traditions, referring to such phenomena as the "Deryn Corff" (lit. corpse bird) that would come flapping at night on a sick person's window and another premonition of death, the "Cannwyll Corff (lit. Corpse Candle), a tiny blue light seen near a house prior to a death and which would then proceed to the cemetery where that person would be buried. He mentions the "toili", a spectral funeral procession, marching in ghastly silence on the road along which the doomed person, whose death was foreseen, would be taken to be buried. The "Nosweithiau Llawen" – impromptu evenings of home-spun entertainment – were not, he argued, without an intellectual element which saved them degenerating into mere sexual orgies.[20] He explains the traditional improvised singing to the harp, known as "Cerdd Dant", the intricate poetic forms known as "cynghanedd" and the "Anterliwtiau", which he describes as "broad farces, or dramatic pasquinades". He eulogises the old melodies of Glamorgan and Gwent, "taken down from the lips of the peasants" by Maria Jane Williams of Aberpergwm; the choral singing … and the Eisteddfod, a favourite target of English journalists:

> The true reason why the Eisteddfodau are held is to be found, partly in the reverence which the common people of Wales cherish for old customs, and partly in the genuine delight they take in such intellectual excitements as are afforded them there, in exercises of oratory, and competitions in poetry and music, just as the common people of England take delight in horse-racing and fox-hunting and pugilism.[21]

And in case the reader might think for one moment that he is not totally unbiased he calls on the opinion of a former Bishop of St David's, Connop Thirlwall, an Englishman who learnt Welsh fluently after his appointment, to such a degree that he was praised for his sermons in the language:

> It is a most remarkable feature in the history of any people, and such as could be said of no other than the Welsh, that they have centred their national recreation in literature and musical competitions.[22]

He writes about literary works motivated or inspired by Eisteddfodic competition, notably the *eisteddfodau* of Abergavenny years earlier which would have impressed the well-educated English reader and awaken a sense of pride in the ordinary Welsh person. He made special reference to Albert Schulz's *Essay on the influence of Welsh Tradition upon the Literature of Germany, France and Scandinavia*, originally written in German and which was awarded first prize at the Abergavenny Eisteddfod of 1840. The adjudicator was the Baron von Bunsen, scholar and diplomat, who had been at various times Prussia's Ambassador to the Vatican, France and Britain. His wife Frances (Waddington) was the sister of Lady Llanover, wife of Sir Benjamin Hall – after whom Big Ben was named. The name of Baron von Bunsen appears often in the politics of that era and when he was Prussia's representative in London he was a regular visitor to the Abergavenny Eisteddfod. It is likely that he and Henry Richard met. In his *Essay on the Eisteddfodau and Similar Institutions* (Letter VI) Richard mentions another prize-winning entry of the Abergavenny Eisteddfod (1848), *The Literature of the Kymry* by the Merthyr Tydfil chemist, Thomas Stephens, "an admirable volume, distinguished alike by sound judgement and solid learning".[23]

He recognised the value of the smaller *eisteddfodau*, the very local ones "diffusing through the whole country a spirit of literary and artistic emulation, which has acted as a powerful inducement to study and mental cultivation … where prizes are offered for the best essays and poems, the best singing and musical compositions". Although he lived his entire adult life in London Richard shows remarkable awareness of how the *eisteddfodau* were changing at the time he was writing from being the preserve of poets and essayists into a celebration of other art forms. Nonconformity had led to hymn-singing festivals and the Welsh choral tradition and this change was approaching a peak when he wrote his *Letters and Essays*. As already mentioned he was remarkably sympathetic in his attitude to folk culture, while aware of how that tradition had languished in the period from 1750 to 1790, a time of Methodist expansion. He knew that William Williams set his hymns to popular tunes sung in the fairs and taverns.

He mentions the Calvinistic Methodists with their own Foreign Missionary Society, and support of missions in India and in Brittany – "having been selected for the very natural reason that the Bretons are the near kindred of the Welsh, a colony driven from their island home to seek refuge in France when the people

of Wales were sorely pressed by the Saxon invaders". In a chapter
on Welsh politics he puts great emphasis on the census figures for
1851, where 21 per cent of the population claimed to be Anglican
and 79 per cent Nonconformists. But there was not one Welsh
Nonconformist Member of Parliament. He provides a sketch of
the Welsh language press in his own time as well as a useful history
of its development and those who had contributed to that development – men like Joseph Harris, founder of *Seren Gomer*, and
David Rees *Y Diwygiwr*. He notes in passing that there was only
one periodical – with a tiny circulation, but which received spon-
sorship from the Tories and the Anglicans – that did not promote
a radical liberal agenda. Whether that was *Yr Haul* or possible *Y
Dywysogaeth* is not clear. He tells the story of William Rees
(Gwilym Hiraethog), editor of *Yr Amserau*, published in Liverpool
and for a short time printed in Douglas, Isle of Man, to avoid the
stamp, advertisement and paper duty – "the taxes on knowledge …
which … weighed cruelly upon a paper struggling with so many
peculiar difficulties". Henry Richard, seething with indignation
and shame tells how the gentry and clergy of North Wales drew
the attention of the Government to the fact that this one Welsh
newspaper was being printed in the Isle of Man. "Surely it is not
easy to conceive of anything more utterly mean, paltry, and despicable, that this act of the parsons and landowners of the country
assembling in solemn conclave to use their combined influence to
try to extinguish, by means of a legal technicality, the only publication through which their countrymen could at that time receive
any regular supply of political intelligence, merely because it advocated opinions different from theirs."[24] *Yr Amserau*, survived this
difficulty, and carried on its campaign for the Disestablishment of
the Church in Wales, which annoyed the Anglicans. The tax, incidentally, was abolished in 1855. Richard could be quite generous
in his praise of the Anglican clergy. He acknowledged the work of
Edward "Celtic" Davies; Evan Evans the poet, antiquarian and
friend of Thomas Grey; and the historian Thomas Price.[25]
However, he enjoys pointing out that of nine living "chaired"
poets, one was an Anglican clergyman, seven were Nonconformist ministers and the other a Nonconformist layman! In Letter
XIII, which deals with the *Political Influence of the Gentry* he gives Sir
Watkin Williams Wynn a hearty reprimand for manoeuvring his
relatives and others of the same political persuasion to be elected
unopposed as MPs for Meirioneth. He was also known for
increasing the rents of tenant farmers who voted Liberal. Richard

Watkin Price of the Rhiwlas estate simply turned Liberal voters
out of their farms. "There is an old Welsh proverb, the meaning of
which they ought to learn if they understood no other scrap of the
language," wrote Richard. *"Trech gwlad nac arglwydd* – which may
be rendered, 'A country is stronger than a lord'."[26] Richard once
quoted that proverb in one of his earliest Parliamentary speeches,
almost certainly the first time Welsh had been spoken in
Parliament.

The Welsh had the reputation for lax sexual morality – one of
the many allegations made in the 1847 *Reports of the Commissioners
of Enquiry into the State of Education in Wales*. Some dirt will always
stick and Henry Richard devoted Letter VIII to *The Charge of Excess
in Illegitimacy Brought Against Wales*. He had gathered an impressive
array of figures, analysed them and concluded that the Welsh were
more moral than the Scots and the English![27] He compared
Anglican Cumbria with Nonconformist Wales to show how the
moral influence of the Nonconformist chapels was much greater
than the Anglican churches. In instances where standards in parts
of Wales were rather lower than he would have expected he would
point out that these were the ports and parts of the industrialised
south-east of Wales which had come under English influences! In
Letter VII he analyses crime figures and again shows that Wales
was a far more law-abiding country than England. Whatever else
may be said of Richard he was a thorough researcher and an adept
statistician![28]

No doubt there are examples of exaggeration in *Letters and
Essays*, but they certainly had an effect on English opinion and
even more so on Welsh self-respect. Even in an old tattered copy
with a sad brown cover and small type, his writing reads well. His
style is crisp and lively and the occasional spark of ridicule can still
send a chill down the spine or send the blood coursing through
the veins. In the introduction to the 1884 edition Richard quotes
the words of William Ewart Gladstone, spoken when he addressed
the 1873 Mold National Eisteddfod, sentiments he repeated on
many subsequent occasions:

> I will frankly own to you that I have shared at a former time, and
> before I had thus acquainted myself with the subject, the preju-
> dices which prevail to some extent in England and among
> Englishmen with respect to the Welsh language and antiquity;
> and I came here to tell you how, and why I have changed my
> opinion. It is only fair that I should say that a countryman of
> yours, a most excellent Welshman, Mr Richard, MP, did a great

> deal to open my eyes to the true state of the facts by a series of let-
> ters which some years ago he addressed to a morning journal,
> and which he subsequently published in a small volume, that I
> recommend to the attention of all persons who may be interested
> in the subject.[29]

Although over 30 years had elapsed since he lived in Wales the letters show how closely he had maintained his relationship with the
country of his birth and his awareness of its religious, cultural and
political changes – particularly with the rural, Welsh-speaking
parts. His nation was becoming ever prouder of him.

He was, said Ieuan Gwynedd Jones, "consistent on the great
themes of nationalism and there was no contradiction in his mind
between his utter rejection of liberal national movements on the
continent and the nationalism he was advocating for Wales … The
second he could advocate because it was based on a Christian doctrine of man and society, and used methods for achieving its aims
which were compatible with Christian ethics, that is to say, that
were non-violent and not self-regarding."[30]

In 1866, at the age of 54 Henry Richard took an important step
in his personal life. On 20 December he married Augusta Matilda
Farley, third daughter of John Farley, a successful wine merchant
in Kennington Park Road. According to C. S. Miall "the interesting ceremony, at which his friend, the Rev J. Baldwin Brown officiated, took place in Stockwell Congregational Church". Brown
and Richard held similar views on many things, particularly education – although Brown was fiercely opposed to Methodism.
Henry Richard and his wife had been friends for many years and
had many common interests, similar tastes and religious convictions. She identified herself completely with her husband's public
and private aspirations and as his health deteriorated later she
became his constant companion and "her pleasant face was as
familiar to Welsh audiences as that of Mr Richard."[31]

It should be remembered that Henry Richard was not a wealthy
man and MPs were not paid for their work in those days, and a
wife from an affluent family would be a considerable asset to him
as he was preparing – as he very obviously was – for a career in politics. He was now, if not exactly rich, at least a man of independent
means, who did not have to rely on his salary for his keep. Before
too long the two were able to settle in 22 Bolton Gardens, a fine
house belonging to his wife's family in a fashionable part of
London.

Chapter 12

From London to Merthyr and back

After their marriage Henry Richard and his wife first settled in Tottenham, then moved to Clapham Road and finally, in 1874, to fashionable Bolton Gardens. Messages of good wishes flooded in from all parts of Wales, a reflection of his increasing popularity in the land of his birth, and, no doubt, some concern for his life and welfare. There has already been mention of the conference arranged by the Liberation Society in Aberaeron in the autumn after the General Election of 1866 when Edward Miall claimed that Nonconformists were unhappy with Sir Thomas Lloyd, the newly elected MP for Cardiganshire. It was obvious, he had said, that his friend Henry Richard was the man to represent the county, a statement enthusiastically received by his audience.

The Representation of the People Act (1867) added greatly to the number of people with the right to vote. Every male house-holder in a borough constituency now had a vote as well as any tenant paying a minimum of £10 a year in rent for unfurnished accommodation. This increased the number of voters in con-stituencies such as Cardiganshire to challenge if not overturn the old order. In urban industrialised constituencies this represented a sea change. In Merthyr Tydfil the number of the enfranchised increased from 1,387 to 14,577.[1] A traditional middle-class con-stituency had become, almost overnight, a working-class con-stituency. Merthyr represented a new concept in democracy. The Liberation Society had been preparing the ground for Henry Richard in Cardiganshire for some time. Then came whispers that the constituency of Merthyr and Aberdare, which with the huge increase in the number of voters would be granted two Members of Parliament, was considering extending an invitation to Henry

Richard. Also, a local committee would be prepared to meet his entire election expenses, a great advantage.[2] (Henry Richard, in all his years in Parliament never once had to meet that cost.) This seat was one to be won. Back in Cardiganshire Sir Thomas Lloyd was having to admit that he could not afford the expense of fighting another election so soon after 1866.[3] He was, however, invited to stand as a Liberal for the Borough and with the support of the Gogerddan and Nant-eos squirearchy was returned unopposed. The County then invited Evan Matthew Richards, the first non-conformist to be elected mayor of Swansea, to fight the seat against the Conservative, E. M. Vaughan, nephew of Lord Lisburne of Trawscoed. Richards, with the formidable support of David Davies eventually won with a small majority.[4] So no harm was done to the ambitions of the Welsh Nonconformists and the efforts of the Liberation Society did not go to waste.

A name that kept appearing in radical circles in that period was that of the Rev Dr Thomas Price of Aberdare. He was a prominent Baptist minister, a supporter of Friendly Societies and an active member of the Liberation Society. He spoke at the two-day con-ference arranged by the Society in Swansea in September 1862, where he drew attention to the practical problems of choosing MPs to represent nonconformist Wales. "Let us work for a few years, and the result will be different from what it is now," was his message in 1862. He had not been optimistic about the quality of nonconformist candidates.

Price obviously had a high opinion of Richard – "a radical politician of some eminence" – and had hoped that he would have fought the Brecon Borough constituency in 1866.[5] In the event Price himself contested the seat – without success. Following the 1867 Act, and the allocation of an extra seat for Merthyr and Aberdare it was anticipated that Price would have given Richard his full backing. Instead he busied himself persuading Richard Fothergill to contest the new seat.[6] Although inexperienced, an Englishman and Anglican, this ironmaster would be a formidable candidate. He was popular, too, according to a poem eulogising him by Evan James.[7] With Bruce, a popular and "excellent" man already established in one seat, things were getting interesting.[8]

In the middle of July 1867, it was decided to formally invite Henry Richard to contest the constituency, although Thomas Price was now worrying that Richard's intervention would endan-ger Bruce, rather than Fothergill. The ironmaster and coal owners were confident that their men, Bruce and Fothergill, could take both seats without difficulty. They concentrated on Fothergill, confident that Bruce would retain his seat comfortably, assuming a Nonconformist could not possibly be elected. Also, they were both moderate Liberals, Fothergill more so than Bruce. Dr Thomas Price evidently shared the view of the wealthy industrialists. Only in the event of Fothergill refusing to contest the constituency was Price prepared to see a Nonconformist standing. He worked assiduously in support of Fothergill, placing the Nonconformists in a difficult position. Openly challenging the powerful Fothergill in Aberdare was not a step to be taken lightly.[9] The Nonconformists were furious, Price was criticised locally and by members of the Liberation Society in England.[10] Recalling again his speech in Swansea urging discretion his behaviour was confusing. The time had come to take advantage of the 1867 Act and Price was undermining the opportunity to elect a Welsh Nonconformist. Worse, Price believed that Nonconformists *en bloc* would follow his lead. Apart from a few Baptists, his own denomination, this would not be the case. The Liberal election committee in Merthyr, however, were in turmoil. The secretaries of the committee consisted of one Baptist and three Unitarians.[11] In July 1867, it was rumoured that Henry Richard could be persuaded to contest the seat. There were 81 Nonconformist chapels affiliated to the committee and after an anguished debate they took a chance. They sent for the complete outsider, a man without money or parliamentary experience, but who was none the less a politician through and through. A pacifist, nonconformist and a Welshman of strong – extreme, even – opinions. In the middle of the month they invited Henry Richard to be their candidate with a suggestion that they would also be supporting the candidacy of Henry Austin Bruce. Aberdare followed, although it had been overtaking Merthyr in population, wealth and influence for almost two decades. There was a stormy meeting chaired by David Davis of Maes-y-ffynnon – acrimonious thanks to the presence of Thomas Price who argued that inviting Henry Richard would endanger Bruce, although he himself was supporting Fothergill![12] With an election likely in September 1868, preparations for Richard's campaign got under way. The constituency included Merthyr, Aberdare, Hirwaun, Mountain Ash and the southern tip of Penderyn in Breconshire. Richard took his time. He visited the constituency and addressed five packed public meetings to ensure that he had the support of the people.[13] He explained his beliefs in detail and he received numerous pledges of support. One of the issues of the day was the Disestablishment of the Church in Ireland, a matter of great interest to Henry Richard and to the people of Wales, who suffered the same injustice. What was being proposed for Ireland was being seen as a first step towards Disestablishment in Wales.

David Davis, a coal owner like his father, was a keen supporter of Henry Richard. He belonged to the new rising plutocracy, which was dominating society in the coalfields – the Nonconformist philanthropists who were patrons of cultural activities. Whenever Richard and his wife visited the area they stayed at Maes-y-ffynnon. Father and son supported Richard and Fothergill. It was becoming increasingly obvious that if there was a split in the vote Richard would not be the one to suffer. A great swell of enthusiasm swept over Merthyr and Aberdare. Large halls were full to overflowing and he addressed meetings on the mountainsides near Hirwaun where during the Merthyr Rising of 1831 the red flag was raised, apparently for the first time in Britain. He spoke the language of the people – in Aberdare, prior to 1870, almost the entire population originated from West Wales and spoke Welsh. Most were Nonconformists – and those who were not had a solid understanding of the religious tradition of the valleys. His audiences knew exactly what Richard stood for and where he was coming from. In the name of the Welsh-speaking Nonconformists he openly challenged the English-speaking landowners who had ruled Wales's social and political life for 300 years. It was a heady message. The descriptions are electrifying. Richard and his wife would arrive in a horse-drawn carriage but as soon as they approached the next venue the pony would be unhitched from the shafts and the men pulled their hero to the next engagement.[14] Flaming torches and bonfires lit the hills and meetings closed to the stirring sounds of *Hen Wlad Fy Nhadau* (Land of My Fathers) composed just 12 years earlier. The heather was well and truly alight and Richard would fan the flames for the next two decades.

He arrived breathing radical fire. He came as a Welshman, a progressive Liberal and a Nonconformist. "The Nonconformists of Wales," he announced, "are the people of Wales."[15] He incorporated the most radical Nonconformist demands in his manifesto and embraced Chartism – although he had been critical of the Chartists in the early 1840s. He pledged to work for the full Chartist programme, towards full democracy and welcomed Chartists to speak on his platform. He worked to build a united

popular front within Liberalism and stood as the candidate of
Wales and the working man.[16] In Merthyr Henry Richard was free
to present his own fiery brand of unfettered radicalism, something
he would not have had the freedom to do had he been fighting an
election in Cardiganshire. And his audience could respond to his
message free from the prying eyes of the landowners and their
spies. At that moment in the development of Welsh radicalism and
political loyalty to the working class Henry Richard, Apostle of
Peace, friend of Cobden, the Nonconformist, incomparable
democrat could present himself as the representative of the
worker and Welsh Nonconformity. The uncompromising politician, the pure ideologist had arrived. Unique circumstances had
brought forward the unique man. A politician who could not be
ignored, one Wales could be proud of. Richard could afford to
speak respectfully – perhaps condescendingly – of the other two
candidates. He was not competing with them for the votes of the
people, they were scrambling for the votes that would secure one
of them the second seat!

It was true that he had spent most of his life in London, he
argued in a meeting in the Drill Hall in Merthyr, but it was the
people of Merthyr and Aberdare who had come and asked him to
be their representative. He could say:

> You know that although my lot was cast in London, yet I had
> been loyal in heart to the old land of my birth, the scene of my
> childhood's joys, and the place of my fathers' sepulchres; and
> you knew that I had never missed an opportunity to do what I
> could to promote the religious, educational and political interests
> of my country; and you knew that I had done all in my power to
> repel the base and groundless calumnies by which our national
> reputation has been defamed. And I think I know you. I have
> kept up my acquaintance with our old language and flourishing
> literature. I know your many social and religious virtues. I know,
> and have had pleasure in proclaiming the fact in the presence of
> Englishmen, that you here, out of your abundant poverty, when
> you have been neglected by those who ought to have taken
> charge of your spiritual interests, have provided a more perfect
> machinery for religious instruction than is to be found in any
> other part of the empire.[17]

He had been described – disparagingly – as a preacher. Richard's
response was:

> Yes, I am a preacher and the son of a preacher. I know no occupa-
> tion and no name more honourable. Some of the best and great-
> est men the world ever saw – far better and greater than those

who sneer at the name – have belonged to that profession. …
And One infinitely greater than they all, whose name I will not
profane by introducing it on this moment, came to preach liberty
to the captives and the opening of the prison to those that were
bound. I cannot help thinking that it was bad tactics on the part
of my opponents to fling this word as reproach at me – of all
places in the world in the Principality. Welsh people know that
they owe much – almost everything – to their Preachers.[18]

It was alleged that he was not a rich man. In that his critics were
absolutely correct, he replied. But was that not a qualification in
itself? There were far too many rich men in the House of
Commons, and they were most certainly not the most suitable
people to legislate for the poor.[19] He was quickly developing the
electioneering skills of turning attacks to his own advantage.

This period in his life saw him develop his already considerable
skills as an orator. He delighted the people with the purity and
beauty of his Welsh. Professor Ieuan Gwynedd Jones gave a
detailed analysis of a speech delivered by Richard on the eve of the
election. It was a speech expressing all the national, religious and
democratic aspirations of his audience. The balanced rhythms of
his sentences were awe-inspiring. Here was an orator who could
adapt the eloquence of the pulpit to the political platform. He was
even more effective on the platform, even more so as he spoke in
the Welsh language.

> What of the people who can speak this language, who read its lit-
> erature, who claim this history, who are the inheritors of these
> traditions, who respect these same [heroes of Welsh history], and
> have created and upheld and sustained these wonders [the
> Nonconformist chapels] – people who account for three-quar-
> ters of the population of Wales, have they not the right to insist:
> we are the Welsh nation? Have they not the right to reproach the
> handful of landowning, privileged, quietly and courteously yet
> clearly and firmly: we, not you, are the Welsh nation? We, not
> you, own this land, and it is our right that our principles and
> desires should be heard and represented in the House of
> Commons. (It is not so just yet!) I maintain that our representa-
> tion in that House is not complete if it is our earthly interests
> alone that receive considerations there; the soul of the nation
> must also be safeguarded, its character, its conscience, and those
> values of Wales have never had anyone to defend them, to the
> great detriment to our country. Remember, the Nonconformists
> are the main body of the nation, and every time Bills have been
> presented to Parliament to promote justice for them it follows
> that they would also be to the benefit of the whole of Wales, yet

without exception all those elected to represent us voted against
these improvements. Those Welsh Members had no sympathy
for your principles, no pride in the history of your nation, no
desire to guard your religion, your dignity, your good name, and
when you were continuously under attack on the floor of the
House, and in the English Press, of the 32 who were sent as your
representatives to Parliament not one opened his mouth to
defend his fellow-countrymen from injury and contempt.[20]

For the evening of nominations a huge, but peaceful, crowd of
men from the ironworks of Dowlais, Penydarren, Cyfarthfa,
Ynys-fach and the Plymouth gathered in the square of Merthyr
Tydfil. Colliers from the Cynon Valley arrived by train from
Aberdare. Of Henry Austin Bruce's address, not a word could be
heard, and not much more respect was shown towards Richard
Fothergill. Henry Richard was nominated by David Davis, who
spoke in Welsh. He ended his address with the words: "May the
great Apostle of Peace be a vehicle to bring peace to reign in your
hearts."[21] Henry Richard also addressed his audience in Welsh:
"Remember, the eyes of Wales are now riveted on the electors of
Merthyr Tydfil and Aberdare, willing them to fulfil their duty.
One more word. Victory is ours, but we must win it not by the fist
or the cudgel but through the power of principle and reason. So,
fellow-countrymen, do not quarrel amongst yourselves as to who
else will be elected. The other candidates are not worth quar-
relling about. Our battle today is about truth, justice, freedom, and
for peace."[22]

By now Richard was completely confident that his audience
had understood his message and were delighted to hear a sophisticated politician articulating their aspirations in their own language. Welsh was the language of the majority of those present at
that meeting, although it was beginning to be take a secondary
position to English in matters relating to technology and trade in
the area. It was still the language of the early trade unions and
where a coal owner spoke Welsh – which, unlike the ironmasters,
many did – it would be the language of negotiation. The Chartists
in the area spoke Welsh. Welsh was a political tool and Henry
Richard used it with confidence to present a message brim-full of
radicalism rooted firmly in the French Revolution. A language
adapted and expanded in the literary and political clubs by the likes
of William Owen (Pughe).[23] Even though the *Times* proclaimed
two years earlier that Welsh was the "curse" of Wales.

Richard's confidence was totally justified. To the strains of *Hen*

Wlad Fy Nhadau he swept majestically to top the poll with a majority that stunned even his own supporters. The former Member, the Honourable Henry Austin Bruce, languished at the bottom, having lost his seat:

Henry Richard	11,667
Richard Fothergill	7,613
The Honourable H. A. Bruce	5,797

The new electors enfranchised by the Reform Act of 1887 would not be loyal to the old middle-class leaders. Local issues and traditions would be more important than "national" ones. And although Bruce had backed the campaign to extend the franchise, it was of no benefit to him. If Merthyr and Aberdare were tactically ready for Henry Richard, the people were also ready for his uncompromising radical Nonconformist philosophy. It has been suggested that Richard had to adapt to a form of radicalism that was foreign to him. The truth is that his contribution to Merthyr's unique radicalism – in his election campaign in 1868 and afterwards as an MP – was considerable and much of what was unique to the experience of Merthyr emanated from Henry Richard himself. Keir Hardie, when he won the seat in 1900, attributed his victory to the "uncorrupted" disciples of Henry Richard.[24]

Henry Richard's majority of 4,000, in those days, was huge, among the largest in the entire election. He had polled 46 per cent of the votes in Merthyr and 49 per cent in Aberdare. The whole of Wales celebrated his success as a victory for the nation. The "Apostle of Peace" was now being acclaimed also as "The Member for Wales". Bruce's failure was considered unfortunate. However, the coal industry had been in a depressed state in the period leading up to the election, and the colliers had been organising to oppose, not so much the wage reduction but the proposed introduction by the coal owners of the double shift. Bruce, as the sitting Member, was seen as not having looked after their interests and getting rid of him was one objective of the colliers. The supporters of Bruce and Fothergill were also blamed for their insulting behaviour towards Richard's supporters. But above all, there was among the voters a unity of purpose to elect Henry Richard. Bruce accepted the verdict of the people with good grace and a seat was swiftly found for him in Renfrewshire. He was, it should be said, one of Gladstone's closest friends and he was eventually elevated to the House of Lords with the title of Lord Aberdare. He and

Henry Austin Bruce, later Lord Aberdare

Richard later worked closely together for the development of secondary and higher education in Wales.

Henry Richard was not a lonely figure when he entered the House of Commons. Instead of 17 Liberal MPs from Wales – mostly inept and unconcerned about the problems of Nonconformity – there were now 23. Among the new ones, for the first time, there were three Nonconformists – Henry Richard, E. M. Richards in Cardiganshire and Richard Davies for Anglesey. Davies, incidentally, was the son-in-law of the celebrated Rev Henry Rees of Liverpool. The reliable Lewis Dillwyn had been returned for Swansea and among the new Members was George Osborne Morgan for Denbigh, who although the son of an Anglican clergyman, would prove himself a stout defender of Nonconformist causes, particularly with his Burials Bills. The number of Conservative MPs from Wales dropped to ten and the Gladstone Government had a majority in the House of 120. Among the Liberals there were 95 who supported the Liberation Society, and of those 63 were Nonconformists.

Chapter 13

Parliament and the Tenant Farmers' Campaign

After the opening of the Parliament in February 1869, the majority of the Welsh Members attended a celebratory dinner in the Freemasons' Tavern, where Edward Miall noted that Wales had now found its voice.[1] Henry Richard spoke and referred to a telegram he had just received informing him that the parish priest at Menai Bridge, Anglesey, had refused to allow a Nonconformist minister to speak at the graveside at the burial service of the Rev Henry Rees of Liverpool.[2] Rees, as already noted, was the father-in-law of Richard Davies, the newly elected MP for the island. Richard expressed his hope that a Bill would soon be passed allowing Nonconformists to be buried in the cemeteries of parish churches and that Nonconformist ministers be allowed to officiate at the graveside. He also spoke of his concern that landowners were punishing tenants who had voted Liberal and his hope that a Bill providing for a secret ballot would soon become law. A little later, Richard spoke at another celebratory dinner – in Bristol – where he said that he had just spent his first week in the House of Commons and had found matters "uncommonly dull" but he had great hopes that matters would improve thanks to the much greater proportion of eager men than in the previous Parliament.[3]

The time prior and after the 1868 election was a golden era in the move towards religious equality much as the years 1848-1851 had been good years for the peace movement. Nonconformists of a political tendency were motivated by the activities of the Liberation Society to make their presence felt in the constituencies and soon their efforts were being reflected with moves for greater religious equality in Parliament. In 1858 Jews had been allowed to become Members of Parliament and two years later the Edinburgh Annuity Tax was abolished, a tax created by Charles I to pay for an Anglican priest in Edinburgh and Montrose. Other arrangements were made to raise the funds which proved equally unpopular resulting in another Bill in 1870 to abolish those, too. The grammar schools were opened to Nonconformists in 1860 and in 1868 the Compulsory Church Rate was abolished. The Church Rate was particularly unpopular with Nonconformists, especially in parishes where the Nonconformists were numerous and active. The Church of England also received financial support from Parliament, while the Nonconformists were totally dependent on voluntary contributions for building and the upkeep of their chapels. They had no wish to support a parish church as well as their own. After the General Election of 1868 with Gladstone as Prime Minister the Irish Church Disestablishment Act was passed. It was during the Second Reading of this Bill, on 22 March 1869, that Henry Richard made his maiden speech.[4] He drew many comparisons between Wales and Ireland. In fact, it was a speech entirely from the Welsh perspective presenting useful information outlining the successes that had emanated from the work of the Nonconformist churches and urging the Irish to study and imitate their methods. He spoke as a representative of the Welsh Nonconformists and with the authority of a man with convictions rather than opinions on the subject. It was, said the *Spectator*, a striking and eloquent speech with the promise that Richard would take a prominent position in the House and make himself heard and known.[5]

Of even greater significance than the success of the Liberals in 1868 – particularly in the longer term – were accusations against Welsh landowners of misconduct. The House of Commons set up a Select Committee to examine reports of threats coming in from all parts of Wales. Henry Richard had told the publisher, Thomas Gee, that he would have made similar allegations public from Merioneth in 1859 if only he had had more compelling evidence. But this time, after contacting progressive Liberals from all parts of Wales, he had the proof he needed. The situation escalated during the spring of 1869 as tenant farmers received eviction notices for voting Liberal. The Welsh Liberals met and decided, not only to present their evidence to the Select Committee but that Henry Richard should present a motion on the floor of the House condemning those landowners. That motion was presented on 6 July.

Richard spoke firmly and with great deliberation. Never within memory, as far as he knew, had any issue to do with Wales ever taken up the time of Parliament.[6] [In a re-print of *Letters and Essays on Wales*, in an appendix entitled *Welsh Education and the Established Church in Wales* Richard mentions a man with connections to a Welsh college who wrote to a Welsh MP asking for a copy of all Parliamentary papers relating to Wales. In time he got his reply – there were none!] It gave him no pleasure, he said, to draw the attention of the House, to accusations made against a class of his fellow-countrymen but matters had got to a stage where justice, electoral freedom, order and peace demanded it. It was a speech to make Tories squirm, although he avoided naming any current Member. Colonel Powell, a former MP for Cardigan Boroughs, was mentioned, however, for threatening his tenants unless they voted for E. M. Vaughan in Cardiganshire. He read out letters from landowners threatening tenants with evictions if they did not vote for the Tories. Among them was one from the agent – an Englishman – of Deri Ormond Estate in Cardiganshire, which Richard read aloud, emphasising contemptuously the incorrect English:

> Derry Ormond, Friday – Sir, –I am given to understand that you and Mr. Oliver as (sic) been about selecting votes for Mr. Richards among the Derry Ormond tenants. What business dare you to interfeer (sic) with the tenants on the Derry Estate, and I trust you won't do so again. But mind your own business. If not, I will mind you before the 24th of next March. I am now desired to tell you, from Mr. Jones, that he expects you to vote at the coming election for his cousin Mr. E. M. Vaughan,[7] and if you refuses (sic) to do so, you will have to leave and all others that refuse to vote according to Mr. Jones's wish. – Sir, yours truly, W. COTTRELL

Henry Richard said that he had verified that the threats had been carried out in 43 instances in Cardiganshire and 26 in Carmarthenshire. They had to leave their farms without compensation for all the improvements they had done at their own cost to their landlords' farms. He mentioned the case of Caleb Morris, "a man with ten children, who had notice to quit. He besought his landlord's agent to let him retain the farm, but was met with a refusal, and the disappointment so weighed upon his mind that he died."

As part of his introductory remarks he said that:

An impression prevailed in England, which some landowners in Wales were willing enough to encourage, that the people had a sort of blind feudal attachment to the lords of the soil, whose lead they were prepared to follow in political matters without inquiry ... They looked on the vote apparently as coming within the operation of the Game Laws, something like a pheasant or a hare, which nobody was to dare touch unless they gave permission; and if any one presumed to canvass their farmers he had no doubt they looked upon, and would like to treat him as a poacher.

They should remember, he continued, that:

Education and political intelligence had spread among the people; but that was precisely what certain classes of the Welsh landlords could not or would not understand. They would not understand that they were no longer lords over serfs of the soil, or chiefs among clansmen, but men among men, with certain advantages of wealth, station, and superior education; but surrounded by an intelligent, improving, reading, and reasoning population, who could be guided and influenced only by an appeal to their understandings and consciences, and not by feudal and social coercion ... The Welsh had a large literature in their own language; nine newspapers were published in it, all of them advocating Liberal principles, with the exception of one which called itself Conservative-Liberal, which had a very small circulation, and was sustained by subsidies from the Welsh landowners. There were, besides, sixteen other periodicals, all supported by the Nonconformists, which, so far as they had any politics at all, were Liberal.

The motion was seconded by George Osborne Morgan (Denbighshire) and there was enthusiastic support from E. A. Leatham (Wakefield) who showed his familiarity with events in earlier elections in Merionethshire. His source was the Congregationalist Michael D. Jones, the man behind the establishment of the Welsh colony in Patagonia. Richard was also supported by E. M. Richards (Cardiganshire), Sir Thomas Lloyd (Cardigan Boroughs) who himself owned lands in Cardiganshire and Carmarthenshire, and Colonel John Stepney (Carmarthenshire Boroughs). Only two speakers opposed the resolution, J. H. Scourfield (Pembrokeshire) and Charles Watkin Williams-Wynn (Montgomeryshire), both Tories who had been elected unopposed, although Williams-Wynn revealed his true colours by suggesting that landlords should avoid letting farms to anyone who was not an Anglican and a Tory!

Since a Select Committee had already been formed to discuss the matter Henry Richard agreed, on the suggestion of H. A. Bruce, the Home Secretary, to withdraw the motion. Bruce praised his former adversary's speech, emphasising the importance of bringing these allegations to the attention of the House and congratulating him on his "powerful and remarkable" speech. Some Tories had complained that "the Notice he had given had not been sufficiently long ... for the purpose of enabling hon. Gentlemen opposite to make inquiries and prepare themselves to rebut the charges". Richard answered that he had presented the motion two months earlier and had postponed presenting it twice to give them additional time to prepare their answers. In any case he had not named anyone – although some had identified themselves in the course of the debate.

The point was made, and the Liberal newspapers, particularly Welsh ones such as *Baner ac Amserau Cymru*, were delighted. Edward Miall who sat alongside Richard throughout the debate, described the scene:

> Much of what Mr Richard told to the House must have been new to the ears of those who heard it, but simply because Wales has not, until now, sent a Member fit in all respects to represent her. His descriptions of the political and literary sympathies of the Nonconformists, or, in other words, the people of the Principality, the depth and consistency of their political feelings, and the extent of their reading and their education was listened to, we are afraid, with that sort of curious interest with which persons always listen to entirely new information. When the speaker proceeded to describe how education and political intelligence had spread amongst the people, and how the landlords could not, or would not, understand this, he hit upon what we believe to be the real secret of landlord intolerance.[8]

His style of speaking received enthusiastic praise from the *Illustrated Times*:

> He spoke from the first bravely, vigorously, eloquently, without a taint of the conventicle in manner, tone, or language. He has only been in the House a few months, and yet he spoke as if to the manner born – nay, better than that, for he not only kept clear of the pulpit style, but also of the conventional tone and manner of the House of Commons, which, if we were not so used to it, would be almost as unpleasant. In short, he just spoke naturally; and to be able to do that is here and everywhere, and always has been, a rare accomplishment.[9]

This moment was the beginning of a chapter in Welsh history. Henry Richard was pronouncing publicly that Wales should be acknowledged as a nation of Nonconformists, a nation with a different political agenda to the other nations represented in the House of Commons. It was the birth of a "new" Wales, and it was due to Henry Richard. From now on it was understood, at least in radical circles, that the work of Welsh MPs was to represent Wales's interests in the same way as those representing Scotland and Ireland. Now, such issues as civic equality for Nonconformists, the Welsh language and land rights would define what was expected of the MPs who represented Wales. Henry Richard had fired the first shot.

This speech by Richard, according to Edward Miall, inspired the new intake of Liberal MPs – Welsh and English – with a new confidence. When Henry Richard sat down on that night of 6 July 1869, two facts were obvious; he had made a reputation for himself, and Wales, at last, had a worthy representative in Parliament. Two years later the Select Committee made its recommendations and the principle of the secret ballot accepted. Richard's speech undoubtedly helped to move matters along.

By the autumn a fund had been set up to compensate the tenant farmers who had been evicted for voting Liberal. The main protagonist was John Griffith, an influential journalist who had settled in London – initially to work for Sir Hugh Owen – and wrote under the pseudonym of Gohebydd (Correspondent) for *Baner ac Amserau Cymru*. He was also the nephew of Samuel Roberts and fervent supporter of the Liberal Party. A committee was formed, and Griffith, with the aid of Henry Richard and E. M. Richards, MP for Cardiganshire, formed an association to help the farmers. Valuers were appointed for Cardiganshire and Carmarthenshire and they submitted their reports to a conference in Aberystwyth on 16 December. It was a well-attended conference with many influential people present, but with few Liberal MPs although some had sent letters of support.[10] It was suggested that some were nervous of associating too conspicuously with such a campaign. The conference was chaired by E. M. Richards and among the speakers was Samuel Morley, MP for Bristol, who had been an enthusiastic supporter of the campaign. Henry Richard proposed the creation of a guarantee fund of £20,000 to be raised by chapel collections. As well as compensating those deprived of their livelihood this would prove that the Welsh people were more than prepared to help themselves. In a meeting the same evening in one of the town's chapels, Morley, who had been generous in his support to many Nonconformist causes in Wales, expressed his sympathy with the tenant farmers who had suffered for providing Europe's leading statesman (Gladstone) – "one of the most sincere, enlightened, and earnest men in England" – with so large a majority in the House of Commons.[11] Meetings were held throughout Wales and in a number of towns and cities in England, such as Liverpool and Birmingham and a fund-raising committee of prominent Welshmen set up in London.[12]

The South Wales radical paper, *Cambria Daily Leader*, sent a reporter to visit 41 farms in Cardiganshire and Carmarthenshire where tenants had been evicted. The reporter failed to find a single family who had been evicted for any reason other than for voting Liberal. In every instance the farmer was found to be conscientious, respected by his neighbours and never late paying his rent.[13]

In a speech in Parliament on 8 August, on the Third Reading of the Ballot Bill, Henry Richard revealed that £4,000 had been collected to distribute among the tenants who had been evicted from their farms.[14] The total, he said, consisted of a little under £2,000 in sums received from individual donators and a little over £1,500 in collections organised by the chapels. The largest sums came from chapels in Cardiganshire (£412) and Carmarthenshire (£216), two counties that had suffered particularly badly from the evictions. According to Gohebydd,[15] 15 shillings in every pound was paid to every claimant. In Cardiganshire 63 payments were made, 21 in Carmarthenshire, 25 in Caernarvonshire and one in Denbighshire. The collection had been a considerable logistical feat by the committee. It was worth noting that the efforts and the meetings had been instrumental in drawing together from all over Wales people of similar politically radical tendencies. Gwilym Hiraethog (William Rees)[16] referred to those who had been evicted from their homes as people to whom the whole of Wales owed a debt of gratitude. The evictions inspired strong nationalistic emotions in the Welsh people and there were suggestions that Henry Richard was considering establishing a Welsh parliamentary party to strengthen Wales's rights and rectify past injustices.

In his speech on 8 August the Member for Merthyr was not afraid of making some barely veiled threats as to what might happen if the Secret Ballot were not adopted. The House of Commons had never before heard such talk from a Welsh MP speaking on behalf of his people:

You send your Judges of Assize from England to our country
year by year, and their testimony is uniformly that of delighted
astonishment at the paucity and almost total absence of serious
crime in many parts of the Principality. Let me call particular
attention to the case of Cardiganshire. That county was the scene
of the worst class of the political persecutions of which I have
spoken. There were between 40 and 50 cases of evictions or
oppression of other sort, and some of them under circumstances
of peculiarly exasperating character. We know what would have
taken place in Ireland under such circumstances. The Irish people would have taken the matter into their own hands. And I am
not at all sure that something of the same sort would not have
taken place in England, for John Bull is by no means so long suffering an animal under provocation as he sometimes takes the
credit of being. But what did take place in Cardiganshire? When
the Judge went down to the Assizes immediately after these evictions, there was not a single prisoner to be tried. Mr Justice
Hannen, in charging the Grand Jury, said that a perfectly clear
calendar was a circumstance he had never before met with since
he had been on the Bench, and he understood from his brother
Judges 'that only in the Principality of Wales was such a thing
known, and that there it was frequent'. And yet these are the people who are worried and persecuted in the manner I have
described. But why is it that the Welsh people are so patient and
forbearing? Not because they do not feel intensely these wrongs;
but it may be ascribed to two causes. First, the moral and religious influence exercised over them by the Dissenting chapels
and Sunday schools, and by which their minds have become
largely imbued with the principles and precepts of Christianity.
But there was another cause in this instance. They believed that
there were some of us who would take care that their case should
be fairly stated to this House, and that Parliament, if it did not
grant them redress for the past wrongs they had endured, would
interpose its protection as a shield to them against future wrongs.
We ventured to promise them that the legislature would pass a
Ballot Law, under shelter of which they might hereafter freely
and securely exercise the franchise which it had conferred upon
them. But if you disappoint them, it is impossible to say what
may happen. If another General Election takes place without the
Ballot, and is followed by similar scenes to those I have
described, we cannot tell what men, stung to desperation and
hopeless of redress, may be driven to.[17]

The Bill was passed by the House of Commons and became law
in September of the following year, but not without furious
attempts to delay it in the House of Lords.

Chapter 14

The Franco-Prussian war

Henry Richard's eyes may have been on other matters but his position as Secretary of the Peace Society allowed no time for relaxation. Richard – aided by Cobden and Bright – managed to keep Britain from interfering in the American Civil War as well as the Schleswig-Holstein war between Denmark and the Germanic states, and the uprising in Poland. In October, 1865, there were troubles in Jamaica, where a drop in the price of sugar had caused widespread and serious poverty. The troubles started when a man was imprisoned for brawling in the Court of Petty Sessions in Morant Bay and was then rescued by local people. On another occasion locals were imprisoned for trespassing on an abandoned plantation. Again the protesters were rescued by demonstrators and this time the magistrate, Baron von Ketelhodt, and a number of Europeans were killed. The island Governor, Edward John Eyre, declared martial law and for several days the militia and volunteers hunted the "rebels" and those who were not shot on sight were tried by court martial and executed. Official figures showed that 439 people were killed – other sources put the number at 2,000 – many without trial, 600 men and women were flogged and nearly 1,000 homes destroyed. George William Gordon, a popular member of the island's Assembly, was accused of inciting the uprising, and although he had not been responsible for any of the violence, he was hanged without trial.[1] Richard, with the aid of the Anti-Slavery Society, prepared an address which was signed on behalf of the Peace Society by himself, Joseph Pease and Samuel Gurney MP, a Quaker whose family had been active in the anti-slavery movement. The address was presented to the Foreign Secretary, Lord John Russell. The following year Richard's pamphlet *The Troubles in Jamaica: A Condensed Statement of Facts*, was published by Jackson, Walford & Hodder. Copies were sent to MPs, newspaper editors and others of influence which stirred up public opinion:

> It was impossible to read this shameful record without feeling the pulse throb with indignation, and the brow flush with shame, at such a grotesque farce enacted in the name of justice, at such a wicked wrong inflicted on an innocent man, at such deep dishonour done to the British name.[2]

Richard knew how to stir British passions. He believed, as did the Anti-Slavery Society that Gordon had been executed for his sympathy for the rights of the black population. Richard's efforts had some success. A Royal Commission sailed to Jamaica and concluded that Governor Eyre should be replaced. However, when he was put on trial the verdict of the Grand Jury was one of "not found". Eyre had been acquitted of the charge of "wilful murder". Richard, although not satisfied, felt that at least something had been achieved by hauling Eyre in front of a Criminal Tribunal.

Britain was again embroiled in a war in 1867, this time in Abyssinia (Ethiopia). In another of those interminable instances of British incompetence, negligence and arrogance some of "Her Majesty's subjects" had found themselves in prison. Britain declared war on 19 November with the unanimous approval of Parliament – even members of the Peace Society supported the decision. Henry Richard's researches resulted in another of his pamphlets.[3] It was, he said, another instance of typical "English" interference in matters which were none of their business. In 1840, a man named Walter Plowden had persuaded Lord Palmerston to appoint him British Consul to Abyssinia. The following year Plowden had negotiated a treaty in England's name with Ras-Ali, the Ruler of Gondar. Ras-Ali at the time was at war with one of his rebellious subjects. In 1854, Ras-Ali's regime was overthrown by his son-in-law, Theodore, and the treaty made by Plowden was rescinded. Soon after Plowden fell into the hands of King Theodore's supporters and was executed. It would have been sensible not to appoint a successor to Plowden, but Captain Charles Duncan Campbell took his place, a man, in the opinion of Richard and others, quite unsuitable for the post. King Theodore refused to recognise him and asked him to leave Magdala, the capital. Despite Lord Russell's instruction to him to withdraw to Massowah, Campbell stayed in Magdala where he continued to interfere in the country's administration and sided with the king's enemies. Theodore wrote a polite letter to Queen Victoria explaining the problem, and although the letter was passed to the Foreign Office it was filed and forgotten. Inevitably Campbell was imprisoned and when a deputation arrived demanding his release they were imprisoned, too. This was followed by the usual response – dispatching an army to release the prisoners. When the war ended in May 1868 it had cost Britain – as Richard noted – £8,000,000.[4] And that because Theodore's letter had been ignored.

In the run-up to the 1868 General Election Henry Richard was as busy as ever with his work for the Peace Society. In June 1868, he and the President, Charles Pease, attended a meeting of the International League of Peace and Freedom – *Ligue internationale de la Paix et de la Liberté* – in Paris. The President of the conference was Jean Dollfus, Mayor of Mulhouse in Alsace, and a good friend of the peace movement.[5] Dollfus was a successful textile manufacturer, economist and politician with similar ideas to those of the Quakers about providing good accommodation and facilities for his workers and a pioneer of the *cité ouvrière*. He also developed the mortgage system for house purchasing.

Richard met and shared the platform with his old friend the lawyer and philanthropist from Belgium, Auguste Visschers. Also present was Frédéric Passy, the French economist and founder and first President of the French Peace Society, or the *Société française pour l'arbitrage entre nations*, as it was re-named in 1889. Passy was an admirer of Richard Cobden's ideas about Free Trade as a means of promoting and perpetuating peace.

Before departing Richard called a meeting of friends of the peace movement to urge the movement in France to promote a friendlier relationship with the German states.[6] The prospects for the future did not look promising. The contention between France and Prussia over Luxembourg early in 1867 showed just how fragile was the relationship between the two countries. A treaty had been agreed through arbitration on 11 May 1867, which made Luxembourg a neutral country. But it was becoming increasingly obvious that the two contentious states might not be so ready to go to arbitration over matters of greater importance, and there was a need to intensify peace campaigns in the two countries.

Passy had written an article which was published in *Le Temps* on 26 April 1867. A month later, on 30 May, he founded, with the aid of British, American, Italian, Danish and Swedish pacifists a new

French peace movement, *La Ligue internationale et permanente de la Paix* (International and Permanent League of Peace). The new organisation, while acknowledging that war was contrary to civilisation, made specific reference to the balance of power in Europe, and the duty of those powers to refrain from threatening or attacking other countries. In order to maintain and promote the principle of respect of nations towards one and other he appealed to men of goodwill in all countries for their support.[7] Henry Richard agreed with the aspirations of an organisation that had no desire to interfere politically, nor to enter into an alliance with any political party. It should be noted that another organisation, the League of Peace and Freedom, was founded in Geneva in September of the same year. This was more radical than Passy's movement and had the support of intellectuals advocating the establishment of a United States of Europe. Henry Richard wished it well and watched developments with interest.

Richard addressed a Social Science Congress in London in September 1868 on the subject of *Standing Armies and their Influence on the Industrial, Commercial and Moral Interests of Nations*. He spoke of the vast numbers of men continuously under arms, estimated at 3,926,957 which with the addition of auxiliary workers would come to a total of over 8,000,000. He claimed that the total cost of these military establishments, including capital interest and the loss of these young men to agriculture and other industries, was in the region of £282,000,000.[8] This cost was a great weight on the nations of Europe, an expense they could ill afford. After referring to the physical evils which were inseparable from such a system he urged the greater powers to come to an agreement and arrange a gradual, simultaneous disarmament. Such a proposal, he said, had been advocated by Richard Cobden, Sir Robert Peel and, in particular, by Emperor Louis-Napoleon of France, who in 1863 had made a clear statement:

> Have not the prejudices and rancours which divide us lasted long enough? Shall the jealous rivalries of the great powers unceasingly impede the progress of civilisation? Are we still to maintain mutual distrust by exaggerated armaments? Must our most precious resources be infinitely exhausted in a vain display of our forces? Must we eternally maintain a condition of things which is neither peace with its security, nor war with its happy chances?

The congress passed a resolution asking its committee to prepare propositions to put pressure on the Government to consider what would be "practicable for the reduction of the burdens of standing armies".[9]

As had been anticipated by Frédéric Passy, although conditions seemed ripe for the development of pacifism, there were signs that war was increasingly likely due to the policies of the greater powers. After the Austro-Prussian War – or Seven Weeks War – of 1866, the unification of the Germanic states seemed increasingly likely, with Prussia becoming the dominant force. In diplomatic circles there was no doubt that soon there would be conflict between the young German Empire flexing its industrial and military muscles, and the French Empire determined to hang on to its dominant position in Europe. In the Paris exhibition of the summer of 1867, France gave a proud display of its industry and art. But in the industrial pavilion visitors could admire the latest creation from the Krupp factory – a cannon proclaiming German military might.

Henry Richard was not unaware of such possibilities. Now an elected MP, when Parliament rose for the Summer Recess of 1869 he set off with his wife on a peace-promoting tour of Europe. They visited Paris, Brussels, The Hague, Prussia, Bavaria and Florence. The purpose of the journey was to initiate some kind of agreement on disarmament. He could see little hope that governments would instigate such a move. For some time he had been inclined to the idea of appealing directly to the people who could put pressure upon their representatives who would in turn seek to influence their governments. Twenty years earlier – between 1849 and 1851 – Richard Cobden had tried to take the matter to the House of Commons, with Henry Richard researching and promoting the Bill outside Parliament. They had been able to raise people's awareness of the subject and stimulate support from many quarters but the campaign had no practical success. Richard was of the opinion that it was time to try again to bring pressure on governments to consider the possibility of simultaneous disarmament. As on previous occasions he kept a detailed journal of their journey:

> My object was to get into communication, as far as I could, with leading members of the different Legislatures of [the] various countries, in order to ask them whether they would be prepared to bring forward a motion in their respective Chambers in favour of mutual and simultaneous disarmaments between the nations. I had the satisfaction of coming into contact with many intelligent men in all those countries, and the feeling of every man was

the same – that the burden of these armaments was becoming
utterly intolerable. There was a desire on all hands to do something to mitigate the terrible burden that was crushing the life
out of the nations.

And what was the result of this visit of mine? In two or three
weeks after I left Berlin, there was a motion introduced into the
Chamber of that country proposing that the Government be
addressed by the Legislature, urging upon it the immediate
reduction of armaments, and at the same time that it should
communicate with the other Governments of Europe with a
view to a general European disarmament. The motion was sustained by ninety votes. A similar motion was submitted to the
Saxon Chamber at Dresden, and it was carried by a considerable
majority. A similar motion was brought forward in the Chamber
in Austria, and it was supported by a vote of fifty-three against
sixty-four.[10]

On their return through France a reception and banquet had been
arranged for them by members of *La Ligue internationale et permanente de la Paix* who were anxious to know what response Richard
had received on his journey. He talked to the politician and member of the French Academy, Jules Favre, who the following year
distinguished himself by opposing the Franco-Prussian War. Later,
after the defeat of France, he had the unenviable task of bargaining
the peace treaty on behalf of France's Provisional Government.
Richard also met Jules Simon, another passionate Republican,
who was born in Lorient, Brittany, and represented Gironde in the
French Parliament. He was another who would oppose the war
and like Favre become a member of the post-war Provisional
Government. Both had openly opposed Louis-Napoleon's *coup
d'etat* and subsequent self-elevation to Emperor. Richard quizzed
both about French attitudes to war. Simon replied:

> I can give you the best possible answer to the inquiry by pointing
> to what took place at the last election (held in May, 1869). I
> examined carefully the addresses that had been issued by the var-
> ious candidates for the suffrages of the French people, and in all
> of them – or in nearly all of them – the candidates, knowing the
> feeling that existed among the French people, were obliged to
> put in their programme the promise to vote for a great reduction
> of the military establishment of France, and for the total aboli-
> tion of standing armies.

Favre promised to do all in his power to work with Richard and
countries that supported his campaign. "I have every reason to

believe," wrote Richard in his journal, "that just before this suicidal war broke out, those gentlemen were preparing to submit a resolution to the Legislative Body of France in favour of universal European disarmament."[11] In a speech delivered some years later in Manchester on "The War and its Lesson" Richard revealed that after Louis-Napoleon had been deposed the Provisional Government had uncovered in the State Archives answers to questionnaires sent to the *Departements* requesting information on popular attitudes to the war with Prussia. Of the 89 replies, 78 reported that the people were strongly opposed.[12]

Like most wars the War of 1870 – as the French usually refer to the Franco-Prussian war – was started for the most trivial of reasons. As has been suggested, distrust and jealousy had smouldered between France and Prussia for some time. After the enforced abdication of Queen Isabella of Spain following constitutional problems no one had sat on the Spanish throne since 1868. In 1869 Spain began trawling the courts of Europe for a likely candidate. Eventually they came across Prince Leopold Sigmaringen, one of the younger sons of the Royal Court of Hohenzollern, a colonel in the Huzzars on the look-out for something better.[13]

France put on a show of indignation at not being consulted and the French Ambassador, Earl Vincent Benedetti, was ordered to seek an explanation from the Prussian Chancellor, Bismarck. Bismarck was unwell and confined to his bed and his deputy knew nothing of the matter. Benedetti was curtly ordered to go and raise the matter with the king, Wilhelm I, who was at Ems. When Benedetti saw the king enjoying his morning stroll, dispensing with diplomatic niceties, he accosted him aggressively. As it happened Prince Leopold had by now decided that he did not want to be King of Spain and had declined the offer. The fact had even been published in the *Cologne Gazette*, and the paper was given to Benedetti to read. But the Ambassador was still not satisfied and demanded assurances from the king that the matter would never be raised again. Wilhelm refused to give such an assurance and told Benedetti to go away.[14]

When Bismarck returned to work he found a report of the incident waiting for him. This report, known as the Telegram of Ems, was used by Bismarck to stir up trouble. His attitude was that if war with France was inevitable, this would be as good a time as any. He published an edited version of the report in the Government's official paper, the *Norddeutsche Zeitung*, hinting that Wilhelm I had insulted the French Imperial Ambassador, who in turn had responded with equal insolence. In no time a report of the insults had appeared in the main newspapers of all the cities of Europe. French papers whipped the politicians into a state of fury and France declared war on Prussia on 19 July 1870.[15]

Henry Richard did all in his power to avoid a calamity, and to cooperate with Frédéric Passy, who was trying to cool passions. On 16 July, three days before the hostilities began, the peace movement in France made a pressing appeal to Wilhelm and Louis-Napoleon as statesmen and Christians not to go to war. But the fury was now in full flow and all restraint in vain.[16]

War was inevitable and Henry Richard turned his sights in another direction, namely keeping Britain from interfering. In the *Herald of Peace* he appealed for calm:

> It would be easy to write a book on the subject, but as defenders of peace, it would be better to be sparing with our words, so that nothing we say might excite the warring parties, those who may easily be the cause of agitation between this country and one of the Powers. It is clear to anyone who has read the Parliamentary papers, as we have done, that the source of the evil lies deeper than the choice of Prince Hohenzollern for the throne of Spain. Every war, as Kant said, begets another war.[17]

Now that war had begun between France and Prussia, it presented an opportunity for warmongering politicians and the military to campaign for increased expenditure. On 1 August 1870, Disraeli raised the matter, arguing that Britain was in a defenceless state. Richard responded sarcastically, accusing Disraeli of abandoning "that wise, reticence and admirable self-control that had always hitherto distinguished him in discussing questions of peace and war". He went on to accuse Members on both sides of the House of dwelling on the defenceless condition of the country. He had, he said, paid attention to these matters over the last 25 years and noticed how the army and navy never seemed to be up to standard:

> Some years ago a great outcry was raised in favour of that great constitutional Reserve Force, the Militia. Well, the Militia Force having been established was now declared to be utterly worthless ... An Honourable and gallant Member opposite had stated that our infantry, our cavalry, and our artillery were in a most unsatisfactory state. If that statement were correct the country had a right to ask what had become of the hundreds of millions of money that had been poured into the lap of the naval and mili-

tary authorities for the purpose of providing us with an adequate
naval and military force ... It had been said that the best means of
preserving peace was to be prepared for war; but there could not
be a greater fallacy. If anybody wanted a proof of the folly and
absurdity of that maxim let him look to either bank of the Rhine.
Europe, in acting upon that mischievous maxim during the last
14 years, had found herself engaged in four bloody wars, and was
now about to enter upon a fifth, which threatened to be the most
disastrous of all.[18]

He referred to a speech once made by Sir Robert Peel who had
warned the House against listening to the opinions of military
men "who were naturally prejudiced on this subject, they would
involve the country in an outlay that no revenue could bear".
There was no shortage of men who wished to join the war in order
to prop up the ailing administration of Louis-Napoleon. Richard
also ensured that the readers of the *Herald of Peace* were aware of
the facts and of the horrors of the war. The efforts of the Peace
Society were scorned by the majority of the popular papers. "Look
at what effect the Peace Society has had on Europe," they taunted.
Exactly, responded Richard in a public meeting in Newcastle on
24 September, inviting them to look at the catastrophe that had
been caused by the War Society:

> ... a quarter of a million men, in the prime of life six week ago,
> were now either lying in bloody graves or for ever damaged. You
> can see the results of their work in the miles of anguish lying in
> the hospitals and houses on the banks of the Rhine and the
> Moselle, in the ravaged and wretched houses in France and
> Germany, where heartbroken wives wait in vain for the fathers,
> husbands, sons, brothers cut down in the prime of their lives, not
> by some law of nature or command of God but by the wanton
> wickedness of their fellow-men ... You can see the work of the
> War Society in the fields that have been destroyed, the towns that
> have been plundered, the villages that have been burnt and dev-
> astated, where the unfortunate inhabitants can be seen wander-
> ing terrified amidst the ruins of their houses their terrible cries
> begging the nations of Europe to come and save them ... What
> does the Peace Society have to say? This – that there are better
> and wiser ways, more reasonable ways, more compassionate,
> more Christian to end disputes between nations, than this way of
> making them murder each other. Although various means are
> used to try and conceal the fact, war is nothing but murder on a
> vast scale. The Peace Society tells you that all the storing of mul-
> tiple arms in Europe by the various governments is irrational and
> criminal, because, rather than achieving their declared purpose
> of keeping peace they are a continuing spur to fight. While they

continue to exist there can be no permanent peace and wars are certain to happen from time to time. There are 5,000,000 soldiers in Europe and I protest against them because they are a danger to peace.[19]

The war was a disaster for France. On France's declaration of war, the other Germanic states joined in support of Prussia. It became evident that the effective use of railways and the Krupp steel cannon gave the German forces a swift advantage and a number of victories on France's eastern front. In the Battle of Sedan on 2 September Louis-Napoleon and his army were taken prisoner, although this did not end the war and the fighting continued under *Le Gouvernement de la Défense Nationale* (Government of National Defence) and afterwards under the Government of Adolphe Thiers. The fighting continued for another five months, after which Paris capitulated in January 1871, following a lengthy siege. It was a terrible psychological jolt to French self-respect, and the pain and dejection caused by such a total defeat at the hands of Prussian forces with their more powerful and sophisticated arms can be felt in Émile Zola's *La Débâcle*, a novel about the shambolic brutality of war written from the point of view of the common soldier, and Alphonse Daudet's *Robert Helmont*, an autobiographical novel of the Paris siege.[20] And the indignity of surrendering Alsace to the new united Germany is poignantly portrayed in Daudet's short story *La Dernière Classe*[21] (The Final Lesson), where the schoolmaster gives his last French lesson before they were forbidden under German rule. It was also a seminal moment in Germany history. On 18 January 1871, ten days before Paris surrendered, Germany was united into one state.

Henry Richard managed to influence Gladstone sufficiently to keep Britain from entering the war, although he failed to persuade him to offer Britain's services as arbitrator before the war had begun, which might have brought success. It is possible that Britain's non-intervention prevented the war from spreading into a European conflict. But despite Richard's pleas the warmongering faction in the House of Commons persuaded the Government to hand £2,000,000 over to the military, and increase the number of men under arms by another 20,000, it was argued, was for the defence of Belgium and Holland. A foolish waste of money in the opinion of Richard, but only seven members voted with him.[22]

Chapter 15

Education and English judges

In 1870 William Edward Forster, with the full support of the Liberal administration, presented an Education Bill to establish more elementary schools, create a more effective system of inspection and to ensure religious equality. It was a first step towards ensuring that all children in England and Wales, between the ages of 5 and 12 should receive compulsory elementary education. It would not be free, although no child would be refused if its parents could not afford to pay. The Denominational Schools – the vast majority being Church of England – would receive increased funding from the Government, and local school boards would be set up to finance education from the rates. These new school boards would establish non-denominational schools where there was a need and these would provide religious education that was non-sectarian. Voluntary and charity schools would continue with the same rights as before.

It was not a new system, rather an attempt to fill the gaps. Where there was inadequate provision, or room for improvement, an elected school board should be established with the responsibility to build a school. Forster presented his Bill on 17 February 1870. Then, on 14 March George Dixon, MP for Birmingham, proposed – unsuccessfully – an amendment that school boards should not have responsibility for religious education in schools funded from the public purse. He had lifted the lid on an aspect of the Bill which would be contentious for years.

It was not so much that there was disagreement between the Tories and the Liberals, but that there was no agreement within the Liberals themselves. Many on the Radical Nonconformist wing of the party wanted to go further than what was being pro-

posed by the Bill. Among them were Henry Richard and Edward
Miall. Henry Richard was well aware that in Wales there was
opposition to the influence Anglicans had on the education system. He argued that education should be secular and that religious
"agencies" should get on with their work outside the schools.
Religious instruction should be left to parents and the Sunday
schools.

On 20 June, and representing the opinion of many within his
party, Richard proposed an amendment: "The Grants to existing
denominational schools should not be increased; and that, in any
national system of elementary education, the attendance should be
everywhere compulsory, and the religious instruction should be
supplied by voluntary effort and not out of Public Funds."[1]

It was not a matter of whether or not children should receive
religious education, he argued, but rather how and by whom. The
Government, he argued, was proposing that everyone should pay
for each other's religious education. The only satisfactory solution
would be to take a secular approach to education. He proposed
that the State should provide a literary and scientific education,
and let the Churches and the religious denominations supplement
that education by teaching religion. There were more than 50,000
ministers of religion in England, many (the Anglicans) paid largely
out of State endowments, and if their responsibility – and that of
the 320,000 unpaid Sunday school teachers – was to be given over
to the schoolmaster, why not give the latter a portion of the religious endowments received by the clergy? Not all the Nonconformist Liberal MPs agreed with him. Samuel Morley, Bristol,
argued that the Bible should be read in schools and that religious
education should be taught, but that it need not be compulsory.
Richard's amendment was defeated by 421 votes to 60, with the
Conservatives voting solidly with the Government.

The Bill went through the committee stage, more or less
unchanged, and at the third reading on 11 July, Henry Richard and
Henry Winterbotham, MP for Stroud, the grandson of a Baptist
minister and another on the radical Nonconformist wing of the
Liberal party, made their final statements on the matter.
Winterbotham opposed denominational schools in general, and
he saw this Bill as being excessively favourable to the schools of
the Established Church. Richard's speech, even by his standards,
was unusually bitter and sarcastic. The Opposition, he said, had
rushed into the open arms of W. E. Forster where they "had been
clasped in a fond embrace and not without a considerable effusion

of tender sentiment" while other Liberals looked on in dismay at their interests being betrayed. Even the Prime Minister had praised the Conservatives for their generous concessions, thundered Richard. There was not one body representing Nonconformists in England or Wales who did not oppose the Bill in its present form. It had been pushed through in the teeth of opposition from the entire Nonconformist community, which constituted half the population of Britain. He went on to accuse Forster of "cantering over the education difficulty … by mounting the good steed 'Conservative', and charging into the ranks of his friends and riding them down rough-shod". The Government, he concluded, would, no doubt, carry the Bill through Parliament, as a Government might carry any measure by using the votes of its adversaries to defeat the wishes of its friends; but one or two more such victories would be disastrous for the Liberal party.[2] Henry Richard's efforts proved futile and the Bill was passed without difficulty.

Henry Richard made his position even clearer in a speech he delivered in his constituency in December:

> The first edition of the Bill I liked better than the second, for under that there was a possibility of bringing all the schools of the country – those that are called denominational as well as the new ones to be established – under the cognisance and direction of the School Board, and so in the process of time I thought it would be possible to have a uniform and universal system of national education; and I believe it would have been a great advantage for young Englishmen and Welshmen to be brought together on the forms of the same schools to learn certain things in common, without having thrust on them the sectarian differences by which society is racked. It seems to me that the new form of the Bill established a complete and lasting distinction between two kinds of schools in the country – the denominational schools and those that were to be under the School Boards; and with reference to the latter, the Bill gave to the Boards the power of dealing with the question of religious instruction, with no protection whatever for the rights of conscience except such as were afforded by the clause forbidding the catechism to be taught in schools. That is not an adequate protection, because in hundreds of parishes in the rural districts of England the Board School will be the clergyman and the squire, and they will have the power to order any kind of religious instruction to be imparted in the school … They may teach as much as they like if it is not in the form of the catechism, and there are scores of catechisms prepared by clergymen a thousand times worse than the catechism of the Church of England. There

should be perfect liberty of teaching for all men. But I do object
to a man putting his hand in my pocket and taking my money to
teach that which I believe to be deadly error. This is the cardinal
injustice of this Bill..[3]

Henry Richard's warning that the Government would ignore the
desires of the Nonconformist community at its peril proved correct. The advantages given by the Bill to the denominational
schools became more and more apparent, in particular through
Clause 25 which made public funds available to them. The clergy
also made a concerted – and successful – effort to control school
boards and the Nonconformists were banished even further from
the administration of an education system which already favoured
the Established Church. When the Gladstone Government lost
the 1874 General election, one reason may have been the lack of
enthusiasm from Nonconformists disillusioned by the 1870
Education Act.

A large conference of representatives of the Nonconformist
denominations – chaired by Henry Richard – was held in the Free
Trade Hall, Manchester, early in 1872 to discuss the subject of religious education in the elementary schools with particular reference to Clause 25. Around 2,000 people were present,
representing over 800 chapels and organisations representing
Nonconformists. Richard was again in a sarcastic mood and
scornful of the Government. By now it was possible to see the
Education Bill for what it was and now was the time to remind W.
E. Forster again how he had forgotten and betrayed his old friends,
the Radical Nonconformists, to further his own ambitions. "But
never," said Richard, "have I seen such symptoms of unity and
earnestness in the Nonconformist camp as now." A resolution was
passed that "the responsibility of the religious education of each
district should be thrown upon voluntary effort". Nonconformists were also urged to organise themselves to elect to Parliament
members who would overturn the Government's education
policy.[4]

An opportunity to make the Government aware of these mis-
givings came on 5 March 1872, and this was done once more by
George Dixon. He listed failings in the administration of the
Education Act, namely: that the membership of the school boards
was not representative of society in general; the attendance of children in schools was not compulsory; the payment of school fees
was being administered in ways that were irregular and inconsis-
tent; that it was permitted for school boards to pay school fees out

of the rates to denominational schools over which the rate-payers had no control; that the Act allowed school boards to use rate-payers' money to provide dogmatic religious instruction in schools established by school boards; and that these powers provoked religious discord throughout the country and violated rights of conscience.

The Resolution was seconded by Henry Richard who concentrated on the denominational aspect of the Act, or rather the part of it that troubled the Nonconformists. He outlined the history of the British and Foreign School Society which grew from the early efforts of the Nonconformist Joseph Lancaster and were in existence years before the National (Anglican) School Society. But as soon as the Church of England began to take an interest it left everyone else behind in the numbers if not the efficiency of their schools. The Church of England, said Richard,

> had every possible advantage in that work. They numbered the wealthiest part of the community in their ranks. While the Dissenters had to build and repair their own chapels, maintain their own ministers, erect and support their own colleges, and sometimes to subscribe large sums of money to protect or promote their own civil and religious rights, the Church of England had all the Ecclesiastical edifices for their sole and exclusive use; they had large Parliamentary grants for the erection of new churches; they had compulsory church-rates to maintain the Church fabrics, and meet other incidental expenses; they had all the enormous national endowments for the support of their ministers, and they monopolized nearly all educational and charitable endowments from the Universities down to the smallest parochial or charity schools.[5]

When Parliament began to provide grants for education the clergy were not restrained by any conscientious scruples from taking any public money the State placed at their disposal for building purposes and teaching their own denominationalism in schools, he added. With all these resources to hand they built thousands of schools over the whole face of the country. The Government had patronised and promoted the Church Schools in every possible way at the expense of every other kind of school.

A prodigious stimulus was given to denominational schools by continuing the building grants to the end of 1870, argued Richard. W. E. Forster must have known how favourable this arrangement would be to denominational schools, particularly the denominational schools belonging to the Church of England. Richard had

warned him of the likely consequences. There were 3,337 applica-
tions for grants in aid for building or enlarging schools. Of these,
2,286 had been approved by the Department; and nearly all were
denominational schools and schools belonging to the Church of
England. On the other hand 91 new schools had been built by
school boards, and 100 had been transferred to them.
Congregational, Wesleyan and schools established by other
Nonconformist denominations tended to transfer to the school
boards. Also, we may assume that the Anglicans understood the
processes of applying for state assistance better than the others,
which could explain why they had grabbed such a large slice of the
available cake. This argument would not have cut any ice with
Henry Richard. To him, Forster's conduct was a mystery. He had,
said Richard, professed to be anxious for the extension of school
boards yet he voluntarily put in the hands of the opponents of
school boards the power to defeat that desire. Why? The only
shadow of a reason Richard had heard was that it relieved the
ratepayers. Well, he supposed that voluntary contributions raised
in order to obtain grants also came from the pockets of the
ratepayers; the only difference was that, under the rate, the assessment would be more equitable. At least, it was refreshing to find
concern for the ratepayers or taxpayers among the Members of the
present Government – a Government that had added an extra
£7,000,000 to the military expenditure in that year alone. Why be
so fastidious about taking £1,500,000 out of the pockets of the taxpayers for building schools?

He referred to an additional 50 per cent given to the denominational schools as compensation for their severance from school
boards, even though the boards still had the power to subsidize
them! He raised the question of the appointment of school inspectors. The two inspectors visiting the schools of Anglesey, one of
the most Nonconformist of Welsh counties, were Anglicans who
went around the island discouraging the formation of school
boards. Also, of the 12 Inspectors appointed during the previous
Parliamentary session, every one was an Anglican.

★ ★ ★

It would be appropriate here to give a brief history of education in
Wales to put Henry Rchard's concerns in context. Wales had a system of education based on the Anglican tradition but which had
evolved in its own way. Griffith Jones of Llanddowror, founder of

the Circulating Schools, had persuaded organisations, such as the Society for Promoting Christian Knowledge, when they were establishing Charity Schools, to ensure that the children were taught through the Welsh language. This had not been the case in Gaelic-speaking Scotland and Ireland. Jones realised that teaching children – or adults for that matter – through a language they did not understand would not succeed. Later, the British and Foreign School Society and the National School Society forgot that lesson and with the infamous *Welsh Not* – where children were punished for speaking Welsh – did try to teach Welsh children through the medium of English. This was a disastrous policy, although it did not undermine the Welsh language as there were so few of these schools.[6] They did not leave much of a mark on Welsh education either, certainly not in the first half of the nineteenth century. It was not until 1843 that the British and Foreign School Society realised how much work needed to be done in Wales. By then the National School Society had taken steps to establish schools in the larger coastal towns, but not in the Welsh-speaking heartland.

Up until 1870 education in England and Wales had operated under a system that was referred to as a voluntary system, although it was voluntary in name only. Before the state in 1833 began to provide assistance for building schools, day schools, where they existed at all, relied on the National School Society and the British School Society. It was a system that relied on the generosity of the nobility – with the state operating as another patron from 1833 onwards. Out of this grew what became known as a Voluntary System. When a Committee of the Privy Council on Education was formed in 1839 the aim of that committee was to provide education by promoting the work of these voluntary agencies. Sir Hugh Owen, an Anglesey man who went to London to make his fortune but instead became an influential bureaucrat, was in charge of the Poor Law Commission. He was a man close to the centre of those movements which were changing society and became a figure of importance in the development of Welsh education, particularly the Bangor Normal College and Aberystwyth University. Owen had been a Calvinistic Methodist – he had attended Jewin Crescent until he married. But his English wife was unable to cope with the Welsh language, whereupon he joined Claremont Congregational Chapel, Pentonville. He was an enthusiast for the British School Society as a means of counteracting the National (Anglican) Schools. In 1843 he sent a letter to the Welsh papers advocating the establishment of British Schools, a letter which had a dramatic response in North and West Wales.[7]

Henry Richard, however, had different ideas on what kind of education system was best suited to Wales and was an advocate of a different voluntary tradition. His grandfather had been one of Griffith Jones's teachers, and his father a stalwart of the Sunday school movement in South Wales. In London, he caught the Congregationalists' enthusiasm for education. Not that Welsh Congregationalist attitudes to education differed to those in England. Before Wales ever dreamt of a system of elementary and secondary education, Congregational ministers, wherever they could, tried to set up schools, or sponsor others to do so. This was the voluntarism embraced by Henry Richard, the voluntarism of the old Radical Congregational Dissent. A Radicalism with a firm social base, but Radicals – like those Henry Richard got to know in London and through the peace movement – sufficiently well-off to be able to afford to be Radical. It also fitted better in South Wales with its greater self-confidence, the product of a greater ease and security in society. The grammar schools of the Congregationalists and other denominations were his ideal – he had been educated at two in Aberystwyth and Llangeitho. It had been a dream of the Congregational Fathers to develop a network of voluntary schools totally free of the state.[8] They may have misunderstood what the relationship between the Government and education should be, but they had good reasons for being suspicious of governments.

Richard, too, had been active in establishing schools in London before becoming involved in education in Wales in 1844. He may have campaigned in Merthyr and Carmarthen even earlier. But in 1844, accompanied by the Rev John Blackburn, minister of Claremont Chapel, the chapel attended by Hugh Owen, he had visited Congregational Chapels in South Wales, to prepare two reports. One was for the Congregational Union of England and Wales on the state of religion in Wales and the other for the denomination's Education Board. In response to the second report a Conference on Education was held in Llandovery, jointly organised with the Wesleyans. A direct result of the conference was the formation of a Normal School to train teachers in Brecon – later moved to Swansea – and the establishment of a number of schools in South Wales.[9]

Henry Richard was keen to establish teacher training colleges in Wales although Hugh Owen advocated sending them to Borough Road College in London, a training college set up in 1817 and linked to the British School Society. According to Owen they would benefit from "the more lively and vivacious Englishmen"! He made other – equally strange – assertions, not least that it was cheaper to live in London. Another of his assertions was that it would be difficult to select a principal for a Normal College in Wales. "If a Wesleyan, or a Congregationalist, or a Calvinistic Methodist, or a Baptist were appointed there is room for fear," he said, "that the denominations outside his own would not place full confidence in him."[10]

Henry Richard for all his long and somewhat eccentric adherence to the principle of voluntarism had a rather holistic view of education. In his fourth chapter in *Letters and Essays on Wales* he explained the difference – and superiority – of the Sunday Schools in Wales compared to those in England:

> One peculiarity of the Sunday-schools in Wales is this, that they comprise not the children of the country merely, but a large proportion of the adults. It is a matter of constant lamentation among the promoters of Sunday-schools in England that the elder scholars, when they have acquired a tolerable proficiency in reading, leave the school, and are withdrawn from the salutary influence which might be otherwise exercised over them by their teachers at the most critical period of their life. But in Wales, however perfectly the young people may learn to read, they do not dream of quitting the school.[11]

An interesting fact about the Welsh Sunday schools – not dwelled upon by Richard – was that they tended to produce readers and public speakers, but not so many writers. The annual religious gathering known as *Y Gymanfa Bwnc*, which he mentions and praises in the same article, may have contributed to that problem. It encouraged readers to learn a chapter from the Bible by heart to be recited by the whole Sunday school and discussed in detail, often from a historical, philosophical and moral perspective.

After 1853 the position of those who believed in the principle of pure voluntary schools had weakened – money, patience and energy were needed to organise and maintain such schools; their advocates, among them David Charles, David Rees and even Henry Richard – were having a re-think. And Welsh people were beginning to see the British Schools as either non-sectarian or simply Nonconformist.

The core of Henry Richard's argument for a voluntary education system independent of any assistance from the Government was his opposition to what he saw as the corrupting influence of the state on the people through its links with the Established Church. He fought a long battle to keep religious instruction out of day schools during the passing of the 1870 Act and afterwards. We can only wonder what his response would be to the growth in our time – particularly in England – of sectarian schools and the way they are promoted and sustained by the Government.

Watkin Williams, the MP for Denbigh Borough, on 24 May 1870, presented a resolution seeking religious equality and parity for Wales with Ireland where Church Disestablishment had now taken place. He argued that all public endowments enjoyed by the Church in Wales should be used to support a secular system of education for Wales.[12] After centuries of neglect, Welsh MPs were following Henry Richard's confident example. George Osborne Morgan, the MP for Denbighshire, who spoke in support of Williams's motion, was another who took up Welsh issues, re-introducing his Burials Bill year after year. Williams's speech makes interesting reading, a lecture in Welsh history to the House of Commons of the kind Henry Richard would deliver from time to time. "The ancient British Church is a Church of pure Christianity, very different from that which is claimed for the Church of England, and that is in many respects curiously analogous to the ideas and opinions of the Nonconformist Churches in Wales at this moment," he said. "The Church of the Britons, or the Church in Wales as it may be called, was in its origin, its inception, and its spirit, a totally distinct Church – a Christian Church which existed many centuries before the Church of England, and which only by fraud and violence was subjected to the Church of England, a proceeding confirmed by Act of Parliament in the reign of Henry VIII." He quoted the French historian Thierry who claimed that in the time of Henry VIII translations of the Scriptures into Welsh had been "carried off from the churches and publicly burnt". This is interesting since William Salesbury's translation of the New Testament was not published until 1567, twenty years after the death of Henry VIII. However, parts of the Gospels had been translated into Welsh much earlier – part of the Gospel according to St Matthew before 1250 and that of St John before 1350. Whatever the veracity of Williams's assertion – or that of his source – it showed Welsh MPs were finding their voices.

Williams's resolution, although unlikely to succeed, was doomed because he had failed to canvass the support of those MPs sympathetic to Disestablishment. Henry Richard had intended to support the motion, but the Prime Minister, Gladstone, unexpect-

edly got up as Williams was sitting down. He suggested that sepa-
rating Wales from England in this special case was impractical. He
also insinuated that Williams's speech was an attack on the English
establishment. The Tories were delighted to see that Gladstone
was not prepared to give to Wales that which he had conceded to
Ireland. Only 45 Members supported Williams's resolution.
Henry Richard was not pleased by Gladstone's intervention in the
debate which probably delayed Disestablishment in Wales by
some decades. Nor was he happy with the position Gladstone had
taken in the Forster Education Act debates and had subjected the
Prime Minister to some stinging rebukes. They were, however, on
good terms and there is no doubt that Gladstone had great respect
for Richard's uncompromising principles.

A report of a boat trip to Greenwich organised by the Cobden
Club which appeared in the *Illustrated Times* gives some indication
of their relationship: "Mr Gladstone was in the boat, and the eloquent Member for Merthyr, who it will be remembered, had
recently censured the Government as severely as Mr Miall did,
was there also. But did the Prime Minister and Mr Richard scowl
at each other? Not a bit of it. When the Prime Minister came
aboard the Member for Merthyr was sitting quietly at the stern,
and very soon after the arrival of the former, he quietly went up to
Mr Richard, cordially shook him by the hand, and then dropped
down at his side and chatted with him ... Such is the way with
political combatants in the House; and long may it be so."[13]

It would be appropriate here to recall the establishment of the
University of Wales and Henry Richard's role in that process. On
15 October 1872, he was present at the opening of Aberystwyth
College. Initially he had been slow to take up the University cause
and it had taken some persuasion to get his support. As already
shown it took a long time to shake off his adherence to the idea of
education being provided through a form of voluntarism and his
resistance to state funding for education. Did he have sympathy
for St David's College, Lampeter, the college his mother's cousin
had been so active in establishing and to which his brother, the
Rev Thomas Richard of Fishguard, had sent his own son to be
educated? There had also been a campaign to establish a
University of Wales based on St David's College. It is unlikely that
he had given much thought to these arguments.

There had been for decades an active group calling themselves
"The Association of Welsh Clergy in the West Riding of the
County of York", patriotic Welsh-speaking clergymen who had

lost patience with the practice of appointing Englishmen to Welsh
bishoprics and likewise clergy who could not speak or understand
Welsh to Welsh-speaking parishes. These clergymen, who formed
an association in 1821, felt free to criticise such practices without
fear of episcopal censure or injury to their own prospects. They
had petitioned the Prime Minister, Sir Robert Peel, on the matter
of appointing English bishops to Welsh sees in 1835; they had
written to the Englishman Connop Thirlwall urging him to
decline the offer of the Bishopric of St David's in 1840; and the
following year they wrote to Prince Albert advocating – among
other things – Welsh and Celtic Professorships at English
Universities. In the 1850s and 1852, being concerned that St
David's College, Lampeter, was "too contracted in its principles to
meet the growing and pressing needs of the Principality" they
petitioned Parliament for a Welsh University. They expressed the
opinion that "the peculiar state of the Principality where four-
fifths of the inhabitants are estranged from the established church,
nothing short of a university founded on broad and liberal principles combining the same privileges and immunities as those of
Oxford, Cambridge, London, Durham and others, can meet the
present necessities of the country, or raise the moral and intellectual character of the people, be they Churchmen or Dissenters".[14]
The petition also provided detailed suggestions for a constitution
and senate for a national university.

In 1852 Hugh Owen, who in 1845 had been advocating
Borough Road as the ideal college for training Welsh teachers, was
also occupying his mind with the idea of a college or colleges for
Wales. Unlike Henry Richard he had no qualms about using public money for educational purposes. Another Welsh expatriate who
made an important and generous contribution towards establishing a National University for Wales, was William Williams, MP for
Coventry and, later, Lambeth. Williams is best remembered for
initiating the 1847 *Report of the Commission of Enquiry into the State of
Education in Wales* (The Treason of the Blue Books). He deserves to
be remembered for more positive contributions to Welsh education. In April 1854, Hugh Owen called a meeting of some prominent London Welshmen, convened at the home of the surgeon
Thomas Charles – of the same family as Thomas Charles founder
of the Welsh Sunday schools.[15] Among those present were Lewis
Edwards, the Rev Henry Rees, George Osborne Morgan, Richard
Davies, David Charles (Trefecca), Samuel Roberts (SR) and
Enoch G. Salisbury. Was Henry Richard there? Perhaps, although

he is not mentioned. A sub-committee, consisting of Morgan, Salisbury and Owen, was formed to draft a blueprint for a University for Wales. Osborne Morgan in his address at the official opening of Aberystwyth College, on 15 October 1872, nearly 20 years later, recalled that meeting and the work of the sub-committee.

It appears that what Owen and his friends had in mind was something similar to the Irish Queen's Colleges model, or possibly London University. The Queen's Colleges, established under The Queen's Colleges (Ireland) Act 1845, were endowed by the state, and set up in response to the demands for education from the Catholic community. (With Protestant opposition to such theology and the Pope officially condemning them, the colleges survived if not as originally intended.) However, the University for Wales project had to be shelved for some years. There were other complicated educational issues – such as establishing teacher training colleges and Hugh Owen busied himself setting up the Bangor Normal College. In 1854 the Crimea War began, followed by the Indian uprising – all requiring the Government's undivided attention. In the Swansea Eisteddfod of 1863, Dr Thomas Nicholas of the Carmarthen Presbyterian College gave a lecture with the title "High Schools and a University for Wales", which brought the National Eisteddfod into the University movement for the first time.[16] Hywel Teifi Edwards saw this as an articulation of the "utilitarian mindset" of Hugh Owen and his friends, namely "a solid, factual higher education that would allow the offspring of the middle class to compete with their contemporaries in England and Scotland for the most respectable jobs ..."[17] The intention was certainly to provide higher education for the Welsh middle class.

When the Castle Hotel, Aberystwyth, was bought in March 1867, as a suitable building for the college the dream was beginning to come true and the idea into an institution. After a disappointing start the response to the appeal for money began to gather pace. Dr David Charles and others scoured the country in 1868 looking for contributions. Another person busily involved in the campaign whose name has been forgotten was David Thomas (1813–1894), a minister in Stockwell, a prolific author, compiler of *A Biblical Liturgy for the Use of Evangelical Churches and Homes*, and editor of the expository in many volumes, *The Homilist*. Thomas was born near Tenby and he was also founder of the Working Men's Club and Institute. A General Committee of 100 was estab-

lished on 14 May 1868, and presented its first appeal for Government assistance. Disraeli refused to receive the deputation. Then,
following the election of a Liberal Government at the end of the
year campaigning began in earnest and the Welsh MPs, Henry
Richard in particular, began to lobby Gladstone. The Prime
Minister at first appeared sympathetic and said that Wales had
every right to expect favourable consideration.[18] In a report of a
meeting Henry Richard and George Osborne Morgan had with
Gladstone on 28 May 1870, the Prime Minister "admitted that it
was impossible to place Wales, with its clearly marked nationality,
and its inhabitants divided from England by a strong line of
demarcation both of race and language, upon the same footing as
an English town or district however populous or important."[19]
However, although a precedent had been set with the Irish and
Scottish colleges, Richard and Morgan had no success. The
Government, it is worth noting, objected to contributing to or
recognising any colleges in England, apart from Oxford and
Cambridge – to maintain standards, so they argued. Throughout
the nineteenth century only three universities were established in
England: Durham (1832), London (1836) and Victoria, Manchester (1880) – while Wales established four, Lampeter, Aberyst-
wyth, Bangor and Cardiff.

A meeting was held at the Westminster Palace Hotel, London,
on 25 December 1869, where it was reported that contributions to
the Aberystwyth college fund were still less that what had been
promised and some were refusing to contribute until they were
assured that Government aid would be secured. The wealthy
classes had contributed little – although David Davies eventually
contributed the princely sum of £3,000 towards the building fund.
But the report also noted that "the Quarrymen of Merionethshire
and Carnarvonshire had set an example to the gentlemen of Wales
in the stimulus which they had given to the movement."[20] Henry
Richard's strong non-denominational line probably did not help.
Although the individual denominations had made great sacrifices
to build chapels and theological colleges, such as the Presbyterian
College in Bala and the Congregationalist College in Brecon, they
were not quick to unite to create a non-denominational college.
And when Thomas Charles Edwards – son of Lewis Edwards and
great-grandson of Thomas Charles – was appointed the first
Principal of Aberystwyth, the other denominations became suspi-
cious that the college was under the control of the Calvinistic
Methodists.[21] In August 1869, the Committee expressed the hope

William Williams

that the college would open soon. Henry Richard was one of 60 men present at College House on 17 November 1869, where Dr David Charles, the Secretary of the Committee, had his headquarters. Also present was Samuel Morley, the Bristol MP who had been generous with his money and energy to educational, Nonconformist and social developments in England and Wales. He contributed £1,000 to the college fund. Another MP to contribute £1,000 was William Williams, instigator of the 1847 "Treason of the Blue Books" Report. The main subject over breakfast at the 17 November meeting was "the present position and future prospects" of the national movement.[22]

Thomas Charles Edwards accepted the Committee's invitation to be the college's first Principal in July 1872, and the college was officially opened on 15 October. It was a "gala day" with Aberystwyth "nicely decked with bunting", a choir, brass band and numerous speeches. Among the Welsh MPs were Sir Thomas Lloyd, E. M. Richards, George Osborne Morgan and Henry Richard. There was one sour note – the Principal of St David's College, Lampeter, found an excuse for not attending and could not find anyone to represent him.[23] A letter from Gladstone was read which assured everyone of his best wishes for the college's future. Henry Richard made two speeches during the day, the one in the morning delivered immediately after Gladstone's letter had been read. The next step, he said, had to be to ask for a grant from the Government. He referred to the Prime Minister's interest in the college and his full approval of its non-denominational nature. Richard added that the Committee would be quite happy to receive the monetary equivalent of two or three Armstrong guns and for the college to be given the same consideration as that received by the Universities of Scotland and Ireland.[24] "We Welsh do not ask for favouritism, but merely to be placed on the same footing as other countries, so that our young men may be fairly started in the race of life," he said, suggesting that he, like Hugh Owen, viewed Aberystwyth as a place to prepare the sons of the Welsh middle-class to compete in the jobs market with those of England and Scotland. Despite Henry Richard's optimistic words, Aberystwyth received no assistance from the Government for years. When Gladstone spoke at the official opening of Nottingham University in September 1877 – Nottingham was actually founded in 1798 – he praised the love the Welsh people had for education. "With no assistance at all from any public fund of any kind they have within the last five or six years founded a large and important College at Aberystwyth," he said.[25] The college was sustained almost entirely for 10 years by the contributions from the middle and working classes – with the quarrymen and coalminers contributing generously. In 1882 Aberystwyth received £2,000 from the Government – it was the first grant it ever gave to a Welsh college. It will be necessary to return and look at the development of University education in Wales and Henry Richard's role in that process.

★ ★ ★ ★

The demands on Henry Richard's time in matters to do with Wales were increasing. He was prominent in establishing the Welsh Congregational Union (Undeb yr Annibynwyr Cymraeg) as a separate denomination, but maintaining its links with the Congregational Union of England and Wales. Since 1837 there had been efforts to encourage the Welsh Congregationalists – their chapels were almost totally Welsh-speaking – to take a greater interest in the affairs of the Congregational Union centrally.[26] A series of revivals had swept through Wales and the Congregationalists in England watched these developments with some envy and no doubt hoped to capitalise on this fervour which was not reflected in England. But the Welsh were reluctant to take an active part in the work of the Union. At one point the English wanted to discipline the Welsh for their lack of enthusiasm by deleting the word Wales from the title, Congregational Union of England and Wales. Henry Richard persuaded them to desist.

The Congregational Union of England and Wales held their 1871 Autumn meetings in Swansea and this time the English delegates were surprised to find that for once Wales was well represented. On Wednesday, 11 October, in a meeting at Zion Chapel, a motion was presented to establish a Union of Welsh (language) Churches. Henry Richard, who had been for 15 years a Congregational minister in London, and remained a prominent member of the denomination in England, was enthusiastic in his support. A committee was formed to draft a constitution and a public meeting was held the following night in Ebenezer Chapel chaired by Henry Richard. The motion presented had all the hallmarks of the skilled politician, and was carefully worded and equivocal, leaving room for change at some future stage. It was approved almost unanimously. The important decision was to establish the Welsh Union – and this had been done.[27] Five years later, in 1876, Henry Richard was elected President of the Congregational Union of England and Wales – the first layman to be so honoured by the denomination.

On 24 July 1871, Richard was present at a meeting to honour the Merthyr composer, Joseph Parry, who would soon be returning to America. Richard spoke with great enthusiasm of the pleasure to be derived from music and its benefits to the people of Wales. Dulais Rhys in his biography of Joseph Parry says Richard and Parry were related – distantly – their paternal ancestors coming from Moylegrove and Trefîn, both villages in Pembrokeshire. He also attended a gathering the following year to celebrate the success of Caradog's Choir.[28] Caradog, Griffith Rhys Jones of Aberdare, conducted the South Wales choir which won the choral prize at the Crystal Palace in July 1872 and 1873. In 1872 the Welsh choir defeated Sir Joseph Proudman's London Choir, one of those successes which did much to cement Wales's reputation as the Land of Song. After that the competition was disbanded as no choir dared challenge Caradog's. The £1,000 trophy can still be seen at St Fagan's Museum of Welsh Life, near Cardiff.

With the Franco-Prussian War continuing Russia saw an opportunity to put right the injustice it perceived to have suffered in the Paris Treaty of 1857. With France in trouble and Britain to all appearances not going to the aid of its former ally, Russia, in October 1870, moved to annul the agreement which allowed other countries to sail their warships through the Dardanelle and

Bosphorus Straits and restricted Russian right to organise its navy
in the Black Sea. Russia informed the other signatories of the 1857
Treaty of its intentions. Although Britain was readier than most to
ignore or dishonour treaties, and although the part of the Treaty
relating to the Straits and the Black Sea was of no military or political relevance to Britain, the newspapers were whipping the political hawks into a state of frenzy. After all, Russia was not seeking
re-negotiation, it was simply announcing its intention to revoke
the Treaty. Richard battled against the militarist mob and his
attacks on some prominent humanitarians and Christians who
were advocating war, men like Lord Shaftesbury and the Bishop of
Carlisle, were quite personal. However, with Gladstone as Prime
Minister and the Liberals in Government Richard was able to
exert sufficient influence to persuade Britain not to go to war
against Russia. A conference was arranged and held in London
where it was agreed to restore Russia's rights prior to 1857.[29]

George Osborne Morgan raised the controversial appointment
of a non-Welsh speaking judge, Homersham Cox, to the Mid-
Wales County Court Circuit on 8 March 1872. Cox was an
Englishman, arrogant, and impatient with those who spoke Welsh
and assumed that anyone able to speak a few sentences in English
would be able to give a fair account of themselves in the language
in court. Following a series of complaints and Osborne Morgan's
campaign, Cox was replaced. This was the second occasion for a
matter uniquely relevant to Wales to be brought before
Parliament, another sign of the growing confidence of the 1868
generation of Welsh MPs.[30]

Osborne Morgan distanced himself from any suggestion that
the Welsh were moving towards self-government – all they
wanted was "the natural and inalienable birthright of every subject
of the Queen – the right to have justice dealt out to them so far as
circumstances would permit promptly, cheaply, and efficiently".
He explained that the Mid-Wales County Court Circuit, com-
prised the whole of the county of Meirioneth, and parts of the
counties of Caernarfon, Cardigan, and Montgomery – the most
exclusively Welsh parts of Wales. For the benefit of "Saxon friends
as had never penetrated into those remote localities", he noted that
at least four-fifths of the people habitually spoke the Welsh language, and, as a rule, spoke and understood nothing else. He went
on: "They carried on the daily business and intercourse of life,
they wrote their letters, they concluded their bargains, and they
made their wills in that language." He related an incident that

George Osborne Morgan by Spy

occurred not many years previously of a very learned judge who had been explaining "with great lucidity" the law in an ejectment case, when he was interrupted by the foreman of the jury, who called out in Welsh – "Tell that old gentleman to cut his speech short – we haven't understood a word he has been saying, and we settled yesterday who was to have the property over a glass of claret at the Mostyn Arms." Matters had not changed much since the time of that incident, added Morgan.

Henry Richard spoke in support of Osborne Morgan, if not as amusingly. It was well laced with sarcasm. The Welsh people, he said, were anxious to learn English to the extent "that in all the schools throughout the Principality – not merely National and British schools, which were supposed to be more or less under the influence of the Government – but in all private adventure schools, the English language was taught, not merely with, but even to the exclusion of, the Welsh language … In most of the day schools in Wales, wherever a child was overheard talking Welsh during school hours he rendered himself liable to punishment." There were, he went on, a considerable number of Welshmen who had learnt to write and speak it fairly well. "But it was true that, while willing and ever anxious to learn that language, the

EDUCATION AND ENGLISH JUDGES   177

Welsh people were yet strongly attached to their mother tongue; and why should they not be? Was there anything monstrous, unnatural, criminal, or barbarous in a people desiring to retain the language of their forefathers? Even Englishmen, though they had not such a language as the Welsh, were attached to the language of their fathers." He proceeded to tell the story of a Dr Bowles, an Englishman who had been appointed by the Bishop of Bangor to a living in Anglesey:

> In 1773 the churchwardens, aided by a society called the Cymmrodorion ... brought an action in the Court of Arches, and attempted to deprive Dr. Bowles of the living, on the ground of his ignorance of the Welsh language. And on that occasion the arguments used by the advocates of Dr. Bowles were to the effect that, although the Doctor did not understand the language, he was in possession of the living and could not be turned out; that Wales was a conquered country, and that it was the duty of the Bishops to promote English clergymen in order to introduce the language, and that that had always been the policy of the Legislature. That was the policy; but what was the result? Not to make Englishmen of Welshmen so much as to make Dissenters of them.

As a Nonconformist, Richard had no objection to that result; but clearly that was not what the promoters of that policy wished or expected. If they wanted to force the Welsh people to become English by laws which pressed hard on their rights, they would fail.

Apart from the Conservative John Henry Scourfield, of Pembrokeshire, who complained of having to listen from time to time to sermons in Welsh – to which Richard retorted that he should learn "the language of the people among whom he moved" – Morgan had the support of all the Welsh MPs. The conclusion of the debate was the passing of the following resolution:

> That in the opinion of this House, it is desirable, in the interests of the due administration of justice, that the Judge of a County Court District in which the Welsh language is generally spoken, and as far the limits of selection will allow, should be able to speak and understand that language.

It was a weak resolution. But with Home Secretary Henry Austin Bruce, who was – in the words of Osborne Morgan, half Welsh, if not unfortunately wholly Welsh – there was hope that the arguments would be understood. Bruce, also, had experience of

administering the law in Merthyr Tydfil where a substantial per-
centage of the population were monoglot Welsh speakers. Not
long afterwards he appointed Welsh-speaking Gwilym Williams of
Trecynon – son of the coal owner and poet, David Williams (Alaw
Goch) – Stipendiary Magistrate for Pontypridd and Rhondda.
Williams was later, in 1884, appointed judge of the Mid-Wales
County Court Circuit.

After Parliament went into the Summer recess in August 1872,
Richard and his wife set off for Ireland – combining work with
pleasure.[31] They crossed from Holyhead and it appears that Henry
Richard was delighted to find nearly all the crew were Welsh, and
that they enthusiastically welcomed their celebrated compatriot.
Richard took the opportunity to deliver speeches on peace and
arbitration in Dublin, Cork and Limerick and visiting as many
places as possible in the course of three weeks. He met a number
of Quakers, most of them wealthy men but in the main politically
conservative and lukewarm on the subject of peace. Few came to
listen to him and he had to present a very basic case as they were
not well-informed on the subject. The sister of Augusta Matilda,
Henry Richard's wife, and her husband, came to join them, and
they travelled together down the Shannon in an uncomfortable
boat to Kilrush and by bus to Kilkee where Richard describes the
wild coastline, its caves and natural bridges in some detail. At
Limerick he visited a school organised by the Congregation of
Christian Brothers, a lay Catholic order established in Waterford
in 1802. It was dedicated to educating the poor and had, at the
time, about 2,000 children in its care as well as industrial schools
where pupils received instruction in a variety of crafts and trades.
"It is clear to me," he wrote, "that these Catholic Orders study to
win the hearts of the children, whom they rule by love. It was
pleasant to see how fondly and familiarly some of the little creatures clung to the hand of the good brother who accompanied
me." Richard was equally favourable in his opinion of the Society
of Vincent de Paul convent and orphanage, and he was happy to
admit that the managers of these Catholic institutions on the
whole did valuable work, and did it well.

The head of an infants school, based on the outskirts of Dublin,
and connected to the Anglican National Society, told him that the
chief opponent of the principle of united secular and separate religious instruction was Thomas Carlyle, one of the first commissioners. He, by introducing scripture lessons and a religious
element into books on other subjects into the National Schools

caused the degeneration into narrow denominationalism. "It is an instructive history from which English Nonconformists would do well to take warning," wrote Richard.[32] The original intention had been to create an education structure that was multi-denominational, with a clear divide between literary and moral education and religious education.

Chapter 16

The International Arbitration Resolution

Henry Richard's greatest Parliamentary success came in July 1873. Five years after he was first elected to the House of Commons, the opportunity came for him to present his resolution on International Arbitration, a question that had occupied his mind for the best part of his life. His success placed him in the front rank of Parliamentarians as an orator and legislator.[1] Two years elapsed between 11 August 1871, when Richard placed his notice of motion in the House of Commons Notice Book on, and its actual submission on 8 July 1873. Two years of great activity, with three agents researching and preparing information, organising petitions and addresses and articles for the newspapers. A time of excitement and agitation, with meetings held at many of Britain's large towns and cities, Henry Richard speaking at most of them.

In a House of Commons where half the members had some connection with the military establishment, attracting attention to the subject of peace and arbitration would be no easy task. "I recall Mr Cobden, when he gave notice of a similar motion over 20 years ago, telling me that the idea was so new, and to the majority of Members appeared so foolish, that a quiet laugh went through the House," Richard told the Congregational Union of England and Wales at the meeting in Swansea in October 1871. "But we did all in our power outside Parliament to stir some excitement in favour of the resolution." On that occasion, said Richard, Cobden had testified that other MPs had approached him asking for more information "as very Quaker in my borough had written to me about it".[2] Richard trusted that not only every Quaker would write to his MP but that every Nonconformist in England and Wales would do so, too. Whether or not he succeeded in his aspiration, it was an intense campaign. It was a fine example of outside pressure combining with meticulous activity within the House of Commons.

It was also a time of forging significant alliances. The Franco-Prussian War had launched another rush of rearming. But it was also a period of consolidation in the peace movement. A month after France had attacked Prussia the carpenter and trade unionist W. Randal Cremer (1828–1908) established the Workmen's Peace Committee.[3] There were no fundamental differences between the objectives of Cremer's soon to be re-named Workmen's Peace Association and the Peace Society, of which Henry Richard was the Secretary. They advocated the settlement of all international disputes by arbitration and the establishment of a High Court of Nations for that purpose. Like Henry Richard they stressed the danger, immorality and the cost of standing armies and called for mutual and simultaneous reduction of armed forces with a view to their entire abolition. Cremer was elected Member of Parliament in East London in 1885 and was awarded the Nobel Peace Prize in 1903. The Workmen's Peace Association and the Peace Society joined forces to campaign and work together after Henry Richard had given notice of his motion. It was another interesting step in Richard's life as it brought him into close contact with trade unionists and other working-class leaders to the left of the Peace Society.[4] Men who had their own contacts in the radical Continental peace movements. Although rather distrustful at first, Richard soon showed a readiness to work with any independent initiatives for peace.

This gave new life to the peace movement throughout Britain and sparked one of the movement's most dynamic periods in nineteenth-century Wales. When Henry Richard asked members of the Congregational Union of England and Wales in October 1871 to write to their MPs urging them to support his resolution he had an enthusiastic response. SR, who had returned to Wales from the United States in 1867, took a prominent role in the campaign.[5] He, and others, addressed public meetings in Tywyn, Talybont, Carmarthen, Llanelli, Aberdare, Tredegar, Llanbryn-mair, Llansadwrn, Machynlleth and Wrexham. There was support from the Congregational Chapels of Caernarfon, Denbigh and Flint. In November 1871, in a Liberal Party conference at Aberystwyth the subject of International Arbitration was discussed. Henry Richard spoke about the resolution and the two radical MPs, George Osborne Morgan (Denbighshire) and E. M.

Richards (Cardiganshire) were both present.

"If in the time of the Saxons the kingdoms which formed the Heptarchy found it expedient to form themselves into one kingdom, governed by one common law, there is no reason why kingdoms no further apart than England, France and Germany, should not unite under one law for the settlement of their quarrels," argued Richard. He was warmly applauded when he suggested that governments should appoint their most eminent jurists to create an international code of conduct, to establish a court of arbitration of distinguished men, independent of political considerations, so that when there was a dispute between nations it could be taken to that court. He proceeded: "Let the nations at variance employ counsel, let evidence be taken, the dispute fully discussed, and let a discussion be given according to the dictates of reason and justice, not settled by an appeal to brute force. The question is quite unconnected with either political party. The staunchest Tory or the most rabid Liberal may help it on, and I entreat my brother Welshmen to assist in doing away with the horrors of war."[6]

Two years seems a long time between Henry Richard giving his notice of motion and presenting his resolution to the House of Commons. There was a good reason for the delay – the *Alabama* dispute, which had been simmering since 1863, appeared to be coming to a conclusion in 1872 and Richard and some of his friends decided it would be tactically wise to let the matter be settled before presenting the International Arbitration resolution to Parliament.[7]

The CSS *Alabama* was a steamer built in Birkenhead by Laird and Son. The ship had been ordered by Captain James D. Bulloch of the Confederate States Navy during the American Civil War. There was no doubting its purpose – it was a robust vessel and, powered by sail and steam, it was capable of 13.25 knots and could inflict great damage to the North's merchant shipping. The United States Ambassador to London, Charles Francis Adams, had ample proof that the *Alabama* was intended for hostile purposes and he wrote to Foreign Secretary Lord John Russell requesting that the ship be prevented from sailing. In spite of the request the *Alabama* sailed out of Birkenhead on 29 July 1862, with a number of guests on board what was deemed to be a final test voyage. But when the ship was a few miles out at sea, the guests were put in a tug and taken back to port. The *Alabama* sailed on to near Moelfre, Anglesey, where it lay at anchor for a couple of days on the pretext of waiting to find out if it had permission to sail onwards. When orders eventually arrived ordering the ship to be detained, it had gone. It sailed to the port of Terciera in the Azores where it was met by two British ships with arms and was refitted as a warship. It then sailed on towards the United States where it proceeded to capture or destroy 65 merchant ships before it was itself sunk by Northern battleships. Another burning issue was that the *Alabama* allegedly sailed from time to time under the Union Jack, attacking ships from other countries as well as merchant shipping from the North. There were strong reactions from the North who viewed this as an act of treachery, not just by the ship's captain, but by the British Government for their negligence in allowing the ship to be built and then to sail unhindered out of Birkenhead. Lord Russell accepted responsibility and declared "that the *Alabama* ought to have been detained during the four days in which I was waiting for the opinion of the Law Officers. But I think that the fault was not that of the Commissioners of Customs; it was my fault as Secretary of State for Foreign Affairs, of an error of judgement."[8]

In spite of initially admitting responsibility, when the United States sought compensation for the destruction done by the *Alabama* Russell ignored all subsequent appeals from the USA. On 23 October 1873, Ambassador Adams wrote again to Russell gently suggesting that the US might be amenable to seeking a neutral and independent body to arbitrate. For two years Russell ignored Adams's friendly and reasonable approach, then, on 30 August 1865, he dispatched an arrogant and peremptory response in which he declared that "Her Majesty's Government are the sole guardians of their own honour".[9] The matter had been raised from time to time in the House of Commons and tension was increasing on both sides of the Atlantic. After two more years of delay the matter was re-opened early in 1868 when Reverdy Johnson replaced Adams as the US Ambassador to Britain. Before he had been elected to Parliament Henry Richard had been trying to put pressure on the Cabinet to put the matter to arbitration. Also at the beginning of 1868, Richard prepared a memorandum and a deputation to present it to the new Foreign Secretary, Lord Edward Henry Stanley, who was more amenable than Russell. Stanley welcomed the memorandum, in fact he was the first of the Ministers of the Crown to agree to the principle of arbitration and it is likely that he would have settled the matter. But at the end of 1868, the Tories lost the General election. With Gladstone now Prime Minister, the Liberals in Government and Henry Richard himself an MP, he was not going to let the matter slide further. Richard made contact with Lord Clarendon, who had been so helpful in getting the arbitration clause, Protocol 23, inserted in the 1856 Paris Peace Treaty. He also contacted Reverdy Johnson and with both those men in favour of arbitration it appeared that the matter would soon be resolved. Then Clarendon died in 1870, Johnson was recalled to America and there was another delay before the matter was raised again. Lord Granville (Leveson-Gower) was appointed to replace Clarendon and he informed the USA immediately of Britain's intention to settle the dispute as quickly as possible. A Joint High Commission of the two countries met in Washington and it was agreed to ask an Arbitration Tribunal, meeting in Geneva, to adjudicate. A Tribunal of five men was nominated, representing Britain, the USA, Italy (Count Frederick Sclopis, who chaired the Tribunal), the Swiss Confederation and Brazil. The Tribunal met in the Town Hall in Geneva, in a room that was subsequently re-named the Alabama Room. The dispute was resolved in 1872 with Britain having to pay $15.5 million (£3,100,000) in compensation to the USA.[10]

The result was much to Henry Richard's satisfaction, because at one stage the relationship between Britain and the US had deteriorated so much it seemed likely that the two countries would go to war. The establishment of this Arbitration Tribunal set an important precedent and was proof that it was possible to settle disputes between two powerful countries. Not everyone, however, was satisfied, and this was a blow to the idea of arbitration in Britain. English pride was badly dented when the adjudication became known. The *Western Mail*[11] was of the opinion that "no-one but a child would venture to assert that England would have yielded to Spain or Denmark what she has now conceded to the United States". Even the most pacifist of Welsh language papers, *Y Cronicl*, was unhappy. Henry Richard responded with a speech in Merthyr in December 1872 when he praised the Gladstone administration for its readiness to settle the dispute, adding: "If anybody imagines that arbitration is a cheap and easy method of having our own way under all circumstances and at all times, then I admit it would be of no use."[12] The adjudication of the *Alabama* Tribunal may have been another reason why the Gladstone Government lost more of its support in 1871–1872. However, it gave hope and confidence to the peace movement and the supporters of Henry Richard's resolution. It also renewed interest in the subject of international arbitration. The West of England and South Wales International

Arbitration Association was established as an auxiliary of the Peace Society. The Association had the support of ministers of religion of all denominations, many businessmen, educationists and trade unions on both sides of the Bristol Channel. Petitions were collected by the Methodist Free Churches in South Wales, the Baptists in Meirionethshire and the Workmen's Peace Association in England and Wales collected 1,038,000 signatures.[13]

On 8 July 1873, Richard presented his motion to the House of Commons. It was nine in the evening when he was called to speak. He sat on the far end of the third bench, exactly where Richard Cobden sat when he presented a similar resolution in 1849.[14] There were not many Members in the House when he began speaking – speaking slowly, in measured language – but soon more MPs arrived until there were around 200 present. The visitors galleries, however, were full. The wording of the motion was as follows:

> That an humble Address be presented to Her Majesty, praying that She will be graciously pleased to instruct Her Principal Secretary of State for Foreign Affairs to enter into communication with Foreign Powers with a view to further improvement in International Law and the establishment of a general and permanent system of International Arbitration. [15]

He referred to the many petitions organised by the denominations and the churches – including the Church of England – and gave a special mention to the work done by the Workmen's Peace Association in support of the motion. Richard could confidently claim that there was hardly a Member in the House who had not had a petition presented to him.

He described how Christian and civilised countries, when there was disagreement would rush at each other's throats in the most barbaric manner. The reason was that no "regular and recognized means" existed to settle these disputes. And since the sword was "the only acknowledged solvent of international disputes", these nations believed that their only choice was for each and every nation to provide itself with the largest possible force. As a result, there were between 4,000,000 and 5,000,000 of Europe's finest men in the prime and vigour of life in the armies of Europe, at a cost that was an enormous and an almost intolerable burden on tax payers. The total cost of all these armies was an astounding £550 million a year. He spoke of the working class labouring, below and above the ground, on the surface of the oceans to earn money which was then swept into the bottomless abyss of military expenditure. He referred to those countries engaged in the tyranny of conscription to force men to serve in their armies and navies and the resulting misery to their families.[16] Such waste, he said. After all a soldier produces nothing – he eats and destroys the produce of other men.

"While spending so much of time, thought, skill, and money in organizing war, is it not worth while to bestow some forethought and care in trying to organize peace?" he asked. He listed the countries that were nearly bankrupt because of the burden of armaments. He also listed examples of instances where arbitration had resulted in conciliation. "Perhaps it may be said in reference to the cases of successful arbitration I have cited that they referred to comparatively small matters," he said.

> My answer is, that they could not possibly refer to smaller matters than those which have often led to long, bloody, and desolating wars between nations. They were not smaller matters, for instance, than the question whether the cupola of a particular church at Jerusalem should be repaired by Greek or Latin monks, and yet that was the quarrel which, through the infinite un-wisdom of some of the Great Powers, led to a war which cost Europe, according to Mr. Kinglake,[17] 1,000,000 of human lives and some four or five hundred millions of money. But. I may be told, in reference to this and similar cases, that the avowed and apparent causes of a war are often not the real ones, that they are mere superficial pretexts, but that there are occult forces at work which impel nations irresistibly into collision with each other. But all this talk is mere fatalism, the elaborate attempts of men to find some justification for their follies and crimes by referring them to the operation of natural or providential laws, instead of their own evil passions. Men love to believe that they are driven into ill-doing by necessity … And I can quote the authority of the most experienced statesman of his time as respects, at least, all recent wars. Lord Russell has said, 'On looking back at all the wars which have been carried on during the last century, and examining into the causes of them, I do not see one of these wars in which, if there had been proper temper between the parties, the questions in dispute might not have been settled without recourse to arms.'

He cited the acceptance of Protocol 23 in the 1856 Paris Peace Treaty as an indication that even the Great Powers were beginning to recognize that there is some principle in the world besides force for regulating the intercourse of States. The successful recourse to arbitration in the matter of the *Alabama* had been another positive

Henry Richard by Spy

step. The importance now, he added, was that every arrangement for arbitration should take place before the quarrel escalated and the passions of the people were aroused.

The motion was seconded by Anthony John Mundella, MP for Sheffield, and then Gladstone got to his feet. He looked tired and appeared incapable of any great effort.[18] In spite of that he spoke for 45 minutes giving warm praise to Henry Richard's speech. Nevertheless it was a strange contribution. He sympathised with Henry Richard's intentions, but would not support his method of achieving those aims. He argued that it would be better for the Government to give its full attention to the matter of arbitration. He reminded Henry Richard how Lord Palmerston had advised Cobden in 1849 to refrain from calling for a division and that his decision to ignore that advice had been unwise. Gladstone had just one reason for opposing Richard's attempt to get support for the motion: that it could put in jeopardy any chances of proceeding with such an important cause. At the same time he admitted that he was conscious of the importance of the motion and convinced that "this country" had a great and honourable destiny in relation to this subject and that it was necessary to proceed carefully, step by step, taking care to act moderately, with good will and justice. He insisted that the time was not yet ripe for such a motion as "public opinion was not yet prepared for such a desirable way of settling questions in which the national honour and prestige were at stake". He then urged Henry Richard to withdraw the motion. Fine words to charm the pacifists in the visitors gallery.

The next speaker, Sir Wilfrid Lawson, MP for Carlisle, was not so easily charmed, and was surprised that Gladstone had been so complimentary of Henry Richard's speech while at the same time asking him to withdraw the motion. While Lawson was speaking Richard held a hurried consultation with his supporters and it was decided not to prolong the debate. When Lawson sat down Richard got to his feet, thanked the Prime Minister for his friendly words and announced that he wished to seek the judgement of the House on his motion. The fact that Henry Richard had ignored the appeal of the Prime Minister came as a complete surprise to the supporters of the Government and Lord Enfield quickly got to his feet and moved "The Previous Question", thus ending the debate and voting to decide whether to have a division on Henry Richard's motion. Many of the Conservatives were absent as were many of the Government's more loyal supporters. July 1873 had been a particularly warm month, and many of the Liberals, having been assured by the Whip that there would not be a vote that evening, had gone off to enjoy themselves at some festivities in connection with the visit of the Shah of Persia. The House divided on "The Previous Question" and to loud cheers is was announced that the "Ayes" were defeated 88 to 98 – a majority of 10. Henry Richard's motion was then presented and the House approved it without division. The old fox had won a famous, if unexpected, victory. Of the 33 Welsh MPs, he received the support of 11, three were against and two were accidentally shut out.

A few days later the Queen's response was read out in Parliament:

> I am sensible of the force of the philanthropic motives which have dictated your address. I have at all times sought to extend, both by advice and by example, as occasion might offer, the practice of closing controversies between nations by submission to the impartial judgement of friends, and to encourage the adoption of international rules intended for the equal benefit of all. I shall continue to pursue a similar course, with due regard to time and opportunity, when it shall seem likely to be attended with advantage.[19]

This was all that could be expected in an official response from the

Queen, but Henry Richard was satisfied. Apparently 125 Liberal MPs had endorsed the motion, some having paired with the Tories and others unavoidably absent. But with over 600 MPs he would not have succeeded without a combination of quick thinking, cunning and luck. Richard's speech was widely praised, with only the *Times* and *Spectator* critical, the *Times* arguing it was premature while the *Spectator* argued that arbitration could only be effective if backed up by force. The Welsh language papers showed little enthusiasm apart from *Baner ac Amserau Cymru*, which confidently proclaimed that Henry Richard's victory would have a great moral influence on the Governments of Europe and the world at large.[20]

When Europe got the news that the British Parliament had supported Henry Richard's motion there was considerable excitement and praise in the Continental papers. The entire debate was translated into French and German. He received many letters from people who had worked with him in the cause of peace – men like August Visschers from Belgium and Frédéric Passy from France – all showering him with praise. The responses from Denmark and Italy were particularly warm. A letter arrived from the American Senator Charles Sumner:

> I thank you for making this motion, and also for not yielding to Mr Gladstone's request to withdraw it. Your speech marks an epoch in a great cause. It will make your Parliamentary life historic. How absurd to call your motion Utopian. There is no question so supremely practical, for it concerns not merely one nation but every nation, and even its discussion promises to diminish the terrible chances of war.[21]

The letters and the response convinced Richard to go on a tour of Europe to seal the success. But before departing he and his wife visited the little Mid-Wales spa of Llanwrtyd where they met his sister Hannah Evans – now widowed – and her daughter Margaret, who suffered from poor health. From there they went briefly to Cardiganshire with the intention of proceeding to the National Eisteddfod in Mold where Richard was one of the Day Presidents. They were still in Cardiganshire when news came of the death by drowning of two of Mrs Richard's nieces – the only daughters of her widowed sister, Mrs Fell – while on holiday in Ilfracombe. It was a dreadful shock for the family. "We immediately joined our stricken ones," wrote Mrs Richard in her diary, "and during the few days that had to be spent there before proceeding to London, all were strengthened and comforted by my dear husband's soothing influence and tender sympathy."[22] During the following year the families of the sisters, including Richard and his wife moved from Kennington Park to Bolton Gardens, one large family in accord. Over the next 14 years he was looked upon by his wife's sisters as the brother they never had, "a true friend, and wise counsellor, ever ready to share every burden, full of tenderest sympathy in all our sorrows." After the death of Hannah, Henry's sister, in 1884, her daughter Margaret was adopted by them and she, too, became part of the extended family.

Chapter 17

Pilgrimage of Peace

The family tragedy made it necessary to postpone the journey to the continent until September. Then on 18 September Henry Richard and his wife set off on their tour of Europe, on what would be his great pilgrimage of peace. His intention was to make personal contact with the parliamentarians and senators of Europe and urge them to support and promote his campaign for international arbitration. They arrived in Brussels where Richard renewed his friendship with Auguste Visschers, who had presided over the 1848 Peace Congress. Visschers was busy with the Americans, David Dudley Field and the Rev James B. Miles, the Secretary of the American Peace Society, who were planning a Conference of Jurists to consider matters of international law to be held the following month. He met the politician and journalist Auguste Couvreur, who had connections with the *Independence Belge* newspaper, and who proposed to present the Belgian Legislature with a motion similar to that which Richard had successfully presented to the British Parliament.[1]

Richard and his wife then visited The Hague where they were warmly received by the Dutch politicians. It is doubtful whether any British politician on an unofficial visit to a foreign country ever received such a sympathetic and enthusiastic welcome. A splendid carriage was sent to take them to the Freemasons' Hall. "When we entered," he wrote in his journal, "a gentleman presented Mrs Richard with a splendid bouquet, the music struck up, and all the audience rose as we passed up to our seats … At the upper end they had my portrait … Around it there was a sort of ornamental frame, with the motto 'Peace on Earth' in Dutch, and the date of my Motion in the House of Commons." Richard gave a 30-minute speech after which he received an Honorary Membership of the Dutch Peace Society diploma presented – to his amusement – to *Sir* Henry Richard.[2]

The following evening a public banquet was held in his honour and two Deputies pledged to bring the matter of Arbitration to the attention of the Dutch Parliament at the earliest opportunity.[3] He visited a number of schools in The Hague among them a community school where the education was free and secular. He noted that "a committee of gentlemen" would visit the parents of poor children urging them to send their children to the school. He praised the school for the way it was managed and that children were not beaten as a punishment. The classes consisted of both sexes and the pupils included Catholics, Protestants and Jews. There was no religious instruction, apart from singing a hymn and a very general prayer at the start of the day. However, there were classrooms set aside where local ministers at certain times of the day could come to provide religious instruction. Even in the denominational schools which were maintained by voluntary subscriptions catechisms were not used as part of the religious education and the style of teaching was similar to that of the British and Foreign Schools.

Richard was disappointed when he arrived at Berlin and found the German and the Prussian Parliaments in recess. However, he did manage to meet a number of influential men, among them the historian and one of the leaders of the Democratic Party, Maximilian Wolfgang Duncker. He also met 75-year-old August Wilhelm Heffter, Professor of Law at Berlin University, the author of influential volumes on European international law and how soldiers should treat prisoners of war. He met the philosopher Johann Heinrich Löewe and they discussed the moral effect of standing armies. Richard was interviewed by Eduard Loewenthal who had just been appointed editor-in-chief of *Neue Freie Zeitung*. Loewenthal was the author of a number of books on subjects to do with peace which had been published in French as well as German. Richard described him as "an earnest and excellent man".[4]

He visited a gymnasium on 20 September where he had a long conversation with the headmaster, Dr Zumpt, about the Prussian education system. Again he reveals his interest in religious education and Dr Zumpt evidently was describing a system in accord with Richard's opinions:

The Bible is taught. There is a prayer and a hymn sung at the commencement of school and if the teacher chooses, at the commencement of class. In Protestant schools Roman Catholics and Jews are not required to be present at such religious services, though usually they do not object, because, as he intimated, it is of so general a kind as to give no offence ... I asked Dr Zumpt if the religious instruction given in the schools made the children religious. He answered promptly and with great emphasis – 'No, religious life does not come from the school, but from the family. The children acquire religious knowledge in school, but not a religious life'.[5]

He met Eduard Lasker, a popular and influential radical in the German and Prussian Parliaments on 1 October. "He received us with much courtesy and kindness, recalled what he said to me four years ago, that the danger to peace was from France, and asked if his prophecy had not come true," wrote Richard. Lasker said that he had followed Richard's work in "England" and the success of his International Arbitration Motion in the House of Commons. "He assured me repeatedly and with great emphasis that his sympathies were with me," wrote Richard in his journal. "But when I suggested whether he would not bring the question of Arbitration forward in the German Parliament, he hesitated, doubted if it would be expedient and opportune to do so by direct resolution, but he would consult some of his political friends ... Declared very positively that the policy of Germany is a peace policy, and pointed out to me ... a really striking paragraph inserted on his proposal, after strong opposition, but by a great majority, in the first address of the German Parliament to the Emperor, in favour of absolute non-interference in the internal affairs of other nations."

Richard and his wife proceeded to Dresden and then to Vienna, capital – at that time – of the Austria-Hungarian Empire. There they met the American Ambassador, John Jay. Jay, who would prove far more helpful than the British Ambassador, drew his attention to the great exhibition – World Fair – which was being held there at the time and hoped that he would have the time to pay it a visit.

When Richard and his wife visited Brussels at the start of their journey they were invited to the International Law conference which was to start on 10 October. Brussels and Ghent were important centres of International Law. Both cities had law schools with professors of vision and an international perspective, such as Alphonse Rivier and the legal historian François Laurent, both authors of standard text-books on international law. Another man of influence and a friend of Rivier and Laurent was the lawyer and radical liberal politician from Belgium, Gustave Rolin-Jaequemyns, organizer of the conference where the *Institut de droit international* (Institute of International Law) was established in Ghent, on 8 September, weeks before the conference in Brussels. Richard was aware of these events and he decided to return to Brussels. On 8 October he and his wife were in Vienna, and to get to Brussels by the 10th they faced a 36 hour journey – two nights and a day without a break. It would not be a pleasurable journey, especially for a man who was now 60 years of age. But with so many of Europe's foremost public figures present, Richard decided it was a journey worth the trouble. Dr Johann Kaspar Bluntschli, a native of Switzerland, but by then Professor of Constitutional Law in Heidelberg and one of the founders of the *Institut de droit international*, would be representing the German Emperor. Also there would be the former Minister, Professor Pasquale Stanislao Mancini from Rome. He was the Chair of the Ghent conference. Professor Charles Giraud of the Collège de France, holder of the only Chair of International Law in France, and Frédéric Passy, founder of the *Ligue internationale et permanente de la paix* in 1867, also of France, were present. These were not men who dealt with such issues in the abstract – they were involved in the political, economic and social developments of their countries. There were members of parliament, some were ministers in their Governments, men who were anxious to extend the franchise and enlighten public opinion with the aim of ensuring peace and European progress. Montague Bernard, first holder of the Chichele Chair of International Law at Oxford, the only Chair of its kind in England, established in 1859, was present. Also present were Dudley Field and the Rev James B. Miles from the USA, as well as a number of Government Ministers and politicians from Belgium, among them Émile de Laveleye and Auguste Visschers – both of whom knew Henry Richard well.

The conference lasted three days and Henry Richard was given the opportunity to present his message. Not everyone was in favour of the principle of arbitration but the following resolution was approved:

> That this Conference declares that it regards arbitration as a means essentially just and reasonable, and even *obligatory* on all nations, of terminating international differences which cannot be settled by negotiation. It abstains from affirming that in all

cases, without exception, this mode of solution is applicable, but
it believes that the exceptions are rare, and it is convinced that no
difference ought to be considered insoluble until after a clear
statement of complaints and reasonable delay, and the exhaustion
of all pacific methods of accommodation.[6]

The original resolution as drawn up by Montague Bernard, did
not include the phrase with the word *obligatory*, but the
Englishman yielded to the opinion of Mancini and others.[7]
Richard said that he would have preferred a resolution without
any qualifying clauses, but the inclusion of the word *obligatory* was
a great improvement. But, he said "exceptions were like a crack in
a bottle; no matter how you corked and sealed it, the essence and
liquid would leak out."[8] This was the most knotty subject discussed at the three day conference. It was also agreed to establish
an Association for the Reform and Codification of the Law of
Nations. Before the proceedings were formally closed, the
Conference passed a resolution that an address of congratulation
be presented to Henry Richard for his services in the cause of the
peaceful settlement of national disputes. The address was signed
by Émile de Laveleye and Auguste Visschers.

Henry Richard wrote in his journal that he had a long and private interview with Mancini who said that he was about to propose an arbitration resolution in the Italian Parliament and he
urged Richard to be present at that occasion and to visit the other
principal Italian cities during his journey:[9]

> Professor Mancini gave me an account of an official mission in
> which he was engaged, I think, in 1867, with a view to negotiate a
> Treaty relating to many points of private international law
> between Italy, France, and Germany. On this occasion the Italian
> statesman proposed that all questions of dispute that might arise
> between the Governments on the matters contained in the
> Treaty should be settled by arbitration. His own Government
> most readily accepted his proposal to that effect. The scheme was
> laid before [the reactionary Eugène] Rouher and the Emperor at
> Paris, both of whom seemed to be quite favourable. He then
> went to Berlin and submitted the suggestion to Prince Bismarck,
> who, after some hesitation, also accepted it. But if I understood
> Mancini aright, the French Government at the last moment
> withdrew from the proposal.[10]

Henry Richard and his wife returned to Vienna in mid-October.
It was not the best time to visit the city as Hungary was in the middle of a general election and many of the politicians he had hoped

to see were busy in their constituencies. It would be no easy matter for him to present his arbitration message, but it was suggested
to him that he should send German copies of his pamphlet on the
subject to Prince Adolf von Auersperg, President of the Upper
Chamber, with a request for him to distribute them.[11]

He managed to meet Professor Leopold Neumann of the
University, who was also a member of the Parliament who praised
Richard for his peace campaigning. He also met the political journalist and Member of Parliament, Ignaz Kuranda, considered to be
one of the founders of the free press in Austria.[12] He, too,
expressed a desire to present a motion on the matter of arbitration,
but it would have to be done indirectly as the Chamber could not
discuss foreign affairs. Another person he met, unexpectedly, was
Somerset Beaumont, Liberal MP for Wakefield, one of the
founders of the Anglo-Austrian Bank. In his diary Richard noted
that Vienna, and indeed Austria, was in the middle of a serious
financial crisis due to a building mania and the formation of spec-
ulative companies and the failure of many investment projects.[13] It
is not clear whether Somerset Beaumont was in Vienna because of
any problems his bank may have been experiencing, but he promised Richard every assistance in his campaign. Richard also noted
that Austrian men were not hard workers and spent much time
eating, drinking and playing billiards in the cafes. In the American
Embassy – who appear to have been more helpful than the British
Embassy – he met a General Eber. The General told him that
Ferenc Deák, an influential man known as "the wise man of the
nation", living in Budapest, was anxious to meet him. "This was
good news," wrote Richard in his diary, "for M. Deák is the one
man in Hungary whose support it is important to gain. He occu-
pies a very peculiar position. He is not in office and never has
been, except for a short time after the revolution of 1848. But his
political power is far greater than all of the Ministers put together.
The Government indeed, seem to depend for their existence upon
his patronage and support, and he could, it is said, at any time
defeat them. But in general he loyally supports them."[14]

The General Eber duly came on 30 October to take Henry
Richard and his wife to the Queen of England Hotel in Pesth, on
the eastern side of the Danube, where Ferenc Deák was waiting
for them. There was a bishop present, who soon departed, and
Baron Béla Wenckheim, a Minister directly responsible to the
Emperor. Baron Wenckheim, a liberal and progressive politician
served in a number of administrations, was, for some months in

1875, Prime Minister of Hungary. After the departure of the un-
named bishop, they were joined by Count Ferenc Zichy, the
Minister of Commerce. "Whether their presence was accidental,
or he had invited them to meet me, I don't know," wrote Richard
in his diary.

> After general greetings, I explained in English, the object of my
> mission, which was translated by General Eber. Then M. Deák
> replied in Hungarian, which was also translated by the General.
> M. Deák said he was most thoroughly penetrated with the
> importance of the idea of which I am the advocate … not merely
> on humanitarian and philanthropic grounds, and in its bearing
> on civilisation, but also on financial grounds. For not only is war
> more expensive than peace, but present circumstances make the
> state of peace almost as bad as that of war. He finds it just and
> proper that England should take the lead in this question, for
> England has always acted a leading part in the affairs of nations,
> and its circumstances are specially favourable to its action in a
> matter of this sort. But the idea is one that can only triumph
> gradually, for it is necessary that it should be propagated not only
> among the nations of Europe, but in America and Asia, between
> which and Europe there were now many important relations.
> Therefore, he was very glad to hear what I had said about the
> probability of other legislatures taking up the question. He was
> quite in favour of bringing the question forward in the
> Hungarian Legislature, but he thought it could not be done with
> advantage immediately. They were deeply preoccupied with
> financial questions. They had to settle their budget, or, rather, to
> find the means to meet their expenses, and it would be difficult
> for the moment to get men's attention fixed on other subjects.
> But when that was disposed of, then he thought it would come
> in very fitly, as bearing on the future of those finances them-
> selves, as the adjustment of their financial difficulties would
> depend on their ability to reduce their military establishments ...
> As a supporter of the Hungarian Government, he could not do
> anything that would be inconvenient or disagreeable to it. He
> would speak privately to his friends about bringing forward the
> question, and though he would not bring it forward himself, he
> would certainly support it. But it must be coupled with the
> understanding that they will be always prepared to do everything
> that was necessary for the security and defence of their country.[15]

That afternoon Richard and his wife crossed the Danube by the
suspension bridge from Pesth, on the flat eastern side of the river,
to Buda and climbed the hill to enjoy the view of the river and the
countryside. He felt contented that he had argued his case and had
received the promise that his vision would be put to, and dis-

cussed, by the parliaments of Austria and Hungary.

The following day, Ágoston Trefort, the Minister of Public Instruction called on them – "a very pleasant man, simple and perfectly unaffected in his manners". Trefort, who would be responsible for public education for 15 years, was one of Hungary's most important figures with regard to the country's nineteenth-century cultural policy. An important milestone in his career was the country's Higher Education Act passed in 1883, establishing a regularized system of secondary schools which remained almost unchanged until 1945. Trefort believed that it was impossible to reform higher education separately from the issue of teacher training.

After visiting the Hungarian capital, Richard and his wife returned to Vienna where the Exhibition was coming to an end. The sight, wrote Richard, "was a brilliant one", and no doubt the people must have been saddened that such a magnificent collection of the products of commerce, industry, and art, was doomed to dispersal. Richard had intended to proceed to Italy but Baron Max von Kübeck, a member of the Parliament, the Reichsrath, expressed a keen desire to meet him. Some years later, von Kübeck became closely involved with other promoters of international peace. So they spent another two days in Vienna and on 4 December the Baron took them to the opening of the new Parliament and Richard described the oath being taken in four languages – German, Italian, Polish and Slavonic.

There had evidently been some discussion as to whether to table a question regarding arbitration but after von Kübeck had talked to his colleagues the decision was to postpone it for a few months – perhaps until February. The custom with the opening of a new Parliament was for the Emperor to summon the Members to the Imperial Palace, and Richard was anxious to witness the ceremony. However, none of his Austrian friends could provide him with tickets, and again the British Ambassador, Sir Andrew Buchanan, was nowhere to be seen. But the American Ambassador, John Jay, who had shown great kindness to them on this and the previous visit provided them with two tickets for the diplomatic box. He was evidently greatly impressed with the splendour of the occasion.

Afterwards Richard visited the editors of the Vienna daily newspapers, presenting each one with a copy of his pamphlet on arbitration, then spending the evening with Baron von Kübeck and his family. On their last Sunday in the city they attended a church

service and met the Anglican priest, a dejected Rev Dunlop
Moore, who was quite disheartened about freedom to worship
and the future of Protestantism in general. He said there were
20,000 Protestants in Vienna but that they were a lukewarm lot.[16]
    Of all the countries visited by Henry Richard nowhere wel-
comed him with greater warmth than Italy. It was there that he
received the greatest honours. Wherever he went the most famous
and prominent citizens would be there to meet and welcome him.
On 10 November the two went via the Semmering Railway –
which had been open for less than 20 years – across the Alps to
Trieste and on to Venice. Having crossed the border into Italy
Richard now felt himself to be among friends. In Austria the
encouragement was cautious and the front rank of politicians did
not wish to be seen associating too openly with the Apostle of
Peace. But the position of Italy was different, so much so that one
statesman said that his greatest wish was for Italy to be a neutral
country. The professors of the universities had studied international relations, and there were no dynastic interests and traditions
in this newly united country to distract the people. The inhabitants, taught by the philosopher, politician and patriot Giuseppe
Mazzini, and then by the soldier and politician, Garibaldi –
although he was no pacifist – had an understanding of the follies
and calamities of foreign wars. In Italy Henry Richard was greeted
as the Apostle of Peace by all sections of society, with unanimity
and enthusiasm bordering on embarrassment. Even before he had
left Vienna, Richard had received from Italy a letter of introduction that was unimaginably complimentary:

    To Henry Richard, Esq., MP

    Sir,

    Allow us to transmit to you, from the country of Federico
    Sclopis, a few words of congratulations on the success obtained
    by you in the House of Commons, on the 8th July, with refer-
    ence to the hallowed and truly humane principle of International
    Arbitration, one destined to become a custom and a rule in the
    new Law of Nations.
        Although the best reward of your incessant labours is the
    prospect – presaged by so many signs – of the fulfilment of your
    magnanimous plans, you will not be displeased to find that we, as
    Italians, and men cordially rejoiced when the Parliament of
    England, acting as the interpreters of the wishes of mankind in
    general, give their sanction to that generous design, and by their
    example excited everywhere an intense desire for tranquil pur-

suits, an earnest belief in prescribed progress, and in the sovereignty of Right, and a natural revulsion from the blind fatality of
brute force. That joy was also felt by us as friends to concord
amongst all peoples, and as friends of peace, that peace which is a
boon to all, a bane to none, whilst being the most potent instrument of ordained progress and of all true liberty.

Still continue, honoured Sir, the advocate of all those generous ideas which ever found willing audiences in the country of
Wilberforce and Cobden, and which in you now find the eloquence of a venerated interpreter. Receive the good wishes of all
who invoke the reign of universal justice on earth, and from us a
cordial grasp of the hand, for yourself and your companions in
victory, Mr Mundella and Sir Wilfrid Lawson.[17]

This remarkable statement, dated 14 September 1873, the first
anniversary of the Alabama Arbitration, had been signed by a long
list of prominent Italians, including Garibaldi; the Marquis
Torrearsa, President of the Parliament; Count Casati, the former
President; Giuseppe Biancheri, President of the Chamber;
Giuseppe Pisanelli, the Deputy President; Mancini, and a number
of Members; university professors, presidents of scientific and
artistic societies; barristers; and presidents of chambers of commerce of all the Italian cities.

Richard was very flattered by the address and in a written
response expressing his deep gratitude for this "signal honour"
which afforded him such great encouragement "to persevere in a
work which has received this testimony of sympathy and approval
from such a select body of enlightened minds and generous
hearts". He regarded this as a "*national* demonstration" as a fresh
impulse for him to continue working for the cause which was so
near to his heart. "The voice of Italy, speaking with such profound
conviction and such harmonious unity, in the interests of justice
and humanity, cannot fail to command the attention and to influence the opinion of the civilized world," he said.[18]

In Venice he was invited to a banquet in his honour organised
by the municipal authorities. As none of those who would be present understood English he was asked to speak in French, which he
understood well, but knowing that he would have to make a public speech in the language made him miserable for days. While
worrying over that, he and his wife went to the Duke's Palace,
crossed the Bridge of Sighs, and visited the prison and the chamber of torture. He noted that the streets swarmed with beggars and
was informed that 11,000 of the inhabitants of the city lived on
public charity.

The banquet was held in the largest hotel in the city and among those present were representatives of the principal magistrates, merchants, educationists and artists. He delivered his speech in French to a warm ovation and noted in his diary that his wife also praised his delivery adding that she was probably not an impartial witness. A telegram arrived from Count Federico Sclopis, who chaired the Alabama Arbitration Tribunal in Geneva. Sclopis, it is worth recalling, was one of the authors of the Sardinia Charter, which was later accepted in its entirety as the Italian Constitution. His message was cordial and ended with the words (in English): "Welcome, and hearty compliments to the Champion of Peace".[19]

Richard received a sympathetic address from the International Working Men's Association – the First International – in Venice assuring him of the confidence and respect with which the people of the Italian peninsula had watched his mission. Richard's message struck a chord with the working class and he was gaining their admiration much as he had gained the respect of members of the middle classes. He replied that one of his dearest desires in the peace movement was to be able to do something "to relieve the sufferings, and improve the condition of the millions of the industrial classes, who have been so long and so sorely oppressed by the heavy burdens of all kinds imposed upon them by the war system in Europe."[20]

After a few days in Verona and a few hours enjoying the sights at Lake Garda Richard and his wife hurried on to Milan to find a telegram waiting for them from Rome. It was from Mancini with the news that he was going to present his arbitration resolution in two days. Short of money, and unable to cash his travellers cheques, he had to rely on the generosity of the owner of the Hotel Cavour who lent him the necessary funds; they then set off on their 18 hour train journey. They arrived on the morning of 24 November to hear that the resolution would be presented that afternoon.

At the agreed time, Senator Augusto Pierantoni, Professor of International Law at the University of Rome, came to escort them to the Chamber and to take them on a tour of the Parliament and introduce them to a number of the Members. The Americans Dudley Field and James B. Miles were there and the group were led to the President's gallery.[21] Professor Mancini and other Members came to meet them and they witnessed various duties including the election of members to various committees – elected, Richard noted, by secret ballot. Then, at three o'clock,

Mancini got up to speak. The Professor's son-in-law sat with them and translated the speech into French. It was an event that made a deep impression on Richard:

> He made several allusions to my motion in the House of Commons, and in closing referred to the presence of Mr Field and myself in the gallery. He was listened to with the greatest attention throughout, though there was not much cheering till the close, when general signs of approval came from all parts of the Chamber. It was an able speech, and adapted with great skill to the feelings of his audience. He spoke for about an hour. The Minister for Foreign Affairs followed, and announced, on the part of the Government, that the motion was accepted without reserve. After him the reporter of the Committee on Finances, in a few earnest sentences, supported the resolution, which was then put by the President. They vote by rising, and the whole assembly, including those on the Ministerial benches, rose with one accord. M. Mancini's motion did not go so far as mine, and did not prescribe any immediate action by the Government. But it involved a full approval of the principle of arbitration, and its acceptance by the Government, and the unanimous vote of the House was a great triumph.[21]

It was an event which gave Henry Richard deep satisfaction and he mentioned how many people had come to congratulate him personally, including the *Times* correspondent, Antonio Carlo Napoleone Gallenga, an Italian who had been himself a Senator at one time. The wording of Mancini's motion was as follows:

> The Chamber trusts that His Majesty's Government will endeavour, in their relations with Foreign Powers, to render arbitration an acceptable and frequent mode of solving, according to the dictates of equity, such international questions as may admit of that mode of arrangement, as well as to introduce opportunely into any Treaties with those Powers, a clause to the effect that any difference of opinion respecting the interpretation and execution of those Treaties is to be referred to Arbitrators, and to promote Conventions between Italy and other civilised nations of a nature to render uniform and obligatory, in the interests of the respective peoples, the essential rules of Private International Right. [Private International Right meant a series of rules privately agreed between one nation and another.]

Henry Richard and his wife spent some days in Rome and Richard took the opportunity to visit the studio of Penry Williams, the Merthyr artist who had lived over 30 reclusive years in the city. Richard and Williams had apparently met at the gathering on 24

July 1871 to honour Joseph Parry in London. To Richard's disappointment Williams could no longer converse with him in Welsh. Three days after Mancini's success a banquet was held in his honour at the Hotel di Roma, where the couple were staying. About 80 men attended, senators, deputies, professors, representatives of the municipality and journalists. The occasion worried Richard somewhat as he had a cold which had been aggravated by the journey as the result of which his voice was gone. Mancini spoke in glowing terms of Richard's work, quoting Gladstone who had said that Cobden's mantle had now dropped on the Welshman's shoulders. When it came to Richard's turn to speak, he spoke a few sentences in French before switching to English with the correspondent of the *Daily News* translating. Thanks to the excitement, the warmth of the room or the excellent meal Richard felt his voice returning and he spoke for 15 minutes and, according to his own testimony, he was warmly applauded.[22]

Two days later Richard received a deputation from the Freemasons thanking him for his work for peace and humanity. He also received a flattering address from the Agricultural Society of Lombardy, men of the plains who understood well the carnage that war had wrought on their land over the centuries. They pointed out that peace was a matter of the utmost importance to those who made their living from cultivating the land. The address was signed by more than 500 landowners and farmers. To those signatories were added that of the President of the Agricultural Commission of Milan and other similar committees in Mantua and other parts of Lombardy. As usual, Richard managed to visit a technical school where there was no religious instruction, and elementary schools under the auspices of the Roman municipality where the children of Catholics, Protestants and Jews were taught side by side. He also met the translators and writers, William and Mary Howitt, and their daughter, Margaret.[23] They were former Quakers who had taken an interest in spiritualism and the literature of northern Europe. Mary Howitt had translated some of the novels of the Finnish feminist Fredrika Bremer. The day after he met the Howitt family, Richard met the Prime Minister, Marco Minghetti, whom he described as "a pleasant and affable man". They met in the chamber where Galileo had appeared before the Inquisition and been forced to recant his theory that the sun was the centre of the universe.

From Rome the two proceeded to Florence where Richard received an address from the women of Italy, designed to "answer the twofold purpose of expressing our thanks to Mr Richard, the House of Commons, and good Queen Victoria, and of beseeching our Government to co-operate with England in promoting the principle embodied in Mr Richard's motion." The two then returned to Milan where another reception awaited them. A banquet was presided over by the Mayor and Senator, Giulio Belinzaghi, and a number of parliamentarians were present, together with members of the City Council and leaders of the Freemason lodges of Northern Italy. In his speech Henry Richard referred to the miraculous revival of national life and great steps taken in education since the unification of the country in 1861 – a process completed when the Vatican became integrated into the state in 1870. This was particularly evident in Milan, he said. If Italy was prepared to become the apostle of peace of the nations, he promised that Britain and America would be ready to give her every support. *Courier*, the city's newspaper, said that the meeting had shown signs that men of differing political persuasions were ready to set aside their differences and to talk in a friendly manner and shake hands at the end of the evening – something which had not been witnessed in living memory.[24]

Turin was the last Italian city visited and Richard was particularly keen to meet Federico Sclopsis, who had presided over the Geneva Alabama Tribunal, he "whose name is imperishably associated with an event that will be regarded hereafter as forming a great landmark in the history of civilisation." He was not disappointed. He found the distinguished man as devoted as ever to the cause of peace.[25] Richard and his wife spent two of their three nights in Turin.

Richard had promised to visit his friend Frédéric Passy in Paris before returning home. They arrived at the French capital on 19 December and two days later a public banquet was arranged in Richard's honour. About 70 writers, politicians, journalists and some of France's most prominent jurists attended the banquet, according to the *Daily Telegraph*. There were also economists and the heads of commercial firms. The banners of Britain, France, the USA and Italy had been placed around a shield and on it the words "8th July 1873", the date of Henry Richard's unexpected triumph in the House of Commons. Among the dignitaries present were Joseph Garnier of the Economist Society, professor, journalist, politician and a campaigner for free trade and peace; Adolphe Franck, the Jewish philosopher and theologian and one of the founders of the *Ligue de la Paix* (the League of Peace); the respected American diplomat, John Meredith Read; and Edmond de Pressensé, the Protestant theologian and politician. Presiding over the evening was Augustin-Charles Renouard, Procurator-General of the Court of Cassation. Frédéric Passy spoke warmly of the philanthropic nature of Richard's work and of his journey around Europe to promote disarmament. He referred, also, to the work of Cobden and Gladstone who deserved like Henry Richard "to be numbered among the heroes of Peace in Europe".[26] He spoke of Henry Richard's previous visits to Europe in 1869–70 and his campaigning for disarmament, a campaign that might have succeeded but for "the mad enterprise" of 1870 – the Franco-Prussian war.

Henry Richard then got up to express his thanks. He first spoke in French then – according to the reporter of the *Daily Telegraph* – "in beautifully articulated English". Richard thought, maybe, that some of the guests had come to see the madman who had been scurrying around Europe suggesting legal ways of keeping the peace while the various countries were adding to their armies and sharpening their arms. Some believed that his aims were impractical, utopian, forgetting that he himself did not hope to see his plans come to instant fruition and that he knew very well what the difficulties were. The first step, he said, was to popularise the idea, and it was a matter of great joy to him that he had friends in various countries who were helping him to do so. The work would take time, and he was not confident that he would see the day when it would be achieved. Nobody knew better than he how deeply the military system had struck its roots into the moral soil of all nations. But while he knew that prejudice and emotions were there to be defeated by reason and justice, those who spoke of his work as Utopian were hiding behind a word, the meaning of which they did not understand. Was it not Lamartine who said that Utopia was merely truth from afar? There was a time when it was said that abolishing slavery was Utopian and likewise the Corn Laws. The latter had once been called an absurd idea, but Henry Richard himself had seen Richard Cobden turning an Utopian idea into reality. He ended his speech with the words: "As far as my share in the work is concerned, if I do not live to see it rewarded with success, I shall not despair, for there are some enterprises in which it is more glorious to fail than it would be in most others to conquer."[27]

On 25 March 1874, three months after he had returned to London, an evening was arranged to welcome him back, chaired by his friend the MP for Sheffield, A. J. Mundella. When called to speak Henry Richard was very modest. No one could have been more surprised, he said, than he was himself to find that his feeble voice, which had been raised in the House of Commons in favour of justice, reason and humanity, had awakened so great a feeling as had been found to be the case. Everywhere he had gone he had been received with open arms, as the friend and Apostle of Peace. He rejoiced greatly that working men in various countries were taking up this question, for, whoever else might gain by war, they at least were sure to suffer. The blood and bones of working men had covered every battlefield in Europe. Others had carried off the spoils, the titles, the honours, the emoluments of war, but everywhere and always the working men came in for the main share of its sufferings – they and their families. Richard said that he had returned with the strongest conviction that there was throughout society, in all parts of the Continent, an intense abhorrence of the war system, and a longing to be delivered from it. He was not so foolish as to claim that the thousand year dawn was about to break, but he believed that his motion in the House of Commons and his Continental journey had made some little contribution towards promoting that blessed era.[28]

Chapter 18

The 1874 Election and Tory rule

Henry Richard returned from his well-received peace pilgrimage to find the Gladstone administration in disarray. The Nonconformists among the MPs were unhappy with Forster's education policies. The electors disapproved the Government's acquiescence to the establishment of the Alabama Arbitration Tribunal – and more so, that they had accepted its verdict. Mentally and physically worn out – yet without warning – Gladstone dissolved Parliament on 23 January 1874, and appealed to the electorate to show renewed confidence and trust in his Government.

Henry Richard immediately set about publishing the Peace Society's manifesto, a manifesto aimed at the entire electorate of the United Kingdom.[1] A manifesto proudly proclaiming that the Government had settled its dispute with the United States – the *Alabama* issue – and the moral support given to his International Arbitration motion. With an eye on the future, he wrote of the burden and waste of the huge military installations, of the benefits of disarmament, and of cheaper methods to settle disputes than by resorting to arms. Richard and his friends distributed election literature and posters crammed with information and statistics. He stressed the importance of electing to Parliament men ready to argue the case for peace and to promote a comprehensive and permanent system of international arbitration. He took instant advantage of the election to spread his message of peace. Was this at the expense of his own constituency? Probably. He topped the poll comfortably, as he did throughout his parliamentary career, but without the overwhelming majority he had enjoyed in 1868. Richard polled 7,606 with Fothergill second with 6,908 – both reelected – and in third position came Thomas Halliday, General Secretary of the Amalgamated Association of Miners. Halliday put up a brave challenge attracting a respectable 4,912 votes.[2] It should also be remembered that the tide was running against the Liberals and that Richard's campaign, as always, relied totally on unpaid volunteers. Yet it was a significant drop from his majority of 4,000 over Fothergill in 1868.

There had been at least one occurrence that damaged his vote. There was a strike by colliery and iron workers in Merthyr in January and February 1873 and Richard came in for scathing criticism for not getting involved. Halliday was able to refer to Richard's "discreet absence". His failure, as the great advocate of arbitration, to try and settle the dispute by that method, prompted some genuine contempt. (He may have been badly advised on this occasion by one of his Merthyr sponsors, Charles James, who later became his fellow MP for Merthyr and Aberdare.) The Conservative *Western Mail* was particularly critical, with scornful references to Richard's tour of the Continent "gorged with dinners and flattery in half the capitals of Europe". It was certainly unwise during an election campaign to boast – as he did in a meeting at Mountain Ash on 27 January – of the enthusiastic receptions he had received in Europe. This again attracted the ire of the *Western Mail*. According to the Anglican and Conservative *Yr Haul*, Henry Richard was afraid of alienating both workers and masters.[3]

The Liberal *South Wales Daily News*, however, stressed that European statesmen and trade unionists had supported Richard's ideas. And not just abroad. In March 1874, 60 delegates representing 50,000 trade unionists in South Wales and the West of England had gathered at a conference organised by the Workmen's Peace Association. The founder, W. J. Cremer, spoke of the change in attitude towards international arbitration and "how the mantle of Mr Cobden had worthily fallen upon the shoulders of Henry Richard".[4] The question remains as to how effective a constituency MP was Richard. Eleazar Roberts's book, for instance, makes occasional references to "Henry Richard's annual visit to Merthyr" and the rapturous welcome he regularly received. The luxury of another MP for the constituency may have taken some of the load off his shoulders. It is fair, also, to say that the rural, Welsh-speaking Tregaron of his childhood was the Wales with which he identified and sympathised.

Henry Richard was safely back in the House of Commons. But the Liberals were no longer in power. The Tories, with Disraeli as

Prime Minister, were in Government with a majority of 46. In Wales 19 Liberals and 14 Conservatives were returned, the Liberals losing four seats. E. M. Richards was defeated in Cardiganshire. Edward Miall, who had been the MP for Bradford, decided to retire because of ill health. So Henry Richard was deprived of two of his closest friends in Parliament. He and Miall could be described as life-long friends, and Richard had worked closely with E. M. Richards during the previous Parliament. Gladstone announced that he needed some respite and that he did not wish to lead his party in Opposition. The Liberals were in considerable disarray and after much internal wrangling Spencer Cavendish – Lord Hartington – was appointed leader. Some had advocated W. E. Forster, but he could not command the support of the Nonconformist Liberals nor of the independently minded MPs.

The Gladstone administration had left the public finances in credit to the tune of £6,000,000.[5] One of Gladstone's election promises was to abolish income tax, but Disraeli convinced the voters that it was nothing more than a bribe and empty promise. In spite of the healthy state of the country's coffers the Disraeli Government soon set about spending it. Disraeli, during the election campaign had made much of the need for "a spirited foreign policy". The navy was the first to make a grab for the cash in the coffers and soon the newspapers were announcing that the British navy was good for nothing. It was, as Henry Richard often pointed out, the eternal cries of the high command of the military. Eventually the Admiralty settled for £100,000.[6]

The first months of the new Parliament was a strange period. On 20 April 1874, the Archbishop of Canterbury, a Scot named Archibald Campbell Tait, presented a Bill to stop what he considered the spread of Catholic rituals in the Church of England.[7] He presented his Public Worship Regulation Bill to the House of Lords, a huge waste of House of Commons' time. Disraeli and Queen Victoria, who approved of the Protestant aims of the Bill, were supportive. As a result much of the first session of the new Parliament was spent arguing over the fine detail of church creed, catechisms, rituals, the Book of Common Prayer and such matters. It was evident that Henry Richard had little patience, nor much inclination, to participate in such debates in a House Commons which included men of a variety of beliefs and some of no beliefs at all. Nevertheless, he delivered a typically prickly speech on 15 July during the Second Reading of this lengthy Bill, where he set out the Nonconformist position. He insisted that he was no enemy of the Church of England but he believed with the utmost sincerity that it would be a great advantage for it to be disestablished from the state. "I believe, rightly or wrongly – such is my profound and earnest conviction – that such a consummation would conduce to the interests of truth and freedom, and charity and peace; and that ultimately, it would confer inestimable advantages upon the Church itself, which would far more than compensate for the loss of the injurious and invidious patronage of the State," he said. Adding: "I feel also, of course, that as a political institution, the Church of England has been a hard and cruel stepmother to the Nonconformists, inflicting upon them for generations wrongs and sufferings, disabilities and humiliations which have burnt a deep mark into the memory of Nonconformists, and which you cannot expect us to forget or condone in a day."

The *Times*, he said, had shown that a clergyman of the Church of England "might teach any doctrine which only extreme subtlety can distinguish from Roman Catholicism on the one side, Calvinism on another side, and from Deism on a third side." But this was a Bill directed against one particular class of persons in the Church of England – Anglicans of Catholic tendencies. "It might appear pleasant to the outward eye," he said, "to have 20,000 men obliged to speak and do the same thing. But at what cost do you get this uniformity; at what a cost of intellectual servility, of violence done to conscience, of temptations to disingenuous sophistry in putting such strained interpretations upon the Articles and offices of the Church, as would, if applied to any other documents, and in any other department of life, be branded as fraudulent and dishonest?" He went on to argue that one of the dangers and difficulties of the Church arose from such attempts to prescribe an enforced uniformity. But it could not be otherwise while there was an Established Church. There was only one way out of this embarrassment – Disestablishment.[8]

After much debating the Archbishop's motion became law on 3 August 1874. As Henry Richard caustically suggested in a speech in Wales that autumn the first term of the new Parliament was "much more like a Church Convocation that a political legislature".[9] After all the splitting of ritualistic and theological hairs an Act was created which was impossible to administer, which the Episcopal Bench, in general, chose to ignore. There were some court cases, and a total of five clergymen were actually imprisoned – but for Contempt of Court. Prosecutions ended when a 1906

Royal Commission recognised the legitimacy of pluralism in worship but the Act remained in force until it was finally repealed on 1 March 1965. This was the result of a whole term of debating, during which time 18 Bills were discussed, each one to do with regulating the services and practices of the Church of England!

Henry Richard's first speech of real importance in the new Parliament came in support of an amendment tabled by Sir Wilfrid Lawson during a debate on the African Gold Coast and the Ashanti[10] War – in today's Ghana, more or less. Britain, like the other colonisers, had been interfering regularly in the affairs of West Africa. In 1871, Britain had bought the area known as the Dutch Gold Coast from the Netherlands, to add on to the area already in its possession. Among the lands sold by the Netherlands to Britain was the coastal kingdom of Elmina – a country the Ashanti claimed as their own. Before the arrival of the colonisers, the Ashanti was one of the most powerful empires in sub-Saharan Africa. The Ashanti and the British were soon at war over the kingdom of Elmina. In 1873 General Garnet Wolseley, with an army of 2,500 British soldiers and thousands of soldiers from the West Indies and Africa, and with their superior arms created their customary devastation, including the destruction of Kumasi, the capital. The British, apparently, were astounded at the size of the city and the magnificence of the palace of the Asantahene, the king of the Ashanti, and his superb library of books in many languages. Nevertheless, the city was razed to the ground. The war was over in a few months and the Asantahene forced to sign a cruel treaty in July 1874 allowing the British to hurry away before the arrival of the "unhealthy" season.

Robert William Hanbury, Conservative MP for Tamworth, proposed a motion on 4 May that it was not desirable in the interests of civilisation and trade for Britain to withdraw from the Gold Coast. Sir Wilfrid Lawson, Liberal MP for Carlisle, tabled an amendment proposing the exact opposite:

> That this House is of opinion that, in the interests of civilization and commerce, it is desirable to withdraw from all equivocal and entangling engagements with the tribes inhabiting the Gold Coast.[11]

Henry Richard supported Sir Wilfrid's amendment with a typically detailed overview of Britain's plundering of West Africa. He had concluded, he said, after wading as patiently as he could through the chaos of reports that had been thrown before the

House in connection with the matter, that it was neither a just nor a necessary war and that it arose from a contemptuous disregard of notorious and acknowledged rights on the part of the Ashanti. There was no doubt:

> that the Kings of Ashanti had sustained relations with, and exercised a kind of suzerainty over Elmina, almost from time immemorial. That was acknowledged on all hands. The King of Elmina admitted it by the payment of a tribute of £80; and when the Dutch assumed the Protectorate, they also acknowledged it by continuing to pay the tribute, although they called it a stipend. Our administrator there, Mr. Ussher, stated his conviction that the King of Ashanti [Kofi Karikari] had certain claims upon Elmina, and warned Her Majesty's Government against completing the negotiation for the transfer of the Protectorate to themselves from the Dutch until that point had been cleared up.

Richard condemned the war as a waste of lives and money, that the way the military campaign was administered was a disgrace and that the result was not a triumph of civilisation but of barbarism and brute force. Both the Gladstone and Disraeli administrations were criticised for their handling of the war. As expected, Lawson's amendment was defeated by 311 votes to 75. It should be noted that the Ashanti troubles had begun when Richard was on the Continent. Had he not been away on his peace mission he would have campaigned energetically against it and the outcome might have been different.

The London Welsh gathered at the Cannon Street Hotel on 25 May to congratulate Henry Richard on his European success. The colourful and patriotic Welshman, John Henry Puleston, newly elected Conservative MP for Devonport presided. Although of different parties, Richard no doubt approved the choice. Puleston, born in Plasnewydd, Llanfair, in the Vale of Clwyd, had spent some years in the United States where he had edited the Pennsylvanian *Phoenixville Guardian*, and had been the proprietor of the *Pittston Gazette*. It is likely that he also had links with the Welsh language paper *Baner America*, then published in Scranton. He left a load of debts behind him Phoenixville, but he returned and repaid the lot in 1879.[12] He had been secretary of the Peace Commission before the Civil War, becoming a well known figure in the USA. In the printed address he presented to Richard there were references to Richard's efforts over 20 years in many spheres of public life – such as the National Eisteddfod, Aberystwyth University, as well as the Peace Society. In reply Richard said that he had, over 40 years, done his best to promote Wales, defend its good name, and try to persuade John Bull that the Welsh in quality, religion, morals, language and literature were not one whit inferior to their neighbours. He told a story of John Gibson, the sculptor, who was presented to the Queen as a Scotsman when he was about to carve her statue. Gibson drew himself up announcing, "May it please your Majesty, I have the honour to be a Welshman". Likewise, said Richard, "I say to all my English fellow-subjects, I have the honour to be a Welshman."[13]

W. E. Forster's 1870 Education Act and the notorious Clause 25 allowing school boards to pay for the children of the needy who attended denominational schools remained a matter of annoyance to Nonconformists. In practice, they objected to Church of England schools receiving money from the rates. Henry Richard, Samuel Morley and other Nonconformist MPs had tabled a resolution demanding the abolition of Clause 25. When proposing the Second Reading on 10 June 1874 Richard argued that the clause was causing great bitterness and discord. The obligations of the Act had not been understood until it had been in existence for some time, he said. The debate was moderate in tone, and although Forster, the architect of the Act, spoke against the resolution a number who had been ministers in the previous Liberal administration, including the party's new Leader, Lord Hartington, supported Richard and his friends. Nevertheless, they were defeated by 373 votes to 128.[14]

There was far more bitter debate over the Endowed Schools Act (1869) Amendment Bill introduced by Lord Sandon. This Amendment would transfer responsibility for endowed grammar schools from the Endowed Schools Commission – which had been established under the 1869 Act – to the Charities Commission. Gladstone was particularly vehement in his attack, viewing it as an attempt to undo the work of his Government. The Endowed Schools Commission was an interim and it was not unreasonable to try and bring stability to the arrangement. But by making the Charities Commission responsible for the administration of the endowed schools the interests of the Church of England would be in safer and even more sympathetic hands. A sure way of raising Henry Richard's ire. This Bill, in fact, succeeded in unifying the Liberals who saw it as a shameless attempt to pacify certain malcontent clergy. Even Forster spoke out against the proposition![15] It is fair to say that the Endowed Schools Commission had been unpopular, particularly with the wealthy. A number of senior Liberals – Gladstone and Henry Austin Bruce among them – had admitted that the 1869 Act was another cause for the 1874 election defeat. This philosophical and political argument between the Conservatives and the radicals developed over a disagreement between the Endowed Schools Commissioners and London Council over one particular endowed school. The Commission resented the interference while the radicals resented the waste of money and keeping ineffectual teachers in jobs for life thanks to some ancient endowment. Some MPs saw the Endowed Schools Commission as an opportunity to bring order to old irrelevant endowments or those that were badly administered. At the same time there was a danger of interfering in the affairs of well-run charities.[16] The Tories won this bitter political argument and the Liberals lost support among the wealthy class.

Speaking on the Amendment on 21 July, Henry Richard noted that the Endowed Schools Commissioners could not be accused of being anti-Church of England since every one of them was an Anglican. To be truthful, he said, they were being dismissed for being unpopular with the trustees of the endowed schools. It ran counter to what was taking place in Europe where the policy was to restrict and control, and not extend, the power of ecclesiastical corporations in dealing with the education of the people. This was a Bill to shut out the Nonconformists, the true Protestants, from all share in the management of those endowed schools, which were to direct the education and to influence the character of the middle classes of the country, and to deliver them over into the hands of the clergy. All the principles of the 1869 Act which had been unanimously adopted by both sides of the House without a division were now to be abolished. He referred to the frequent accusation made against himself and others of "political Nonconformity". He continued: "We are not the aggressors in this matter. I am sometimes told – 'Why can't you leave the Church alone?' My answer is, the Church will not leave us alone. It meets us at every point; it crosses our path in every direction. We cannot engage in any work, religious, charitable, educational, social, or political, but we are thwarted, embarrassed, and worried by the exclusive pretensions of this dominant Church."[17]

Following this storm of opposition and three days of debating the Bill moved to the committee stage with a majority of 262 to 193. Despite changing a number of clauses, it was eventually agreed to transfer the administration of the Endowed Schools to the Charities Commission.

At the end of the second parliamentary session Henry Richard and his wife set off again for Geneva. Richard had the luck to be present at two Congresses, the first was the *Institut de droit international*, and the second the Association for the Reform and Codification of the Laws of Nations, founded by the Americans David Dudley Field and James B. Miles. As already noted both organisations had been established the previous year. The *Institut de droit* was founded in Ghent with the aim of promoting progress and uniformity in international law as they affected private rights, and the relations of international commerce, property and civil procedure. The Association for the Reform and Codification of the Laws of Nations, founded almost simultaneously in Brussels, aimed at setting up a general code to be administered by a Central Tribunal. As the *Institut de droit* was a congress of jurists, Henry Richard could not participate and attended as an observer with an interest in international law.

On the third day of the congress of the Association for the Reform and Codification of the Laws of Nations he delivered a paper on *The Gradual Triumph of Law over Brute Force*. He, too, looked ahead to a time when Europe would be united:

> We have seen how, in course of time, the domain of law has been continually enlarging, and banishing brute force further back in an ever-widening circle. First, individuals have laid aside their arms, and submitted their differences to judicial reference. Then the feudal barons, with their large following of clients and vassals, acknowledged a similar jurisdiction, and were merged into one compact community. Then separate tribes of the same nation became merged into one. Then distinct nationalities, although aliens to each other in race, language, and religion, obeyed the same powerful law of assimilation. But if this tendency to bring larger and still larger communities of men under the authority and protection of general law is thus clearly traceable in all history, is there any harm, is it not, indeed, a clear duty, to employ all practicable means to facilitate and hasten this consummation as respects the great nations of Europe and the world?[18]

In a public meeting at the end of the congress Richard delivered another speech, followed by the fiery orator, Père Hyacinthe Loyson, a priest who left the Catholic Church after preaching against the infallibility of the Pope and established his own *Eglise Gallicane*. He rejoiced that the work of promoting peace and goodwill amongst the people, which the ecclesiastics had started, was now being taken up by jurists, learned men and philanthropists.

Chapter 19

The Cobden Letters and Liberal recovery

With his work in Geneva completed Richard and his wife left for a few days in Lausanne and on to Aigle. Richard wanted to put the late Richard Cobden's letters in some kind of order. It is probable that among them were a number of letters Cobden had written to Gladstone – letters which Gladstone valued greatly and was anxious that they should be passed on to his children.[1] Cobden, as already mentioned, died in the Spring of 1865, and within three months the Cobden Club was established. It was later that Cobden's widow became a problem. Catherine Anne (née Williams) was the daughter of a well-off timber merchant in Machynlleth. Her brother – we also recall – was Hugh Williams, the Carmarthen solicitor connected to the Daughters of Rebecca, destroyers of the toll-gates in south-west Wales in the early 1840s. Hugh was truculent, obstinate, yet capable of great charm when more persuasive methods were more likely to succeed.[2] It was not for nothing that he was known as "Hugh of the hundred bastards"! His sister certainly had his prickly obstinacy.

Cobden was a prolific letter writer, and in his clear, homely yet dignified style he set out his political and social ideas. He would write to all kinds of people on a variety subjects, a habit that his wife often found trying. But if Cobden's profligate letter writing inconvenienced his wife, that was not the view of John Bright and other members of the Cobden Club. They realised the value and importance of the letters and were eager for them to be published in a popular volume so that a new generation could share a political and economic vision they considered would be of benefit to Britain. They worried that the letters would be published piecemeal in many volumes by the many proud recipients thus reducing their impact. Bright and others set about collecting the letters and all seemed to be proceeding satisfactorily. But they forgot to contact the widow and inform her of their intention. It soon became evident that she did not share their enthusiasm, insisting that the letters were her copyright – which legally was not so. It was quickly decided not raise that issue as she, too, had many valuable letters in her possession.

It appears that Mrs Cobden had "conceived a violent prejudice"[3] against Thorold Rogers, a clergyman, economist, statistician and – eventually – Liberal MP. Rogers was a friend and keen advocate of Cobden's ideas, but her sudden disapproval of the man developed into a concern that he would be asked to edit her husband's letters. The reasons for her dislike of Rogers are a mystery, as he had officiated at the marriage of one of her daughters and had preached the sermon at her husband's funeral. A person of tact was needed to manage the awkward widow. The Cobden friends quickly decided on Henry Richard. Everything was in his favour: he was the Secretary of the Peace Society; he was the advocate of arbitration, the author of Joseph Sturge's biography and a wholehearted admirer of Cobden. Even more importantly, in the opinion of the predominantly English members of the Cobden Club, he was Welsh, and might gain the sympathy of the fickle widow. Early in January 1873 Thomas Thomasson[4] was given the task of visiting Mrs Cobden and suggest to her that Henry Richard be asked to edit the letters. Mrs Cobden vacillated – at first enthusiastic, she would then change her mind and suggest other names. Then she would raise the subject of how the letters should be classified, chronologically or should they be grouped according to subjects. It was becoming obvious that she wanted to keep control of the project. The patient Thomasson was getting to the end of his tether and no one knew for sure if Mrs Cobden wanted any money from the book or just the prestige of being associated with the project; the Club offered her the roylaties, assuming money to be the motive. On 5 February 1873 Thomasson wrote to Mrs Cobden asking her to communicate henceforth with Henry Richard. He was washing his hands of the matter.[5]

Thomasson's letter had the desired response – a letter from Mrs Cobden, dated 8 February 1873, sent directly to Henry Richard. She wrote that she was busy putting her late husband's papers in order and suggested "that an advertisement ought now to be one of the first steps taken simultaneously with a circular to his correspondents" inviting them to submit letters they had received from

Cobden which could be considered for publication. Richard's response was worthy of an advocate of conciliation! He had hesitated greatly before accepting what he saw as "a very honourable, but also, a very delicate and difficult task" requiring great wisdom. "I consented only on condition that I should have the entire confidence of Mr Cobden's principal friends interested in the matter, and above all and before all, of course your confidence."[6] He offered suggestions of people who might help with the copying and mentioned Henry Catford who worked in the Peace Society office. Soon, she was again raising problems, such as who would print the book. She proposed W. Ridgway, but in the opinion of the Cobden Club he was expensive and not renowned for the quality of his work. They had a preference for John Cassell. Richard said that he had no view on the matter but in order to get agreement he suggested that they should ask two or three companies to tender for the work. Very soon, Mrs Cobden's unhurried responses to letters and lengthy silences were causing concern for the Cobden Club and to Henry Richard. This was also the time leading up to his motion on International Arbitration and we can imagine Richard rapidly losing patience. In an attempt to hurry matters along, she was assured that any profit from the publication would be hers and in the event of the publication making a loss, the Club would accept responsibility.

There were other problems. People promised letters, but did not keep their promises. Then there was the problem of gathering the many letters Cobden had sent to French politicians and friends. As for Henry Richard, his European peace pilgrimage which began in September 1873 and continued right to the end of the year, followed by the General Election, must have made him put the Cobden letters project on hold. According to H. R. Evans[7] few letters survived from 1874 that indicated any progress. Contact between Richard and Catherine Cobden are even rarer – not one letter between 25 August 1873 and 8 March 1875. Evans suggests that it was unlikely that they met in this period.

It would appear that he had taken a fair number of letters with him on his 1874 alpine holiday to read and put in order. "If I am not mistaken their publication will produce a sensation, and I would fain hope help bring about a Liberal revival," he wrote in his diary.[8] "They cannot fail to raise Mr Cobden's reputation both for ability and high moral qualities." Richard's opinion of the value of the letters was certainly justified, but he was not to edit them. In fact, we still await the complete volume of Cobden's letters. Many were published in John Morley's *The Life of Richard Cobden.*[9] Letters by Cobden relating to international matters were published in J. A. Hobson's book, *Richard Cobden: The International Man.*[10] Nor did Henry Richard write Cobden's biography, although, according to Eleazar Roberts,[11] Catherine Cobden had invited Richard to write it. Miall[12] insisted that his busy public life had prevented him from doing the work and it had to be done by John Morley, a well known journalist – and later MP – from Blackburn. Both were probably incorrect. It is accepted that Catherine Cobden was the stumbling block respecting publishing the letters – and work continues to this day.[13]

Regarding the biography, Richard appears to have done some work, as John Morley in his preface to *The Life of Richard Cobden* acknowledges that "much of the correspondence had already been sifted and arranged by Mr Henry Richard ... who handed over to me the result of his labour with a courtesy and good-will for which I am particularly indebted to him". Sadly, Richard was not always in receipt of the courtesy and kindness he offered others. Very little happened about publishing the complete collection of Cobden's letters, but when Catherine Cobden died in April 1877, there was some hope that the great obstacle had been removed. But soon Richard got confirmation that he did not enjoy the confidence of the Cobden family – in the unkindest way imaginable. In the *Carmarthen Journal* of 18 May 1877, the following announcement appeared:

> It is stated that the Misses Cobden are about to undertake the preparation for the Press of the late Mr Cobden's letters and papers. They will be assisted by Sir Louis Mallet and Mr Caird.[14]

It was a great insult to Richard, done in the name of Richard Cobden, who had no greater admirer. H. R. Evans[15] suggested that the civil servant and active member of the Cobden Club, Sir Louis Mallet, knew nothing of the announcement in the *Carmarthen Journal*. A letter dated 6 February 1878, sent by Mallet to Richard appears to confirm that he had never been approached.[16] As for the Mr Caird, the name J. Caird (possibly the philosopher John Caird) had been put to Catherine Cobden at an early stage in the discussions as a possible member of a committee to help Henry Richard with his work, but she had opposed it. We can be assured that Hugh Williams played no part in the Cobden daughters' decision as he had been dead for three years.

As well as handing over the letters and the work he had done to

John Morley, it would be reasonable to assume that Richard had made a greater contribution to the biography. "Your biography of Cobden is a miniature that I have perused with entire sympathy and admiration," wrote Morley to Richard on 8 April 1878. "Both the spirit and the execution make it all that such a vignette should be."[17] Undoubtedly he was referring to the entry contributed by Richard to the *Encyclopaedia Britannica*, a splendid essay in the opinion of Eleazar Roberts,[18] who went on to claim that many had suggested that Richard should have written the biography.

But these were disappointments that lay ahead. Richard was able to enjoy the autumn break in 1874, a few weeks of quiet happiness. He and his wife enjoyed the splendours of the mountains while Richard immersed himself in the letters of his political hero. They left Aigle, visited Berne, Interlaken, Lucerne, saw the sun rise over the Righi – there was no railway to the summit in those days – and watched it set.

He returned to his busy round of public activities, setting off almost immediately to the autumn session of the Congregational Union of England and Wales where he gave a speech on Religion and Politics. Nonconformist spiritual prosperity, he said, had come hand-in-hand with an active discharge of their duties as citizens. Over the previous 40 years, when there had been remarkable political activity, the Congregationalists had built more chapels, founded more schools and missions, and engaged more in charitable enterprises than ever before. In an address to the Liberation Society in Manchester shortly afterwards he made a rather surprising comment, alluding to a rumour that there had been a disagreement between himself and Edward Miall, and that they were rarely seen on the same platform. Richard announced that there was no basis at all to the whispers. "If those gentlemen who make these unworthy insinuations only knew on what terms of affectionate brotherhood Mr Miall and I have lived for so many years, without a cloud in our friendship, or a jar of jealousy – I always ready and willing to act as his humble lieutenant, and recognising him as our captain – they would not anymore repeat these absurdities."[19]

He was at the Colston Celebration in Bristol in November, presumably to celebrate the life of Edward Colston.[20] His friendship with the Bristol MP, Samuel Morley, explains Richard's presence but it would appear a strange event for him to attend. Born 2 November 1636, Colston, who had been briefly a Tory MP for Bristol, was a generous benefactor to the city – establishing schools and workhouses – but his money had been made in the slave trade. Colston has always been a controversial figure in Bristol, with the many buildings, schools and monuments perpetuating his name. Richard also addressed the annual dinner of the Anchor Society, another of the societies founded in Bristol in memory of Colston, a political society, supporting the Whigs, then the Liberals. The other speakers were Samuel Morley and Lord Ducie (Henry Reynolds-Moreton), who for a short time had been a Liberal MP for Stroud, before inheriting his father's titles.

Richard addressed the failure of the Liberals in the General Election earlier in the year. It was because, he said, that they had gone "down to Egypt for help".[21] A reference to Clause 25 of the 1870 Education Bill and how Forster had ignored the wishes of the Nonconformists and relied on the support of the Tories to get the Bill passed. But Richard was not one to lose heart. When the first reformed Parliament (1832) had succeeded to pass a number of progressive bills, the Whigs were heavily defeated by the Tories in 1834 and Sir Robert Peel became Prime Minister. Their followers, said Richard, were very dejected, and one of them, Sydney Smith, had doubted whether the laws of nature still operated. Smith had gone out to his garden and sown some cress and mustard seeds, and after a few days he felt better when he saw the green shoots come from the ground! At the time Richard was making his speech the Liberal front bench, now in Opposition, was in complete disarray. But in his opinion there was no possible leader, he said to a resounding cheer, no one but Gladstone.[22] John Bright was not a credible alternative because of the state of his health. Gladstone surpassed all as an orator and statesman. Also, because of his religious earnestness, Richard saw him as a man to be trusted. True, Gladstone was High Church, preferring a "richer ritual" than that which satisfied Richard and his Nonconformist friends but that was no reason to refuse him. Although the great Whig families were the *crème de la crème* of creation – Richard again in derisive mood – as leaders he thought them effete, and he believed that the progress made in recent years had been achieved under the radical wing, and their faithful leader Gladstone. He did not wish to split the Liberal Party, but while some would wallow in the Slough of Despond others would hurry on to the Delectable Mountains, Richard wished that they would march together, adapting their steps to each other's pace under the banner and on it the words, "Onwards! Onwards"!

The Liberals, following the 1874 general election, were, as

Henry Richard suggested, in considerable confusion and disarray.
But events in foreign parts helped restore unity. Between 1874
and 1876 there was a series of uprisings in the Balkans, cruelly
suppressed by Turkey. The Ottoman Empire, as will be recalled
from the Crimean War, extended deep into Eastern Europe.
Turkey had lost much of the sympathy it might have had for not
honouring its part of the 1856 Paris Treaty – to respect the rights
of Christians within its Empire. Its treatment of the Christians
had provoked rebellion amidst the Slavs of Bosnia and
Herzegovina. In 1875 Austria-Hungary, Russia and Germany
tried to calm matters down, and the following year the
Dreikaiserbund – Three Emperor's League – produced the "Berlin
Memorandum" calling for a cessation of hostilities for two
months which would allow negotiations to take place. There were
also suggestions of threatening Turkey with sanctions if it continued to disregard the promises it had made nearly 20 years earlier.
France and Italy approved the proposal but Disraeli refused his
support because "England" had not been consulted. Disraeli's
response gave Turkey new confidence, convinced that Britain
would not allow its empire to be threatened. The insurgency
spread from Bosnia and Herzegovina to Bulgaria where the
Turkish soldiers committed their worst atrocities.

Gladstone became infuriated with Disraeli's indifference and
he leapt back into the political fray, leading a campaign against the
barbaric actions of the Turks and re-establishing himself as the
leader of his party. He published the booklet, *Bulgarian Horrors and
the Question of the East*,[23] a scathing attack on the Ottoman empire.
They were not, he wrote, the mild Mahometans of India, nor the
chivalrous Saladins of Syria, nor the cultured Moors of Spain.

> Wherever they went, a broad line of blood marked the track
> behind them; and, as far as their dominion reached, civilisation
> disappeared from view. They represented everywhere govern-
> ment by force, as opposed to government by law.[24]

He accused Disraeli and his Government of deliberately conceal-
ing what was happening and keeping Parliament and the people in
ignorance. It was thanks to the *Daily News*,[25] wrote Gladstone, that
the British people became aware of the atrocities committed by
Turkey.

Henry Richard and the Peace Society would not be silent on
such a matter. As more and more details became known the

Society held a series of meetings and protests which came to a climax in the middle of 1876. Among the main agitators were the Liberals and the Nonconformists while the Conservatives, the Church of England and Queen Victoria opposed the protests. Disraeli's cool response was that the Bulgarians got what they deserved for their audacity and that the British people should have no sympathy for them. But the Liberals were leading – and controlling – the argument, leaving the Tories with no room to manoeuvre or respond. Among the intelligentsia – of both parties – there was hardly a person who was silent. For an issue that had nothing directly to do with Britain, the response was electrifying – unique even. One of the difficulties was the attitude of the Tories towards Russia. Eventually, in 1877, Russia went to war with Turkey following the failure of international diplomacy to secure peace. Even some Liberals were worried that this would strengthen and extend Russia's influence – one of Britain's reasons for siding with Turkey in the Crimean War. Henry Richard had argued consistently since the start of the Crimean War that the Russians had no intention of extending its territories nor its sphere of influence. His pamphlet *History of the Origin of the War With Russia*, first published in 1855, was reprinted. In order to throw "light on the cause of that War, an opportunity should be afforded to the young generation that has come into political life since those days, to judge for themselves what really was the nature and amount of those Russian demands in 1853-4".[26] Copies were distributed to MPs and Members of the House of Lords, and to newspaper editors, and we can assume that it played an important role in reminding the public what a blunder the Crimean War had been.

Richard also a played a prominent role in establishing the Eastern Question Association which became increasingly important in view of the intransigence of Disraeli. There was disagreement even within the Tory administration – one group wanting to stay neutral and not get involved, the other group anxious to take arms for the honour of "England", although they could not agree on which side! The peace lobby kept up the pressure, urging the Government to hold a neutral position while seeking opportunities to mediate in an attempt to end the bloody conflict. Members of both Houses joined in the campaign, as did leaders from all the religious denominations, mayors, magistrates, university professors and industrialists in one united front to form public opinion. The Eastern Question Association, formed with the aim of watching events in Eastern Europe and to give voice to public opinion, provided useful information and was a restraining influence on the Government. It was officially launched in St James's Hall, London, on 8 December 1876, at a conference following one of the most powerful series of protests that had ever been seen in Britain – a conference sometimes referred to as the "Anti-Turkey Conference". The Duke of Westminster presided at the afternoon meeting with the Earl of Shaftesbury presiding in the evening. Henry Richard was among the afternoon's speakers with Gladstone speaking in the evening. When Richard called on the conference to declare that not a penny of British money, and not a drop of British blood, should be expended on upholding "that organised barbarism called the Ottoman Empire", the entire conference erupted to loud cheers of approval. The activity and excitement was reflected in the letters pages in the newspapers and the pamphlets and booklets flowed from the presses. Among the first was a reprint of Henry Richard's *Evidences of Turkish misrule*, another pamphlet he had first published in 1855. The pamphlet was praised by the Liberal *South Wales Daily News*:

> Mr Richard has rendered valuable service to humanity ... civilisation itself is indebted to him for bringing into one compact whole such an array of evidence from historians, travellers, diplomats, statesmen and Government officials, who were witnesses of what they describe, in proof of the incurable and deadly misrule of Turkey.[27]

The agitation in response to the atrocities committed by Turkey was at its greatest in Wales, the South-West and North of England – strongholds of Nonconformity.[28] The vast majority of British people – with the exception of Henry Richard and his small band of followers in the Peace Society – had supported the Crimean War. They had been particularly hostile towards Russia and supportive of Turkey. Welsh radicals were no exception, but Turkey's failure to respect the Paris Treaty of 1856 had changed public opinion. Henry Richard made a point of this shift in public opinion in a speech in Merthyr Tydfil on 13 September 1876,[29] when he said that the majority of the British people, including the Liberal Party, apart from a tiny minority, had supported the war. It may be that many in his audience had read *Evidences of Turkish Misrule* and remembered his opposition to the Crimean War. Maybe they also recalled the physical threats to which he had been subjected. This time the flow of public opinion was with him. Britain had fought a useless and unnecessary war in the Crimea to protect the Turkish Empire and "maintain the balance of power ... a cabalistic phrase the politicians use when they want to throw dust in the eyes of the people," he said.

This time Richard and his colleagues succeeded in keeping Britain from becoming involved, although Britain was politically and financially supportive of Turkey. There was another faction within and outside Parliament who wanted to support Russia. As Richard said in a speech in Merthyr in December 1877,[30] John Bull always believed that wherever in the world there was a quarrel it was a matter of honour that he should be there with his stick stirring up trouble. Other countries, this time, had been doing all they could to secure peace. After Turkey had defeated the uprisings in Serbia and Montenegro in 1876 Russia insisted that it should agree to a cease-fire and a Conference was held in Constantinople on 23 December 1876, at which Germany, Austria, France, Britain (Lord Salisbury), Italy and Russia were all represented. Turkey was asked to make reforms to ensure peace within and beyond its borders. Although Turkey's Foreign Affairs Minister, Safvet Pasha, was present and was party to the agreement, the Sultan and his ministers resisted and refused to ratify the recommendations. Britain, France, Germany and the other countries failed to bring pressure on Turkey. Russia acted independently, and in an alliance with some of the Balkan nations, declared war on Turkey on 24 April 1877. Turkey, by the end of 1877, faced defeat and appealed to Britain to act as arbitrator. At first, Russia refused, but after three months of frantic diplomatic negotiations, the problem – if not the debate – was resolved in July, with the Berlin Treaty.

Henry Richard, accompanied by Frédéric Passy, Professor Leone Levi of King's College, London, and a number of representatives of the peace movement from France and the Netherlands, went to Berlin hoping that a clause on international arbitration would be included in the treaty as in the Paris Treaty of 1857. This time, in spite of the number of peace representatives who went to Berlin compared to the three – Richard, Sturge and Hindley – who had gone to Paris in 1856, they did not achieve the same success. There was disagreement now between Austria and Britain on the one hand and Russia on the other. Count Luigi Corti of Italy and others argued that France, Germany and Italy had donned the mantle of arbitrators. The efforts of Richard and his friends were not altogether in vain since Article 63 of the Treaty declared much to their relief "that the Treaty of Paris of 1856 and the Treaty of London of 1871 are maintained in all such of their provisions as are not abrogated or modified by any of the stipulations in the Treaty of Berlin".[31]

A significant outcome of the Berlin Treaty was the application of the principle of self-determination for oppressed national minorities – a principle Gladstone and Henry Richard adhered to throughout the crisis. Romania, Serbia and Montenegro were given their independence from the Ottoman Empire and Bulgaria was re-formed as an independent state after four centuries under Ottoman rule.

This had the effect of Welsh radicals identifying with Bulgaria, and other Balkan countries who desired to be free from the Ottoman Empire. It has been suggested that Richard, who had supported the principle of self-determination for small nations throughout the Bulgarian crisis was emerging as a leader of Welsh nationalism as well as Welsh Nonconformity in the House of Commons.[32] This was not so according to Goronwy J. Jones, although he suggests that Richard may have been an unwitting catalyst in the emergence of Welsh nationalism and that the Bulgarian tragedy was a significant turning point in the attitude of the Welsh people towards self-government. Could it also be said that his *Letters and Essays on Wales* had a similarly unintentional effect? As has already been suggested, Richard claimed that the purpose of those articles first published in the *Morning Star* in 1866 was to educate the English about the Welsh. But they proved even more effective in raising Welsh pride and confidence.

Richard's successful parliamentary resolution of July 1873, was still reverberating around the political world. The Swedish Parliament in Stockholm had approved a motion supporting the principle of International Arbitration. News also came that the Dutch Second Chamber in The Hague had given qualified support to a similar motion – a willingness to co-operate if not to take the initiative – by a majority of 35 votes to 30.[33] In the United States on 17 June 1874, the House of Representatives adopted the following resolution, which was later approved by the Senate:

> That the people of the United States, being devoted to the policy of peace with all mankind, enjoying its blessings, and hoping for its permanence and universal adoption, hereby, through their representatives in Congress, recommend such arbitration as a national substitute for war; and they further recommend to the treaty-making of the Government to provide, if practicable,

hereafter, in treaties made between the United States and
Foreign Powers, that war shall not be declared by either of the
contracting parties against the other, until efforts shall have been
made to adjust all alleged causes of differences by impartial arbitration.

The House also adopted the following resolution:

Resolved by the Senate and House of Representatives, that the
President of the United States is hereby authorised and
requested to negotiate with all civilised Powers who may be willing to enter into such negotiation for the establishment of an
international system whereby matters in dispute between different Governments agreeing thereto may be adjusted by arbitration, and, if possible, without recourse to war.[34]

Also in 1874, news came of the death of two who had worked diligently alongside Henry Richard for the cause of peace – Visschers,
who had provided such support in organising the three European
peace congresses, particularly the first one in Brussels, and Senator
Charles Sumner of the United States.

Chapter 20

The Burials Bill and relations with China

The demands on Henry Richard's time were ever increasing. It is doubtful whether any Nonconformist layman ever played a more prominent role in religious affairs. On 19 January 1875, he attended the official opening of the Congregational Memorial Hall and Library in Farringdon Street. By 1850 the Congregational denomination had developed a network of 3,200 flourishing chapels, many of them prominent in the high streets of England, Scotland and Wales. In 1862, on the bicentenary of the expulsion of Dissenting Ministers from their homes and livelihoods within the Church of England a decision was taken to build new chapels and a memorial hall and library to house the valuable books and manuscripts collected by Joshua Wilson.[1] He was the son of Thomas Wilson, the influential treasurer of Highbury College, with whom Henry Richard had had a tetchy relationship in his student days.

The good and the great of the Congregational and other Nonconformist denominations were present at the opening, among them Samuel Morley, the Bristol MP, who had contributed £5,000 towards building the Memorial Hall and Library. Joshua Wilson's nephew, John Rimington Mills, with £12,000 the single most generous contributor to the project, presided. Among the speakers were Henry Richard who spoke of "The Contention of Modern Nonconformity for Religious Equality". He admitted frankly that their forefathers, with notable exceptions had not accepted the principle of religious equality. The outstanding exceptions, he said, were the early Baptists who held just views with regard to the role of the civil magistrate in religious affairs. The history of Dissent, he said, showed that Nonconformists in the first instance had not opposed the Establishment theory, and had only done so in response to injustice. It was so in the history of the Calvinistic Methodists in Wales, the Wesleyans Methodists in England and the Free Church of Scotland. As for the last two named denominations they were only beginning to realise that the evils of which they complained were not accidents but sprang from the very heart of the Established Church system.[2]

The library was relocated to its present building at 14 Gordon Square in the last quarter of the twentieth century.

On 29 January, ten days after the official opening of the Memorial Hall and Library in Farringdon Street, Henry Richard was elected Chair of the Deputies of the Three Denominations – the Presbyterians, Congregationalists and Baptists – in London. The association was formed in 1727 and was effective in defending the civil and religious rights of Dissenters. The – unanimous – election of Henry Richard, following the resignation of the printer and politician Sir Charles Reed, was an indication of the respect he enjoyed among London Nonconformists. In his first address from the chair he gave a brief history of the work and success of the Deputies, success that came from constant vigilance and not putting too much trust in political parties. They had been loyal to the Liberal Party and while openly admitting their disagreements with Gladstone, they did not plot against him and Richard was confident that much more would be achieved for justice, freedom and Liberal progress. He said that he had recently heard John Bright say that the question of Disestablishment was coming to the fore again and that politicians needed to be alert to respond wisely to that great problem.[3] In his book, Charles Miall[4] quotes extensively from the testimony of the Secretary of the Deputies, Alfred J. Shepheard. While listing Richard's many favours to the organisation he mentioned in particular his diligence in "watching the almost innumerable Bills relating to ecclesiastical matters introduced into the House of Commons (in many of which clauses are constantly inserted prejudicially affecting Nonconformists)".

George Osborne Morgan plugged away with his Bill to allow Nonconformist services to be conducted at burials, whether in parish churchyards or cemeteries. He presented it again in 1875 – he did so every year from 1870 until he finally succeeded in 1880. Osborne Morgan was the son of an Anglican clergyman, the Rev Morgan Morgan of Conwy. Morgan Morgan's parents were both from Cardiganshire, his father David Morgan from Llanfihangel Genau'r Glyn and his mother, Avarina Richards, connected to the interesting Ffos-y-bleiddiaid family, Swyddffynnon, six miles from Tregaron, Henry Richard's birthplace. Osborne Morgan and Henry Richard co-operated on many campaigns, particularly ones of special relevance to Wales. Richard, as ever, supported Morgan's Burials Bill and spoke at the Second Reading on 21 April 1875.

Osborne Morgan argued that it was a civil, not a religious right, for a person to be buried in a parish cemetery. There were in England and Wales between 12,000 and 13,000 graveyards, and for millions of inhabitants the only place of burial was the parish churchyard. Opponents of the Bill argued that allowing Nonconformists to conduct part of the service at the graveside was a step away from demanding the right to conduct marriage cere-monies within parish churches. Morgan's response was that Nonconformists had no difficulty in getting married in accor-dance with their religious beliefs, as they could do so in a Nonconformist place of worship, or at a Registry Office. The problem with burials was that the great majority of Noncon-formist chapels did not have a cemetery so there was no choice but for people to be buried in the parish churchyard.

Gladstone, although a High Churchman, supported Morgan's Bill, as did Henry Richard at the Second Reading with a vigorous and factual speech. Richard could see no difficulty. He had attended scores of Nonconformist funerals and found that for the most part the service followed the same order as that of the Church of England and for a very good reason: it was based on verses from the Scriptures, a choice made with "admirable judge-ment and taste". "And it is remarkable," he added, "that the com-paratively small portions of the service not taken from the Bible are just those to which not only Nonconformists, but many Churchman have strongly taken exception."

One reason why the Church of England has lost its hold on large sections of the people, was its unyielding rigidity and adher-ence to forms. "Your system is hard, inelastic, unaccommodating," he argued. "You insist upon putting your own ministers – highly intelligent and educated gentlemen – into a strait-waistcoat of uni-formity, and do not give them the slightest power or discretion to vary or alter the services they perform according to the circum-stances of the case."

There was, he continued, a large class of people, consisting of Nonconformists of every denomination, who were forbidden to have their dead buried by their own ministers, and in accord with the religious forms of their preference. "It seems to us as if the Church took advantage of its position to lay its hand on the Dissenter and claim him as its own when dead, though through life he has conscientiously refused her his allegiance," he said. Were it not for the labours of the Nonconformists there would be a deplorable destitution of religious instruction among large masses of the people, he continued, adding that some Anglicans did not hesitate to join with the Nonconformists in religious and philanthropic campaigns. "Yet when we come with our dead to the graveyards, which are the property of the nation, and ask to have them interred by our own ministers, and with such religious serv-ices as are most consistent with our consciences and preferences, you meet us with uplifted hands, and exclaim – Procul, O procul, este profani!"[5]

He proceeded to list very county in Wales, with the exceptions of Radnorshire and Monmouthshire, noting the numbers of Nonconformist chapels that had a cemetery. Of a total of 1,658, only 532 had a cemetery.[6]

Interestingly, although George Osborne Morgan's opening speech suggested that, with the Conservatives in power, he was not hopeful of success, the vote was very close, 234 in support and 248 against – a majority of just 14. It was the smallest majority since Disraeli's administration had come into power the previous year. As well as Gladstone, W. E. Forster and John Bright spoke in favour of the Bill and a small number of Conservatives voted with the Liberals, while others abstained.

Henry Richard had the opportunity to speak up on the issue of Disestablishment during the Second Reading of the Bishopric of Saint Albans Bill, 11 May 1875. This was a Bill presented by the Government to create a new bishopric, to which Richard tabled an amendment to postpone the debate. It may be thought that, he as a Nonconformist, had no right to meddle in a matter relating to the internal organization and government of the Church of England, he said. But in the eye of the law, they were all members of the Church of England, whether they liked it or not. He went on:

> I acknowledge the anomaly. I confess that it appears to me a fla-grant absurdity, that a Body constituted as this House is – and it cannot be otherwise constituted, if it is to be a fair representation of the people of this country – a House consisting of members of the Church of Rome, of the Greek Church, of Presbyterians of

various denominations, of Independents, Baptists, Wesleyan and
Calvinistic Methodists, members of the Society of Friends,
Unitarians, Jews, and I know not how many other forms of religious faith or no faith, should have committed to it the duty of
regulating everything pertaining to the faith and practice, to the
doctrine, discipline and worship of a Protestant Episcopal
Church ... I remember the Right Honourable Gentleman the
Member for the University of Oxford some years ago, under the
pressure of this difficulty, suggesting that the Roman Catholic
and Nonconformist Members of the House might be asked to
abstain from taking any part in discussing and voting on questions connected with the Church of England. But that, of course,
was only a momentary thought ... If Roman Catholics and
Nonconformists are to abstain from taking part in discussing and
deciding Church of England questions, then the members of the
Church of England must in like manner abstain from interfering
in questions affecting the rights and interests of Roman
Catholics and Nonconformists. I remember, also, [Mr.
Gladstone], on the same or a similar occasion, saying that ecclesiastical legislation has become very difficult in this House, and
that it may become impossible. But all this is inevitable so long as
we have the Church connected with the State.[7]

It is an entertaining and readable speech with references to curates
and clergy living in penury while Bishops in their splendours
blindly supported the Government with "an elasticity of conscience to which only Episcopacy can attain". It need hardly be
said that Richard's amendment was defeated by 273 votes to 61.
Richard Davies, the Liberal – and Calvinistic Methodist – MP for
Anglesey was the only Welsh MP to support him on that occasion.

Henry Richard and his wife set off for The Hague after the
House broke up for the summer recess in August 1875 with the
intention of attending the meetings of the two International
Juridical Associations. They arrived on the last day of the month to
find that the conference of the *Institut de droit international* had
ended, but the pacifist and politician Jan Pieter Bredius, who came
to welcome them said that the Queen of the Netherlands had set
that day aside to receive the delegates of both conferences. When
she was introduced to Henry Richard as "the author of the celebrated motion on arbitration in the British Parliament", she
replied, "I am happy, Mr Richard, to make your acquaintance;
your name is well known to me, as it is over the world".[8]

The following day the Association for the Reform and
Codification of the Law of Nations met under its President David
Dudley Field. Henry Richard spoke on the subject of international

arbitration. He argued for the need for consistency and unity to
the law of nations, and if that were achieved there would be more
hope of establishing a great tribunal to adjudicate between
civilised nations, just as the Supreme Court of the American
Confederation adjudicated between the States of the Union, and
between the Federal Government and the different States. The
subject of establishing an International Tribunal, Disarmament
and Non-intervention were discussed. Two resolutions were
agreed – both drafted and presented by Henry Richard. The first
was on the subject of International Arbitration, praising those
countries that had approved the principle and others who had
adopted it. The second resolution deplored the enormous and
ever-increasing armaments budget, urging the Governments to
agree a mutual reduction of this dangerous extravagance.[9]

In this practice Britain was as guilty and extravagant as any
country. In the two years that Disraeli had been in Government,
the military expenditure had increased by £2,300,000. And when
the Government in 1876 presented its estimates for the following
year, proposing a further rise of £600,000, Sir Wilfrid Lawson, seconded by Henry Richard, proposed an amendment opposing the
increase. They were also supported by Jacob Bright (John Bright's
younger brother), Joseph Whitwell Pease of the Quaker, pacifist
and Liberal family, and Peter Rylands, another of the North of
England industrialists.[10]

And for what purpose do we need these armaments? asked
Richard. To defend ourselves from attacks? But from whom?
France had been the great threat, whether as a constitutional
monarchy, republic or empire – it was irrelevant. Whatever the
condition of the French Government, whether in the agonies of
revolution at home, trying to create a constitution out of earlier
ruins, or at war with Austria or Italy, or entering into trade treaties
with Britain, the British people were constantly being urged to
believe that France was always meditating some mischief against
us. He went on:

> Then, for what other purpose do we want a large Army? We have
> renounced the policy of intervention in the quarrels of the
> Continent, at least all our statesmen have done so – Conservative
> as well as Liberal. In proof of this I may cite the words of Lord
> Derby, the Foreign Secretary. In addressing his constituents at
> King's Lynn, when he was a Member of this House, adverting to
> the debate on the Dano-German War, which had taken place in
> 1864, he said: 'The ostensible object of that debate was to take

the sense of this House as to whether the Danish negotiations had been mismanaged, but the object with which many Members – I among the rest – went into it, was to obtain from Parliament a distinct and decided expression of opinion in favour of a policy of non-intervention in Continental disputes; in that we perfectly succeeded.' The Right Honourable Gentleman himself the Secretary for War made an admirable speech in the same debate, in which, referring to the facts of the Dano-German War, and the part we had taken in the matter, he said, 'I say that facts point to the conclusion that the position of England, free from Continental complications and embarrass-ments, fits her for being the mediator of Europe. They point out that, having nothing to gain from the oppression of the smaller States, nor from the damage of the larger, she is qualified to occupy a position of dignified neutrality, a position in which she can wield more influence than she could ever gain by war'.

Richard ended his speech by urging the Government to put an end to the disastrous system of wild expenditure and agree to the reduction of arms and that "peace is really our policy".

The amendment was defeated by 192 votes to 63. Defeated, said Richard, by a majority closely connected, either personally or by family relations with some of the services, into whose hands these enormous sums were poured in increasing amounts year by year.

Richard was given the opportunity to return to the same subject in just two months in support of an amendment by Peter Rylands opposing the raising of income tax. This again because of the insa-tiable thirst of the armed services. Turning to the Book of Proverbs[11] the services, he said, were "like the daughter of the horse-leech, whose cry is continually 'give, give,' and the misery is, that however much you give them, they have nothing to show for it. To pour money into the hands of the services is like pouring water into a sieve. According to my calculations, we have during the last 20 years, from 1856 to 1875, spent £550,000,000 on our defences, and yet at the end of that time we are constantly told that we are absolutely defenceless."[12]

Towards the end of June, Richard brought before Parliament the state of Britain's trade relations with China and on the 27th he tabled the Resolution:

That, having regard to the unsatisfactory nature of our relations with China, and to the desirability of placing those relations on a permanently satisfactory footing, this House is of opinion that the existing Treaty between the two Countries should be so revised as to promote the interests of legitimate Commerce, and to secure the just rights of the Chinese Government and people.[13]

There was no part of our history upon which an "honest Englishman" with an unprejudiced mind could look at without mortification and shame. "That is to say, if we are to be judged by the ordinary rules of international morality," he said. The problem stemmed from a class of Englishmen who were always looking for occasions of offence, invariably trivial, and when found they would seize upon them and make them the foundation for invoking measures of vengeance, aggression and annexation. They were always pushing Britain into war with Oriental nations; wars in which they themselves did not fight, nor paid for.

> In our first quarrel with the Chinese in 1838, which led to the war of 1840, we were wholly in the wrong. It was occasioned by the fixed, obstinate, audacious determination of British merchants to smuggle opium into China in flagrant violation of the laws of the Empire, and in open defiance of the reiterated proclamations and protests of the Chinese Government. That war had been called, and justly called, the Opium War. Some had objected to that designation; but no one can read the history of the events that led it to it without seeing that opium was the most important factor in the war. The Home Government, in the first instance, laid down the sound principle that 'Her Majesty's Government cannot interfere for the purpose of enabling British subjects to violate the laws of the country to which they trade, and that they must take the consequences'. But when Commissioner Lin seized and destroyed the contraband opium, which he had as perfect a right to do as our Custom House officers would have to seize and destroy a cargo of smuggled French brandy, we went to war with the Chinese on that issue, and compelled them, among other things, to pay $6,000,000 as compensation to the smugglers.

He proceeded to quote the work of Harriet Martineau[14] in his attack on this disgraceful episode in British history – "an humiliating story, and the wonder of a future generation will be, how we bear the shame of it as easily as we do". Treaties were made, and broken by Britain in a series of actions as despicable and arrogant as any in the entire history of the British Empire. The poppies were grown in north-east India and the opium prepared on a huge industrial scale in the famous Sudder factory in Ghazipur – "the most valuable gem in Queen Victoria's crown" – which the Chinese were then forced to buy to feed Britain's greed for money.[15] Ever since the 1840s, said Richard, this evil – opium – had been a stain on British policy and the main source of the ill-will towards Britain from the Chinese Government and its people. Treaties were broken by British merchants with the full support of the Government:

> For 14 years, from the Treaty of Nanking (1842) to the Treaty of Tientsin, the British Government habitually violated the Treaty by monopolizing the manufacture of opium in India, preparing it for the Chinese market, and selling it for exportation. It allowed opium to be received ... in the ports at which our Consuls resided, and at Hong Kong it permitted opium to be carried along the coast in armed vessels, with the British flag flying; it granted registers to lorchas engaged in smuggling cotton and opium, and these, having the British flag, could bid defiance to Chinese authorities. It may be said that the Chinese Government connived at this trade. Connived at it! What else could they do? They had already bitter experience of what would befall them if they attempted a rigorous execution of their own laws. Sir Rutherford Alcock, in a remarkable Memorandum which he wrote in the year 1857, says that every privilege gained by us has almost invariably taken the shape of some evil or abuse attaching to the exercise of our acquired rights ... Foreign merchants in direct Custom House relations with Chinese authorities, all more or less venal and corrupt, launched into a wholesale system of smuggling, and fraudulent devices for the evasion of duties. Chinese laws and Treaty stipulations were alike disregarded ... The Imperial Revenue was defrauded by both; and foreign trade was demoralized, and converted into a game of hazard and over-reaching.' And he justly remarks that if the Chinese were then loath to make those concessions, how much less disposed they must have been to extend them with the knowledge they possessed that no conscientious payment of duties, or respect for Treaty stipulations can be looked for at the hands of foreign merchants, if the Chinese themselves cannot find the means of making the evasion impossible ... Contempt for all Chinese authority, and disregard of inherent rights, habitual infraction of Treaty stipulations, license and violence, wherever the off-scum of the European nations found access, and peaceable people to plunder; such were the first-fruits of this important concession, and time only served to increase their growth. Our whole intercourse since the Treaty of Nanking has been carried on under a perpetual menace of hostile collision and interruption of trade.

And people wondered why the Chinese had no desire to embrace Christianity. Henry Richard's motion had the support of many in the Liberal Party and following assurances that his Resolution had the approval of the Government, Richard agreed to its withdrawal. However, there was little improvement in the British attitude towards China.

Chapter 21

Religious instruction in schools

A little earlier in the same month that Henry Richard tabled his resolution on China, the Bill to extend Elementary Education went to its Second Reading. The Nonconformists in the House of Commons opposed the Bill as it would, particularly in rural areas, compel Nonconformists to send their children to Church of England schools creating more opportunities for the clergy to promote sectarian education at the expense of the state system. And this would be funded from public sources. On 19 June 1876, during the Second Reading, Richard complained that parts of the Bill had only received the most superficial attention. He complained of the extra influence placed in the hands of the denominational schools – of which the Church of England schools were by far the most numerous – and how this would affect the rights and freedom of a large section of the population who were not Anglicans. It was his duty, he said, to inform the House that every Nonconformist organisation throughout Britain opposed the Bill with such unanimity and seriousness as had ever been seen. The question was not, said Richard, whether religious training was desirable or not. "On that point there is no difference of opinion," he said. "There is none, at least, so far as I am concerned. I yield to no man in this House in my anxiety to have children religiously educated. I go further, and agree ... that there ought to be distinct, clear, positive, religious teaching. I do not believe in a neutral religion that has no blood in its veins – something that will please everybody and displease nobody. But the question is, when and by whom it is to be given?" He gave notice that he would continue to oppose the Bill when it went to Committee.[1]

True to his word, on 10 July he tabled an amendment that "the principle of universal compulsion in education cannot be applied without great injustice unless provision be made for placing public elementary schools under public management."[2]

He explained how the subject of popular education had been a cause close to his heart and that he worked humbly and earnestly for it for over 35 years. "Thirty years ago I took an active part in the establishment of a school for boys, girls, and infants in one of the populous districts of the metropolis, through which school I believe up to the present time some 15,000 or 16,000 children have passed," he said. "In the year 1845 I had the pleasure of starting a movement in favour of day school education in Wales, which has led to the formation of the first Normal school ever established there, and of many scores, if not hundreds, of day schools in various parts of Wales. After that I had the honour of being honorary secretary of the Voluntary School Society, which established normal schools in London, and largely aided by means of grants of money, the maintenance of voluntary schools in various parts of the country."

He begged the House to excuse his little bit of egotism, but he wished the Members to understand that he was not one to object to, nor obstruct, education, but an active worker in that great cause. It would have given him great satisfaction if the Government had introduced a Bill allowing everyone, regardless of sect or political party to work together to promote the work of national education. Unhappily, this Bill promoted sectarian, not national education. He continued: "The object of the Bill is obviously, I may say avowedly, to discourage the formation of school boards, and all that more liberal and unsectarian class of schools that spring from school boards, and to strengthen and extend to the utmost possible extent the denominational schools."

It was not difficult to see how this would annoy Nonconformists. He explained that out of 14,000 parishes outside the boroughs only 1,749 had school boards. This left over 12,000 parishes, where, if there were any schools at all, would of necessity be denominational schools. He accused the Government of subsidising these – Church – schools with generous grants from public funds often amounting to twice the income of the school from every other source. This was substantially increased as the local authorities had the power to compel all children in the district, whether they be Roman Catholics, or Nonconformists, or Jews, to attend the denominational schools.

And if any "sturdy Dissenter or Roman Catholic" refused – on grounds of conscience – to send his child to the school, the court had the right to fine him five shillings. It was also more than likely that the Justice of the Peace was the very clergyman who was the manager of that school. And if the "sturdy Dissenter" persevered in his refusal, the child could be taken away to an industrial school until he is 14 or 16 years of age, and the parents compelled to pay for his keep.

It was true, Richard acknowledged, that Nonconformist denominations could establish schools and he noted that a Nonconformist, Joseph Lancaster, had been the first provider of popular education. In Wales, Congregational ministers had, wherever possible, set up schools, or sponsor someone else to do so.[3] It was later that the Church of England began to establish schools and do good work. But the Church had wealth, endowments to the salaries of clergymen, buildings, money from the state, social influence, and the ear of men in power to aid them. The Church had nothing else to do with its money except build schools. The Nonconformists, on the other hand, had to build and maintain their chapels, maintain their ministers, colleges, Sunday schools without assistance from anywhere. Yet, despite the disadvantage, Nonconformists in Wales had built between 400 and 500 day schools. Nor was it correct to say that no unfair influence was exerted on the minds of Nonconformist children attending Church schools, claimed Richard. "The learning of the Church catechism, and the attendance of children at church on Sunday, were *sine quâ non* conditions in many cases for admission into the Church schools."

It had been a fierce and long debate and Henry Richard's amendment was defeated by 317 votes to 99, a majority of 218. Still he refused to give in and contributed regularly to the discussions during the Committee stage, sometimes supporting other times opposing clauses. But when the Bill returned to the floor of the House for its Third Reading on 5 August he was as defiant as ever, declaring it "the worst Bill, the most unjust, the most reactionary, the most tyrannical in spirit, that has been brought before Parliament since Lord Bolingbroke proposed his Schism Bill in the reign of Queen Anne."[4] [The Schism Bill of 1714 prohibited Nonconformists and Catholics from educating their children in their own schools by making it necessary for every schoolmaster to have a Bishop's Licence proving that he had taken the Anglican sacrament within the previous year.] "The object of that measure was the same as this – to put the education of the people of this country in the hands of the Church of England by discouraging and suppressing all other kinds of education," roared Richard. "That failed utterly and ignominiously, as it deserved to fail, and as I hope this also will fail." He accused the Tories of aiming at the very existence of school boards and if all the amendments they had tabled had been carried, it would have jeopardised the existence of those boards.

In Britain, where the diversity of religious opinion was so great, he argued, "you cannot, in rate-supported or State-supported schools, give religious instruction without trenching on the rights of conscience; that, therefore, the religious instruction must be given at other times and by other persons – in a word, that there must be united secular, and separate religious, instruction."

It should be said that Henry Richard was never a keen sup-porter of compulsory education and he had found it difficult to depart from the principle of freedom from state intervention. The old Congregationalists had a vision of covering the country with a system of voluntary education free from state interference.[5] It may be that they never really understood the relationship that should exist between government and education, but they had cause to be suspicious. In Richard's opinion the schools describing them-selves as "voluntary" were not worthy of the name. In the preced-ing 16 years Church schools had received £10,500,000 of public money, while the income from voluntary sources amounted to £600,000 a year.[6] In his final act of resistance when the House divided, Richard was defeated by 119 votes to 46.

Also during the spring of 1876 Richard was elected to the chair of the Congregational Union of England and Wales, his period of office beginning the following year (1877). It was the first time for a layman to be Chair of the Congregational Union – Richard had stopped using the title of Reverend 25 years previously.

It was getting to the end of September 1876 when Henry Richard and his wife set off on what was becoming their annual visit to Europe. Their destination this time was Bremen, now one of the German Government's main trading and ship-building ports in the north of the country, and the fourth conference of the Association for the Reform and Codification of the Law of Nations. The number of those attending, despite a good represen-tation from Germany, France, Austria, Denmark, Norway and Sweden, was down on previous meetings. The Americans were absent as it was a Presidential election year and the German Society of Political Economists were also meeting at the same time in Bremen. Also, soon after the 1875 Conference, James B. Miles, the Secretary, died and his meticulous planning was sorely missed. Henry Diedrich Jencken had been elected in his place. Richard noted that there was much eating and drinking. He mentioned a banquet at the Hall of the Künstlerverein where wine was drunk, which had lain in the Rathaus (City Hall) cellar since 1620 . He did not appear particularly impressed by it and noted that it resembled a "less noble beverage".[7] Among the topics discussed were bills of exchange, a subject of interest to Jencken; the Principles that should regulate the Intercourse of Christian and non-Christian peoples, a subject of much interest to Richard; and the Exemption of Private Property at Sea from Capture, which was presented by Professor Sheldon Amos of London University.

Henry Richard's twelve month period as President of the Congregational Union of England and Wales began in May 1877, not the most opportune time as he was also distracted by matters relating to the "Eastern Question". For his inaugural address from the Chair he chose the subject of "The Relations of the Civil and Spiritual Powers in various countries in Europe".[8] He outlined, in some detail, the relationship existing between Church and State in France, Germany, Italy, Austria, Belgium and Switzerland. His address contained much original research, what he had seen and discussed with eminent men on his European journeys. He talked of the character and conflict in which Nonconformists were engaged. The scepticism he had found on the continent, he claimed, was due to the sinister alliance of Church and State which had damaged the spirit and inclination of Christianity so that it had become alienated from a large section of the best elements of European society. He continued: "Despotism and priest-craft have always been faithful allies, leagued in an eternal conspiracy against the rights and liberties of mankind. Yes, we have a right to say to popes, cardinals, and prelates, and other representatives of official religion all over the world 'The name of God is blasphemed among the nations through you'." The lesson to be learnt, he said, reversing the words of the Gospel according to St Mark, was to "let no man join together what God has put asunder". The address stimulated great interest on the continent. It was translated and published in the *Revue Politique* in Paris and translated into Dutch and other languages.[9]

The first meeting of the Assembly under his presidency was not without controversy. The "Eastern Question" was raised by Dr Robert William Dale, a Congregational Minister from Birmingham and ardent supporter of the Liberal Party. He proposed a resolution of sympathy with Gladstone who advocated a policy of coercion against Turkey, compelling the country to accept the recommendations of the Constantinople Conference of 23 December 1876 – which the Sultan had chosen to ignore.[10] Dale was supported by five of the most eminent delegates. Henry Richard, in the chair, was in a difficult position. The resolution implied approval of the use of force to compel Turkey to comply with the Constantinople recommendations. With great diplomacy Richard praised Dale's proposal and expressed his appreciation of Gladstone's contribution to humanity and freedom. He approved Dale's belief that "England" would give no material nor moral support to Turkey, as it showed how far public opinion had changed among those who had supported the Crimean War and the policies that led to that war. He trusted that those who were so mistaken in 1854 would not now, in 1877, go to the other extreme and advocate going to war with Russia against Turkey. What could have been a contentious issue was averted.

In the autumn Assembly of the Congregational Union at Leicester, on 18 October, he spoke on "The Application of Christianity and Politics". Many of the evils of society, he said, could be traced to the fact that the teachings of Christ had never been fully applied to politics.[11] He spoke of slavery, how governments were treating indigenous population and taking their lands, and of war. He spoke again of the relationship between Church and State and of religion and education. He also spoke of the influence of Christianity.

"I don't believe that Christianity is dead or dying," he said. "Some of the ancient dogmas in which former generations of Christians embodied their conceptions of Christian truth may be dying, and perhaps it is time they should be, and buried out of sight." Christianity as a permeating power in world affairs, he argued, was more alive and powerful than ever. "I ask you to look upon its action upon society, and to consider how much it is doing to elevate, to refine, to humanise our race. Think of the innumerable institutions of benevolence and charity scattered over the face of this and other Christian countries – for the poor, for the orphan, for the sick, for the ignorant, for the blind, for the crippled, for the idiot, for the insane, for the fallen, for the criminal, for every conceivable form of human sin and suffering, which are fed by the sympathy and compassion that Christianity begets, and tell me if this can be accomplished by a dead or dying religion."[12]

Again, he expressed dismay that ministers of the Gospel were not prepared to discuss the subject of Peace and asked them to set aside at least one sermon a year to condemn the warring, revengeful and cruel spirit which so often possessed the people. The Prophets of the Old Testament did not shun from censuring their rulers, why did today's preachers do so? he asked.

During Richard's stay at Leicester the Workmen's Peace Association took the opportunity of presenting him with an illuminated address expressing their admiration of his services for the cause of Peace. In his response to the presentation Richard said that few things had given him greater pleasure than the formation of this association, and the efforts of its members in promoting peace. No class suffered more from the effects of war than the working class.[13] He ended his speech quoting the words written – possibly by Henry Andrews, also known as Francis Moore, of *Old Moore's Almanack*:

"What is it after all, the people get?
Why – Widows, taxes, wooden legs, and debt."

Again, in 1877, George Osborne Morgan presented his Burials Bill – but this time it raised a major storm. The Conservative Government decided, following the Bill's narrowest of defeats the previous year, that something had to be done. The task of guiding a Bill through Parliament which would put an end to the troublesome Morgan's efforts was entrusted to the Home Secretary, Sir Richard Cross. He made a complete hash of it, offering Nonconformists burials without a service – silent burials, as provided at the time for those who had not been baptised or had committed suicide. It was a reactionary Bill – in fact, laughable. It also allowed the Local Authority Boards to close cemeteries if they were full, or on health grounds, and to open new ones paid for by the rate-payers. It was being suggested, too, that most churchyards were very nearly, full. New ones would have two mortuary chapels, consecrated and unconsecrated sections and, presumably, be unconnected to parish churches. It was an attempt to side-step the issue of allowing Nonconformist ministers to officiate in Anglican churchyards. The Nonconformists were furious. In addition to the silent burial insult, it was not true that cemeteries were full, 10,000 remained open and fewer than 1,000 had been closed. The Deputies of the Three Denominations and the Liberation Society jointly organised a conference in April, chaired by Henry Richard in which around 30 MPs were present. John Carvell Williams, the London Welshman, who – with Henry Richard – had taken a prominent part in the Liberation Society's meeting in Wales in the early part of the 1860s, detailed the objections to the Bill. These objections were embodied in a series of resolutions which included a call on the Liberal Party to unite and defeat the Bill. This was done and a mortified Home Secretary forced to with-draw it.[14]

Chapter 22

The Eastern Question, Afghanistan and the Boers

Henry Richard, his wife, and his niece – Margaret Evans – attended the Annual Congress of the Association for the Reform and Codification of the Laws of Nations held in Antwerp from 31 August to 4 September. Richard read a paper on "The Obligation of Treaties". He argued that international morality would be more effectively raised by the gradual growth of public opinion than by appeals to brute force. Later he moved a resolution urging the insertion of an Arbitration Clause in all future International Treaties. It was seconded by Professor Sheldon Amos and unanimously adopted.[1]

From Antwerp they proceeded to Brussels and then to Switzerland. In Zurich they went, as observers, to the Institute of International Law which was meeting for the duration of 10-13 September 1877, travelling to Geneva where the first ever *Congress on the Social Evil* was held.[2] It was a significant event, widening the appeal of the organization and saw the establishment of the International Federation for Aid to Young Women as a protection agency for young women travellers or foreigners. This was a campaign to repeal the humiliating 1864 Contagious Diseases Act "designed to supply soldiers and sailors with an adequate number of safe harlots, slaves of the State, who are to be cleansed as mere sewers – things not person," in the words quoted by Carolyn Evans Campbell in *Soiled Doves of Colorado and the Old West*. Richard met up again with some old friends, among them Sheldon Amos. Also present was Josephine Butler, one of the century's great feminists who was greatly concerned about the fate of prostitutes and a campaigner for better education for young women. Although seeing prostitution as a sin, Butler realised that men took particular advantage of poor women, something she had seen when she did voluntary work in the poor houses of Liverpool. She had often visited France and Switzerland where she suffered persecution from the authorities – but had been warmly welcomed by feminists. Henry Richard addressed the congress in French on the subject of "Standing Armies as a Source of Social Immorality". As prostitutes would converge on military camps, this was a subject pacifists – including Henry Richard – would address from time to time.

The Turkey-Russian war was becoming more prominent as an issue in Parliament. On 28 January 1878, Sir Stafford Northcote, the Chancellor of the Exchequer proposed "that a sum, not exceeding £6,000,000, be granted to Her Majesty, beyond the Ordinary Grants of Parliament, towards defraying the Expenses which may he incurred, during the year ending on the 31st day of March 1878, in increasing the efficiency of the Naval and Military Services at the present crisis of the War between Russia and Turkey". The Liberals were furious. W. E. Forster, put down an amendment opposing the proposal. Since Britain had not taken sides in the war, and there was no justification for doing so, there was no justification for pouring more money into the military coffers. The matter was adjourned and the debate continued until 11 February.

Henry Richard entered the fray on 8 February, the day after the British Fleet had been ordered to sail past the Dardanelles "for the protection of the lives and properties of British subjects in Constantinople". He attacked the appointment of Austen Henry Layard as British Ambassador to Constantinople. Those listening to him recalled that during discussions prior to, and after, the Crimean War Layard had shown himself to have been particularly hostile towards Russia and well disposed towards Turkey. Since his appointment to his new posting to Constantinople he had made no attempt to conceal his prejudices. "Sending such a man at such a time to such a place" under such circumstances "was an act of perverseness, amounting to infatuation", stormed Richard. He then switched his attack on Disraeli. There was a feeling abroad, he said, that there was a disturbing element at work which greatly counteracted the declaration of those Members of the Cabinet "who had endeavoured to keep England out of that desolating war in the South-east of Europe". That "disturbing element" was believed to be the influence on Disraeli. Mr. Richard said that he would not accuse Disraeli of any wish to plunge the country into war; but he could not acquit him of "a propensity to use great swelling words calculated to excite the feelings of his countrymen and to breed resentment in the hearts of other countries". If the Government were not for war, asked Richard, was it not odd that they should come down to the House and say – "Express your confidence in us as a peace Ministry by granting us £6,000,000 for war purposes?" As for the matter of sending the Fleet to the Dardanelles, what British interests were being threatened to justify such an action? The Russian Government had pledged not to direct military operations against Gallipoli, unless a Turkish force assembled there. Yet, in the teeth of all that, and behind the back of the House of Commons, the Government had dispatched the Fleet to the Dardanelles, and that prior to a Peace Conference. "[I]t was as if the [arbitration] adjudicators each went into Court with a loaded pistol in his hand."

Richard ended his speech with a reference to unemployment and poverty:

> Thousands of men in this country are not employed; thousands more cannot earn a scanty subsistence for themselves and their families; thousands, as in the case of South Wales, would have actually starved but for the generosity of the British public. Is this a time to ask for £6,000,000 of the people's money to be expended in armaments?[3]

Richard was referring to the suffering in his own constituency. Some of the ironworks had closed and more suffering had been caused by the coal owners locking men out of the pits. That year Richard and Lord Aberdare (Henry Austin Bruce) set up a fund – which raised £5,000 – to relieve the suffering of the workers and their families. Richard himself took responsibility for acknowledging the hundreds of letters received daily with contributions to the fund.[4]

The Government announced on 8 April its decision to call up the reserves and militia in case Britain went to war alongside Russia – although the Cabinet was split as to which country should be supported, Turkey being the favourite but by very little. Sir Wilfrid Lawson proposed an amendment the following day to the effect that there was "no great emergency ... and that such calling out of the Reserves [was] neither prudent ... nor warranted by the state of matters abroad." Richard joined in the debate, supporting Lawson. He ridiculed the British "fits of terror and aversion" towards other nations. This time it was a "blind, unreasoning hatred and fear of Russia". Sometimes it had been directed against the French – "very often it is the French" – and Turkey, the United States and other countries in turn. He had no patience with these double standards. "If we are philosophically inclined, we say that the Anglo-Saxon race is fulfilling its destinies; if we are piously inclined, that we are following the leadings of Providence. But you may depend upon it there are other nations who are not prepared to allow us to set up this double judgment, one for ourselves and another for others; who look upon our aggressions and aggrandizements with as much jealousy as we do upon those of Russia." In an other part of his speech, he said: "I know the maxim finds much favour in this House, that England never does wrong." He made a comparison with Wales which was not well received by some English MPs, even on his own side:

> I belong to a suppressed nationality myself. It is really amusing to observe the quiet way in which we apply one standard of conduct to ourselves, and another to the rest of the world. My Honourable Friend the Member for Newcastle (Mr. Cowen) told me the other day, with horror and indignation depicted in his countenance, that the iniquity of Russia in her conduct towards Poland had now culminated. In. what respect? In this respect – that the Russian Government had suppressed the use of the Polish language in the Courts of Law, and obliged them to use the Russian language. 'Are you aware,' I said to my hon. Friend, 'that that is precisely what the British Government is doing in Wales. Any poor Welshman is liable to be tried for his life, and hundreds of them have been tried for their lives, in a language of which he is absolutely ignorant.' This did not seem to strike my hon. Friend as anything out of the way when done by Englishmen in Wales, but when done by Russians in Poland it is horrible oppression.[5]

He added: "We go into hysterics of indignation, and say – 'Look at this aggressive Russia!' But, with regard to the countries we ourselves have swallowed, we are like the [adulterous] woman in the Proverbs, who 'wipeth her mouth and saith, I have done no wickedness'."[6]

Sir Wilfrid Lawson's amendment was defeated 64 votes to 319, a majority of 255.

The fiftieth anniversary of the repeal of the Test and Corporation Acts was celebrated in 1878. The Corporate Act of 1661 prohibited anyone who had not taken Communion in accor-dance with the rites of the Anglican Church during the twelve months after being elected to any office relating to the government of a city or corporation from continuing in that office. The Test Act of 1673 extended the prohibition to include civil and military office. This meant that all Catholics, Dissenters, Unitarians, Jews and Quakers were excluded from any form of public office. The exact date of the repeal was 9 May and on that day representatives of the Deputies of the Three Denominations called on Lord John Russell at Pembroke Lodge, Richmond, to present him with an address of appreciation for the part he had played in the 1828 repeal of the Acts and his life-long advocacy of religious freedom. Henry Richard, although his period as Chairman of the Deputies had just ended, led the deputation – which, incidentally, as well as Congregationalists, Presbyterians and Baptists, also included two Unitarians. Russell was too unwell to receive them and Lady Russell accepted the address and read a response from Russell which stated that of all his political successes none was dearer to his heart that the repeal of the two Acts and the emancipation of Dissenters from these "odious disabilities". The Act as applied to Catholics was not repealed until 1829 and restrictions on Jews were not completely abolished until 1890.

The Paris Universal Exhibition of 1878 provided an opportunity not to be missed by the Peace Society and the peace movement in general. The Workmen's Peace Association, particularly Benjamin Lucraft and W. Randal Cremer, took a leading role in organising a Peace Congress, held at the end of September. The International Peace Congress met at the Pavillon de Flore, once a cornerstone of the Palais du Louvre and Palais des Tuileries complex until the latter was destroyed in the Paris Commune uprising of 1871. The Peace Congress lasted five days and there was a strong representation from Britain, which included Henry Pease, President of the Peace Society, Alfred Illingworth, the Vice-president, and Henry Richard. Twenty-nine years had elapsed since the Paris Peace Congress of 1849, the organisation of which Henry Richard had played such a prominent part. Others who had been prominent in 1849 attended the 1878 Congress, including Joseph Garnier and Frédéric Passy of France. Richard chaired the second meeting in which he referred to the previous 25 years – a time when the nations of Europe had increased their military power to an extent never previously seen in the history of the world, but there had been no peace, rather there had been six wars, more terrible than anything seen in the history of humanity. But Richard would not despair because in the preceding 40 years there had been 20 successful examples of arbitration. If only the people could be educated in the principles of peace, and the press to dedicate its massive influence to the same cause and if ministers of religion would cooperate, then reason would supersede might.[7] There were speeches and resolutions on matters peripheral to peace – such as Free Trade and religious freedom – and opportunities to express opinions on liberal issues apart from peace. Among the speakers were women, working men, politicians from many countries and French Government Ministers. A committee was formed which included: Frédéric Passy; Charles Lemonnier, founder of the League of Peace and Liberty in Geneva in 1867; Henry Richard; and Auguste Couvreur, of Belgium, with the aim of making plans for a Universal Federation of Peace Societies.[8]

Among the many resolutions passed there were two on disarmament:

1. That an International Commission, composed of representatives of each nation, be appointed to secure a reduction of the armaments of each nation.
2. That the Governments of civilised peoples should open as soon as possible negotiations to arrive at a proportional and simultaneous disarmament in each country.[9]

The two propositions attracted much attention and a number of politicians supportive to the question of peace set about presenting them to their own parliaments. The first to do so was Jean Dollfus of Alsace who raised the question in the Reichstag at Berlin. Gustav von Bühler, presented a practical proposal to the Reichstag the following March in which he suggested "a general reduction, and disarmament of the armies to about half of their present average strength, when on a peace footing … to last for the term of 10 to 15 years". The actions of Dollfus and Bühler stirred up interest in other countries, particularly Austria and Italy.

The nineteenth century was a time Britain seemed to be constantly skirmishing or at war in some far-flung corner of the globe. Even before the issue involvement in the war between Turkey and Russia was fully developed it was becoming more obvious by the day that Britain was preparing to attack Afghanistan – time for Henry Richard to get involved in another campaign. It is difficult to imagine how he could keep an eye on all that went on in British foreign policy. Britain began a campaign of threatening Afghanistan – an independent country – in order to establish a "scientific frontier" for India, which neither the people of Afghanistan, nor their leaders, had agreed to. What worried Britain was that Russia was extending its sphere of influence and had already taken possession of Tashkent, Samarkand and Khiva. Clearly, in the opinon of some English observers, neither the mountains of the Himalayas nor the Gobi desert were good enough protection against Russian interference in British interests in India. Well before the Paris Congress, Pease, Wise and Richard had published an address calling on their friends in the peace movement to oppose any attack on Afghanistan.

After the 1878 Treaty of Berlin, some the tension between Britain and Russia had eased. But matters deteriorated when Russia sent a delegation to Kabul. Sher Ali Khan, the Emir of Afghanistan, failed to stop the delegation from entering the country. The British demanded that Kabul should receive a delegation from them too. This time the Emir stood firm and the delegation was stopped before it got to the Khyber Pass and politely told to turn back. The British Government was furious, the press fanned the flames and Parliament was called to debate the issue on 5 December. Britain had already declared war on 20 November and sent a powerful army to attack Afghanistan, beginning a war from which Britain would eventually emerge victorious but failing to control a country that has proved stubbornly resistant to foreign interference.

As expected, the debate in the House of Commons on 5 December 1878, was furious. The Liberals argued that Britain – again – had gone to war without the authority of Parliament. Public opinion was also being guided by members of the House of Lords who took the same view as the Liberals. Prior to that Henry Richard had been prodding the Peace Society into action and organising meetings all over Britain. He set out his arguments carefully and presented them in a way that showed the injustice of the war, the suffering and the waste in lives and money. He wrote a series of letters which were published in *Christian World* – and later as a pamphlet entitled *The Afghan Question*. He denounced the Afghan War in a series of speeches in Merthyr shortly after the debate in Parliament, which were praised and published in the *South Wales Daily News*.[10] Evidently his anti-imperialist attacks on Disraeli were welcomed by his constituents who invariably passed resolutions congratulating him on "the calm, dignified and Christian tone of his speeches".[11] The Congregational Union of

England and Wales also protested against the war on Afghanistan. The Government which had proudly returned from the 1878 Berlin Treaty boasting of "peace with honour" soon found its credibility undermined. It had rushed into an unnecessary war, costly in blood and money and terrible suffering for the Afghan people. The Disraeli administration left its finances in a mess, and in many parts of the world an inheritance of suspicion and hatred of the British Empire.

Hardly had two months elapsed before Britain embarked on another minor adventure that would carry on for decades, this time it was in Southern Africa. It began as a border dispute in the Transvaal between Cetshwayo, king of the Zulu nation, and the Boers. A commission was appointed to mediate between the Zulus and the Boers, which resolved the border dispute in favour of the Zulus. But Sir Henry Bartle Frere[12] announced that the decision was one-sided and unfair to the Boers. Frere had done some good work as Governor of Bombay (Mumbai) in the previous decade, where he had shown great sympathy for Indian culture, and unlike most of his fellow countrymen he had not tried to impose Christianity on the population. Unfortunately, after a period in London and Zanzibar he was appointed High Commissioner for Southern Africa and ordered by the British Government to create a confederation of the untidy group of British colonies in that part of the continent. The Zulus were independent and Frere decided that if the confederation were to succeed, the Zulu nation and its large and disciplined army had to be destroyed. He was offensive towards Cetshwayo, making impossible demands with the threat of war if he did not comply. On 11 January 1879, a British army crossed river Tugela, and a fortnight later, at Isandlwaba, 2,000 British soldiers came face to face with 20,000 Zulus. Despite the far superior fire-power of the British – the Zulus had very primitive weapons – the British were annihilated, a traumatic defeat at the hands of a native force. The English papers were enraged, calling it murder while Sir Wilfrid Lawson's argued in Parliament that the Zulus were only defending their land.

Henry Richard took the opportunity to attack Frere on 24 April when the MP for Burnley, Peter Rylands, tabled a resolution questioning the increase in public spending. It was a chance to attack the Government's entire policy which had dragged the public finances to such a state that it was necessary to squeeze £83,000,000 from the pockets of tax payers. Trade was in a dreadful state, industry and enterprise paralysed, the (London) *Gazette* full of bankruptcy announcements, thousands out of work and tens of thousands of those who were in work hardly able to earn enough to feed themselves or their families. All these because the Government had adopted a "a spirited foreign policy" which Richard interpreted as a policy of aggression and meddling, of bluster and blood invariably leading to war or national humiliation, generally to both.

> Sir Bartle Frere said it was necessary to make war on the Zulu Chief, because be maintained a standing army of celibates which was a menace to his neighbours. But if that justified war with Zululand, it would equally justify war with France, with Germany, with Austria, with Russia – in fact, with all the nations of the Continent, for they all maintain standing Armies of celibates which are a menace to their neighbours.

He had often heard it alleged, he said, and doubtless he would hear it again, that it was unfair to attack Sir Bartle Frere, a distinguished public servant placed in a difficult position. He had been reprimanded, but he had not been ordered to return to Britain, and had not been dismissed from office. Richard had no sympathy for him:

> … let who will sympathize with Sir Bartle Frere, I am free to confess that my sympathies are with the 1,200 or 1,500 families who have been plunged into anguish and desolation by his means. Yes, my sympathies are with the mothers, wives, daughters, sisters, who in those desolate homes are sobbing and breaking their hearts over the brave and the beloved who at Isandlana, and elsewhere, were hurled into bloody and premature deaths by his headlong and reckless policy. Yes, and I feel sympathy for the relations of the unhappy Zulus – for they also had wives, mothers, and sisters – thousands of whom, we are told, have already perished while bravely and patriotically, as we should say of others, defending their country against a wanton and unprovoked invasion.

There was hardly a nation on earth, savage or civilised, he pronounced with which Britain had not been in hostile conflict. "There is scarcely a country whose soil we have not manured with human flesh; scarcely a sea whose waters we have not crimsoned with human blood." Since 1816, Britain had been engaged in 73 wars – 73 wars in 63 years! And this was an era sometimes called "an era of peace"! During this time Britain had spent

£1,300,000,000 on wars and in preparations for war. That was, he said, pretty good for a country that was said to be in danger of being corrupted by the Peace-at-any-price Party. What party was that, he pondered. Certainly nor the Tories, despite the bench of bishops in its ranks. Not his own party, where there were men as fierce and ready as anyone to go to war, men with the insane war of 1854 against Russia and the even more shameful war of 1867 against China still on their consciences.

> We are told, with reiterated emphasis, that we are an eminently amiable and pacific race. We never encroach on other people's rights. We never invade other people's territories. Still, there is a vulgar prejudice in society, that when you find a man always getting into loggerheads with his neighbours all round, it affords some presumption that he is himself of an arrogant and quarrelsome disposition. No, it is not the love of peace which is dangerous to a nation. The danger to a country arises when men in high places, and who exercise necessarily great influence upon the character, as well as upon the destinies, of a nation, take such a course as is calculated to deprave and demoralize the public sentiment by habitually tampering with the truth, by exciting a rowdy war feeling through artful appeals to the lowest passions of the lowest classes of the people, by erecting national selfishness into a supreme rule of State …

Jacob Bright rising to speak when Richard sat down, noted that as no member of the Government Ministerial Bench got up he presumed that Henry Richard's speech was unanswerable.[13]

Despite Frere's attempts to keep on good terms with the indignant Boers, in December 1880 the first war against the former Dutch colonists began. And it proved disastrous for Britain with defeats in a series of battles – Bronkhorstspruit, Laing's Nek, Schuinshoogte and Majuba. The Boer Republics were established and Frere's plans for a confederation of British states in southern Africa were shattered.

Chapter 23

Disarmament campaign and the 1880 election

The resolutions passed in the Paris Peace Congress of 1878 had inspired some agitation for peace on the Continent. Henry Richard, in his continuing battle to persuade the nations to agree to reduce their oppressive levels of spending on arms and armies, initiated his own campaign in 1879. He set out his arguments in a speech he delivered to the Congress of the Association for the Reform and Codification of the Law of Nations, held in London in August of that year. On 11 August, he addressed an audience of representatives from Belgium, the Netherlands, France and Sweden on the subject of "International Reduction of Armaments" – a comprehensive statement in which he reiterated his well-rehearsed moral, political and financial arguments.

He was preparing the ground to present a motion on disarmament to Parliament, and in October he spoke in support of the proposal at a meeting in Warrington. Among his supporting speakers were Peter Rylands MP, and John Gordon McMinnies who was elected the following year as MP for Warrington. Richard addressed at some length the European military condition, in which he condemned the prolific waste of the money wrung from the toiling millions and the tyrannical conscription system which forced young men to leave their communities and join armies, often in foreign lands. The meeting adopted a resolution protesting against the war system and pledging support to Richard's motion.[1]

The following month Richard began his campaign of disarmament in Wales. An audience of 500 delegates from all parts of

Wales gathered in the Guildhall, Swansea, to listen to him and Lewis Dillwyn, MP for Swansea, and John Roberts, MP for Flint, another of the Liberal radicals. Richard was confident that if Parliament supported his motion, other European countries would follow. Dillwyn proposed the meeting pass a resolution supporting Henry Richard and called on all present to organise petitions in Wales and to use any influence they had to promote this international campaign. Nevertheless, Dillwyn urged Richard not to hasten too much as there would soon be a general election. The Disraeli administration had lost all respect and was rapidly running out of steam, the Liberals had regained their confidence and felt certain that they would be back in Government in a matter of months. But to the Conservative *Western Mail*, Henry Richard's voice was that "of one crying in the wilderness … crying 'disarm' to the armour clad millions of warlike Europe".[2]

There were, however, signs that the time might have been ripe for such a campaign. On 26 January 1880, a firm proposal was supported in the Austrian *Reichsrat*, expressing "the wish that the Imperial and Royal Governments … consider the idea of a general, proportionate and simultaneous army reduction, which will not alter the respective strengths of the different States." This was promising and there were similar signals coming from other countries sagging under the weight of maintaining their armies. But Richard heeded the advice of Lewis Dillwyn and with the problems piling up Disraeli, on 24 March, called the election.

In his election address Henry Richard emphasised the need for disarmament and arbitration, for religious equality and justice for the Irish. Although Disraeli's foreign policy had been a matter of concern for many, it was issues closer to home that were foremost in Welsh minds – anger over the Burials Bill, the problems of trade and agriculture and Disestablishment of the Church. Polling took place on 2 April, and Henry Richard, as always, headed the list in the Merthyr and Aberdare constituency.

Henry Richard	8,035
Charles H. James	7,526
W. T. Lewis	4,445

Charles Herbert James had been a faithful supporter of Henry Richards, a prominent public figure in Merthyr, a Unitarian who had received his early education at the school of Taliesin Williams – son of Iolo Morganwg. The unsuccessful candidate, W. T. Lewis, was officially an independent. He was Lord Bute's mineral agent and could expect the support of the industrialists and their agents.

Just two Tories clung on to their seats in Wales – Sir Watkin Williams-Wynn in Denbigh and Lord Emlyn, and if only the Liberals had had the confidence to field a second candidate in Carmarthenshire, Lord Emlyn would probably have lost his seat as well. The reason for the Liberals' success, according to Henry Richard, was that the mass of the people were Nonconformists, they trusted the secret ballot, and their anger at the unjust wars instigated by Disraeli.[3] In the new Parliament there were 352 Liberals and 237 Conservatives. There were also 63 Irish Home Rulers – who would generally support the Liberal Party. Within the Liberal ranks there were around a hundred Nonconformists.

After the resignation of the Disraeli Government on 28 April Queen Victoria called on Lord Hartington, who had been leader of the Liberal Party since the 1874 election, to form a Government. He refused, telling her that Gladstone was the only person suitable to be Prime Minister. The Queen, who disliked Gladstone intensely, then called Lord Granville (Granville Leveson Gower) who had been Foreign Secretary in the previous Gladstone administration. He, too, gave the same response and advised her to call Gladstone.[4] She had no choice but to call on "the grand old man". Forming a Government would be no easy task because the more conservative wing of the Liberal Party did not share the progressive wing's admiration of Gladstone. The new Parliament did not meet until 29 April, although that, in part, was due to the Easter recess.

A Parliamentary Breakfast was held for the friends of religious equality at the Cannon Street Hotel at the end of May, organised by the Liberation Society and the Deputies of the Three Denominations. It was also an opportunity to celebrate the success of the Liberal Party in the General Election and the Nonconformists among them. There were about 30 MPs present with Henry Richard presiding. Richard's address attracted much press attention – generally favourable, especially from the *Times*. Richard, in sarcastic mood, commented afterwards that he was moved almost to tears by this new sympathy shown by the Tory press towards Nonconformists. Especially as that element of the press had referred to Parliament as "their Parliament".[5] In his speech at the breakfast Richard mentioned Gladstone's generous and appreciative acknowledgement of the Nonconformists' contribution to the election success, calling them "the backbone of the Liberal

Sir Watkin Williams-Wynn – an endangered species

Party". Richard warned against making extreme and unpractical demands on the Government and damaging confidence in the Party when those demands were shown to be impossible. He expressed readiness to be patient with the Government, which had succeeded to a dismal inheritance of blunders, complications and crimes and to remember also that they were members of the great British community, interested in everything that concerned peace, prosperity and honour. When the Government presented good measures they would be assured of firm support from the Nonconformist Members. Nevertheless they would not forget that the gains made during fifty years of alliances with the Liberal Party in the acquisition of civil and political rights had happened through their own efforts. Richard also reminded his listeners that only two of the hundred MPs appointed to offices in the new Liberal Government were Nonconformists. They did not desire offices, he said, but there were disadvantages to being excluded from public life. They did not present it as a grievance, they were merely noting the fact.

The following month there was a large gathering of 4,000 Welsh people in the Crystal Palace with carriages from all over Wales bringing supporters to celebrate the Liberals' election success. Henry Richard addressed the gathering in Welsh where he suggested that Sir Watkin Williams-Wynn might be selected as a specimen of an almost extinct species, a Welsh Conservative MP. The gathering was chaired by Lord Sudeley of Gregynog, the retiring MP for Montgomeryshire. The constituency's new MP was Lord Sudeley's brother, the Honourable F. S. A. Hanbury-Tracy.

George Osborne Morgan was appointed Judge-Advocate-General in the new administration and swiftly took the advantage of the opportunity to present his Burials Bill giving Nonconformists the right to officiate in Parish churchyards. This was the tenth occasion for him to present the Bill and, again, it was a long and, at times, bitter battle. The Bill became Law on 3 September, having been watered down by compromises during its passage through committees and the various Readings in both Houses. Henry Richard tried unsuccessfully to extend the scope of the Act in 1883, but it was some years after his death that a satisfactory conclusion was agreed.

With the Liberals back in Government, and Henry Richard having heeded Lewis Dillwyn's advice not to present his motion on arms reduction until the Tories had been ousted, it was now time to do so. On 15 June he tabled the following motion:

> That an humble Address be presented to Her Majesty, praying that She will be graciously pleased to instruct Her Principal Secretary of State for Foreign Affairs to enter into communication with other Powers, with a view to bring about a mutual and simultaneous reduction of European Armaments.

He was not, he said, going to proclaim "any dangerously pacific views" and promised not to ask the House to assent to anything which the most devout believer in the right of war may not consistently support. The rampant militarism which pervaded and overshadowed the nations had grown to such enormous dimensions that it was impossible to use exaggerated language to describe it. It was, he went on, "an affront to reason, a scandal to civilization, a scourge upon humanity, and, above all, that it is a reproach to that holy religion which the nations of Christendom profess to accept and reverence."[6]

He was appealing not only to pacifists, but also to those who believed the need for arms for defensive purposes to be essential, yet who believed that the spending on defence was excessive. Any celestial visitor would have to conclude that man's main purpose on earth was to "fight and to prepare for fighting", he said, with cutting sarcasm. There were, he claimed, at any one moment 12,000,000 men under arms in Europe of which 4,000,000 were permanently standing armies at an annual cost of £500,000,000.

He pleaded with Gladstone not to turn his back on this great question. "No greener wreath ever surrounded any man's brow than that which will encircle his if he will only consent to grapple with this high argument, and endeavour to bring the various nations of Europe into general concert to reduce those armaments," Richard said. "Above all, he will earn the grateful benedictions of millions of the people who are now groaning under this baneful system of militarism." In another intriguing suggestion he said that "if the various States of Europe pursue the process of increasing their armaments on a principal of emulation, if they can add to forces, batteries, ships, guns, fortifications, &c, against each other; why, in the name of common sense, cannot they reverse that process, and begin to undo the mischief they have been doing so long?"

At the end of the debate Gladstone got to his feet doing what he did in 1873, asking Richard to withdraw his motion and not push it to a vote. However much he sympathised with the idea the time was not ripe to get into discussion on the matter with foreign powers and the House should not force the Government into a position where it might have to disrespect the authority of the House. Richard felt that he had been placed in a perplexing position. He might well have carried his motion as he had done in 1873, but this would have been very embarrassing for Gladstone – although that does not seem to have worried Richard unduly on the previous occasion! But an answer came. The influential John Bright beckoned Richard and placed in his hand another form of words and said, "If you will accept this instead of your own, I think Mr Gladstone would let it pass." The motion, now in the form of a resolution and not an address to the Crown, was accepted by Henry Richard. It was a declaration of sympathy with the principle of Richard's but not binding the Government in any form. As Richard could not propose an amendment of his own motion, he passed the paper to Leonard Courtney, the MP for Liskeard, who was sitting next to him. Courtney duly tabled the amendment, Richard withdrew his motion, and the following amendment was unanimously accepted "amid general cheering":[7]

> In the opinion of this House, it is the duty of Her Majesty's Government on all occasions, when circumstances admit of it, to recommend to Foreign Governments the reduction of European Armaments.

Baner ac Amserau Cymru[8] took the view that the Government had adopted the motion in spirit, if not in the letter. The *South Wales*

Daily News took a more realistic line, making the point that all attempts at reform went through many stages – from being treated with contempt, then patronisingly, then as it moves into the stage of attracting some success it rouses opposition, but when men start denouncing it and swearing that it will never succeed, that is when victory is in sight. Henry Richard's ideas were still at an early stage and it would be wise to remember that and not yield to despair.[9] Richard was not one to despair, although there was no doubt disappointment to find that Gladstone was no readier to raise the matter with foreign powers than Disraeli had been before him.

In fairness to Gladstone he was stuck with the distastrous policies of his predecessor. Disraeli in 1877 had annexed the Transvaal – an action that was criticised by Gladstone in a series of famous speeches he made during his election campaign in Midlothian. After the Liberals came to power in 1880 the Transvaal Boers, on the evidence of the Midlothian speeches, were expecting to have their independence restored. December 1880 came, and after eight months of Liberal rule and no response from Gladstone, the Boers revolted.[10] The first significant battle between the Boers and the British took place near the town of Bronkhorstspruit on 20 December. The Boers did not have an army, the farmers would just get together as the need arose. But they were terrific riders, hunters and excellent shots with the experience of occasional skirmishes with the natives. While they did not have the modern repeater rifles of the British in their every day clothes they blended into the landscape and were more than a match for the lines of British soldiers in their scarlet uniforms. The Bronkhorstspruit battle lasted just 15 minutes during which time 156 British soldiers were killed or injured before they surrendered and taken were prisoner by the Boers. Of the Boers, two were killed and five injured.

That, and similar skirmishes over the following two months, was enough to persuade the British that it was time to start discussing matters with the Boers. Gladstone ordered Major-General Sir George Colley, the British High Commissioner in the Transvaal, to make contact with Paul Kruger, their leader. Colley took his time communicating with Kruger, seemingly disobeying the orders of the Government. He ordered his soldiers to engage the Boers at Majuba Hill on 27 February 1881, which turned out to be the climax of the series of disasters suffered by the British in the Transvaal in the course of a few months. The British were annihilated and Colley was killed. It was a significant battle for more than one reason. The Boers showed themselves to be tactically advanced in military conflict. It also gave them the confidence to challenge the British in the future, whom they concluded were not much good at fighting.

In Britain Queen Victoria, the Conservative opposition and the press were enraged and baying for revenge. However, the Workmen's Peace Association and the Peace Society stood firm in their opposition to the use of military power to prevent the Boers from regaining their independence. Protest meetings were held in England and Scotland. At the beginning of January 1881, Henry Richard led a deputation of 25 MPs and other prominent men to meet Lord Kimberley, the Minister for the Colonies, and present him with an address which Richard had prepared as Secretary of the Peace Society. The address stated that the Transvaal had been possessed by subterfuge, and that "England" should put an end to these acts of bloodshed immediately by giving then Boers their independence. Even the absolutist pacifists in Wales were reluctant to follow Richard's lead and criticise Gladstone on this occasion. Gladstone's good name, as far as Richard and his friends were concerned, was restored with the Pretoria Treaty giving the Boers independence in internal affairs while Britain took responsibility for external matters. This satisfied the pacifists and those who were uncomfortable with Gladstone's policy – but not the Conservatives, as might be expected.

Henry Richard was obviously satisfied that a peace treaty had been signed with the Boers, but he was perturbed with Sir George Colley's actions and on 29 April he put a motion to the House "that the power claimed and exercised by the representatives of this Country in various parts of the world to contract engagements, annex territories, and make war in the name of the Nation without authority from the Central Government is opposed to the principles of the British Constitution, is at variance with recognised rules of International Law, and is fraught with danger to the honour and true interests of the country." He listed the wars, great and small – some of which have already been referred to in this book – that had been started in this way and some horrific instances, for example, the town of Batanga, in West Africa, burnt in an act of wanton vandalism on the flimsiest of excuses. He inquired whether Britain was in control of its destiny or at the mercy of "small, irresponsible officials in all parts of the world" who seemed to think they were at liberty to go to war without

264   HENRY RICHARD: APOSTLE OF PEACE AND WELSH PATRIOT

even the consent of the Executive and to spill blood and waste vast
sums of money in the name of a State of 32 million people. Such a
course, he said, was at variance with the recognized rules of
International Law. Again, Richard did not get the support of
Gladstone, merely expressions of sympathy. Gladstone said that
central Government was as guilty as its representatives in foreign
lands of starting wars. Richard should take comfort from the fact
that better communications – through the telegraph – ensured
that central Government was able to keep a tighter grip on its foreign agents. Which was some kind of acknowledgement that these
men needed to be kept under control. A number of MPs supported Richard, among them Peter Rylands who spoke particularly about the attacks on China. Only one member spoke in
support of Gladstone's position, a Conservative, Charles Warton.
There does not appear to have been much interest in the debate,
only 136 went to the trouble of voting and Henry Richard's
motion was defeated by a majority of eight votes – 72 to 64.[11]

Chapter 24

Lord Aberdare's Departmental Committee

For far too long schools and education in Wales were organised on a similar pattern to that of England and the 1870 Education Act had changed nothing. Then in 25 August 1880, the Government appointed a Commission, or Departmental Committee, to inquire into the condition of Intermediate and Higher Education in Wales and recommend measures for improving and supplementing that provision. The issues to be examined would be:

1. Providing more amenities for Higher Education, in addition to Aberystwyth College which had been opened in 1872.
2. Establishing a network of Intermediate Schools.

Much to his surprise Henry Richard was invited to be a member of the committee. Not that he had no interest in education. On the contrary, he had for years been campaigning for primary education in Wales and he had played an important role in establishing Aberystwyth College. That the Government had set up such a committee at all to consider education in Wales was something of a miracle. That Richard, a Welsh Nonconformist, had been appointed to it was even a greater shock. The Chairman was Lord Aberdare (Henry Austin Bruce) and the other members were John Rhys, Professor of Celtic at Oxford, Lord Emlyn, Lewis Morris, the solicitor and Anglo-Welsh poet from Carmarthen, and Canon Hugh George Robertson, Principal of the Diocese of York Teachers' Training College. The name of Sir Hugh Owen had been discussed but he had declined to let his name be considered as he was in poor health. In fact, Owen died in November 1881. "When I was invited by Lord Spencer I was concerned that I was the only Nonconformist on the Committee," said Richard. "At least, I was not sure of my friend, Professor Rhys. He was once a Nonconformist, but he is now a Professor at Oxford and I am afraid that I could only consider him, at best, as neutral."[1] Richard tried to get Lewis Edwards on to the Committee, without success.

It appears that Richard had no cause for concern – they all seemed to get on well with one another. The inquiry lasted from October 1880 until February 1881 with the report published in July. The Committee visited many of the larger towns in Wales and held 50 meetings from Newport to Holyhead. They interviewed 275 witnesses, lords, four bishops, members of parliament, teachers, Anglican clergy, Nonconformist ministers of all denominations and working men. Richard and John Rhys ensured that Welsh speakers gave their testimony in their mother tongue, although Welsh language education was not part of the inquiry.

They soon found that the provision for the middle classes – the grammar and private schools – was woefully inadequate. A moderate estimate suggested that 15,700 boys in Wales required education higher that elementary, but there were only 27 endowed grammar schools providing accommodation for only 3,000 pupils. Of these places only 1,540 were filled.[2] With regard to higher education, apart from denominational academies, there were only Aberystwyth College and St David's College, Lampeter. There were only two endowed schools for girls. Henry Richard noted that the grammar school endowments, whatever the stipulations of the original trust, had dropped into the hands of the Church of England.[3] The vast majority of the governors of the grammar schools in Wales, according to the Commission's report, were Anglicans. At Ruthin, Cowbridge, Monmouth and the two schools for girls – Llandaff and Denbigh – all the governors were Anglicans. At Bangor, of the 20 governors, four were Nonconformists. As the governors were Anglicans, it followed that they would appoint headmasters who were Anglicans, who would in turn appoint members of staff who would also be Anglicans. Were not the pupils, asked Richard, "surrounded by an ecclesiastical atmosphere calculated to alienate them from the faith of their fathers?" The Commissioners evidently agreed as the report called for a reorganisation of the schools and endowments for the special needs and requirements of Wales; that grammar schools, science schools and a superior kind of elementary school be planted in various parts of Wales, and that these schools should be non-denominational. Another recommendation was that scholarships would be established allowing clever children of poor families to progress from the elementary schools to the grammar schools and from there to university. It was also recommended that another college should be established, either in Cardiff or Swansea in South Wales, and that Aberystwyth should continue either as the college of the north or relocate somewhere further north. This proved extremely controversial, but the end result was the etablishment of three colleges. A bitter and successful battle saved Aberystwyth, Cardiff college opened in 1883 and Bangor in 1884. The Aberystwyth affair will be looked at later. As for the proposed Intermediate Education Bill for Wales, despite the efforts of Henry Richard and other Welsh MPs, this did not get on the Statute Book until 1889, a year after Richard's death.

Richard never stopped worrying at the way members were selected to the school boards and he was insistent that there had to be a better relationship between the Anglicans and the Nonconformists. The Boards remained heavily under the influence of the Church of England. He expressed his opposition to giving religious instruction in the State schools – a view that was not shared by the other members of the Departmental Committee.

In March 1882 there was a meeting of the clerics of the Bangor diocese at the Cathedral who were of the opinion that the members of the Departmental Committee had been misled by prejudiced witnesses wishing to promote their own political agendas. Henry Richard responded the next month when he addressed the English Congregational Union of North Wales. He had been the only Nonconformist on the Committee and he did not accept that he could have had that great an influence over them. He certainly did not accept that Anglican clerics had a better understanding of the desires of Nonconformists than the Nonconformists themselves. On the whole, it can be assumed, that Henry Richard had been an influential voice on the Departmental Committee.

Later in the year there was an anonymous attack on the Departmental Committee's Report in the *Church Quarterly Review*, although it was more of a personal attack on Henry Richard, rather than on what was perceived as the Report's sympathetic treatment of Nonconformists. Richard, also writing anonymously, responded in the *British Quarterly Review*.[4] He admitted being the author of the reply in the *British Quarterly Review* in a re-print of *Letters and Essays on Wales* (1884), his response also being included as an appendix to the book. It became known eventually that the author of the attack on Richard in the *Church Quarterly Review* was the Bishop of Llandaff, Dr Alfred Ollivant, an amiable enough character but extremely hostile towards Nonconformists.[5]

Be that as it may, Richard in his introduction to the 1884 edition of the *Letters and Essays* considered it "a vehement attack upon myself for the part I had taken on that Committee, and, through my sides, on Welsh Nonconformity and the people of Wales generally".[6] Ollivant, it must be said, had been rummaging diligently among old issues of Nonconformists journals, some going back 40 years, to find some juicy bits with which to attack the chapelgoers: bits – not always too guardedly worded – warning their fellow countrymen against building too many chapels, excessively emotional sermons, drunkenness and sexual morality. Ollivant's attack used past warnings by Nonconformists towards their own flock as a stick with which to beat 1880 Nonconformists. Richard's response, writing about himself in the third person, is a mine of interesting facts and statistics about the condition of Wales at the beginning of the final quarter of the nineteenth century. It still makes entertaining reading thanks to the fluency of his style and the ferocity of his defence. As for Bishop Ollivant, he died in December 1882, shortly after the publication of his own article and before the publication of Richard's response.

It is doubtful whether twenty-first century Wales would give more than a passing thought to the Sunday Closing (Wales) Act of 1881. According to some respected Welsh historians the principal effect of closing public houses in Wales was to create an image of the Welsh as a nation of miserable, teetotal, Nonconformists. Yet, at the time, it was politically important as it formally acknowledged the separate character of Wales and set a precedent for future legislation. The temperance movement had worked diligently in support of the Bill and Henry Richard had expressed his support for it in a meeting at Soar schoolroom, Merthyr Tydfil. The Bill was presented to Parliament by John Roberts, MP for Flint, on 6 February 1880, and he was supported by Henry Richard, George Osborne Morgan, Henry Hussey Vivian, MP for Glamorgan, and Samuel Holland, MP for Meirioneth. Henry Richard spoke at the Second Reading of the Bill on 30 June noting that a similar Act that had existed in Scotland for 27 years had proved to be a blessing, likewise the Act that became law in Ireland in 1878. All the Welsh Members of Parliament supported the Bill, apart from Lord Emlyn, who would not have been in the House at all were it not for the incompetence of the Carmarthenshire Liberals.[7] The Act became law the following year. The National Eisteddfod was held in Merthyr in the autumn of 1881 and it was to be expected that Henry Richard would preside at the principal meeting and on that day a public holiday was proclaimed in the town. The pavilion, which held 6,000, was crammed when he came to speak. Unusually, he was presented with an address listing his many contributions to Wales – unusual, as the Eisteddfod was considered a non-political institution. The National Eisteddfod had become anglicised in this period. "English was three parts of four ... if not nine parts out of ten of the speech [publicly] used in the Mold Eisteddfod [1873]," wrote Gohebydd in *Baner ac Amserau Cymru*.[8] It was not unusual even for the language to be denigrated from the Eisteddfod platform itself. David Davies advised his fellow countrymen at the Aberystwyth Eisteddfod of 1865 that "the best medium to make money by was the English." If they were content with brown bread, let them, of course, remain where they were. But if they wished to enjoy the luxuries of life, with white bread to boot, the way to do so was by the acquisition of English. He knew what it was to eat both.[9] Henry Richard would not be proffering any such advice as he addressed the audience in Welsh. When he left Wales for London half a century before he had made three promises, he told his audience: he would never forget the language of his country; he would not ignore the people and the cause of his country; and would neglect no opportunity of defending the character and promoting the interests of his country.[10]

He mentioned the great changes he had seen during his lifetime. When he first went from Tregaron to London, the journey took three days, and no one would embark on it without making a will first! While expanding on the advances in education in Wales he mentioned the importance and advantages of the *eisteddfod*, an institution praised by Gladstone himself when he visited the Mold National Eisteddfod.

For Richard, 1881 was a year of personal sadness. The previous year he had heard of the death of his fellow worker for the cause of peace, particularly the congresses of 1848–1852, the American Elihu Burritt. Edward Miall died in April 1881, then on 20 November of the same year news came of the death of Sir Hugh Owen, with whom Richard had worked for 40 years on matters relating to education in Wales, particularly the establishment of Aberystwyth College. Richard gave the address at both funerals.[12]

Chapter 25

War in Egypt

It is not possible to ignore for long the principal campaign of Richard's life. In 1881 the troubles with the Boers gathered pace and Richard's attempt to prevent British agents abroad starting wars without reference to London failed. In the case of the 1882 Egyptian War it was the London Government that decided to go to war – and a Liberal one at that. This war gave Richard more grief and work perhaps than any in a lifetime of campaigning.

Up to 1862 Egypt had been debt-free, but the following year the country had a new leader, Isma'il Pasha. His ambition was to modernise the country and he began to borrow money to do so.[1] Within a few years his country's debt had grown to £90,000,000 and he was paying huge interest to financial speculators in England and France. He sold his country's shares in the Suez Canal Company for a meagre £4,000,000 to Britain – at the time governed by the Tories. With his country in deep trouble, in 1875 Isma'il Pasha asked Britain to look at Egypt's financial problems. It soon became clear that the position was not stable and instead of letting the speculators – who had been doing very well – take the loss, two representatives, one from Britain and the other from France, were sent to sort out the country's finances. Britain and France took full responsibility for Egypt's internal affairs. They got rid of Isma'il Pasha and replaced him with a puppet, his nephew, Muhammed Tewfik Pasha. Matters proceeded peacefully for two years. Then in February 1881 there was a military insurrection in Cairo – led by Colonel Ahmad Urabi – and the rebellion spread through the country.[2] The people had become hostile towards the British and French – "Egypt for the Egyptians and no foreign interference" was the cry – and a Nationalist Party was formed.

After some diplomatic activity in January 1882, Britain and France began to panic and in May they sent warships to anchor off Alexandria to support the Tewfik puppet government. Urabi and his soldiers, now in control of Alexandria, set about strengthening the fortifications. The situation worsened and the presence of the allied fleet increased rather than decreased the danger to Europeans. A serious riot broke out on 17 June. Admiral Beauchamp-Seymour of the British fleet sent an ultimatum to Urabi demanding that he surrender the city within three days. No reply was received and the bombardment of Alexandria began promptly at 7 o'clock on the morning of 11 July. The French fleet, on orders from Paris and possibly advised by Germany, withdrew to Port Said. The bombardment by the British fleet continued for two days. Urabi and his soldiers withdrew, leaving the city in the hands of the mob. Prison doors were thrown open and between the bombardment and the rioters 2,000 Europeans were killed. The London Government declared war which was ratified by Parliament on 27 July. An army of 40,000 soldiers was dispatched to Egypt and after a series of victories, the last at Tel el-Kebir, Urabi quietly surrendered to the British. Originally Gladstone had intended putting him on trial but he was released and allowed to go into exile, suggesting that Gladstone admitted there was some justification for the uprising. Muhammed Tewfik Pasha's administration was re-instated.

In June, before the attack began, the Peace Society published a strong statement condemning military intervention in Egypt. They pointed out that the right to use the Suez Canal was not endangered and that interference in the internal affairs of another country was contrary to the policy of both the Liberals and the Tories. Also, it argued, neither blood nor money should be expended protecting the interests of speculators and bondholders.[4]

Henry Richard was in aggressive mood in the House of Commons, particularly on 12 July. The previous day he had pressed the Prime Minister to answer one question: was there not an understanding among the powers represented at the Constant-inople Conference, that no separate action be taken by any one power pending its deliberations? And was the bombardment of Alexandria not a violation of that understanding?[5] Gladstone responded lamely that there was a general understanding, subject to exceptional circumstances, and that the Alexandria bombard-ment must be considered as exceptional circumstances. Richard returned to the fray on the 12th when he supported a motion moved by Edward Gourley, MP for Sunderland, and seconded by Sir Wilfrid Lawson, denouncing the bombardment of Alexandria as a "cowardly, cruel, and criminal act". The justification offered by the Prime Minister and the Under Secretary of State for Foreign Affairs were not satisfactory. "They had both said that this was not an act of war," said Richard. "If it was not an act of war, then what was it?" He had always understood that there was no justification for the wholesale slaughter of human beings, unless it was done in pursuance of the rights of war. But here it was denied that there were any rights of war. In that case, he asked, if it was not an act of war, it could not be anything else but murder.

> The Right Honourable Gentleman assigned three reasons in vindication of the proceeding at Alexandria – that it was necessary, first, to defend Her Majesty's Fleet; next to put down military violence in Egypt; and, thirdly, to avenge the massacre committed about a month ago. But what business had Her Majesty's Fleet in the port of Alexandria at all? Further, was the mere fact of an independent nation fortifying its coasts against a threatened invasion by a foreign Power to be regarded as a justification for making an attack upon it? He was sorry to hear the Right Honourable Gentleman referring to the massacre that had taken place about a month ago as another justification of the act of bombardment of Alexandria ... They were told, also, that the bombardment was necessary for the protection of the interests and lives and property of British subjects. My contention, on the other hand, is that all the mischief that had arisen in Egypt, the massacre of last month, the danger to the Fleet, the destruction of Egyptian commerce for the time, the driving out of Europeans, and the jeopardy of the Suez Canal were owing to the wanton act of intervention on the part of Her Majesty's Government in sending the Fleet to Alexandria. If that had not taken place, none of these results would have followed.[6]

That evening John Bright handed his resignation to the Prime Minister. It has been claimed that Bright admitted to Henry Richard that his speech on 12 July had precipitated his decision.[7] According to William Jones's *Quaker Campaigns in Peace and War*,[8] Bright spoke to Lord Granville the afternoon before the bombardment and been assured that all was well in Egypt. The following day news came of the destruction of the defences. "The news struck the Cabinet like a thunderbolt," said Bright. "Everyone was stunned by the turn of events, and I decided I could no longer remain a member of the administration". In resigning he remained true to the principles he had advocated all his life.

Henry Richard was able to return to the Egyptian question on 25 July when Gladstone proposed "that a sum, not exceeding £2,300,000, be granted to Her Majesty, beyond the ordinary Grants of Parliament, towards defraying the Expenses which may be incurred during the year ending on the 31st day of March 1883, in strengthening Her Majesty's Forces in the Mediterranean". Richard took the opportunity to oppose the motion, in the strongest terms. "We can be very zealous, even almost ferocious, Christians in this House on occasion, especially when it concerns the outward and ceremonious acknowledgment of Christianity," he said. "But no one would be safe from ridicule here who would attempt to bring our national policy, and especially our foreign policy, to the test of a severe Christian morality." He had been accused of belonging to "The Peace-at-any-price Party". There was also a "War-at-any-cost Party". These were the ones always ready to inflame public opinion to the point of fighting, but who are careful to keep far away from the privations, the hardships, and the horrors that war entails. They were the ones indulging in 'high-falutin' declamations about national dignity and glory and the honour of the British Flag.

> But when these are brought into peril by their own counsels, they preferred sending forth poor follows, whom they hired at 1s. 4d. a-day, to bear the brunt of the conflict while they stayed at home wrapped in luxury and ease. And yet these are the men who crow over us, who vaunt themselves as the only true patriots, and as the advocates of a spirited and heroic policy. Spirited and heroic! I call it cowardly and contemptible … I have thought that I would move in this House a Resolution to the effect that when a majority voted in favour of war, those who had so voted should be at once incorporated into a regiment, and sent to the front to receive the first fire of the enemy. If that were the law I would answer for it that there would be fewer wars.

He went into considerable detail about the way Egypt was being fleeced in order that the speculators' money should be safe-guarded. " … we had virtually taken the Government of Egypt into the hands of England and France," he claimed. "The Revenue of Egypt is £9,000,000 or £10,000,000. About one-half of this is sent out of the country to pay the foreign bondholders, which is as if £40,000,000 of our Revenues were sent out of the country, while nearly all places of trust and power and emolument in Egyptian administration are monopolized by Europeans." He then turned his attention to the rise of a National Party in Egypt. "Is it any wonder that a National Party should rise?" he asked. "It was time it should rise, and the Egyptians would have showed themselves utterly devoid of dignity and self-respect if they had not revolted against such a state of things ... Of course, all the European office-holders do all in their power to deny or discredit that Party." The Fleet had been sent to protect British subjects and Europeans, he said: "But since the arrival of your Fleet all British subjects and Europeans have had to flee precipitately from Alexandria, leaving their property to the mercy of the fanatical Natives. The Government could not fail to have been aware that the appearance of a British Squadron in Egyptian waters would produce danger to European residents." The idea that Britain should attack Alexandria for strengthening its own fortifications was, he said, laughable. "I find a man prowling about my house with obviously felonious purposes. I hasten to get locks and bars, and to barricade my windows. He says that is an insult and threat to him, and he batters down my doors, and declares that he does so only as an act of strict self-defence."

Coming to the end of his speech he said that he worried that the accumulation of these unfortunate events had cast a shadow over Gladstone's "great and illustrious" career. He ended with the words: "I am determined to record my vote against this proposal, even if I have to walk into the Lobby alone."[9]

Richard's stance received little support in Parliament. But what grieved him most was the withdrawal of the "conditional support-ers" of the Peace Society. The Liberal Government had set out to court the popularity of the people by rescuing money British spec-ulators had lent at high interest rates to Egypt. They succeeded on two fronts with the public – and Gladstone – dazzled by the bril-liant victories of General Garnet Wolseley in Tel el-Mahuta, Kassassin and finally in Tel el-Kebir. As was the case with the Crimean War the Peace Society's fair-weather friends withdrew and despite their admiration for Henry Richard, the Welsh people were no exception. Even the Congregationalist *Tyst a'r Dydd*[10] crit-icised Henry Richard and Sir Wilfrid Lawson for their opposition to the war.

Richard was certainly annoyed by this act of betrayal and a let-ter from him was published in the 23 March 1883 edition. Welsh admiration for Gladstone knew no bounds at this time. Although very High Church, there was much of the Calvinist about him and he was showing a great deal of sympathy towards Wales and the Welsh, thanks partly to Richard's *Letters and Essays on Wales*. He had supported the move towards higher education in Wales and establishing Aberystwyth College. He had been responsible for establishing the Departmental Committee to inquire into intermediate education, of which Richard was a member. He had supported the demand for Welsh-speaking bishops, he was the first prominent politician to visit the National Eisteddfod and had supported the Sunday Closing (Wales) Act of 1881. Henry Richard himself was unstinting in his admiration of Gladstone, but if the choice was between admiration and principles, Richard could be relied on to stick to his principles. "I testify that I respect and like Mr Gladstone as much as any man in the kingdom; but there is one instinct that is rooted even deeper in my mind, and that is a fear of that God that loathes injustice and tyranny," he wrote in his letter to *Y Tyst a'r Dydd*. Although he received little or no support from Wales in his opposition to the war in Egypt, in November, 1883, he received a letter from David Morgan, the influential miners' agent, telling him that 40,000 miners supported the Peace Society and that "a meeting of delegates at Aberdare ... passed a resolution without a dissenting voice, recommending all of the miners of South Wales to send subscriptions to the Peace Society".[11] This was a reprise of the enthusiastic reception Henry Richard had received in October 1883 when he addressed 4,000 miners at an open air meeting in Merthyr on the advantages of arbitration and conciliation to settle industrial disputes.

One other speech of interest by Richard on the war in Egypt merits a mention. It was delivered on 19 April 1883, on the occasion of the Lord Alcesters [Admiral Seymour] Annuity Bill and similarly the Lord Wolseley Bill. Gladstone proposed that both should receive an annuity for life of £2,000 a year, and for their eldest heir after them, as a reward for their distinguished service in the war in Egypt. Richard saw this as glorification of war and an act beneath contempt.

> ... my objection rests on the general principle that it is unwise ... to encourage and stimulate the military spirit, which, in my opinion, is an evil spirit. I should like very much to know why this particular class of our fellow-subjects should be singled for special recognition and honour for doing their duty? Is it because of the supreme excellence of the work they perform? Why, the work of the warrior is one of pure destruction. His work is to scatter havoc and ruin over the earth, to carry into the hearts and homes of men mourning, desolation, and woe. And is that a kind of work that needs to be specially encouraged by a Christian State? But I may be told that they are honoured because they

serve their country. Well, I hope we all try in some humble way
to serve our country. Is not the poor agricultural labourer, who
toils in the cultivation of the soil, and who causes two blades of
grass to grow where only one grew before, serving his country?
Is the plea that shall be put forward thus – that the work of the
soldier is very dangerous work, which is done at the hazard of his
life? So is the work of the miner. There are thousands and tens of
thousands of our countrymen who, every day and night, descend
into the bowels of the earth, carrying their lives in their hands, to
extract for us the means of heat, light, and locomotion, without
which the whole mechanism of society would stand still; and
there are more of these brave soldiers of industry who perish
every year, in pursuit of their perilous occupation, than the numbers which fall in most modern battles. But we never hear of
these being decorated with medals, or made to pass in procession
before the face of Royalty. Shall I be told that soldiers are thus
honoured because they contribute to the glory of our country?
Well, I dare say my view of what constitutes true national glory
may differ from that of many Honourable Gentlemen present.
But I confess that some exploits have been recorded in our
national annals, within the last 30 years, which I suppose are
regarded by some as heroic and honourable, that appear to me to
be simply shameful and humiliating. The burning of Kagoshima,
the bombardment of Canton with red-hot shot – and that on a
quarrel which almost everybody now acknowledges was an
unjust quarrel – the destruction of Magdala and Coomassie, after
the unfortunate people whose country you had invaded had been
completely vanquished, and when no possible plea of necessity
could exist for those acts of vandalism, and I am obliged to say
the bombardment of Alexandria; these seem to me to be proceedings that had no single element of heroism in them, but to
be the simple abuse of the power of the strong against the weak. I
covet no such glory for my country; and it is because measures
like those now before us have a tendency to encourage such acts
and enterprises that I am strenuously opposed to them.

The motion was carried with 217 MPs in favour and 85 supporting Henry Richard's opposing view.[12]

★ ★ ★

In the summer of 1882 Richard and his wife set off to holiday in
Aix-les-Bains and Geneva. While they were away, news came of
the death of his sister, Mary Morris, after a long illness. A telegraph was sent to Vevey but they had left before the message
arrived. As a result he was not able to get to Cardiganshire in time
for the funeral.[13]

Chapter 26

Problems of the Welsh colleges

The year 1883 began with a significant development for higher education in Wales. A conference was held in Chester town hall to discuss how to make the best use of a grant from the Government of £4,000 towards establishing and maintaining a college for North Wales. The conference was arranged by T. Marchant Williams, born in Aberdare, one of the most influential Welshmen of the end of the century – poet, novelist, editor of *The Nationalist* and one of the first students to attend Aberystwyth college. Representatives of all the North Wales towns that hoped to attract the college attended, among them the Bishop and Dean of Bangor, the Bishop of St Asaph, the heads of various educational institutions, and the Duke of Westminster (Hugh Grosvenor), who owned Eaton Hall, Chester.[1]

Henry Richard was asked to formally propose that there should be a college for North Wales and he was seconded by the Bishop of Bangor. An amendment to postpone any decision until a Bill on Intermediate Education in Wales had been introduced to Parliament was defeated. The Dean of Bangor, who was not well disposed towards Aberystwyth, proposed that the college should be sited in one of the six counties of North Wales, and he was seconded by the editor and publisher from Denbigh, Thomas Gee. Cardiganshire was not viewed as being in North Wales. David Davies proposed an amendment in support of Aberystwyth college. He was seconded by Lewis Edwards. With the majority of those present from the North the amendment was easily defeated. A committee was elected to decide where in North Wales the college should be sited and they agreed, more or less unanimously, on Bangor. Their decision was announced in August.

278 HENRY RICHARD: APOSTLE OF PEACE AND WELSH PATRIOT

T. Marchant Williams

This was a devastating blow for Aberystwyth. The Departmental Committee's Report – chaired by Lord Aberdare – had been less than complimentary towards Aberystwyth. Marchant Williams, one the first students to go to Aberystwyth, if only for about five months, was hostile towards the place.[2] Williams had also testified before the Departmental Committee – he was then a schools' inspector for the London School Board – and his testimony was damning. Although Aberdare was himself President of the Aberystwyth college, his support was also lukewarm. He described the town of Aberystwyth as an unfortunate choice for a college, one that would make it difficult to attract sponsors or students in sufficient numbers. He considered his own part of South Wales as being much better suited. Lewis Morris busied himself with other plans for Aberystwyth, such as using the building as a grammar school or a college for girls. It appears that Henry Richard, too, although a native of the county, had lost his enthusiasm. He was throwing his energies behind Cardiff as the suitable site for the South Wales college and, according to Stuart Rendel, MP for Montgomeryshire, Richard, at least for some time after 1881, was unhelpful in his attitude to Aberystwyth College. Another member of the Departmental Committee, Lord Emlyn, had pledged for St David's College, Lampeter, and was described in 1884 as never "favourable to Aberystwyth".[3] Looking back on the testimonies to the Departmental Committee, that of Principal Thomas Charles

Edwards had not been as confident as might have been expected. He may have felt that he was appearing before an unsympathetic court. His performance had been very different to that of Francis Jayne, Principal of St David's, Lampeter, who was given complete freedom to express all kinds of wild prejudices against the Welsh.[4] It would seem that Henry Richard did not assist Edwards as he might have done with questions aimed at putting him at ease and eliciting fuller answers and to be more communicative. Other members of the Aberystwyth staff who testified were also brushed aside. And after the publication of the Departmental Committee report, T. C. Edwards did not leap to the defence of his college.

If Aberystwyth was to be saved someone had to roll up his sleeves and prepare for battle. David Davies was still fuming over the way the amendment he had proposed at Chester had been rudely dismissed and would defend Aberystwyth come what may. Another who surprisingly leapt into the fray was Stuart Rendel, MP for Montgomeryshire, a wealthy Englishman with no connections with Aberystwyth but who considered that the college had been shabbily treated by Lord Aberdare and the Departmental Committee and that the decision taken at Chester was a serious mistake. The people of Aberystwyth were also up in arms, none more so than John Gibson, proprietor and editor of the *Cambrian News*, who kept up a weekly fusillade of comments and criticism in the leader column of his paper, calling for the resignation of Lord Aberdare and Lewis Morris and accusing Henry Richard – even the late Sir Hugh Owen – of being enemies of the college. Although he saw others as being strong as steel in their support of the "college by the sea".

Among Gladstone's closest friends – so far as he had close friends at all – were two with close links to Wales. One was Lord Aberdare. But the one with the greatest influence on Gladstone was Stuart Rendel.[5] Not the greatest or most brilliant of orators, he was a true friend, modest, pleasant with a talent for dealing with people. He was also persistent and his influence was growing among his fellow Welsh MPs. He also used his influence to gain sympathy for the Aberystwyth cause with Liberal and Conservative MPs the other side of Offa's Dyke.

Support was now growing in North Wales, especially from those towns who had hoped – and failed – to provide a home for the College of the North. Thomas Gee of *Baner ac Amserau Cymru*, had done all he could to promote the cause of Denbigh and poured scorn on Aberystwyth in the process. It was he who had seconded the Dean of Bangor's motion that the college should be sited in one of the six countries of the North. But when Denbigh lost out to Bangor, he changed his tune and began a campaign to save Aberystwyth. The whole of Wales was now raising its voice in defence of the college. The counties of Meirioneth and Montgomery were beginning to realise that Aberystwyth was more convenient for them than Bangor. The Education Secretary, A. J. Mundella, agreed small sums of money so that Aberystwyth could be closed down gradually over a period of three to five years.[6] David Davies, as ever, was prepared to put his hand in his pocket.

It is in the nature of a successful politician to sense quickly what direction the wind is blowing. A number of Welsh MPs realised soon enough that turning their backs on Aberystwyth had not been a good move. Henry Richard was one of the first to realise his mistake. In no time at all he was corresponding with his old friend Mundella. Mundella was a slippery character and he preferred to deal with Henry Richard rather than with the amiable, but determined, Stuart Rendel. Mundella assumed that Richard would agree with him that Wales should have just two colleges – one that was due to open in Cardiff, having got the nod over Swansea, on 24 October 1883, and one to open in Bangor a year later, and that there was no room for a third. Richard was also prominent and active with Cardiff and had already been appointed Vice-Chairman of the college. On 14 March 1884, Rendel made the following observation to Parliament:

> That the College of Aberystwyth having, notwithstanding the Report of the Departmental Committee, been left out of the scheme for higher education in Wales, this House is of the opinion that the injury to the cause of education in the Principality, and discouragement to a great portion of the Welsh people, will result, unless measures are taken to place that College, in respect of State recognition and support, on an equal footing with the Colleges at Cardiff and Bangor.

He was supported by Sir Robert Cunliffe, MP for Denbigh Borough. Henry Richard got up to speak immediately after Sir Robert. His two friends, he said, represented "a large body of opinion in Wales in favour of a continued grant to Aberystwyth College". He continued:

> And this is no wonder, because Aberystwyth was the creation of

popular enthusiasm for education in Wales. The fact stated by
my Honourable Friend who has just sat down is a very significant fact to those who know the class of people from whom, for
the most part, the money was got; that upwards of £70,000 has
been contributed by the people of Wales towards this Institution.
The College has an excellent and commodious building, with
laboratories, class rooms, museum, and a library. It has a staff of
most competent and efficient Professors, and a considerable
number of students, who are increasing year by year.[7]

The old fox was changing his tune. Some were arguing that Wales
did not have "a sufficient number of young persons of that class
likely to avail themselves of the advantages of collegiate education". There was no certain way of knowing, the only answer was
by making the experiment. Lord Aberdare, he said, had written a
letter to the *Times* the previous year in response to two Scotsmen –
and others – who had objected to establishing any colleges in
Wales on the basis that its population was to small. In his reply
Lord Aberdare showed that Glamorgan had a larger population
than any county in Scotland with the exception of Lanarkshire,
and that probably the population of Wales and Monmouthshire in
1881 was twice as great as was that of Scotland when its earlier universities were founded. Many counties in the south and north-east
of Wales had large mining and manufacturing industries, that
Caernarvonshire and Meirionethshire had, in their slate quarries,
an intelligent body of workmen, who had shown their appreciation of the value of education in the great sacrifices they had made,
and that in other counties of Wales there was a considerable urban
population. He referred to the success of the Cardiff College, still
in its infancy, where there were 150 students and between 600 and
700 young people attending evening classes. "A short time ago the
Times told its myriad readers that the Welsh read nothing but the
Bible and sermons," said Richard. "With regard to the former part
of the indictment, I plead guilty on their behalf. They do read the
Bible very largely, and I think a nation may do a worse thing than
be familiar with that Book. But as for the other, the fact is that
there are comparatively few sermons printed in Welsh, as the
Welsh prefer hearing sermons to reading them." He proceeded to
analyse the reading habits of the Welsh people which in proportion to population had twice as many periodicals as England, one
and a half times as many as Scotland and four times as many as
Ireland.
Evidently he was conscious that he could be accused of chang-

ing his mind as to whether Wales would be able to support three colleges. After all, he had signed the Departmental Committee Report advocating one college for the north and another for the south. Anticipating such a response he quoted Tennyson:

"And the thoughts of men are widened
With the process of the suns."

It proved an interesting session when even Lord Emlyn, the great defender of St David's College, Lampeter, lost his patience when Mundella tried to waste time by asking for the opportunity to study the Aberystwyth balance sheet.

Earlier that same day Mundella had met Rendel and other Welsh MPs. It was a stormy meeting and his response to their pleadings to save Aberystwyth was a brusque "No!" Then he received a message from Gladstone and he gave way with good grace. Aberystwyth was saved at the eleventh hour.[8] Rendel commented drily that it was well worth seeing Henry Richard, George Osborne Morgan, Hussey Vivian and the Tories joining forces to support Aberystwyth.

As already noted Cardiff College was officially opened on 24 October of that year having got the better of Swansea in a lively, but friendly competition. Lord Aberdare, President of the college, gave the inaugural address and said that Protestants and Catholics, Nonconformists and Anglicans had cooperated in the friendliest possible way to establish this non-denominational college. Other speakers included John Rhys, Professor of Celtic at Oxford, John Viriamu Jones, Cardiff's first Principal, and Henry Richard, the Vice-President. Richard expressed the hope that there would be no jealousies – local, sectarian or national – and that all would unite harmoniously in developing the South Wales College. To those of his friends who appeared opposed to Englishmen taking part in the great enterprise, he said "I am not afraid of the Saxons". He was prepared to fight them, not with swords and spears as in former times, but in the spirit of the college motto, "Goreu arf, arf dysg" (The best weapon, is the weapon of learning). They would meet these Saxons with that weapon, and defeat them.[9]

Soon afterwards an unpleasant sectarian difficulty did arise when the Dean of Llandaff, a certain Dr Rees, proposed that the Professor of Mathematics and Astronomy, the distinguished H. W. Lloyd Tanner should be dismissed for being a member of the National Secular Society.[10] The Dean was told that Tanner's work was limited to scientific matters. It was, however, noted that Tanner had disavowed any sympathies with the social aspects of the movement associated with Charles Braudlaugh, the century's best known atheist, suggesting that he had been put under some pressure. Richard was not present at the meeting to discuss the Dean's proposal, but a letter from him was read in which he objected strongly to any action being taken against Tanner, which he said would be contrary to the college's constitution. Would the next objection be to the appointment of a Catholic, a Jew or Unitarian to the college staff? It could lead to all sorts of denominational problems. The President, Lord Aberdare, agreed and the motion was defeated by 13 votes to 8.

Richard continued to nag away at the lack of Nonconformists in official appointments. He told a meeting of the Deputies of the Three Denominations that he had written a strongly worded letter to Gladstone complaining that Nonconformists in view of their numbers, had nowhere near the kind of representation that they deserved in the official and administrative life of Britain.

There was a time, no doubt, when, owing to their long exclusion from the Universities, and the prejudice – well or ill founded – in favour of University men as most competent for public posts, the number of Nonconformists qualified for such positions may be held to have been very limited. But there are now many scores – I may say hundreds – of men who have had a thorough University education, and who have distinguished themselves greatly, as is indicated by the fact that in 22 years there have been 14 Nonconformist Senior Wranglers at Cambridge. I don't say that there is any studied exclusion of Nonconformists, but by connections and habits of life they have been left out of the running. There have been so few of them within the temple of office, that they would not help to open the gates to others, and so they have been simply forgotten and left out in the cold. And when we poor Nonconformist MPs have tried to help them, we have always found that there have been other and more powerful influences at work to baulk our endeavours.[11]

In an address to the Dissenting Deputies Richard said that he had received a promising response from the Prime Minister urging him to suggest the names of Nonconformists to the Endowed Schools Commission when a position became vacant. This he did and James Anstie, a barrister and Nonconformist who was appointed to the Charities Commission, was probably the first to profit from Richard's efforts.

During 1883 and 1884 Richard twice tried to reform the rights of Nonconformists being buried in Parish churchyards by extending George Osborne Morgan's Burials Bill of 1880 – without success. The Conservatives, by various ploys, managed to obstruct him on both occasions.

Chapter 27

Talk of retirement

With a certain inevitability one war leads to another. The uprising of Colonel Ahmad Urabi having been quashed, Muhammed Tewfik Pasha once more – nominally – ruled Egypt and the Sudan, where for a decade life had been uneasy. European campaigns against slavery had caused economic problems in the north of the country. That, and the oppressive policies of the government in Cairo was the cause of the Mahdi uprising of Muhammad Ahmad ibn Abd Allah. In 1883 Sir Evelyn Baring (Lord Cromer) was dispatched as diplomatic agent and British Consul-General to Egypt. His first mandate was to order Tewfik to withdraw from Sudan. Tewfik did so – unwillingly – but did all he could to transfer power smoothly and peacefully. But there were problems. There were a number of Egyptian garrisons scattered around Sudan, all surrounded by the Mahdi's men. General Valentine Baker let an army of 3,500, mostly Egyptians, to try and raise the siege on the Tokar and Sinkat garrisons. But on 4 February 1884, they were intercepted at El Teb by a thousand Mahdi soldiers. Although heavily outnumbered by a better equipped army, the Mahdi's men crushed and massacred Baker's army. The Gladstone Government yielded to public outrage and an army of 4,500 soldiers was dispatched under Gerald Graham to seek revenge. They engaged with the Mahdi's forces, also in El Tab, and on 29 February Graham's army slaughtered 5,000 Sudanese before returning triumphantly to Britain.[1] In the same month General Gordon had arrived in Khartoum and arranged for women, children and wounded to be evacuated to Egypt. Britain intended to withdraw from Sudan but Gordon disobeyed orders. He secured the defences and prepared to defend the town. On 18 March the forces of the Mahdi arrived. On this occasion the British Government was much slower to respond. It was August before it decided to send an army to relieve Gordon and more months elapsed before that army, led by Sir Garnet Wolseley, set off up the Nile. Wolseley arrived on 28 January 1885, to find Khartoum fallen and Gordon dead.

Henry Richard had been critical of his party's policy from the start. "I can hardly give expression to my feelings from hearing, daily, of the terrible and futile slaughter, which is happening in the Soudan," he wrote to a protest meeting in St James's Hall. "It is inconceivable how some of the men in the present administration can give their support to such a policy."[2] It had all stemmed from British interference in the monetary problems of Egypt and the subsequent bombardment of Alexandria, he argued. He wrote indignantly to Prime Minister Gladstone protesting against any further sanguinary expeditions to the Sudan and against entrusting any issues of peace or war to the naval and military officers in the Middle East. He wrote letters which appeared in a number of newspapers urging the public to write to the Prime Minister condemning what was happening. Evidently he considered Gordon's decision to try and defend Khartoum to be another example of a soldier disobeying orders. As Secretary of the Peace Society, he made public his opposition to sending soldiers to save Gordon's skin. Richard was dissatisfied by Gladstone's response to his letters – he saw it as nothing more than a defence of irresponsible actions by soldiers and he decided to say so in the House of Commons at the first opportunity. That opportunity came on 15 March when Henry Labouchère, MP for Northampton, moved a resolution at the Supplementary Estimates, "that the necessity for the great loss of British and Arab life occasioned by the military operations in the Soudan, have not been made apparent". Richard seconded the resolution.

If any class of persons in the House were entitled to look back with any satisfaction at the course they had taken in regard to "this miserable Egyptian business", he said, it was that small minority who had opposed the armed intervention in Egypt. They were the ones who had denounced it as unjust, unnecessary, and unwise, and as likely to involve dangerous and unforeseen responsibilities.

The true friends of a man, he added, were those who, seeing him enter upon a false and dangerous path, warned him against the first step, and pointed out to him the perils he must incur in that direction, and not those who stood by to goad him on, some by flatteries and some by reproaches. The Government, in his opinion, had committed two capital errors – the first, by going into Egypt; and the second, by going into the Sudan. He continued:

> It was true that the Commanders of those expeditions were, or had been, British officers, but they were not in British service; and, for my part, I have no respect for those mercenary soldiers who sold their swords to whoever would buy them, and were ready to fight anywhere, or for any cause, without the smallest concern as to whether it was just or unjust. These men went at their own risk, and, of their own accord, placed their lives on the hazard of the die, and I protest against our being called upon to protect them when living, or to avenge them when dead.

The only purpose of the attack, he said, was to raise the siege on the Tokar garrison. So said the Prime Minister, and likewise General Graham. But there was no need to liberate Tokar. "It had surrendered nearly a fortnight before we went near it, and a portion of the garrison was found afterwards fighting *con a more* with the enemy against us," said Richard. "And when we took possession of the town … the Secretary of State for War, told us that there were some 700 persons within its walls, who apparently were dwelling there safely and contentedly under the protection of Osman Digna's army … we slaughtered 2,000 or 3,000 Arabs to relieve Tokar, which needed no relief, and to rescue 700 persons, who were in no danger save from our intervention, and we called that rendering a service to humanity."[3]

The Conservatives and the Irish nationalists unanimously supported Labouchère and Henry Richard – but only three Liberals voted with them, Sir Wilfrid Lawson, John Passmore Edwards, MP for Salisbury, and Alfred Illingworth, MP for Bradford. The Government scraped home by 111 votes to 94. Richard was severely criticised by the Liberal Party. But he had stuck to his principles. He argued that the Opposition and the Irish MPs had listened to his arguments, agreed with him and voted accordingly in disgust at the unnecessary bloodshed. It is debatable whether the Conservatives supported Richard and Labouchère because they agreed with them, or because they saw an opportunity to give the Liberal Government a kicking.

Henry Richard had now reached the age of 72 and his health was not as robust as it had been and rumours were going around that his heart was not in the best of condition. It became known before long that he was suffering from angina. Nevertheless he and his wife set off in September 1883, to attend the Eleventh Congress of the Association for the Reform and Codification of the Law of Nations in Milan. On 11 September he gave a lecture on the "Progress of the Principle of International Arbitration".[4] A discussion followed at the end of which a series of resolutions were adopted, expressing satisfaction at the increased disposition of governments to recognise arbitration as a just and reasonable method of settling international differences between "civilized" nations. Richard congratulated the Association on the growth of international arbitration – there had been seven cases since 1870 – and it was encouraging to see European powers working together to achieve objectives of such international importance.[5] During their stay in Milan Richard received an address from various Italian Masonic Lodges in which they expressed their fullest approval of his "noble propaganda in favour of peace".[6] Mancini, the Italian Minister of Justice, whom Richard had met 10 years earlier, was unable to be present on this occasion but sent a message of good wishes and congratulations.

Richard and his wife then proceeded to holiday in Varese, some 50 kilometres north of Milan. He was so invigorated by the place that, in spite of advice to the contrary, he decided to walk to the top of Monte Generoso, the crest of which marked the border between Italy and Switzerland. The mountains were always an inspiration to him and he felt renewed by the physical exertion.[7]

"The duties of England as a Christian Nation towards the non-Christian Races of the World" was the subject of an address by Richard to a conference of ministers and laymen of various denominations at the centre of the Social Science Association in November. (Richard was as guilty as the English of confusing England and Britain on such occasions.) He began by praising those who sowed the seeds of civilization and Christianity in foreign lands, but he was concerned that in their zeal for their mission there was danger of them resorting to the use of arms to facilitate their efforts and by doing so degrade and dishonour a great and holy cause. He spoke of the misery and oppressions that followed the conquests of Spain in Mexico, Paraguay and Peru; the Portuguese in Brazil; the Dutch in South Africa; and England in India, China, Japan, Burma &c. Their actions disregarded the cardinal principles of Christian faith and practice and he advocated strongly that missionaries abroad should recognise more fully the precepts of the Christian religion, and to influence people by moral power and win their confidence by kindness and love.[8]

In the annual meeting of members of the Peace Society in May 1884, the President, Sir Joseph Pease, referred to rumours that Henry Richard was about to retire from his position as Secretary of the organisation. Richard said that he was getting older and that his energy was not what it had been and that there were signs that his health was deteriorating. However, following some pressure from the executive committee he had agreed to continue for another year and resign at the next annual meeting in 1885.[9]

At the beginning of July 1884, at a breakfast in the home of Sir Joseph Pease, many of Henry Richard's admirers gathered to present him with a cheque of 4,000 guineas in appreciation of years of work for peace, education and religious equality.[10] The sum – a very large one in those days – was raised secretly, effortlessly and without appealing to the public. It was organised by Sir Joseph Pease, Samuel Morley and Alfred Illingworth. Among the Welsh contributors were Richard Davies, MP for Anglesey, John Roberts, MP for Flint, and David Davies, MP for Cardigan Boroughs.

The dispute over the Afghanistan borders came up again in March 1885, which brings us back to the cause of the 1878 war when Britain attacked Afghanistan.[11] Russia, to avoid conflict, had been advocating since 1882 that an agreement should be reached to settle the border issue and a British-Russian Commission was set up. But with the commission going so long without meeting the Afghanistan army came up from the south, and a Russian army descended from the north. With both armies camped on either side of the Kushk river, on 30 March 1885 Russia attacked and defeated the Afghans. This was a move guaranteed to infuriate Britain, who viewed Afghanistan as a buffer state between India – under British rule – and the Russian Empire. Henry Richard, since Britain and Russia had both signed the 1856 Paris Treaty at the end of Crimean War, suggested that this was an opportunity to approach some friendly power to arbitrate. Gladstone accepted the principle but as there was already some dialogue he refused to allow a debate. Richard prepared a document outlining the history of the dispute, highlighting Protocol 23 of the Paris Treaty. The document was signed by John Bright, Samuel Morley, James Bryce and over 80 other MPs. Henry Richard also wrote a letter, published in the *Pall Mall Gazette*, asking why the matter could not be referred to arbitration. Then on 4 May Gladstone told the House of Commons that Britain and Russia had agreed to take that action.[12]

At the annual meeting of the Peace Society on 19 May 1885, Henry Richard presented his last report and his resignation. He was succeeded by another Welshman, William Jones,[13] the son of John Jones, a Quaker from Ruthin, who had been living for some time in Sunderland and had been Organising Secretary and Lecturer of the Society. He was yet another in the Society's line of Welsh secretaries or joint-secretaries, Evan Rees of Neath being the first, followed by Nun Morgan Harry of Pembrokeshire, before Henry Richard took on the responsibility. Richard was persuaded to continue in an honorary role for some time to ensure a smooth transition and that his experience and connections might not be lost. The members expressed their appreciation of Richard's work – 37 years as Secretary – promoting the principles of peace and his success in raising awareness of the possibilities of arbitration throughout Europe. A minute referring to Richard's resignation said that the members' regret was "intensified as they look back at the history of the Society, and recall the extent to which its progress had been influenced by [his] indomitable patience, his resolute will, his political sagacity, and his intellectual power." Thanks to his fearless and eloquent advocacy – with pen and speech – the Society had "surmounted the antagonism which it had formerly confronted and had gained a continually growing influence on the national mind". Reference was made to the many occasions where he had done good service to the cause of peace within and outside Parliament and the success he recently had in getting Britain and Russia to agree to go to arbitration over the disputed Afghan border.[14]

In the public meeting which followed, Richard said that now, at the age of 73, thankful that his bodily and mental powers were not more impaired, there were signs of declining powers, and sometimes a failing of health which warned him that he had to husband the little strength that remained. He had survived four Presidents. He was neither tired of the work nor discouraged. If God spared him, he hoped he could continue to be of some service to the cause of peace and he was confident that young men would come forward and take the flag of peace from his failing hand and hold it with a resolute arm. "You are," he said as he concluded his address, "advocating a cause which, in my innermost conviction, I believe to be the cause of truth, reason, justice, and humanity, the cause of religion and, I will venture to say, the cause of God."[15]

True to his word he continued to do all in his power for the cause of peace. In a conference in Darlington in this period he confessed that his hope of an abatement in the war system lay in popular opinion rather than in the policy of Cabinets – which were bound to the rampant militarism of the rest of Europe. He wished for the day when the decisions of Parliament reflected more fairly the wishes and the opinions of the people.[16]

A few years earlier, looking back on the history of the Peace Society Henry Richard was able to claim that it had "helped to create something like a Christian conscience in the nation on the questions of peace and war". He continued:

> It has put the advocates of war on the defence; it has rendered it impossible that any war can now be waged by England, as a matter of course, without question or challenge, or it has to some extent, leavened the public mind – even the minds of those who are professedly most vehemently opposed to its principles – with new ideas as to the responsibility connected with wholesale bloodshed, which they dare, indeed cannot, wholly suppress.[17]

In the period between 14 and 27 November 1885 there occurred the third war between Britain and Burma. For some years France had been at war in Indo-China getting closer to the Burmese border. Burma approached France in an attempt to forge an alliance, which worried Britain, although in the end France declined to come to any agreement. The Burmese Government had also imposed a fine on the Bombay Burmah Trading Corporation for maladministration and failure to pay its employees. The British responded that the accusations were groundless and the court corrupt. Britain insisted on appointing a British arbitrator and when Burma refused, a number of further demands were made. These included having a British diplomatic presence in Mandalay, that any fines imposed on the company be suspended until the diplomat arrived, and that Burma would be subjected to British rule in foreign matters and provide facilities for developing trade between northern Burma and China. Burma rejected the ultimatum and Britain attacked. Burmese forces were in disarray. The attack was unexpected and the country's Minister of Defence had maded it clear that he wanted to discuss peace terms and in the confusion some Burmese soldiers surrendered. The British also spread rumours that they had no intention of governing the country, rather they wanted to depose the unpopular King Thibaw and replace him with Prince Nyaung Yan, Thibaw's older half-brother. But Nyaung Yan, exiled in India was already dead. By the time the Burmese became aware of the trickery the entire country had lost its sovreignty and from 1 January 1886 it was part of the British Empire, the southern part of the country already being under British rule.

Sir Ughtred Kay-Shuttleworth, Under Secretary of State for India, presented the most remarkable resolution to Parliament on 22 February 1886, namely that the cost of the military operations "against the King of Ava" [i.e., Northern Burma] should be defrayed out of India's budget. William Hunter, MP for Aberdeen North, promptly tabled an Amendment: "That this House is of the opinion that it would be unjust to defray the expense of the Military operations in the Kingdom of Ava out of the revenues of India."

The Amendment was Seconded in particularly scathing language by Henry Richard. He sought to extend the debate – not only to debate the matter of forcing India to pay for the war – but the wider issue of Britain's policy in Burma.

> For my part, I must state my opinion that the summary annexation of that Kingdom was an act of high-handed violence for which there is no adequate justification. Recent events and present appearances seem to indicate that it was not only an act of injustice, but an act of flagrant folly. By suddenly overturning the existing Government, it looks as though we had consigned the country to what may prove to be a prolonged anarchy; while there is no little danger of our becoming involved in serious troubles and complications in more than one direction, especially with China. I am sorry that the present Government are disposed to endorse and adopt that policy. I believe it would have been better if they had acted as they did in Afghanistan and the Transvaal, and reversed the policy of their Predecessors, instead of following it as they did in Egypt, with what consequences to themselves and the country is now only too well known. The pretext assigned for this act of wholesale confiscation is the misconduct of King Theebaw. But I fear the real motive was that we coveted his possessions, and were determined to have them at any cost. When Naboth's vineyard is wanted, it is not difficult to make out a case, to our own satisfaction at least, why Naboth himself should be put out of the way.[18]

The two principle reasons for the attack, said Richard, was the greed of military officers to enrich themselves and gain an opportunity for further interference in the affairs of China. As for making India pay for the war, the country had nothing to do with this war "about certain logs of wood", and it certainly could not afford to pay for it. This was a country where 40,000,000 people "had to go through life on insufficient food; and ... in the 19 years between 1861 and 1880 more than 11,500,000 people had died of famine," said Richard. "And is this a people on whose shoulders we should throw the cost of our own quarrels?" As usual, the Amendment tabled by Hunter and Richard was defeated by 292 votes to 82, a majority of 215.

Chapter 28

His last great speech

Richard returned to this subject less than a month later when on 19 March he presented a resolution: "That, in the opinion of this House, it is not just or expedient to embark in war, contract engagements involving grave responsibilities for the Nation, and add territories to the Empire without the knowledge and consent of Parliament."

As with the resolution he had proposed in April 1881, Richard challenged the right of Cabinet to decide to go to war. He rejected the generally accepted view advanced by A. V. Dicey[1] in 1885 that the power exercised by the Cabinet in foreign affairs was constitutionally proper because the "Ministry in all matters of discretion carry out, or tend to carry out, the will of the House."

Richard said that as a people we prided ourselves not a little upon being a self-governing nation viewing people in other countries under despotic rule with pity and a degree of contempt. In matters of minor importance we would defend our rights with great tenacity.

> If any attempt were made to levy the smallest tax, or to impose any civic obligation upon our people, without the authority of Parliament, the country would be convulsed with excitement and indignation. And yet, in regard to one Department of Government, dealing with matters which are of the highest importance, and which involve far reaching issues and consequences, the Department which controls all questions of foreign policy, we are practically, as far as I can see, absolutely powerless and helpless. Any official, acting in our name, in any part of the world, may plunge us into war, with all the sacrifices of treasure and blood, and all the solemn responsibilities which a state of war involves; or may contract engagements on our behalf, entail-

ing grave and lasting obligations; or may make large additions to our dominions, the care of which, and the defence of which, devolve upon the nation; and all this may be done without our knowledge and consent.

He raised the subject of Royal Prerogative which could be used as a constitutional ploy and a licence to go to war, make treaties and extend the frontiers of the Empire without Parliamentary approval.

Perhaps I may be told that the matters I specify belong to the Royal Prerogative, that the Sovereign alone has the right to make war and contract treaties, and enlarge the boundaries of the Empire; but we all know perfectly well that, whatever may have been the case in former times, that is now a mere fiction, and a very mischievous fiction, too, which may enable an ambitious or unscrupulous Minister to hide himself behind the Throne, and so escape the responsibility of his own acts; for, as Sir Henry Maine says, in his recent work on *Popular Government*, speaking of the change that, in this respect, has come over, if not our Constitution, at least our habitual practice. At present the Sovereign can make neither war, nor treaty; he can appoint neither Ambassador, nor Judge; he can do no executive act. All these powers have gone over to what is a sort of Committee of Parliament, calling themselves the Cabinet, who are practically irresponsible.[2]

He went on to list the wars which his generation had witnessed – Afghanistan, Burma, Syria, the Opium Wars, Persia, Japan, Southern Africa, Egypt – showing that in every instance there had been time and opportunity to debate and seek the approval of Parliament and the sense of the country before rushing off to war. Regarding the question of treaties – he noted that 37 had been contracted in Britain's name, all of them involving grave national responsibilities. Here, again, he said, Parliament was absolutely helpless. In other countries – such as France and the USA – the right to make treaties was subject to the approval of the Legislature.

Moreover, in Richard's opinion, the fewer treaties there were between the British and other governments the better. Quoting Cobden, he said that "the greatest possible contact between peoples and the least possible contact between Governments [the better] … contact of peoples promotes peace, and the contact of Governments endangers peace".

At present, it seems to be in the power of any petty officer in the

> Service of the Government, or, indeed, of any private adventurer,
> to take over large territories, and saddle the duty of maintaining
> and defending them on the British people, so lax has often been
> the acceptance of these acquisitions by the Governments of the
> day ... I have lost all faith in the Governments; they seem to have
> delivered themselves up, bound hand and foot, to the power of
> the rampant militarism which is the curse of Europe. The one
> topic which seems really and supremely to interest them, is to
> make preparations for fighting. At this very time, when bitter
> destitution and distress prevail in every country of Europe –
> when there are millions of men, not belonging to the worthless,
> improvident, vicious classes, but honest and industrious men,
> who desire nothing more than to earn their bread by the sweat of
> their brow – who are trembling on the verge of starvation, what
> do the Governments do? The one thing that pre-occupies their
> mind, and on which they are squandering the millions wrung
> from the hard hand of toil, is to add to their armaments on a sys-
> tem of insane rivalry to which there is no limit. So that the con-
> dition of Europe may now be described by two words – arming
> and starving.

But he did look with some hope in the direction of France where
the people were tired of war and where government after government had been overturned between 1881 and 1885, because the
people objected "to a warlike and filibustering policy". In 1882, he
said, the French people had made their voices heard and prevented
their Government from joining Britain in the war in Egypt.

He ended his speech with the words: "Let the men that make
the quarrels / Be the only men to fight." A fierce debate followed,
Randolph Churchill contemptuous, Gladstone sympathetic and
conciliatory and full of praise for Richard's speech but concerned
about the practicalities of the resolution. James Bryce, the Under
Secretary of State for Foreign Affairs, made an appeal to Richard to
withdraw his resolution. But Richard insisted on a division. On
the first vote, that the Speaker leave the Chair and the House go
into division Richard won by 112 votes to 108, a majority of four.
The House reconvening, the resolution became a substantive
motion and Richard was defeated by 115 votes to 109. It will be
noticed that more Members had come in and voted the second
time without hearing Richard speak – saving the Government
from an embarrassing defeat.[3]

Richard's effort was praised by a number of newspapers,
including the *Times*, which described the debate as interesting and
informative, while the *Daily News* noted that it was easier to scorn
than to respond to Richard's arguments.

In a report on the debate in the 1 April issue of the *Herald of Peace*, Richard quoted what Gladstone had to say in Parliament in February 1857 when raising questions about the war in Persia. "I will say, without fear of contradiction," Gladstone had said, "that the practice of commencing wars without associating Parliament with the first measures is utterly at variance with the established practice of the country, dangerous to the constitution, and absolutely requiring the intervention of this House in order to render the recognition of so dangerous a proceeding utterly impossible."[4] It is much easier to make grand statements when in Opposition, it is not so easy when in Government.

This had been the last of Henry Richard's great Parliamentary speeches. He felt his health was failing and on the advice of his doctor to avoid over-taxing himself physically and mentally he made no further great contribution to any debate until his death on 20 August 1888.

Richard's efforts did not receive the attention they deserved in this period. His resolution of 19 March went virtually unnoticed in Wales. The burning issues during 1884-85 were Irish Home Rule, parliamentary reform and extending the franchise with the aim of adding two million to the electoral role. The House of Lords had rejected the County Franchise Bill which would have given the same rights to rural constituencies as those enjoyed by the boroughs. Huge protest meetings and marches were held denouncing the actions of the Lords and the Bill was passed in 1885 after making constituency changes which were acceptable to the Tories. Rumours were put about that the Gladstone administration intended to bring back the restrictive Protection of Person and Property (Ireland) Act which had made it unlawful for the Irish National League – formerly the Irish National Land League – to assemble. As a result of these rumours the Irish Nationalists and Charles Parnell, founder of the re-named Irish National League, crossed over to support the Tories. In June 1885, with a number of Liberals abstaining, an alliance of Tories and Irish Nationalists defeated the Government on a detail of Hugh Childers's Budget. As the electoral registers had not been prepared it was impossible to hold a general election for some months. Gladstone resigned and the Conservatives governed under Lord Salisbury – with the support of Gladstone as the Tories did not have a majority even with the support of the Irish MPs – until Parliament was dissolved on 18 November 1885.

Having resigned from the position of Secretary of the Peace

Society and aware of the frailty of his health, Henry Richard, after 17 years as MP for Merthyr and Aberdare, considered giving up his seat in Parliament. But his constituents would not hear of it and he and Charles James were returned unopposed. Wales kept faith with Gladstone, returning 30 Liberals out of 34. But overall the Liberals had lost 33 seats, the Conservatives had gained 10 and Parnell's Irish Party had gained 23 seats. The Irish now had a total of 86 MPs, the Conservatives 247, and the Liberals with their 319 seats, no longer had an overall majority in Parliament. Parnell had been effective in achieving some of his aims by obstructive tactics. It was in this period that the "guillotine" was introduced as a means of limiting the length of debates.

Gladstone introduced his Home Rule Bill for Ireland on 8 April 1886, and on 8 June it was defeated by 30 votes. The Liberals were not united in their support, with many of the traditional Whigs hostile to the idea, although the progressive wing of the party – Henry Richard among them – was strongly in favour of Irish Home Rule. Also, Gladstone had not anticipated the opposition of the Ulster Protestants, nor the wrath stirred up by the inflammatory speeches of the Conservative, Lord Randolph Churchill. "Ulster will fight and Ulster will be right," was the cry. The Orange Orders had dissipated in the 1830s; now they were regrouping and rearming.

Gladstone chose to call the election. But the failure of the Irish Home Rule Bill in 1886 put British politics in a turmoil.[5] The old Liberal Party was torn apart and destroyed. It lost its majority in England and its grip on the cities was weakened. Worse, led by Lord Hartington and Joseph Chamberlain the Liberal Unionists – many of the old Whig tradition – entered into an informal alliance with the Conservatives. Even in Scotland there was a strong Unionist element in the Liberal Party. Lord Salisbury, between his own Conservative Party and the Liberal Unionists could rely on 393 seats, Gladstone was down to 191 and the Irish Nationalists had 85. Wales, in the main, stayed true to Gladstone, and again Henry Richard and Charles James were returned unopposed. And despite many disagreements, Henry Richard never wavered in his support for Gladstone. "Come what may," he said, "I shall stand by the Grand Old Man."[6] Among the most interesting of the new intake of Welsh Liberals was Thomas Edward Ellis, aged 27, the MP for Meirioneth. T. I. Ellis in the biography he wrote of his father noted that Henry Richard "went out of his way to get to know Tom Ellis."[7] In general, however, the Welsh Liberal MPs were getting older. Only nine were under 50, and Richard, at 74, was the third oldest. He could no longer rely on the friendship and the constituency support of David Davis, who had died in 1884. But still there was Thomas Williams, Chairman of the local Liberal Association, who had been one of the most enthusiastic in getting Richard to represent the constituency 20 years earlier. It appears that Henry Richard had wanted to retire from Parliament before the 1885 election and submitted a letter of resignation to Thomas Williams. But Williams kept the letter in his pocket and never made it public and after an hour-long conversation between them in the House of Commons, Richard yielded to the plea "to die in harness as the senior Member for Merthyr".[8]

Before the general election, and between the debates on the military operations in Burma, Lewis Dillwyn, on 9 March, brought the question of Church Disestablishment before Parliament.[9] The resolution was: "That as the Church of England and Wales, has failed to fulfil its professed object, as a means of promoting the religious interests of the Welsh people and minis-ters, to only a small minority of the population, that its continu-ance as an established Church in the Principality, is an anomaly, and an injustice, which ought no longer to exist." The resolution was seconded by Henry Richard who stated in very clear language that the Church of England in Wales was not, and never had been, the Church *of* Wales. It had failed, he said, to win the love and loy-alty of the people, and had never discharged, in anything approaching a satisfactory manner, its own professed function as the religious instructor of the nation. On the contrary, it had been used, particularly in Norman times, as an instrument for the extinction of the Welsh language and the suppression of Welsh nationality. He gave a snapshot of centuries of Welsh history. It was one of those Welsh history lectures that Henry Richard seemed to enjoy giving to the House of Commons. He quoted a complaint sent by the Welsh Princes to Pope Innocent during the reign of Henry III, that:

> 'The Archbishop of Canterbury, as a matter of course, sends us English Bishops ignorant of the manners and language of our land, who cannot preach the Word of God to the people, nor receive their confessions but through interpreters. And these Bishops that they send us from England, as they neither love us nor our land, but rather persecute and oppress us with an innate and deep-rooted hatred, seek not the welfare of our souls; their ambition is to rule over us, and not to benefit us, and on this

> account they do not but very rarely fulfil the duties of their pas-
> toral office. And, whatever they can lay their hands upon, or get
> from us, whether by right or wrong, they carry into England, and
> waste and consume the whole of the profits obtained from us, in
> abbeys and lands given to them by the King of England.'

He spoke of the Protestant Reformation:

> Some of my clerical countrymen indulge in a fond historical
> dream to the effect that, after the accession of the Tudors, there
> was a golden age for their Church, when it was ruled by native
> Bishops, and enjoyed a season of great spiritual prosperity. But it
> is only a dream, with which the reality does not correspond.
> There was, no doubt, a certain number of Welsh Bishops then
> appointed – as many as 30 in 157 years. But that brought little
> improvement in the religious condition of the country – so far
> otherwise, that I venture to say it is scarcely possible to exagger-
> ate the utter – one might almost say the contemptuous – neglect
> with which Wales was treated during the early years of the
> Reformation.

He referred to the negligence of the Anglican Bishops on the matter of translating the Bible into Welsh. In 1563 an Act of
Parliament was passed ordering the translation of the Scriptures
into Welsh but for 25 years nothing was done. Eventually, when
the Bible was translated it was done not by the Bishops, "but by
the simple vicar of a parish in Denbighshire, Dr William Morgan,
whose name and memory deserve to be held in lasting and grateful remembrance by the people of Wales". He spoke of Rhys
Prichard, Vicar of Llandovery, who had testified that not one in a
hundred of his compatriots could read the Bible, that no copy of
the Scriptures could be found even in the mansions of many of the
gentry; that the country was sunk in ignorance and immorality of
every description, while "the clergy were asleep, leaving the people to sin unwarned and unrebuked".

Then, he said, in the middle of the eighteenth century "there
arose in the Church a most admirable man – the Rev Griffith
Jones, of Llanddowror, founder of the Circulating Schools". Like
Prichard, Griffith Jones also wrote of "lazy vicars and rectors who
have led a careless life from their youth, and have set their minds
on keeping company and going unsteadily from tavern to tavern,
and who are as ignorant of their mother tongue as they are of
Greek and Hebrew; and, therefore, without sense of shame,
preach in English in the most purely Welsh assemblies throughout
the country". It was not entirely the fault of the clergy, he con-

ceded, since their bishops "the alien Bishops, as a rule, lived wholly apart from the people, and even from the clergy. Some of them did not reside in the country, and one, at least, during the whole term of his episcopate, never once set his foot in his diocese." Having detailed the corruption and carelessness of the Bishops he ended by appealing "to the justice and generosity of Englishmen" to liberate the Welsh people from an anomaly that ought to be swept away, for which they would gain the gratitude and loyalty of his countrymen![10]

Albert Grey, Liberal MP for Tyneside, proposed an amendment "That as the Church of England and Wales, has failed to fulfil its professed object, as a means of promoting the religious interests of the Welsh people and ministers, to only a small minority of the population, that this House is of opinion that the time has arrived for introducing, without delay, into its organisation such reforms as will enable it to adapt itself more efficiently to the religious needs and wishes of the Welsh people". The toothless amendment was carried – narrowly – by 241 votes to 229.

The subject of the Disestablishment of the Anglican Church from the State was an issue that was raised ever more frequently. In Wales all the Liberal MPs – bar one – supported Disestablishment. Of all the Liberal Parliamentary candidates, at the time it was estimated that around 400 more or less supported Disestablishment. Also, the energy of the Liberation Society was worrying the Anglican clergy. John Carvell Williams, with whom Henry Richard had cooperated to inspire Welsh interest in the society in the 1860s, had been elected MP for one of the Nottingham seats. The society's pamphlet, *Suggestions on Disestablishment*, was re-printed. Prior to the December 1885 general election a series of articles appeared in the *Fortnightly Review* and then published as a booklet under the title *Radical Programme* – also known as the Unauthorised Programme. This programme advocated a number of radical reforms including Disestablishment. The introduction to the booklet was written by Joseph Chamberlain, at the time Liberal MP for Birmingham. The following year Chamberlain took a leading role in forming the alliance between the Whig wing of the Liberal Party and the Conservatives.

The election of Carvell Williams pleased Henry Richard greatly. As well as being Chairman of the Welsh Members Parliamentary Party, Richard was also the unofficial leader of the Nonconformist MPs. Although Carvell Williams had close connections with Parliament – he had been for many years a lobbyist for the Liberation Society – he was in a position to be far more effective and influential as an MP, as well as taking some of the load off Henry Richard's shoulders. In October 1886 they received – jointly – a request from Sydney Buxton, an East London MP, to write a pamphlet on Disestablishment for the *Imperial Parliament Series*. *Disestablishment*[11] was published in 1886. The Church of England is severely criticised – as is Christianity, or Christianity in the organised or established sense, particularly in its connection with war and the barbarity of war. Where Church and State are inextricably linked, it argued that the Church cannot easily raise its voice to oppose war – and this is contrary to the principles preached by Christ. It contains much about Wales, particularly about the rural areas and gives a strong rebuttal to the argument that Wales would suffer religious deprivation if the Church were to be Disestablished. According to the 1851 census, in the agricultural districts of Cardiganshire, the number of sittings in places of worship provided for 97.8 per cent of the population – of which the Church of England supplied 27.4, and the Dissenters 70.4 per cent.[12] In a letter to Richard, John Bright wrote:

> It is a remarkable book, so small in compass and so readable, and yet dealing with the whole of the great question on which it treats. Your little book is admirable alike in regard to facts and arguments. I have read nothing on the Church Question so complete, and so calculated to influence public opinion in a right direction.[13]

For Henry Richard Disestablishment – the separation of Church and State – was a matter of principle. Yet, he made good use of the condition of Wales to support his argument, namely that the Church of England was becoming more and more irrelevant to Wales as Nonconformity strengthened its grip on the country.

Chapter 29

The Cross Commission on Education

Henry Richard's membership of the Royal Commission to inquire into the state of Education in England and Wales was his final contribution of importance to Wales and to education. At the end of 1885 during Lord Salisbury's brief Conservative administration Richard was invited to be one of the Commission's 23 members, chaired by Lord Cross. Without doubt the purpose of the Cross Commission was to place the denominational – to all purposes, Church of England schools – on the same footing as the Board schools in respect to public aid. Lord Cross virtually admitted it. It was, therefore, vital that the Commission should have a strong representation of men who believed strongly in the principle of non-denominational education. Richard was conscious that he was getting older and his health deteriorating and he thought long and hard over whether to accept the invitation. He wrote to Dr Robert William Dale, the Birmingham Congregational minister, who had also been invited to join the Commission, expressing his concerns. "I am getting to be an old man, and rather shrink from further labour and responsibility ... I am suspicious as to the composition and object of the Commission, and fear to be caught in a snare." On the other side, he said, there were subtle adversaries who were also men of extreme views. However, he had decided to accept, but in his letter of acceptance he said that he had insisted on an assurance that Nonconformists would have fair representation on the Commission.[1]

The Commission was established on 15 January 1886. Of the 23 Commissioners, 15 were known to be hostile to placing education under public control. The other eight were either Liberals or Nonconformists. The Commission met on 146 days and listened to 151 witnesses, about 110 of whom had connections with the Church of England. The work was finished on 27 June 1888. The Commissioners were far from unanimous in their conclusions. The Majority Report was signed by 15, the Minority Report by eight and there was even a second Minority Report. The following extract from the Extended Minority Report gives some indication of the cause of the disagreements: " … their report appears to us too often to approach proposals for the improvement of education from the view point of considering how much such improvements may affect the interests of certain classes of schools rather than how far they are desirable …"

They saw the Main Report as being over-concerned with safeguarding the interests of the voluntary schools, i.e. the Church of England Schools, and a certain class of people. They accepted that it contained recommendations that would benefit education in general, but they were linked to demands for increased public financial support for Anglican schools. This did not do justice to the wishes of the minority who wished to extend the scope and purpose of education in general, and to put it on firm footing with local, public support. Again there is evidence, in both minority reports, of Henry Richard's opposition to schools providing religious instruction and his advocacy of what he had witnessed in Germany, where schools did not provide religious education. In Richard's opinion, teaching religion did not ensure a religious spirit.

According to Dr Dale[2] Richard sat on the Cross Commission as the representative of the Educational interests of Wales and as the Political and Parliamentary leader of the Nonconformists. One thing is clear, Richard was determined to ensure fairness for the Welsh language. He succeeded to such an extent that the only point on which all three reports agreed was that in Wales pupils should be allowed to take Welsh as a special subject, and if desired, that Welsh be studied instead of English as a class subject, based on establishing a graded system of translating from Welsh into English and the teaching of Welsh in addition to English. It was also recommended that the use of Welsh be permitted to examine candidates for the Queen's Scholarship and Certificates of Qualification.[3] This was a huge step forward when we recall that the Education Bill of 1870 legislated that English alone could be used in day schools.

As a result of these recommendations a series of provisions were made by the Department of Education, provisions which had they been acted upon by head teachers and schools' inspectors would have meant that the Welsh language today would be in a far more secure position. The following points were approved in the Code issued by the Department:

1. Bilingual books were allowed to be used in all classes, as well as bilingual writing books;
2. A grant of two shillings was offered for the successful teaching of Welsh alongside English
3. A grant of four shillings per head was offered for every pupil in Classes V, VI and VII who passed Welsh Grammar as a special subject;
4. Translating from Welsh into English was admissible instead of English composition;
5. The teaching of Welsh History and Geography was to be encouraged.[4]

Thanks to "the ardent and enlightened Welshman ... Henry Richard" supporters of the Welsh language got nearly everything they had asked for. But, sadly, schools many years later were still teaching subjects through the medium of English. Prior to 1885 the Welsh language in education had been completely ignored. Thanks to the persistence of Henry Richard, the sole Welshman on the Cross Commission the door had been opened for the development of Welsh education. The opportunity was there. That it was not seized cannot be blamed on Richard who died soon after the publication of the Commission's report.

"There was something pathetic in the quiet heroism with which Mr Henry Richard discharged his duties on the Education Commission," according to Dale. The two often travelled together to the Commission's rooms in Richmond Terrace, and Dale says that not once during those many months was Richard able to ascend the steps without pausing to take the remedy to avert an attack of angina which was the cause of much distress to him in his final years. "More than once, when the proceedings had taken the form of a regular debate and he rose to speak, it was apparent that he was suffering severe physical distress, and that even the slightest excitement occasioned by addressing a short speech of five or ten minutes to a company of 20 gentlemen was perilous to him. He knew his danger, and sometimes spoke of it in deep emotion. But while he lived he was resolved to do all the work that lay within his strength." As already noted the Cross

Commission saw him as the political and parliamentary leader of the Nonconformists and as the representative of the educational interests of Wales. Rarely would he miss a meeting and, according to Dale, his contributions were always weighty and substantial. "He gave the closest attention to the evidence of the witnesses, and when the final Report was under discussion he was always vigilant and alert," wrote Dale. "He was invariably courteous but inflexibly firm. When he had reached a conclusion, it was not easy – I am not sure that it was possible – to move it from him … [H]e wrote some of the sentences that seem to me most admirable in the Extended Minority Report."[5] Although it was the experienced Edward Lyulph Stanley who drafted most of that Report.

Richard gave his last address to the Peace Society in the Annual Meeting in May 1887. He was aware that his life was coming to its end and he called on his fellow workers not to be discouraged:

> [I] believe the powers that are for us are greater than those that are against us. Reason is for us, for war is an outrage on reason; justice is for us, for war tramples justice under foot; humanity is for us, for war desolates humanity, and has written its scroll within and without with mourning and lamentation. Civilisation is for us, for war is the incarnation of barbarism; and, above all, religion is for us, for it is not possible that He who made of one blood all nations of men, can look with complacency upon His children engaged in butchering each other; and we have the benediction of Him … who has said, 'Blessed are the peacemakers, for they shall be called the children of God'.[6]

The 1887 conference, the 13th, of the Association for the Reform and Codification of the Law of Nations was held in the Guildhall, London, in July. It was a noteworthy event because of the presence of many influential men. Richard, speaking on the subject of International Arbitration, gave the second address of the conference. He began with an analysis of the military and financial condition of Europe. There were, he said, 17,000,000 men either at war or training for war, with a further 3,041,054 on a peace footing ready to be called upon if necessary. The annual cost of this in direct taxation on the people was £158,428,740. The indirect costs – the millions of able-bodied men not in productive industry and the loss of interest on the prodigious capital invested in preparations for war was estimated to be £500,000,000 a year for Europe alone. The aggregate national debts of Europe, he said, was £4,649,286,882 and the total annual interest on that capital was £213,640,000.

But there was room for optimism. Since 1883 there had been instances of successful arbitration in disputes between various States – between the Netherlands and St Domingo over the seizing of a ship, between Britain and Germany over claims over Fiji; between Spain and the US, again relating to the seizure of a ship; between Russia and Britain on the Pendjeh incident (Afghanistan, 1885); and between Spain and Germany over a dispute about the Solomon Islands. It would be his last speech to the Association and he ended it with these words:

> We shall find, on looking back over the past, that the charges now brought against us, of being missionaries and preachers of impracticable Utopia, have been brought against others who, in former times, had faith and courage to labour for great reforms against the traditions and customs of their age, but who, nevertheless, by patient continuance in well-doing, did succeed in achieving great and lasting triumphs for civilisation and humanity. None of us are sanguine as to expect that we can accomplish all our hearts' desire by a sudden coup. Nobody knows better than we do, the difficulty of the object we are aiming at; but we must be content to work on earnestly and steadfastly for the right – and most men admit that we have right on our side – with the calm and firm conviction that even in such a world as this, the right is destined ultimately to be victorious.[7]

As would be expected, when the National Eisteddfod was held in London in 1887, Henry Richard was one of the Day Presidents where he took the opportunity to speak on the importance and uniqueness of the Welsh language. He still contributed articles about Wales to the English papers and on 17 January 1888, an article appeared under his name in the *Daily News* – the radical paper established by Charles Dickens in 1846. In the article Richard outlines the Parliamentary progress of Wales during the preceding decades. He assumes no credit for that progress but most of it was due to his example and leadership. The article, typically, is laced with the sarcasm that was a feature of his speeches:

> Wales is rapidly coming to the fore. Some tried a good many years ago, to call the attention of the English public to the condition and claims of the Principality. A few generous spirits, of whom Mr Gladstone was one, paid some heed to our representations. But, on the whole, John Bull had other cares on his mind and other work on his hands. He had to watch over and adjust the balance of power in Europe. He had to maintain the independence and integrity of the Ottoman Empire. He had to estab-

lish a scientific frontier in Afghanistan. He had to subjugate the Boers in the Transvaal to the sovereignty of England. He had to conquer Cetywayo and regulate the affairs of Zululand. He had to bombard Alexandria, to govern Egypt, and slaughter many thousand Arabs in the Soudan. In a word, he had to prosecute a spirited foreign policy in all parts of the world, and compared with those magnificent enterprises, what right had a poor million and a half Welshmen to expect that he would incline his ear to their plaints and pleadings, or indeed have leisure or thought very much to mind his own affairs.

As is always the case in our political history, Wales had to make itself troublesome in order to gain notice. It had to raise its voice pretty loudly on questions relating to the land and the Church and other venerable superstitions before it conquered the apathy of its neighbours. But since it has succeeded a little in frightening the dominant classes it has come to occupy a more and more conspicuous place in men's thoughts and speeches. It is now recognised as having a distinct individuality of its own, and not to be deemed for ever a mere tag to the tail of England. Prime Ministers and ex-Prime Ministers, and all sorts of distinguished statesmen and orators, have turned upon it the light of their countenance and have sought to woo its people with the voice of the charmer. It has had a Government Commission of Inquiry all to itself ... Its case has been partially heard even in Parliament, notwithstanding resolute attempts to stamp it out. As a natural consequence of all this many are running to and fro speaking and writing of the state of the Principality, and if true knowledge is not increased, what pretends to be knowledge is very much noised abroad. Adventurous English journalists have summoned to invade and explore this terra incognita, and some of them have even dared to penetrate to those parts of the country where they tell us 'the people are almost entirely cut off from English civilisation' – whatever that may be. As the result of these excursions they have deluged the pages of newspapers with a variety of sensational reports, more or less apocryphal, of what they have seen and heard, and have delineated the characters of individuals and characters and classes in a very bold style of caricature, which has partly amused and partly also exasperated the people on whom they have thus experimented, who complain with great emphasis that they are misrepresented and maligned. Among the things which the explorers have discovered, and which they proclaim to the world with a delightful naïveté, is the fact that Welsh is the language of familiar conversation among seven-tenths of the inhabitants of "this dark country" – a revelation of itself sufficient to appal the English Philistine, who has a lurking, though perhaps unavowed, conviction that no people can be really civilized who don't talk English.

But that is not all, for they have found out further that there is a large number of newspapers and other periodicals published in the Welsh language, which are, to an alarming extent, in the hands of Nonconformists, and, to give climax to the horror, that many of those are actually edited by Dissenting ministers; and as Dissenting ministers, are little better than reprobates, quite 'fit for treasons, stratagems and spoils', the shuddering reader is allowed to conceive into what peril our institutions may be brought with such men wielding so terrible an instrument as a language which is 'not understanded' of the guardians of 'English civilisation'.

The Nonconformists were criticised for being a collection of sects representing a vast swathe of theology. Richard explained that the main body of Nonconformity consisted of Calvinistic Methodists, Congregationalists, Baptists and Wesleyans, He added:

> Among all these there is far less diversity of doctrine and mutual jealousy than among the sects existing within the Church of England, of which we were told not long ago by the *Times* that 'it is now established that a clergyman of the Church of England may teach any doctrine which only extreme subtlety can distinguish from Roman Catholicism on the one side, Calvinism on the other side, and Deism on the third side.[8]

He ended his article by defending the Nonconformist denominations from accusations of being political establishments, their ministers preaching politics from the pulpits on Sunday and of hostility towards the Church of England. Even at election time when feelings ran high, Richard denied ever having heard a Nonconformist minister preaching politics. "It is not often that I attend the services of the Established Church in Wales, but the last time I did so I heard a purely and intensely political sermon, none the less significant because it was hurled at the head of Mr Gladstone, who was present on the occasion," he said.

This article was published less than eight months before his death. It would be difficult to imagine such an attack on the English establishment being published today in even one of the more liberal of London's broadsheets.

Chapter 30

His last days

Henry Richard never stopped working – it could almost be said that he died in the harness as he had promised. In March 1888 the Council of Aberystwyth College decided the time was ripe to ask the Government for a College Charter. The work of preparing the application was given to a committee consisting of Lord Aberdare, Lewis Morris, Stuart Rendel MP, Morgan Lloyd and Sir John Henry Puleston, the Conservative MP for Devonport. On 13 July news came that the Council of Cardiff College had appointed Lord Aberdare, Henry Richard, Principal Viriamu Jones, Sir Hussey Vivian MP, and others to accompany them in a deputation to meet the President of the Committee of Council on Education, Lord Cranbrooke, on 17 July. It was a large deputation and included Welsh Lords, MPs, governors of the three colleges as well as a number of other prominent dignitaries. This was Henry Richard's final contribution to education in Wales. He had been prominent in establishing Aberystwyth College, although he had been accused of losing interest at one stage and had not been steadfast in defending the interests of the College on the 1881 Aberdare Departmental Committee. He had not opposed the decision taken at Chester for the North Wales College to be based in one of the six North Wales counties. A decision that could have sounded the death knell of Aberystwyth college. But when he saw that Wales was united in defence of Aberystwyth he leapt back into the fray and played a prominent part in the campaign. As Vice-President of Cardiff College, he made an important contribution in the meeting with Cranbrook. The case for Aberystwyth to receive full and final recognition was firmly presented as was Wales's claim for its own University supported by its own Charter.

Cranbrook's response was favourable. Early in August Richard chaired the lengthy and arduous discussions at which the proposed form and words of the Charter was settled. It was to be his last service to Wales and appropriately it would be to Higher Education.[1] He was spared having to witness the squabbling over the eventual name of the University College of Wales, Aberystwyth, and the final acceptance of the Charter.

Less than a fortnight later he and Mrs Richard went to Treborth, to stay for a few days with their old friend, Richard Davies, formerly MP for Anglesey, and then Lord Lieutenant of the county. It has been suggested that Richard had been shaken by the news of the sudden death of his friend, Dr John Alfred Lush who had been elected to Parliament at the same time as Richard and, suffering from the same heart problem, had retired from Parliament some time before. Unknown to his wife, Richard had spent three days putting his personal papers and affairs in order. Then on 9 August they set off for North Wales and Treborth, where he arrived without any real pain or discomfort. Richard Davies described his final days:

> He was ever a welcome guest here, dear to old and young alike. It was evident that he suffered very frequently from spasms – at the heart this time – but he would be so bright and cheery at intervals, ready as ever to enjoy his drive, or to be a most interested spectator of the young people's fun and games. On the Saturday before his death he drove with us to Betws-y-Coed, by Ogwen and Capel Curig, and it is a mournful pleasure to us to remember how he delighted in the air and scenery of that day.[2]

On their way past Llyn Ogwen it was said that Henry Richard had turned to Mrs Davies with the words "This is a day to remember". Among the others in the carriage was Jeremiah James Colman, MP for Norwich (of Colman's mustard). According to Colman they had been discussing the subject of age and that Richard had said that no one should live too long. On Monday, Dr Owen Thomas (Minister of Princes Road Methodist Chapel, Liverpool) called and they spent a few lively hours talking about the great preachers of the past, among them Ebenezer Richard. Anne – Mrs Richard Davies – was the daughter of the celebrated Rev Henry Rees, Liverpool.

On the evening of 20 August at dinner Henry Richard was in great spirits. Then at around 11 he was forced to retire to his room in pain. The pains became worse. Doctors were sent for, but a little before midnight, with his wife and surrounded by a congenial circle of political and dear friends, he died. On the 22nd, after a short service conducted by the Rev David Charles Davies, who was born in Aberystwyth and a former minister of Jewin Crescent, his body was taken from Treborth to Bangor, and then by train to his home at 22 Bolton Gardens, London. He was buried at Abney Park Cemetery on Friday, 24 August 1888. Present were ministers of religion, MPs, representatives of the Peace Society, the Congregational Union, the International Arbitration Society, Aberystwyth College, Brecon College, the Cymmrodorion, the National Eisteddfod and many other organisations and societies with which he had been involved. The service was conducted by the Rev Edward White and Dr R. W. Dale. White chose his verses with care from Psalm 37, "For the end of that man is peace"; Isaiah 32, "The fruit of righteousness is sown in peace of them that make peace"; and from Isaiah 2, "They shall turn their spears into ploughshares and their spears into pruning hooks."

Dr Dale said it was appropriate that he died in Wales within the sound of its waters and in sight of its mountains, the land where he grew up and which he loved so much. Richard, he recalled, had always maintained that the Free Evangelical Churches of Wales were the true national churches of his country, and that he resisted the claims of the ecclesiastical Establishment funded by the State.

> Although he believed that it was no part of the function of the State to maintain the authority of the Christian Gospel, he also believed that it was the function of those who had received the Christian Gospel to cause its spirit to penetrate the legislation and the life of the State. To the last he was a Radical of that early type which has almost disappeared. He believed in trusting the people of a country like this with the management of their own public business ... He thought it safer for the people, if they had any fitness for freedom, to make mistakes in the conduct of their own affairs, than for them to be saved from mistake, even if that were possible, by central government.

Dale then spoke of Richard's relationship with his constituents:

> They recognised his integrity and had boundless faith in him; they recognised his zeal in their service. From the time that he first became Member for Merthyr his seat was never seriously in danger, and of late years no one dared to think of disturbing it. He was more than Member for Merthyr, he was Member for Wales, and for many years he was the authoritative representative in the House of Commons of English as well as Welsh

Henry Richard's tomb in Abney Park cemetery, London

Nonconformity. Of his private life, of which during the last two years I have seen much, I would only say that he was singularly gentle, kindly affectionate, and unselfish. He loved warmly, and he was warmly loved.[3]

The Rev Dr Owen Evans, Minister of Tabernacle, the Welsh Congregational Chapel, King's Cross, gave the address in Welsh at the grave side and spoke of the loss to Wales and of Richard's many contributions to the land of his birth. Then they sang the Welsh hymn with the intoxicating words by David George Jones, the blacksmith from Llanarthne:

Byrdd myrdd o ryfeddodau
Ar doriad bore wawr.

On 4 September, a fortnight later, Gladstone spoke at the Wrexham National Eisteddfod. Much of his address was a tribute to the life and work of Henry Richard:

I have owed to him much of what I have learned about Wales as my experience has enlarged, and I owe a debt to him on that account which I am ever glad to acknowledge. But, gentlemen, he has broader claims upon you. He has upon you the claim of having exhibited to the world a model character, such as any country cannot but regard as a model of sympathy and delight. I have seen him in Parliament, the advocate of decided opinions, the advocate of some opinions, perhaps among the best he enter-

tained – for instance, in respect to peace – in which he had no
great number of sympathisers or followers. I have seen him
always uniting a most determined courage and resolution in the
assertion of his principles and views with the greatest tenderness,
gentleness and sympathy towards those who differed from him
... there was in him what I may call an inner place, which was the
secret of his outward self-command, and of his gentleness as well
as of his courage. It was impossible to see him without seeing
that he was not only a professor of Christianity, but that his mind
was a sanctuary of Christian faith, of Christian hope, and of
Christian love; and all those great powers and principles radiated
forth from the centre, and let his light shine before men ...[4]

Gladstone again referred to Henry Richard when speaking at
Porthmadog on 15 September 1892. Sometime in Parliament – he
could not remember when but there had been a discussion on the
authorized translation of the Bible and Henry Richard got up: and
said words to the effect that

You, English, have an excellent and priceless translation of the
Holy Scriptures, and I hope that you appreciate it, as you should.
But I trust that you will not be offended for saying that we Welsh
people have a much finer translation. It is finer, not because your
translators were negligent in any way but because the Welsh
tongue was finer than the tongue of this country.[5]

He never failed to exalt the land nor the language of his birth.

Tributes and messages of condolences arrived from all parts of
the world. The Executive Committee of the American Peace
Society passed resolutions extending their condolences with his
widow and of sympathy "to our brethren in the London Peace
Society" adding: "*Their* loss is *ours* also, and that of the cause of
peace and arbitration throughout the world. We rejoice that what
Mr Richard accomplished for peace by his forty years of strenuous
and noble activity can never be lost." The English papers, even the
Times, were generous in their commemoration. "He was what
may have been called, perhaps, by his enemies an extremist, and
that, it is likely, because he was a man in earnest," was the opinion
of the *Daily News*. "... he had great influence in the councils of the
Radical class and the Liberal Party, and many of their younger
members were indebted indirectly to his doctrine for their hatred
of war and the unstable diplomacy that leads to war," wrote the
Leeds Mercury. "It is good that there are men who refuse to accept
the influence of convenience, and who hold that pure justice is the
only basis for legislation – Mr Richard was such a man," said the

The statue by Edward Toft of Henry Richard in Tregaron, unveiled 18 August 1893

Birmingham Post. "Mr Richard was the country's conscience on more than one occasion," according to the *London Echo.* And in the opinion of the *South Wales Daily News:* "There was no more typical Welshman. His was a household name. He loved his people, and they loved him."[6]

> Mr Henry Richard," said Thomas Edward Ellis, newly elected Liberal MP for Meirioneth. "was the first real exponent in the House of Commons of the puritan and progressive life of Wales, and he expounded the principles which Nonconformity has breathed into the very life and heart of the Welsh people.[7]

A statue in memory of Henry Richard was unveiled on the square of Tregaron on 18 August 1893. The principal speaker was Sir George Osborne Morgan who spoke of Richard's defence of tenants oppressed by their landlords. "When he sat down, one thing was obvious to everyone, Wales had a worthy representative, and that Mr Richard's Parliamentary career was safe."

> Canys yr oedd yn fawr gan ei genedl, ac yn gymeradwy ym mysg lluaws ei frodyr, yn ceisio daioni i'w bobl, ac yn dywedyd am heddwch i'w holl diriogaeth"

> Because he was great among his nation, and accepted of the multitude of his brethren,; seeking the good of his people, and speaking peace to all his seed.

Notes

Introduction

1 Henry Richard, *Letters and Essays on Wales*, Introduction to the 1884 edition (London), p. viii
2 Ieuan Gwynedd Jones, *Henry Richard – Apostle of Peace 1812-1888* (The Fellowship of Reconciliation, 1988), p. 20
3 Ibid., p. 13
4 The Archbishop of Wales, *Memories* (London, 1927), pp. 116-117
5 Ibid., p. 98
6 Ibid., p. 119

Chapter 1

1 The Circulating Schools was an idea devised and developed by Griffith Jones, an Anglican clergyman from Llanddowror, Carmarthenshire. Itinerant teachers and apprentices would spend three months living and working in poor, rural communities, teaching people to read – primarily The Bible. The teaching was in Welsh and happened within the cycles of agricultural life in the Welsh hills. Backed by the money of Madame Bridget Bevan, wife of a Carmarthen MP, the schools were a great success with adults and children. The schools began in 1730 and ended in 1779 when Madame Bevan died and her will was contested. By 1761 the movement claimed to have taught 160,000 children and anything from 300,000 to 450,000 adults to read. The population of Wales at the time would not have exceeded 500,000. The success of this drive towards literacy attracted the attention of Catherine the Great of Russia, and developing countries as late as the 1950s considered setting up similar schemes. Gwyn A. Williams, *When Was Wales?* (London, 1985), pp. 154–155
2 H. R. Evans, *Dr Edward Richard of Tregaron and Finchingfield*, *The Transactions of the Honourable Society of Cymmrodorion* (London, 1962), p. 93.
3 Ibid., pp. 95–98
4 Ibid., pp. 93–95
5 Ibid., p. 98
6 Carey Jones, *Gyrfa'r gŵr o Dregaron*, (Swansea, 1988), p. 11
6 Evans, *Dr Edward Richard of Tregaron and Finchingfield*, pp. 103-104
8 Ibid., p. 101
9 Ibid., pp. 102-103
10 Charles S. Miall, *Henry Richard, M.P.: A Biography* (London, 1889), p. 89
11 Ibid., p. 104
12 Ibid., p. 103
13 D. Densil Morgan, *Dawn Dweud: Lewis Edwards* (Cardiff, 2009), p. 8.
14 Ibid., p. 10
15 Ibid., p. 19
16 Ibid., p. 23
17 Evans, *Dr Edward Richard of Tregaron and Finchingfield*, p. 120
18 J. J. Morgan, *Cofiant Evan Phillips Castell Newydd Emlyn* (Liverpool, 1930), p. 17
19 Evans, *Dr Edward Richard of Tregaron and Finchingfield*, pp. 106-108
20 Ibid., pp. 110-111
21 Ibid., p. 110
22 Ibid., p. 112

Chapter 2

1 Evans, *Dr Edward Richard of Tregaron and Finchingfield*, p. 112
2 Cited by Eleazar Roberts, *Bywyd a Gwaith y Diweddar Henry Richard*, A.S. (Wrexham, 1902), p. 13
3 These academies were established at a time when Oxford and Cambridge would not accept non-Anglican students. See also Geraint Dyfnallt Owen, *Ysgolion a Cholegau yr Annibynwyr* (Swansea, 1939)
4 Evans, *Dr Edward Richard of Tregaron and Finchingfield*, pp. 113-114
5 Ibid., p. 114
6 Cited by Roberts, *Bywyd a Gwaith y Diweddar Henry Richard*, pp. 13-14
7 Jones, *Gyrfa'r gŵr o Dregaron*, p. 16
8 Cited by Roberts, *Bywyd a Gwaith y Diweddar Henry Richard*, pp. 15-16
9 Evans, *Dr Edward Richard of Tregaron and Finchingfield*, pp. 120-121
10 Cited by Roberts, *Bywyd a Gwaith y Diweddar Henry Richard*, p. 15
11 Evans, *Dr Edward Richard of Tregaron and Finchingfield*, pp. 117-118
12 The cholera had been a matter of great concern in 1832 although it appears that no member of Jewin Crescent died because of it. See Gomer M. Roberts, *Y Ddinas Gadarn: Hanes Eglwys Jewin Llundain* (Bicentenary Committee of the Founding of Jewin Chapel, London, 1974), p. 107.
13 Evans, *Dr Edward Richard of Tregaron and Finchingfield*; pp. 120-121
14 Ibid., p. 121
15 Ibid., p. 123
16 Ibid., p. 123
17 Ibid., p. 124
18 Ibid., pp. 124-125
19 Gwyn A. Williams, *Peace & Power: Henry Richard, A Radical for our time* (CND Cymru, 1988), p. 4
20 Evans, *Dr Edward Richard of Tregaron and Finchingfield*; pp. 127-130
21 Ibid., pp. 126-127
22 Charles S. Miall, *Henry Richard, M.P.*, pp.12-13
23 Evans, *Dr Edward Richard of Tregaron and Finchingfield*, pp. 127-128
24 Ibid., p. 128
25 This would probably have been David Charles (the second), hymn-writer and minister, Editor-in-chief of *Casgliad o Hymnau Hen a Newydd at Wasanaeth y Trefnyddion Calfinaidd* (Collection of hymns ancient and modern for the service of the Calvinistic Methodists) which was published in 1841, although there is a suggestion that the hymnal was ready for press when Ebenezer and Henry Richard called on them.
26 Evans, *Dr Edward Richard of Tregaron and Finchingfield*, pp. 128-129
27 Ieuan Gwynedd Jones, *Henry Richard*, p. 9
28 Evans, *Dr Edward Richard of Tregaron and Finchingfield*, p. 129
29 Ibid., p. 129 -130
30 Ibid., p. 130
31 Ibid., p. 131

Chapter 3

1 Evans, *Dr Edward Richard of Tregaron and Finchingfield*; pp. 131-132
2 Roberts, *Bywyd a Gwaith y Diweddar Henry Richard*, pp. 18-19
3 Ivor Thomas Rees, *Henry Richard – yet another look*, *Merthyr Historian* 20 (2009); p. 129, citation of Edward E. Cleal, *The Story of Congregationalism in Surrey*
4 Cited by Miall, *Henry Richard, M.P.*, pp. 27-28
5 *History Notes of Marlborough*; cited by Ivor Thomas Rees, *Merthyr Historian 20*, p. 129
6 Evans, *Dr Edward Richard of Tregaron and Finchingfield*, p. 133. (Also J. J. Morgan, *Cofiant Evan Phillips Castell Newydd Emlyn*, pp. 131-132)
7 Ibid., p. 135
8 Richard, *Influence of the Eisteddfodau and similar institutions in Wales*; *Letters and Essays on Wales*, Letter VI, pp. 44-52
9 Ieuan Gwynedd Jones, *Henry Richard*, p. 10
10 Ibid., p. 11
11 Ibid., p. 11-12
12 Ibid., p. 12
13 Ibid., pp. 12-13
14 Evans, *Dr Edward Richard of Tregaron and Finchingfield*, p. 137. Letter dated 22nd August, 1843. The

Daughters of Rebecca – an Old Testament reference, possibly Genesis 24, verse 60 – was the name adopted by tenant farmers protesting against the numerous toll-gates on public roads. The men disguised themselves by blackening their faces and dressing in women's clothes when they attacked and destroyed the toll-gates. The protests began in May 1839 and continued until 1844

15   Henry Richard used his influence to persuade the Peace Society to print 10,000 leaflets urging the protesters to refrain from resorting to violent methods. It appears that they had little or no effect. Goronwy J. Jones, *Wales and the Quest for Peace* (Cardiff, 1969), p. 7

16   Richard, *Political Condition of Wales – State of the Representation, Letters and Essays on Wales*, Letter X, pp. 81-82

17   *Y Cronicl* 1, 1843. Cited by T. H. Lewis, *Y Mudiad Heddwch yng Nghymru, The Transactions of the Honourable Society of Cymmrodorion* (1957), p. 111

18   *Yr Eurgrawn*, XXXV, 1843. Ibid., p. 111

19   *Yr Haul*, VIII, 1843. Ibid., p. 112

20   *Y Diwygiwr*, VIII, 1843. Ibid., p. 113

21   H. R. Evans, *Henry Richard and Cobden's Letters, The Transactions of the Honourable Society of Cymmrodorion* (London,1958), p. 57

22   Richard, *Political Condition of Wales – State of the Representation, Letters and Essays on Wales*, Letter X, pp. 81-82

23   From *Y Diwygiwr* (V, 1839) cited by Lewis, *Y Mudiad Heddwch yng Nghymru*, p. 99

24   Richard, *Letters and Essays on Wales*, p. vii

25   Ibid., p. vii

26   Roberts, *Bywyd a Gwaith y diweddar Henry Richard*, p. 25

27   Ibid., pp. 26-27

28   Richard, *Letters and Essays on Wales*, p. viii

29   Ieuan Gwynedd Jones, *Henry Richard*, p. 13

30   Ibid., p. 13

31   *Bywyd y Parch Ebenezer Richard*, London (1839)

32   Evans, *Dr Edward Richard of Tregaron and Finchingfield*, p. 138

33   Ibid., p. 133

34   Ibid., p. 134

35   Gomer M. Roberts, *Y Ddinas Gadarn: Hanes Eglwys Jewin*, p. 75

36   Evans, *Dr Edward Richard of Tregaron and Finchingfield*, p. 139

37   Gomer M. Roberts, *Y Ddinas Gadarn*, p. 99

38   Ibid., pp. 101-106

39   Ibid., p. 106

40   Evans, *Dr Edward Richard of Tregaron and Finchingfield*, p. 139

41   Ibid., p. 139

42   Cited by Evans, *Dr Edward Richard of Tregaron and Finchingfield*, p. 140

Chapter 4

1   Goronwy J. Jones, *Wales and the Quest for Peace*, p. 2

2   T. H. Lewis, *Y Mudiad Heddwch yng Nghymru*, p. 91

3   Ibid., p. 91

4   For a description of the opium trade and its effect on India see the novel by Amitav Ghosh, *Sea of Poppies* (London, 2008)

5   In *Y Dysgedydd* XXIII (1844) the words of J. R. Morrison are cited as an example of attempts to justify the Opium War on religious grounds. His father, Dr Robert Morrison, had been a missionary in China: "And we rejoice in the revelations of His powers in over-ruling the evils of war to extend our opportunities to proclaim to the people of that country, those who wallow in the deepest darkness, the approach of His kingdom of light and glory." See Lewis, *Y Mudiad Heddwch yng Nghymru*, p. 102

6   A reference to evidence provided by an American missionary named Robert A. Hume who said that the people of India viewed missionaries as being related to the soldiers who had humiliated them and this had hardened their hearts against the teachings of Christ. Similarly, the missionary James Long who had worked in India and who claimed that "the main barrier to extending Christianity was the warring spirit of those who professed it". Roberts, *Bywyd a Gwaith y Diweddar Henry Richard*, pp. 322-323

7   Roberts, *Bywyd a Gwaith y Diweddar Henry Richard*, pp. 295-301, provides a fairly detailed synopsis of the lecture.

8   Lewis Appleton, *Henry Richard, The Apostle of Peace* (London, 1889), p. 5
9   Miall, *Henry Richard, M.P.*, p. 35
10 Roberts, *Bywyd a Gwaith y Diweddar Henry Richard*. p. 34
11 Miall, *Henry Richard, M.P.*, p. 33; Appleton, Henry Richard, p. 5
12 Miall, *Henry Richard, M.P.*, p. 36
13 Ibid., pp. 39-40
14 From the diary Richard kept of his journey. Cited by Miall, *Henry Richard, M.P.*, p. 49
15 Miall, *Henry Richard, M.P.*, p. 52
16 Ibid., p. 54
17 Ibid., pp. 53-54
18 To read Victor Hugo's speech see: http://www.cahierseuropeens.eu/cedh004/us/CEDH04 pp. 23-26
19 Miall, *Henry Richard, M.P.*, p. 56
20 Roberts, *Bywyd a Gwaith y Diweddar Henry Richard*. p. 39
21 Miall, *Henry Richard, M.P.*, pp. 59-61

Chapter 5

1   Miall, *Henry Richard, M.P.*, pp. 61-62
2   Ibid., pp. 61-62
3   Ibid., p. 63
4   Ibid., p. 64
5   Ibid., p. 64
6   Ibid., p. 65
7   Ibid., p. 66
8   Ibid., p. 68
9   Morgan, *Dawn Dweud: Lewis Edwards*, p. 24
10 From Henry Richard's diary. See Miall, *Henry Richard, M.P.*, pp. 71-72
11 Ibid., p. 72
12 Ibid., p. 74
13 Ibid., p. 76
14 Ibid., pp. 77-78
15 Ibid., p. 79
16 Ibid., p. 80
17 Roberts, *Bywyd a Gwaith y Diweddar Henry Richard*, p. 45
18 Lewis, *Y Mudiad Heddwch yng Nghymru*, p. 107
19 Miall, *Henry Richard, M.P.*, pp. 82-83. Bunsen was the husband of Frances, sister of Lady Llanover, and he would often attend the Abergavenny Eisteddfodau

Chapter 6

1   Lewis, *Y Mudiad Heddwch yng Nghymru*, p. 107
2   1848, edition VI: cited by Lewis, *Y Mudiad Heddwch yng Nghymru*, p. 107
3   The preface to the 1850 volume, ibid., p. 107
4   1849, edition XIV, ibid., p. 107
5   1850, edition XXXIII, ibid., p. 107
6   1849, edition XIV, ibid., p. 108
7   Cobden would soon be presenting a motion on Arbitration to Parliament on 14 June 1849, where he had gained modest support - he was defeated by 176 votes to 79. Henry Richard had campaigned diligently outside Parliament for the motion, organising meetings and petitions. In a letter to Joseph Sturge, Cobden wrote that the first petitions in favour of Arbitration had been received by MPs with scorn and contempt, but when he presented his motion to the House he was given an attentive hearing. Cobden advised Sturge and Richard to stick to the principle that war was un-Christian – although he himself had always taken a political and practical stance. On a personal level Richard always took that line but he was quite prepared to use Cobden's pragmatic and secular arguments in the *Herald of Peace* and later in Parliament. See Appleton, Henry Richard, pp. 6-9.
8   Lewis, *Y Mudiad Heddwch yng Nghymru*, p. 109
9   Miall, *Henry Richard, M.P.*, p. 84
10 Roberts, *Bywyd a Gwaith y Diweddar Henry Richard*, p. 48

11   Miall, *Henry Richard, M.P.*, p. 85
12   Roberts, *Bywyd a Gwaith y Diweddar Henry Richard*, p. 48
13   Lewis, *Y Mudiad Heddwch yng Nghymru*, p. 110
14   Ibid., p. 110
15   Gwyn Griffiths (Editor), *The Author of our Anthem: Poems by Evan James* (Llanrwst, 2009), p. 72
16   Gwyn Griffiths, *Land of My Fathers* (Llanrwst, 2006), pp. 114-115
17   Miall, *Henry Richard, M.P.*, p. 88
18   W. & F. G. Nash, London, 1853
19   Richard Cobden, *1793 and 1853*, in *Three Letters* (London, 1853), p. iv
20   Ibid., p. 71
21   Roberts, *Bywyd a Gwaith y Diweddar Henry Richard*, p. 51
22   *Y Cronicl* X, 1852. Cited by Lewis, *Y Mudiad Heddwch yng Nghymru*, p. 114
23   Roberts, *Bywyd a Gwaith y Diweddar Henry Richard*, pp. 51-52
24   Ibid., pp. 52-53
25   Miall, *Henry Richard, M.P.*, p. 91. Also – in his report of the Franfurt Peace Congress, SR noted: "We would be happy to see Henry Richard being offered an open door in some part of Wales through which to enter Parliament where he could be a voice for Peace." Cited by Lewis, *Y Mudiad Heddwch yng Nghymru*, p. 107.
26   Ibid., pp. 91-92
27   Samuel Roberts, Y Cronicl (X, 1852), p.375. Cited by Lewis, *Y Mudiad Heddwch yng Nghymru*, p. 114
28   Miall, *Henry Richard, M.P.*, p. 93
29   Lewis, *Y Mudiad Heddwch yng Nghymru*, p. 115
30   Roberts, *Bywyd a Gwaith y Diweddar Henry Richard*, pp. 55-56
31   Miall, *Henry Richard, M.P.*, pp. 96-99

Chapter 7

1   Stephen Frick, *Joseph Sturge, Henry Richard and the Morning Star*, Ann Arbor Michigan (1980), pp. 74, 94
2   Tracey Haggert, *"Blessed are the Peacemakers": Religious Pacifism and the Crimean War 1854-1856* (MA Dissertation, University of British Columbia, 1995, https://circle.ubc.ca/bitstream/handle/2429/3950/ubc_1995-0472.pdf?sequence=1) pp. 19-24
3   Ibid. pp. 21-22
4   Henry Richard gives a totally different opinion in his pamphlet, *Evidence of Turkish Misrule*, (published on behalf of The Eastern Question Association by Cassell Petter & Galpin, London, 1855)
5   Haggert, *"Blessed are the Peacemakers"*, pp. 22-23
6   Henry Richard, *Memoirs of Joseph Sturge*, (London, 1864), p. 464
7   G. F. Mason, *Sleigh Ride to Russia* (York, 1985), pp. 5-6
8   Henry Richard, *History of the Origins of the War with Russia, Drawn up from Parliamentary Documents* (London, 1855), p. 23
9   Miall, *Henry Richard, M.P.*, p. 89
10 Ibid., p. 103
11 Letter cited by William Robertson, *Life and Time of John Bright* (London, 1883), p. 295
12 Published on behalf of The Eastern Question Association by Cassell Petter & Galpin, (London, 1855).
13 Henry Richard, *Evidence of Turkish Misrule* (London, 1855), p. 3
14 Ibid., p. 12
15 Ibid., p. 11
16 Lewis, *Y Mudiad Heddwch yng Nghymru*, p. 118
17 Ibid., p. 120
18 Y Cronicl, (Edition XIII, 1855). Cited by Lewis, *Y Mudiad Heddwch yng Nghymru*, p. 120
19 Lewis, *Y Mudiad Heddwch yng Nghymru*, p. 121
20 Edition XXXVIII, 1855. Cited by Lewis, *Y Mudiad Heddwch yng Nghymru*, p. 118
21 Introduction to Edition XIV, 1855. Cited by Lewis, *Y Mudiad Heddwch yng Nghymru*, p. 118
22 Edition XII, 1856
23 Haggert, *"Blessed are the Peacemakers"*, pp. 15-16
24 Lewis, *Y Mudiad Heddwch yng Nghymru*, p. 121
25 Y Cronicl (Edition XIII, 1855). Cited by Lewis, *Y Mudiad Heddwch yng Nghymru*, p. 120

26 A. J. P. Taylor, *The Troublemakers* (Hamish Hamilton, London, 1957), p. 16
27 28 July 1854. Cited by Lewis, *Y Mudiad Heddwch yng Nghymru*, p. 121
28 2 December 1872
29 8 December 1855
30 *History of the Origins of the War with Russia, Drawn up from Parliamentary Documents*
31 Alfred Bowen Evans, *War: its Theology; its Anomalies; its Incidents and its Humiliations. A discourse delivered in the Church of St Andrew Marylebone* (Ward & Co, London, 1885)
32 Peter Brock in, *The Quaker Peace Testimony 1660 to 1914*, (York, 1990), p. 272
33 Haggert, *"Blessed are the Peacemakers"*, pp. 15-16
34 Evans, *Dr Edward Richard of Tregaron and Finchingfield*, p. 141

Chapter 8

1   Appleton, *Henry Richard*, p. 26
2   Letter dated March 17th, 1856. Cited by Stephen Frick, *Henry Richard and the Treaty of Paris of 1856, The National Library of Wales Journal* (Aberystwyth, Vol. XVII, Number 3, Summer 1972), note 9, p. 311
3   Roberts, *Bywyd a Gwaith y Diweddar Henry Richard*, pp. 84-85
4   Letter dated February 7, 1856. Cited by Frick, *Henry Richard and the Treaty of Paris of 1856* (Aberystwyth, Vol. XVII, Number 3, Summer 1972), note 9, p. 311
5   Stephen Frick, *Henry Richard and the Treaty of Paris of 1856, The National Library of Wales Journal* (Aberystwyth, Vol. XVII, Number 3, Summer 1972), p. 299-300
6   Henry Richard, *Memoirs of Joseph Sturge* (London, 1864), p. 422
7   Frick, *Henry Richard and the Treaty of Paris of 1856*, pp. 301-311
8   Ibid., p. 301
9   Ibid., p. 302
10 Ibid., pp. 302-303
11 Ibid., pp. 306-307
12 Miall, *Henry Richard, M.P.*, p. 109
13 Appleton, *Henry Richard*, p. 32
14 Roberts, *Bywyd a Gwaith y Diweddar Henry Richard*, p. 68
15 Miall, *Henry Richard, M.P.*, p. 111
16 Richard, *Memoirs of Joseph Sturge*, p. 526
17 Ibid., p. 527

Chapter 9

1   David Brown, *Cobden and the Press in Rethinking Nineteenth Century Liberalism*, Editors: Anthony Howe and Simon Morgan (Aldershot, 2005), pp. 87 - 90
2   Letter – not dated – from Henry Richard to an un-named friend - evidently written in 1858. Cited by Miall, *Henry Richard, M.P.*, p. 114
3   Ibid., p. 115
4   Evans, *Dr Edward Richard of Tregaron and Finchingfield*, p. 142
5   Ibid., p. 142
6   Ibid., p. 143
7   Ibid., p. 144
8   Ieuan Gwynedd Jones, *The Liberation Society and Welsh Politics, 1844 to 1868, The Welsh History Review* (Cardiff, Vol. 1, No. 2, 1961), p. 216
9   Ibid., p. 211
10 Ibid., p. 213
11 Ibid., p. 216
12 Miall, *Henry Richard, M.P.*, p. 121
13 Ibid., p. 121
14 Ibid., pp. 122-123
15 Ibid., p. 123
16 Cambrian, September 26th, 1862. Cited by Ieuan Gwynedd Jones, *Dr. Thomas Price and the Election of 1868 in Merthyr Tydfil, The Welsh History Review* (Cardiff, Vol. 2, No. 3, 1965), p. 259.
17 Miall, *Henry Richard, M.P.*, p. 125-126
18 Lewis, *Y Mudiad Heddwch yng Nghymru*, p. 123
19 Miall, *Henry Richard, M.P.*, p. 138. In December 1863 Henry Richard spent some days at the home

of Richard Cobden in Durnford House, Midhurst, and he kept a detailed journal of their conversations, which included discussions on a variety of topics, some contemporary, others from past events. Miall had access to the journal and made good use of it

20   Ibid., p. 138-139. This interesting little tale came from a conversation between Richard and Cobden in July 1861
21   Ibid., p. 138-139
22   XXV, 1860. Cited by Lewis, *Y Mudiad Heddwch yng Nghymru*, p. 123
23   Appleton, *Henry Richard*, p. 50
24   Ibid., p. 51
25   Roberts, *Bywyd a Gwaith y Diweddar Henry Richard*, p. 71
26   Ibid., pp. 72-73

Chapter 10

1   Appleton, *Henry Richard*, p. 57
2   Ibid., p. 58
3   Miall, *Henry Richard, M.P.*, p. 128
4   Roberts, *Bywyd a Gwaith y Diweddar Henry Richard*, p. 77
5   Aled Jones and Bill Jones, *Welsh Reflections: 'Y Drych' & America 1851-2001*, (Llandysul, 2001), p. 153.
6   *Y Drych*, February 14th, 1863
7   *Hunan-Amddiffyniad SR: yn ngwyneb y camddarlunio fu arno drwy adeg cynddaredd y rhyfel cartrefol yn America*. Cited by Jones & Jones, *Welsh Reflections*
8   1861, no. XIX. Cited by Lewis, *Y Mudiad Heddwch yng Nghymru*, pp. 125-126
9   Ibid., p. 126
10   1862, no. VI. Cited by Lewis, *Y Mudiad Heddwch yng Nghymru*, p. 126
11   1860, no. XVIII. Cited by Lewis, *Y Mudiad Heddwch yng Nghymru*, p. 126
12   Roberts, *Bywyd a Gwaith y Diweddar Henry Richard*, p. 76
13   1863, no. XLII. Cited by Lewis, *Y Mudiad Heddwch yng Nghymru*, p. 126
14   1 June 1864. Cited by Lewis, *Y Mudiad Heddwch yng Nghymru*, p. 126
15   1866, no. XLVI. Cited by Lewis, *Y Mudiad Heddwch yng Nghymru*, p. 126. Tregelles Price, by the way, died in 1856
16   Appleton, *Henry Richard*, pp. 63-65
17   Ibid., p. 70
18   Ibid., pp. 71-75
19   Ibid., pp. 76-77
20   Ibid., p. 82

Chapter 11

1   Evans, *Dr Edward Richard of Tregaron and Finchingfield*, p. 145
2   Ibid., p. 146
3   Miall, *Henry Richard, M.P.*, p. 130
4   Ieuan Gwynedd Jones, *The elections of 1865 and 1868 in Wales, with special reference to Cardiganshire and Merthyr Tydfil, The Transactions of the Honourable Society of Cymmrodorion* (London, 1964) pp. 57-58
5   Ibid., p. 59
6   Ibid., p. 59
7   Ibid., p. 62
8   Evans, *Dr Edward Richard of Tregaron and Finchingfield*, p. 149
9   Miall, *Henry Richard, M.P.*, p. 147
10   Ieuan Gwynedd Jones, *The elections of 1865 and 1868 in Wales*, p. 62
11   Evans, *Henry Richard and Cobden's letters*, pp. 55-56
12   Appleton, *Henry Richard*, pp. 89-90
13   Evans, *Henry Richard and Cobden's letters*, pp. 58-59
14   Ibid., p. 59
15   Ibid., p. 81
16   Henry Richard, *Letters and Essays on Wales*, p. 1
17   Ieuan Gwynedd Jones, *Henry Richard*, pp. 12-13
18   Henry Richard, *Letters and Essays on Wales*, p. 26

19 Ibid., p. 33
20 Ibid., pp. 38-39
21 Ibid., p. 47
22 Ibid., p. 47. Quotation of a statement by Bishop Connop Thirwall, an Englishman appointed Bishop of St. David's in 1840 and who learnt Welsh and would deliver sermons and conduct services in the language
23 Ibid., p. 48
24 Ibid., p. 95
25 Ibid., pp. 99-100
26 Ibid., p. 120
27 Ibid., pp. 64-66
28 Ibid., p. 57
29 *Times*, August 20th, 1873. Cited by Richard, *Letters and Essays on Wales*, p. ix-x
30 Ieuan Gwynedd Jones, *Henry Richard*, pp. 20-21
31 Miall, *Henry Richard, M.P.*, pp. 145-146

Chapter 12

1 Ieuan Gwynedd Jones, *The Elections of 1865 and 1868 in Wales*, p. 63
2 Ibid., p. 64
3 Ibid., p. 64
4 Ibid., p. 65
5 Ieuan Gwynedd Jones, *Dr. Thomas Price and the Election of 1868 in Merthyr Tydfil*, p. 260
6 Ibid., pp. 266- 267
7 Gwyn Griffiths, *Cerddi Evan James: Awdur Hen Wlad Fy Nhadau* (Llanwrst, 2006), pp. 116-120
8 Ieuan Gwynedd Jones, *Dr. Thomas Price and the Election of 1868 in Merthyr Tydfil*, p. 259.
9 Ibid., p. 264
10 Ibid., p. 265
11 Gwyn A. Williams, *Power & Peace*, p. 4
12 Ieuan Gwynedd Jones, *Dr. Thomas Price and the Election of 1868 in Merthyr Tydfil*, p. 265, note 149
13 Miall, *Henry Richard, M.P.*, p. 149
14 Roberts, *Bywyd a Gwaith y Diweddar Henry Richard*, pp. 107-108. Quoted from *The Nonconformist*
15 Gwyn A. Williams, *Power & Peace*, p. 2
16 Ibid., p. 2
17 Miall, *Henry Richard, M.P.*, pp. 152-53
18 Ibid., p. 153
19 Ibid., p. 153
20 Ieuan Gwynedd Jones, *Henry Richard ac Iaith y Gwleidydd, Cof Cenedl III*: Editor, Geraint H. Jenkins (Llandysul, 1988) p. 130
21 Ibid., p. 128
22 Ibid., p. 128
23 Ibid., pp. 133-134
24 Ieuan Gwynedd Jones, *Henry Richard*, p. 20

Chapter 13

1 Miall, *Henry Richard, M.P.*, p. 154
2 Ibid., p. 155
3 Ibid., p. 155
4 Hansard 22 March, 1869, vol. 194 pp. 1967-1972
5 Miall, *Henry Richard, M.P.*, p. 157
6 To read all the speeches see Hansard 6 July, 1869, vol. 197 pp. 1294-1329
7 Vaughan was the Tory candidate defeated by E. M. Richards in Cardiganshire
8 Miall, *Henry Richard, M.P.*, pp.160-161
9 Miall, *Henry Richard, M.P.*, p.161 (footnote)
10 Ibid., pp. 163-164
11 Ibid., p. 164
12 Ibid., pp. 164-165
13 Matthew Cragoe, *Culture, politics, and national identity in Wales, 1832-1886* (Oxford, 2004)

14 *Hansard*, 8 August, 1871 vol. 208 p. 1133
15 *Baner ac Amserau Cymru*, 27 July 1870, p. 47
16 Quoted in the *Llandudno Register & Herald* 18 December 1869
17 *Hansard*, 8 August, 1871 vol. 208 pp. 1137-1138

Chapter 14

1   Appleton, *Henry Richard*, pp. 93-94
2   Ibid., p. 95
3   Ibid., pp. 98-99
4   Ibid., p. 100
5   Ibid., p. 100
6   Ibid., p. 100
7   André Durand, *Gustave Moynier and The Peace Societies, International Review of the Red Cross* (Camberidge, October 31st, 1996, no. 314) pp. 532-550
8   Appleton, *Henry Richard*, p. 102-103
9   Ibid., p. 103
10 Miall, *Henry Richard, M.P.*, pp. 167-168
11 Ibid., p. 168
12 Ibid., p. 168 (note)
13 Appleton, *Henry Richard*, p. 110
14 Ibid., p. 111
15 Ibid., p. 112
16 Ibid., p. 112
17 Roberts, *Bywyd a Gwaith y Diweddar Henry Richard*, p. 121. The correct quotation from Kant is "War is bad, it begets more evil than it kills".
18 *Hansard* 1 August, 1870, vol 203, pp. 1286 - 1365)
19 Roberts, *Bywyd a Gwaith y Diweddar Henry Richard*, p. 128
20 *La Débâcle* was published by Charpentier, Paris, 1892, and *Robert Helmont* by Dentu, Paris, 1874
21 In *Contes du Lundi*, 1873, Nelson, Paris
22 Miall, *Henry Richard, M.P.*, p. 177

Chapter 15

1   *Hansard* 20 June, 1870, vol. 202, pp. 495-518
2   *Hansard* 11 July, 1870, p. 203, t. 79 - 83)
3   Miall, *Henry Richard, M.P.*, pp. 178 - 179
4   Ibid., pp. 186-187
5   *Hansard* 5 March, 1872, vol. 209, pp. 1407 - 1418
6   Idwal Jones, *The Voluntary System at Work, The Transactions of the Honourable Society of Cymmrodorion* (London, 1931-32), pp. 82-83
7   W. E. Davies, *Sir Hugh Owen – his Life and Life-work* (National Eisteddfod Association, 1885) pp. 76-78
8   Thomas Rees, *Cenadwri'r Eglwys a Phroblemau'r Dydd* (Wrexham,1923) pp. 20-21
9   Jones, *Gyrfa'r gŵr o Dregaron*, pp. 37-38
10 W. E. Davies, *Sir Hugh Owen*, pp. 80-81
11 Henry Richard, *Letters and Essays on Wales*, tt. 33-34
12 *Hansard* 24 May 1870 vol. 201 pp. 1274 -1291
13 Roberts, *Bywyd a Gwaith y Diweddar Henry Richard*, pp. 117-118; Miall, *Henry Richard, M.P.*, pp.175-176, (note)
14 Iwan Morgan, *The College by the Sea* (Aberystwyth, 1928) p. 7. See also Joseph Morgan, *A Biography of the Reverend David James* (Pontypool, 1925) p. 65
15 J. Gwynn Williams, *Prifysgol Cymru 1893, Transactions of the Honourable Society of Cymmrodorion* (London, 1993) pp. 85-86
16 E. L. Ellis, *The University College of Wales, Aberystwyth, 1872-1972* (Cardiff, 1972) pp. 13-14
17 Hywel Teifi Edwards, *Yr Eisteddfod* (Cardiff, 1976) pp. 65-67
18 Iwan Morgan, *The College by the Sea* (Aberystwyth, 1928) pp. 14 and 343
19 Ibid., pp. 343-344
20 Ibid., p. 14
21 J. Gwynn Williams, *Prifysgol Cymru 1893*, p. 88

22 Iwan Morgan, *The College by the Sea*, p. 14
23 J. Gwynn Williams, *Prifysgol Cymru 1893*, p. 87
24 Miall, *Henry Richard, M.P.*, p. 205
25 Iwan Morgan, *The College by the Sea*, p.17
26 R. Tudur Jones, *Yr Undeb – Hanes Undeb yr Annibynwyr Cymraeg 1872-1972* (Swansea, 1975) p. 24
27 Ibid., pp. 52-53
28 Roberts, *Bywyd a Gwaith y Diweddar Henry Richard*, pp. 137-138
29 Ibid., pp. 131-132
30 To read all the speeches see *Hansard* 8 March, 1872 vol. 209, pp. 1648-73
31 Miall, *Henry Richard, M.P.*, pp. 201-203. It should be noted that Miall set this journey in 1873 not 1872 as it should have been
32 Ibid., pp. 201-202. Footnote

Chapter 16

1 Appleton, *Henry Richard* p. 126
2 Roberts, *Bywyd a Gwaith y Diweddar Henry Richard*, pp. 145-146
3 Jones, *Wales and the Quest for Peace*, p. 43
4 Ieuan Gwynedd Jones, *Henry Richard*, pp. 19-20
5 Jones, *Wales and the Quest for Peace*, p. 43
6 Ibid., pp. 45-46. Quoted from the *Western Mail*, 30m November 1871
7 Appleton, *Henry Richard* p. 128
8 Ibid., p. 115
9 Ibid., p. 116
10 The story is told by Thomas Willing Balch, *The Alabama Arbitration* (1900, Philadelphia)
11 16 September 1872. Cited by Jones, *Wales and the Quest for Peace*, p. 47
12 Herald of Peace, 1873, p. 172. Cited by Jones, *Wales and the Quest for Peace*, p. 47
13 Jones, *Wales and the Quest for Peace*, p. 48
14 Appleton, *Henry Richard*, p. 130
15 To read Henry Richard's speech and the full debate see *Hansard* 8 July, 1873, vol. 217, pp. 52 - 90
16 Britain was an exception at the time
17 Alexander William Kinglake, Author of *Invasion of the Crimea, a history of the war in eight volumes*
18 Appleton, *Henry Richard*, p. 132
19 Miall, *Henry Richard, M.P.*, p. 199
20 Jones, *Wales and the Quest for Peace*, p. 49
21 Miall, *Henry Richard, M.P.*, p. 200
22 Ibid., pp. 206-208

Chapter 17

1 Ibid., p. 209
2 Ibid p. 210. Charles Miall had access to Henry Richard's diary of this journey – as he did of diaries Richard had kept of other journeys, and he quotes extensively from them
3 Ibid., p. 211
4 Ibid., p. 211
5 Ibid., pp. 212-213. From Henry Richard's diary
6 Ibid., p. 215
7 Ibid., p. 215. From Richard's diary
8 Ibid., pp. 215-216
9 Ibid., p. 217
10 This could well have been true since Eugène Rouher had been in and out of the Government on more than one occasion during 1867.
11 Miall, *Henry Richard, M.P.*, p. 218
12 Ibid., p. 218
13 Ibid., p. 219
14 Ibid., p. 219-220. From Henry Richard's diary
15 Ibid., p. 220-221. From Henry Richard's diary
16 Ibid., p. 224
17 Ibid., p. 226

18 Ibid., p. 227
19 Ibid., p. 229
20 Ibid., p. 229
21 Ibid., pp. 231-232
22 Ibid., pp. 233-234
23 Ibid., p. 2345
24 Appleton, *Henry Richard*, p. 137
25 Ibid., p. 137
26 Roberts, *Bywyd a Gwaith y Diweddar Henry Richard*, p. 162
27 Ibid., pp. 162-163
28 Appleton, *Henry Richard*, p. 138

Chapter 18

1 Appleton, *Henry Richard*, p. 139
2 Jones, *Wales and the Quest for Peace*, pp. 50-51
3 Ibid., pp. 51-52
4 Ibid., p. 52
5 Miall, *Henry Richard, M.P.*, pp. 246-247
6 Roberts, *Bywyd a Gwaith y Diweddar Henry Richard*, pp. 168-169
7 Miall, *Henry Richard, M.P.*, p. 249
8 To read Henry Richard's speech see *Hansard* 15 July, 1874, vol. 221, pp 56-57
9 Miall, *Henry Richard, M.P.*, pp. 252-253
10 Appleton, *Henry Richard*, p. 140
11 To read the full debate see *Hansard*, 4 May, 1874, vol. 218, pp. 1592-1664
12 Samuel Whitaker Pennypacker, *The Autobiography of a Pennsylvanian* (Philadelphia, 1918). According to Pennypacker, the reason for him not paying his debts was entirely due to lazy carelessness
13 Miall, *Henry Richard, M.P.*, pp. 254-255
14 Ibid., p. 255-256
15 Ibid., p. 256-257
16 Lawrence Goldman: *The Defection of the Middle Class: The Endowment Schools Act, The Liberal Party, and the 1874 Election in Politics & Culture in Victorian Britain*, Editors. Peter Ghosh and Lawrence Goldman (Oxford University Press, 2006)
17 *Hansard*, 21 July, 1874, vol. 221; pp. 417-425
18 Appleton, *Henry Richard*, p. 144

Chapter 19

1 Miall, *Henry Richard, M.P.*, p. 260
2 Evans, *Henry Richard and Cobden's letters*, p. 58
3 Ibid., p. 59
4 Another of the North of England cotton industrialists, free market and anti-Corn Law campaigner
5 Evans, *Henry Richard and Cobden's letters*, p. 64
6 Ibid., pp. 65-66
7 Ibid., p. 76
8 Miall, *Henry Richard, M.P.*, p. 259
9 Chapman & Hall (London, 1881)
10 T. Fisher Unwin (London, 1918)
11 Roberts, *Bywyd a Gwaith y Diweddar Henry Richard*, p. 83
12 Miall, *Henry Richard, M.P.*, p. 259
13 Two volumes have now been published by the Oxford University Press, with two more in the pipeline
14 Evans, *Henry Richard and Cobden's letters*, p. 80
15 Ibid., p. 80
16 Ibid., p. 80
17 Ibid., p. 81
18 Roberts, *Bywyd a Gwaith y Diweddar Henry Richard*, p. 83

19 Miall, *Henry Richard, M.P.*, p. 261
20 Ibid., p. 261
21 Isaiah 31, verse 1
22 Miall, *Henry Richard, M.P.*, p. 262
23 John Murray, London, 1876
24 Gladstone, *Bulgarian Horrors and the Question of the East* (London, 1876) p. 13
25 Article by the American journalist J. A. MacGahan (August 22nd, 1876 edition)
26 From the introduction to the second imprint
27 Appleton, *Henry Richard*, p. 160
28 Jones, *Wales and the Quest for Peace*, p. 55
29 Ibid., p. 57. Cited from *Herald of Peace*
30 Roberts, *Bywyd a Gwaith y Diweddar Henry Richard*, p. 186
31 Appleton, *Henry Richard*, p. 166
32 Jones, *Wales and the Quest for Peace*, p. 56. Cited from R. T. Shannon, *Gladstone and the Bulgarian Agitation* (Nelson, 1963)
33 Appleton, *Henry Richard*, p. 135
34 Miall, *Henry Richard, M.P.*, p. 264. (Footnote)

Chapter 20

1 Ibid., pp. 265-266
2 Ibid., p. 267
3 Ibid., p. 269
4 Ibid., pp. 269-271
5 Away, away, you uninitiated!
6 For the entire debate see *Hansard* 21 April, 1875, vol. 223, pp. 1363-1421.
7 *Hansard* 11 May 1875 vol. 224; pp. 489-509
8 Miall, *Henry Richard, M.P.*, pp. 273-274
9 Appleton, *Henry Richard*, p. 145
10 For Lawson and Richard's speeches see *Hansard* 6 March, 1876, vol. 227, pp. 1439-1456
11 Chapter 30, verse 15
12 *Hansard* 15 May 1876 vol. 229, pp. 715-721
13 *Hansard* 27 June, 1876 vol. 230, pp. 536-559
14 *History of the Thirty Years' Peace* (G. Bell & Sons, London, 1877)
15 For a portrayal of this disgraceful episode of British history see *Sea of Poppies* by Amitav Ghosh (John Murray, London, 2008)

Chapter 21

1 *Hansard* 19 June 1876 vol. 230; pp. 57-64
2 *Hansard* 10 July 1876, vol. 230; pp. 1186-1207
3 Thomas Rees, *Cenadwri'r Eglwys a Phroblemau'r Dydd*, pp. 20-21
4 *Hansard* 5 August, 1876 vol. 231; pp. 566-673
5 Thomas Rees, *Cenadwri'r Eglwys a Phroblemau'r Dydd*, p. 20
6 *Hansard* 10 June, 1876, vol. 230; p. 1205
7 Miall, *Henry Richard, M.P.*, p. 285
8 Ibid., pp. 282-283
9 Roberts, *Bywyd a Gwaith y Diweddar Henry Richard*, p. 178
10 Ibid., p. 177
11 Appleton, *Henry Richard*, p. 151
12 Miall, *Henry Richard, M.P.*, p. 283
13 Appleton, *Henry Richard*, pp. 151-152
14 Miall, *Henry Richard, M.P.*, pp. 280-281

Chapter 22

1 Appleton, *Henry Richard*, p. 152
2 Miall, *Henry Richard, M.P.*, pp. 301-302
3 *Hansard* 8 February 1878, vol. 237; pp. 1332-1340
4 Miall, *Henry Richard, M.P.*, p. 336

5   *Hansard* 9 April 1878, vol. 239; pp. 997-1008
6   *Book of Proverbs*, Chapter 30, Verse 20
7   Miall, *Henry Richard, M.P.*, pp. 302-303
8   Ibid., p. 303
9   Appleton, *Henry Richard*, p. 173
10 Jones, *Wales and the Quest for Peace*, p. 63
11 Ibid., p. 63
12 Frere was born in Clydach, Llanelli, near Abergavenny, where his father was manager of one of the Crawshay family's ironworks
13 *Hansard* 24 April, 1879, vol. 245, pp. 1040-1048

Chapter 23

1   Appleton, *Henry Richard*, p. 175
2   Jones, *Wales and the Quest for Peace*, p. 64
3   Miall, *Henry Richard, M.P.*, pp. 313-314
4   Ibid., p. 314
5   Ibid., p. 319
6   *Hansard* 15 June, 1880, vol. 253, pp. 80-95
7   Appleton, *Henry Richard*, p. 178
8   June 23, 1880
9   Jones, *Wales and the Quest for Peace*, p. 67
10 Ibid., p. 68
11 *Hansard* 29 April 1881, vol. 260, pp. 1424-1450

Chapter 24

1   Roberts, *Bywyd a Gwaith y Diweddar Henry Richard*, p. 216
2   Henry Richard, *Letters and Essays on Wales*, p. 193
3   Ibid., p. 190
4   April edition, 1883
5   He had been the Vice-Principal of St. David's College, Lampeter, where he learnt Welsh fluently and would preach in the language on Sundays at Llangeler where he was vicar of the parish for a time. He did much to initiate the building of churches in the industrial valleys of South Wales and persuade the industrialists to help fund them
6   Henry Richard, *Letters and Essays on Wales*, p. ix
7   *Hansard* 30 June, 1880, vol. 263, pp. 1167-1181. .
8   Hywel Teifi Edwards, *Yr Eisteddfod*, (Court of the National Eisteddfod, 1976), pp. 79-80
9   E. L. Ellis, *The University College of Wales, Aberystwyth*, p. 15 (footnote)
10 Miall, *Henry Richard, M.P.*, pp. 333-334
11 Appleton, *Henry Richard*, p. 170
12 Miall, *Henry Richard*, M.P., pp. 330-331

Chapter 25

1   Ibid., p. 339
2   Appleton, *Henry Richard*, p. 186
3   Ibid., p. 187
4   Ibid., p. 188
5   Ibid., pp. 188-189
6   *Hansard*, 12 July, 1882, vol. 272, pp. 196-199
7   Roberts, *Bywyd a Gwaith y Diweddar Henry Richard*, pp. 235-236. Quotation from *Herald of Peace*, April 1889, p. 205
8   Ibid., p. 236. (Footnote)
9   *Hansard* 25 July 1882, vol. 272, pp. 1776-1780
10 Jones, *Wales and the Quest for Peace*, p. 71. Quotation from issue of 9 March 1883
11 Ibid., pp. 72-73
12 *Hansard* 19 April, 1883, vol. 278 pp. 686 - 690
13 Miall, *Henry Richard, M.P.*, p. 341

Chapter 26

1 Ibid., pp. 341-342
2 E. L. Ellis, *The University College of Wales, Aberystwyth*, p. 68
3 Ibid., p. 69
4 Ibid., p. 68
5 Kenneth O. Morgan, *Liberals, Nationalists and Mr Gladstone, The Transactions of the Honourable Society of Cymmrodorion* (London, 1960) p. 41
6 E. L. Ellis, *The University College of Wales, Aberystwyth*, pp. 80-81
7 *Hansard* 14 March 1884, vol. 285, pp. 1589-1632
8 E. L. Ellis, *The University College of Wales, Aberystwyth*, p. 82
9 Miall, *Henry Richard, M.P.*, pp. 342-343
10 Ibid., p. 343 (footnote)
11 Ibid., p. 345

Chapter 27

1 Appleton, *Henry Richard*, p. 194
2 Roberts, *Bywyd a Gwaith y Diweddar Henry Richard*, pp. 251-252
3 *Hansard* 15 March 1884, vol. 285, pp. 1666-1671
4 Appleton, *Henry Richard*, p. 200
5 Miall, *Henry Richard, M.P.*, p. 348 (footnote)
6 Appleton, *Henry Richard*, p. 200
7 Miall, *Henry Richard, M.P.*, p. 349
8 Appleton, *Henry Richard*, pp. 200-201
9 Miall, *Henry Richard, M.P.*, pp. 350-351
10 Ibid., p. 351-352
11 See Chapter 22
12 *Hansard* 4 May, 1885, vol. 297, pp. 1501-1511
13 Jones, *Wales and the Quest for Peace*, p. 76 (footnote). See, also, the *Dictionary of National Biography*
14 Miall, *Henry Richard, M.P.*, p. 350
15 Ibid., p. 351
16 Ibid., p.352
17 Jones, *Wales and the Quest for Peace*, p. 76. Quotation from *Herald of Peace*, 1882, p. 144
18 *Hansard* 22 February, 1886, vol. 302, pp. 948 - 954

Chapter 28

1 Jones, *Wales and the Quest for Peace*, p. 73. Quotation from *The Law of the Constitution*, pp. 394-395
2 *Hansard* 19 March, 1886, vol. 303, pp. 1386-1423
3 Roberts, *Bywyd a Gwaith y Diweddar Henry Richard*, p. 257
4 Ibid., 259. See, also, *Hansard* 3 February, 1857, vol. 144, p. 145
5 Kenneth O. Morgan, *Liberals, Nationalists and Mr Gladstone*, p. 44
6 Roberts, *Bywyd a Gwaith y Diweddar Henry Richard*, p. 260
7 *Gwasg y Brython* (Liverpool, 1948, vol. 2) p. 21
8 Miall, *Henry Richard, M.P.*, p. 358
9 Appleton, *Henry Richard*, p. 203
10 To read this interesting speech or, the entire debate see *Hansard* 9 March, 1886, vol. 303, pp. 305-367
11 Henry Richard. M.P., and J. Carvell Williams, M.P., *Disestablishment* (London, 1886)
12 Ibid., p. 66
13 Miall, *Henry Richard, M.P.*, p. 356

Chapter 29

1 Ibid., p. 363
2 Ibid., p. 367
3 Jones, *Gyrfa'r gŵr o Dregaron*, pp. 44-45
4 *Y Gymraeg Mewn Addysg a Bywyd* (HMSO, 1927) p. 66

5 Miall, *Henry Richard, M.P.,* pp. 367 - 368
6 Appleton, *Henry Richard*, pp. 211-212
7 Ibid., pp. 207-208
8 Richard, Henry: *The Religion and Politics of Wales* in *Daily News*, 17 January 1888, p.5, cols, 5 and 6.
   The article was also translated and reproduced in its entirety in Roberts, *Bywyd a Gwaith y
   Diweddar Henry Richard*, pp. 267-274

Chapter 30

1 Iwan Morgan, *The College by the Sea*, pp. 26-27
2 Miall, *Henry Richard, M.P.*, p. 369
3 Ibid., pp. 374-375
4 Appleton, *Henry Richard*, pp. 213-214
5 Roberts, *Bywyd a Gwaith y Diweddar Henry Richard*, pp. 291-292 (footnote). Henry Richard's
   precise words - *Hansard*, 18 March 1870 - were: "And among those who hold this view there are
   many who are most earnestly concerned for the religious character of their countrymen, and who
   hold in as profound reverence as my Right Honourable Friend, Dr. Newman, the old English
   Bible, or rather the old Welsh Bible, which is a still finer version than yours, in proportion as the
   Welsh is a much finer language than the English."
6 Roberts, *Bywyd a Gwaith y Diweddar Henry Richard*, pp. 283-285
7 Miall, *Henry Richard, M.P.*, p.. 361

Bibliography

Appleton, Lewis: *Henry Richard, The Apostle of Peace* (London, 1889)

Balch, Thomas Willing: *The Alabama Arbitration* (Philadelphia, 1900)

Brock, Peter: *The Quaker Peace Testimony 1660 to 1914* (York, 1990)

Cobden, Richard: *1793 and 1853, in Three Letters* (London, 1853)

Cragoe, Matthew: *Culture, politics, and national identity in Wales, 1832-1886* (Oxford, 2004)

Daudet, Alphonse: *Contes du Lundi* (Paris, 1873)

Davies, W. E.: *Sir Hugh Owen – his Life and Life-work* (National Eisteddfod Association, 1885)

Durand, André: *Gustave Moynier and The Peace Societies, International Review of the Red Cross* (Cambridge, October 31, 1996, no. 314)

Edwards, Hywel Teifi: *Yr Eisteddfod* (Cardiff, 1976)

Ellis, E. L.: *The University College of Wales, Aberystwyth, 1872-1972* (Cardiff, 1972)

Evans, Alfred Bowen: *War: its Theology; its Anomalies; its Incidents and its Humiliations. A discourse delivered in the Church of St Andrew, Marylebone* (London, 1885)

Evans, H. R.: *Dr Edward Richard of Tregaron and Finchingfield, The Transactions of the Honourable Society of Cymmrodorion* (London, 1962)

Evans, H. R.: *Henry Richard and Cobden's Letters, The Transactions of the Honourable Society of Cymmrodorion* (London, 1958)

Frick, Stephen: *Henry Richard and the Treaty of Paris of 1856*, The National Library of Wales Journal (Aberystwyth, Vol. XVII, No. 3, Summer 1972)

Frick, Stephen: *Joseph Sturge, Henry Richard and the Morning Star* (Michigan. 1980)

Ghosh, Amitav: *Sea of Poppies* (London, 2008)

Gladstone, William Ewart: *Bulgarian Horrors and the Question of the East* (London, 1876)

Goldman, Lawrence: *The Defection of the Middle Class: The Endowment Schools Act, The Liberal Party, and the 1874 Election in Politics & Culture in Victorian Britain*, Editors: Peter Ghosh and Lawrence Goldman (Oxford, 2006)

Griffiths, Gwyn (Editor): *The Author of Our Anthem – Poems by Evan James* (Llanrwst, 2009)

Griffiths, Gwyn: *Land of My Fathers*, (Llanrwst, 2006)

Haggert, Tracey: *"Blessed are the Peacemakers": Religious Pacifism and the Crimean War 1854-1856* (MA Dissertation, University of British Columbia, 1995)

Hansard: (London)

Jones, A. and Jones, B: *Welsh Reflections: 'Y Drych' & America 1851-2001* (Llandysul, 2001)

Jones, Carey; *Gyrfa'r gŵr o Dregaron* (Swansea, 1988)

Jones, Goronwy J.: *Wales and the Quest for Peace* (Cardiff, 1969)

Jones, Idwal: *The Voluntary System at Work*, The Transactions of the Honourable Society of Cymmrodorion (London, 1931-32)

Jones, Ieuan Gwynedd: *Dr. Thomas Price and the Election of 1868 in Merthyr Tydfil, The Welsh History Review* (Cardiff, Vol. 2, No. 3, 1965)

Jones, Ieuan Gwynedd: *Henry Richard ac Iaith y Gwleidydd, Cof Cenedl III*: Editor Geraint H. Jenkins (Llandysul, 1988)

Jones, Ieuan Gwynedd: *Henry Richard – Apostle of Peace 1812-1888* (The Fellowship of Reconciliation, 1988)

Jones, Ieuan Gwynedd: *The elections of 1865 and 1868 in Wales, with special reference to Cardiganshire and Merthyr Tydfil, The Transactions of the Honourable Society of Cymmrodorion* (London, 1964)

Jones, Ieuan Gwynedd: *The Liberation Society and Welsh Politics, 1844 to 1868, The Welsh History Review* (Cardiff, Vol. 1, No. 2, 1961)

Jones, R. Tudur: *Yr Undeb - Hanes Undeb yr Annibynwyr Cymraeg 1872–1972* (Swansea, 1975)

Lewis, T. H.: *Y Mudiad Heddwch yng Nghymru, The Transactions of the Honourable Society of Cymmrodorion (London,* 1957)

Miall, Charles S.: *Henry Richard, M.P.: A Biography* (London, 1889),

Morgan, D. Densil: *Dawn Dweud: Lewis Edwards* (Cardiff, 2009)

Morgan, Iwan (Editor): *The College by the Sea* (Aberystwyth, 1928)

Roberts, Gomer M.: *Y Ddinas Gadarn: Hanes Eglwys Jewin Llundain* (Committee for the Bicentenary Celebration of Jewin, London, 1974)

Mason, G. F.: *Sleigh Ride to Russia* (York, 1985)

Morgan, Kenneth O.: *Liberals, Nationalists and Mr Gladstone, The Transactions of the Honourable Society of Cymmrodorion* (London, 1960)

Morgan, J. J.: *Cofiant Evan Phillips Castell Newydd Emlyn* (Liverpool, 1930)

Pennypacker, Samuel Whitaker: *The Autobiography of a Pennsylvanian* (Philadelphia, 1918)

Rees, Ivor Thomas: *Henry Richard – yet another look, Merthyr Historian* 20 (2009)

Rees, Thomas: *Cenadwri'r Eglwys a Phroblemau'r Dydd,* (Wrexham,1923)

Richard, Henry, and Williams, J. Carvell: *Disestablishment* (London, 1886)

Richard, Henry: *Evidence of Turkish Misrule* (published on behalf of The Eastern Question Association by Cassell Petter & Galpin, London, 1855)

Richard, Richard: *History of the Origins of the War with Russia, Drawn up from Parliamentary Documents* (London, 1855)

Richard, Henry: *Letters and Essays on Wales* (London, 1884)

Richard, Henry: *Memoirs of Joseph Sturge* (London, 1864)

Roberts, Eleazar: *Bywyd a Gwaith y Diweddar Henry Richard, A.S.* (Wrexham, 1902)

Robertson, William: *Life and Time of John Bright* (London, 1883)

Taylor, A. J. P.: *The Troublemakers* (London, 1957)

Williams, A. G. : *Memories by the Archbishop of Wales* (London, 1927)

Williams, Gwyn A.: *Peace & Power: Henry Richard, A Radical for our Time* (CND Cymru, 1988)

Williams, J. Gwynn: *Prifysgol Cymru 1893, The Transactions of the Honourable Society of Cymmrodorion* (London, 1993)

Y Gymraeg Mewn Addysg a Bywyd (HMSO, 1927)

Index